RAV DOVBER PINSON

Embraced
IN DIVINE
SPACE

The Festivals of Sukkos,
Hoshana Rabbah & Simchas Torah

IYYUN
PUBLISHING

IYYUN PUBLISHING

Published by IYYUN Publishing
650 Sackett Street
Brooklyn, NY 11217

www.iyyun.com

Iyyun Publishing books may be purchased for educational, business or sales promotional use. For information please email: contact@iyyun.com

Editor: Reb Matisyahu Brown
Proofreading / Editing: Yaakov Gershon
Cover and book design: RP Design and Development

ISBN 979-8-9919640-2-9

Pinson, Dovber 1971-
Embraced in Divine Space: The Festivals of Sukkos, Hoshana Rabbah & Simchas Torah
1. Judaism 2. Jewish Spirituality 3. General Spirituality

RAV DOVBER PINSON

Embraced
IN DIVINE
SPACE

The Festivals of Sukkos,
Hoshana Rabbah & Simchas Torah

IYYUN PUBLISHING

IYYUN PUBLISHING

בס"ד

THIS BOOK IS DEDICATED
to

REB AARON & HODAYA HUHEM
and family

To the Huhem family whose home is like an open Sukkah —
not bound by walls,
but expansive like the heart of Klal Yisrael itself.

Just as the sages taught that it is fitting for all of Israel to dwell
together in one great Sukkah, so too, their home welcomes all —
a gathering place for souls from every background
and every path.

Here, young Jews — seekers, wanderers, and students alike —
find warmth, nourishment, and belonging. Under their roof,
strangers become family, and moments become timeless.

———

Contents

PART ONE:

SUKKOS &
THE SUKKAH

Contents

PART TWO:

THE FOUR SPECIES:
What They Represent,
and Intentions for the Waving

Contents

PART THREE:
HOSHANA RABBAH

Contents

PART FOUR:
SHEMINI ATZERES
- SIMCHAS TORAH -

PART ONE:

SUKKOS &
THE SUKKAH

Opening

S UKKOS SHIMMERS WITH A LIGHTNESS OF SPIRIT, A FESTIVAL OVERFLOWING WITH JOY SO TANGIBLE IT SEEMS TO DANCE IN THE AIR. It stands in contrast to the solemn grandeur of Rosh Hashanah and Yom Kippur, the Yamim Noraim, the Days of Awe, when hearts turn inward in reverence and reflection. Now, the weight of those sacred days lifts, giving way to a celebration that is open, unbounded, and radiant with delight.

After the deep and intense self-reflection of Elul, the trembling reverence of Rosh Hashanah, and the profound submission and self-nullification of Yom Kippur, Sukkos offers a sudden sense of expansive relaxation and joy. The spiritual pressure of prolonged and intense prayer and introspection on those Days of Awe created in us a sense of renewal, purity, and lightness. Now, sheltered and embraced by the Clouds of Hashem's Glory, we are lovingly held within the Sukkah, where we celebrate the open horizons of our renewed life. This makeshift structure, with its tenuously balanced poles and walls topped by branches or reeds, open to the elements and swaying in the breeze, becomes a 'container' for the revealed Presence of the Creator of the universe.

Sukkos is, in this way, part of our elaborate process of 'starting over' and regenerating ourselves at the end of the old year and the beginning of the new year.* In fact, the Torah tells us

---

* On the one hand, Sukkos is during the time of "as the year ends," but also וחג האסיף תקופת השנה / "And the Feast of Ingathering (Sukkos) at the turn of the year" (*Shemos*, 34:22), which means at the beginning of the year: Rashi, *ad loc.* The Medrash says, if not for the Golden Calf and the breaking of the Luchos, every month of the year would have had its own Yom Tov: Nisan has Pesach, Iyyar has Pesach Katan, Sivan has Shavuos, Tamuz has *Yom Tov Gadol* / a great Yom Tov, and so forth (אמר רבי לוי בכל חדש וחדש [שבקין] בקש הקב"ה ליתן לישראל מועד, בניסן נתן להם פסח. באייר נתן להם פסח קטן. בסיון נתן עצרת. בתמוז היה בדעתו ליתן להם מועד גדול ועשו העגל ובטל תמוז ואב ואלול, ובא תשרי ופרע להם ראש השנה ויום הכפורים והחג: *Yalkut Shimoni*, Pinchas, 782. Chida, *Devarim Achadim*, Derush 20. See also *Pesikta d'Rebbe Kahana*, Piska 30). Based on this teaching, we can deduce that Rosh Hashanah would have been in Tamuz, Yom Kippur would have been in Av, Sukkos in Elul, and Shemini Atzeres in Tishrei. In other words, if not for the Golden Calf, Sukkos would have been at the "end" of the year, in the month of Elul, but now, after the episode of the Golden Calf, Sukkos is in Tishrei, at the "beginning" of the new year. Hence, Sukkos is conceptually connected both to the end and the beginning of the year.

that Sukkos is a Yom Tov that appears בצאת השנה / "as the year ends" (*Shemos*, 23:16). Similarly, in reference to *Hakhel* / the grand assembly on the eighth year (following the Shemitah year when farmland rests and outstanding debts were waived), the Torah calls Sukkos מקץ שבע שנים / the *Keitz* / 'end' of the (previous) seventh year (*Devarim*, 31:10). And yet, Sukkos is also a culmination of the first ten days of the year, the Yamim Noraim, and therefore, when the Torah speaks about the days of Rosh Hashanah and Yom Kippur (*Vayikra*, 23: 23-32), it immediately follows with the verse, בחמשה עשר יום לחדש השביעי הזה חג הסכות / "And on the fifteenth day of this seventh month there shall be the festival of Sukkos" (*Vayikra*, 23:34).

On the first ten days, Rosh Hashanah and Yom Kippur stir up a new life-force deep within our inner world of desires, yearnings, thoughts, and emotions. On the eve of the fifteenth day, Sukkos arrives and this lifeforce bursts out like the full moon, and we start dancing into the new year and our new sense of self. We are now equipped to leave our inner world and literally go outdoors. When we have moved into our temporary shelter under the stars, rain, and sun, we sit and eat and relax there without fear, despite the tenuous, perhaps rickety structure gently enclosing us. Our mind, heart, and body fill to overflowing with expressive joy, and despite the sometimes raw weather and physical vulnerability, we relish a sense of warmth, protection, and security.

PESACH / PAST. SUKKOS / FUTURE

Sukkos, from this perspective, is the continuation of the Yamim Noraim (*Yalkut Shimoni,* Vayikra, 651). On the other hand, Sukkos is one of the three major *Yamim Tovim* / holy days of the year called *Shalosh Regalim.* Following its description of the Yom Tov of Sukkos and its offerings, the Torah continues: אך בחמשה עשר יום לחדש השביעי באספכם את־תבואת הארץ תחגו / "Indeed, on the fifteenth day of the seventh month, when you have gathered in the yield of your land, you shall observe the festival" (*Vayikra,* 23:39). This description of Sukkos speaks about the Yom Tov of Sukkos as the spiritual and agricultural culmination of the three Regalim (*Devarim,* 16:16. *Rosh Hashanah,* 4a. *Ritva. Meiri,* ad loc). The first of the three, Pesach, comes upon us in the spring, when new growth is sprouting. Shavuos follows in the early summer, when it is already a time of cutting grain. When Sukkos finally arrives, it is a time of gathering in the produce of the land and celebrating the harvest.

Today, Sukkos, though it stands as the grand finale of both the spiritual and agricultural cycles, is often cloaked in mystery and receives far less attention than it deserves. Sadly, its meaning, its joy, and even its observance remain somewhat elusive, particularly in contrast to the widely celebrated Pesach Seder. While Pesach tells a vivid, primal story, our collective and dramatic exodus from Egypt, the breaking of shackles, and the birth of a nation, Sukkos is subtler and more atmospheric. It invites us not with a thunderous narrative but with the gentle rustle of leaves, the scent of the harvest, and the embrace of a temporary dwelling beneath the open sky. Perhaps it is this very subtlety that causes Sukkos to be overlooked, especially by those whose Torah observance is less intense or consistent, for the time being. Sukkos arrives in the shadow of the awe-filled High Holy Days, whose solemnity and grandeur dominate the season. For many, Rosh Hashanah and Yom Kippur have become the heart and the primary seasonal touchpoint for memories of family traditions and national history, while Sukkos lingers quietly just beyond the spotlight, awaiting those willing to step into its delicate beauty, its celebration of presence, vulnerability, and joy.

Perhaps yet another reason for the popularity and ubiquitous celebration of Pesach is that it is predominantly focused on the past and our common memory. Not only are we remembering our departure from Egypt, but spiritually we are performing *Tikkunim* / rectifications and healings on our collective past as a people. We are also touching into our personal past, and revisiting memories of past Seders, for example, how our grandmother made Charoses, and singing old songs and tasting foods that bring us back decades or millennia. By contrast, Sukkos is all about what is yet to come.

Although Sukkos, too, celebrates our communal history, our journeys in the Desert following our Exodus from Egypt, on Sukkos, we imagine, dream, yearn for, and even create our personal and collective future redemption.

Dreaming of the future is subtler than remembering the past, but it can be more joyous as well. It may be true that shared memories can tie us together much more tangibly than shared imaginations of the future, however, when we do come together in shared visions and dreams of a bright future, this can bind us together in uncontainable joy.

Throughout Sukkos, we sing, dance, and celebrate together, and we feel the truth of our Sages' saying that Klal Yisrael is worthy of sitting (conceptually) in one vast Sukkah, all together. This is one reason that Sukkos is called *Zeman Simchaseinu* / 'the Season of Our Joy', and not any of the other Yamim Tovim have this distinction.

Moreover, unique to Sukkos is the fact that we literally enter, with our entire body, 'into' a Mitzvah. All of us — our whole body, mind, and soul, our past, present, and even our future, enter into this vibrant Divine space.

Sukkos is also full to bursting with Mitzvos. We recite the full Halel service of praises every day, and we shake the *Arba Minim* / the Four Species, also known as 'the Lulav and Esrog', every day except Shabbos. In our more distant past, this schedule was even fuller: every day there was a different number of bull offerings brought in the Beis haMikdash.

Sukkos is also uniquely rich in texture, with days of different tone and character. There are 'Yom Tov' days which are similar to Shabbos, intermediate 'Chol haMoed' days, and 'Simchas

Beis Shoeivah' nights when our Sages danced in the courtyard of the Beis haMikdash — and when, in some places today, we dance in the streets. On the seventh day of the festival, there is the unique 'Final Day of Judgment', called Hoshana Rabba, with extensive supplications, and on the final day of Yom Tov, there is Simchas Torah, when we celebrate and dance with the Torah scroll deep into the night, and then begin the new yearly cycle of Torah readings during the day. Each of these days is replete with its own type of joy, and its own particular laws and customs.

A TIME OF MEMORY, RE-LIVING AND IMAGINING

A Yom Tov festival is also called a *Moed* / a 'meeting time', or 'appointment in time'. These days are portals within time into conscious meetings, and heightened closeness, with HaKadosh Baruch Hu, the Holy One. A parable illustrates the nature of these sacred times...

A king was traveling with his beloved son and an entourage in the wilderness. When his son became thirsty for water, he told his father, and immediately, the commander of the royal cavalry sent his fastest horsemen to the nearest town to fetch water. In the worst-case scenario, it would take two hours to fetch water for the prince.

One day, another proposal was put forth by one of the ministers: instead of running horsemen to the nearest town whenever the prince is thirsty, why not have the entourage carry a rig and drill a well right where they were at that moment? The king agreed with this proposal, and the next time the prince complained of thirst, they stopped and drilled. Sure enough, by the end of the day, water was found.

Later on, the prince asked his father why he opted to dig, which was an arduous undertaking, and actually took longer than sending horsemen for water. The king replied, true, it would have been easier and quicker, but perhaps one day you will again be traveling along this path by yourself, and again you will become thirsty, and you may not have able horsemen to retrieve water. Now that we have dug a well, you will always have water for your journey.

The prince replied, "But father, don't you think that after many years the sands will refill the well?" "Yes," said the king, "and that is why we will mark the site of the well on our maps. By observing the map, you will know the exact place where the well was dug, and you will be able to reopen it with minimum effort. In fact, we will dig many wells all along our journey and mark them on our maps. Each well will be marked with the specific nature of the well, and the particular method which is needed to reopen it."

Such are the Yamim Tovim. Each holy day marks a point in the journey we took as a young 'prince' with our Heavenly Father, as we left Egypt and became a nation. Each point, each holy day, is another spiritual well that slakes our spiritual thirst and strengthens us as we traverse the path of the yearly cycle.

Hashem has dug wells for us in various terrains of time, and they are called Pesach, Shavuos, Rosh Hashanah, Yom Kippur, and Sukkos. Each well has a unique characteristic; the nature of Pesach is freedom, and the nature of Shavuos is receiving Torah. The special methods of reopening these wells are the unique Mitzvos of each holy day. On Rosh Hashanah, we open a spiritual well by listening to the sound of the Shofar. On Sukkos, we open a spiritual well by eating in the Sukkah and waving the Four Species.

Additionally, the wells that we find today within each Yom Tov are not in random locations along the path of the cycle of the year. From the very beginning of time, these points along the journey were predestined to be sources of Divine flow, waters with the precise qualities needed to quench the type of thirst we have in each specific season. In Nisan, in the spring, the soul thirsts for freedom. In Sivan, near the beginning of the summer, the soul thirsts for the enlightenment of Torah. On the full moon of Tishrei, after Rosh Hashanah and Yom Kippur, we thirst for the Divine embrace. Each kind of water has a unique quality, taste, and array of nourishments for every soul.

This parable also makes it clear that these special days marked in the 'map' of the calendar are not merely commemorating memories of the 'rest stops' we took on our original journey thousands of years ago. Rather, every year, on the same days in the cycle of the year, the wellsprings of those original events and miracles, revelations, and illuminations, are flowing with fresh, clear water in the present. The same energies that manifested when we left Egypt, when we received the Torah, or when we received atonement, are vividly manifest for us whenever we come upon their corresponding well.

The same inner light of the Clouds of Glory that embraced us in the Desert is revealed again, each year on Sukkos (בשוב תקופת הזמן ההוא יאיר אור מעין האור הראשון: *Derech Hashem*, 4:7). On a deeper level, since Sukkos is not merely a remembrance of the past, but also a celebration of the future, we are celebrating the Clouds of Glory of the future: the Presence of the *Shechinah* / Indwelling Divine Presence that will be revealed to us in the coming Redemption, may it be soon and in our days!

Chapter 1

WHY THE SUKKAH
& WHY THIS TIME OF YEAR:
The Revelation of Rosh Hashanah / Yom Kippur

BEFORE WE EXPLORE THE DEEPER SIGNIFICANCE OF THESE POWERFUL AND TRANSFORMATIVE DAYS OF SUKKOS, WE WILL BEGIN BY REVIEWING THE TORAH'S descriptions of this Yom Tov, then move on to the explanations transmitted by *Chazal* / our Sages, and then to the discussions of the *Rishonim* / early (pre-16th century) scholars. Finally, we can expand our understanding and appreciation through the wisdom of the scholars, sages, mystics, and Chasidic masters down to the present generation.

Regarding the Yom Tov of Sukkos the Torah states: בסכת תשבו שבעת ימים כל־האזרח בישראל ישבו בסכת למען ידעו דרתיכם כי בסכות הושבתי את־בני ישראל בהוציאי אותם מארץ מצרים אני ה אלקיכם / "You shall live בסכת / in *Sukkos* / booths for seven days; all citizens in Israel shall live in Sukkos in order that future generations ידעו / 'may know' that I made the Children of Israel live in Sukkos when I brought them out of the land of Egypt; I am Hashem your G-d" (*Vayikra*, 23:41-43). This is the Torah's description of the Yom Tov of Sukkos.[*]

---

[*] With regards to other Mitzvos of the Torah there is great debate whether proper intent is indispensable, and if a person performs a Mitzvah without intention whether they have fulfilled their obligation or not: *Berachos*, 13a. *Eiruvin*, 95b. *Pesachim*, 114b. *Rabbeinu Yonah*, Berachos 12a. *Tosefos*, Sukkah, 39a. *Tosefos*, Pesachim, 7b. *Shulchan Aruch*, Orach Chayim, 60. *Magen Avraham*, 3. *Beis Yosef*, Orach Chayim, 489. Regarding the Mitzvah of Sukkah, the Bach (*Orach Chayim*, 625, based on the words of the Tur) rules, that without *Kavanah* / intention, namely knowing that one is sitting in the Sukkah as a remembrance of the going out of Egypt, the Mitzvah of sitting in the Sukkah has not been fulfilled: See also *Bekurei Yaakov*, 625:3. *Derech Pikudecha*, Hakdamah, 1:5. It seems that the Beis Yosef, in *Orach Chayim*, 625, rules that we also need Kavanah, but according to the Beis Yosef, the required Kavanah is specifically remembering the miracle of the Clouds of Glory: See also *Kaf haChayim*, ibid., 2. Although see *Likutei Sichos*, 32, Emor 3. The Mishnah in Sukkah opens with the ruling of the Sages that סוכה שהיא גבוהה למעלה מעשרים אמה פסולה / if the *S'chach* / 'roof' of the Sukkah is higher than 20 Amos (approx 30 feet), the Sukkah is not Kosher for three reasons. The first reason is as follows: אמר רבה, דאמר קרא למען ידעו דורותיכם כי בסוכות הושבתי את בני ישראל, עד עשרים אמה, אדם יודע שהוא דר בסוכה, למעלה מעשרים אמה אין אדם יודע שדר בסוכה, משום דלא שלטא בה עינא / "Rabbah said, this is because the Pasuk says, "So that your future generations will know that I caused the Children of Israel to reside in Sukkos when I took them out of the land of Egypt." In a Sukkah up to twenty Amos high, even without a concerted effort, a person is aware that he is sitting in a Sukkah (his eye catches sight of the S'chach). If however, it is more than twenty Amos high, a person is not aware that he is in a Sukkah because his eye does not involuntarily catch sight of the roof. There are two possible implications of this

As we read these *P'sukim* / verses, questions arise. Why, for example, do we need to sit for seven days in a Sukkah in order to "know" that Hashem made us live in Sukkahs when we left Egypt? What type of Sukkahs did Hashem make us dwell in as we journeyed from Egypt? All the Torah says is that Hashem "sat us in Sukkahs," but what are these 'booths' and what do they represent?

While the Torah is clearly telling us that we need to remember that we sat in booths as we left Egypt, there are two opinions regarding what it is referring to when it uses the term *Sukkos*. Rebbe Akiva says that Hashem sat them in literal 'booths', and we need to remember those. Rebbe Eliezer argues that "Sukkos" refers to the Clouds of Glory that shielded and protected us as we left Egypt, and we need to remember those, as distinct from the 'booths'.*

---

reckoning: either the Sukkah itself is *Pasul* / invalid, or the person sitting in the Sukkah has not fulfilled his obligation. It would seem that according to Rabbah, such a Sukkah is not Pasul, rather, the person sitting in it does not fulfill his obligation, because he cannot see and "know" the S'chach, which is the defining feature of a Kosher Sukkah. Yet, Rashi, and more acutely Rabbeinu Chananel, write that the P'sul is in the Sukkah itself — it is not really a Sukkah at all. Rashi: עשה סוכה שישיבתה ניכרת לך. Rabbeinu Chananel: כל סוכה שאינה ידועה דהאי סוכה דמצוה היא, אינו סוכה. In other words, without the awareness of the *Gavra* / person, there *is no* Sukkah.

* *Sukkah*, 11b. This is the *Girsa* / version in our Gemara, yet the Medrash has these two sages giving the opposite interpretations — ר' אליעזר אומר סוכות ממש היו. ר' עקיבא אומר, ענני כבוד היו: *Sifra*, Emor, 17. 11. *Mechilta*, Bo. *Sefer Rokeach*, 219. ר' עקיבה אומר אין סכות אלא ענני כבוד: *Mechilta DeRashbi*, 13:19. *Bikurei Yaakov*, Orach Chayim, 625:2. *Chelkas Yoav*, Orach Chayim, Siman 27. The version in the Medrash seems more consistent, as generally, the Halachah follows Rebbe Akiva (*Eruvin*, 46b), and the Halachah is that

BASIC QUESTIONS

Rebbe Akiva's opinion, as above, is that we are remembering that Hashem sat us in booths when we left Egypt. Obvious questions about this idea arise, although our sitting in a Sukkah today could be considered a *Chok* / super-rational Mitzvah, in which case questioning it could be 'irrelevant'. Questions, however, are necessary to deepen our learning and understanding, so, we should ask: what is so special or amazing about sitting in booths as we left Egypt; why is there an obligation to 'remember' or commemorate this event?*

---

when sitting in the Sukkah, one should think about the Clouds of Glory — והסוכות שאומר הכתוב שהושיבנו בהם הם ענני כבודו: *Tur*, Orach Chayim, 625. Rashi, *Sukkah*, 2b: אלא בידיעות דורות הבאין היקף סוכות ענני כבוד הנעשה לאבות. However, see *Shu'T Toras Chesed*, Orach Chayim, Siman 35:2, Rashi, *Vayikra*, 23:43. The version in the Medrash is also more consistent with the general principle of Rebbe Akiva, who normally follows a more interpretive and creative interpretation, albeit one in which every word of the Torah has deep significance, as distinct from a purely literal meaning (the general principle of Rebbe Yishmael is that the Torah speaks 'literally', in the language of man): See *Tosefos*, Sotah, 24a. Yerushalmi, *Sotah*, 7:5. Note: *Shavuos*, 19a, Rashi ad loc. These are the two opinions, yet, the Pasuk uses the term סכות / Sukkos, plural and with a Vav, suggesting that the two opinions of the Sages are simultaneously both accurate.

* The Ramban writes, החלו לעשותן (סוכה יא) ועל דעת האומר סכות ממש עשו להם בתחילת החרף מפני הקור כמנהג המחנות ולכן צוה בהן בזמן הזה והזכרון שידעו שידעו ויזכרו שהיו / במדבר לא באו בבית ועיר מושב לא מצאו ארבעים שנה והשם היה עמהם לא חסרו דבר "And according to the opinion of the sage who says that *Sukkahs/Sukkos* means booths in the literal sense (the reason why this commandment is to be observed at the onset of the winter season, and why it is celebrated at all to begin with), they began to build Sukkahs at the beginning of the winter, on account of the cold, as is customary in camps. Therefore, He commanded (that we also build) them at that time. The sense of the remembrance is that we should know and remember that we were in the wilderness and did not live in homes, "and they found no city of habitation" for forty years, but Hashem was with us and we lacked nothing: *Ramban*, Vayikra, 23:43.

In fact, the booths seem inconsequential to the Exodus from Egypt and being freed; perhaps it would be just as relevant to commemorate the type of sandals that *Klal Yisrael* / the Community of Israel wore when they left Egypt. Why is the structure they sat in so relevant? Secondly, neither the miracles of the Well of Miriam nor the daily appearance of *Mon* / Manna warrant even a one-day Yom Tov, so why do the booths, even if they commemorate the miraculous Clouds of Glory, demand a full seven-day celebration?

Moreover, what does it actually mean that we sat in *Sukkahs* / booths as we left Egypt? People who journey through the Desert pitch tents in the sand; they do not make booths to shelter themselves. Indeed, throughout the Torah description of the journey through the Desert, the Torah speaks about the "tents" of Klal Yisrael, as in, *Mah Tovu Ohalecha Ya'akov* / "How beautiful are your tents Yaakov," and "Return to your tents!" If we assume that an *Ohel* / 'tent' and a Sukkah are two distinct types of shelter, what does it mean that we sat in Sukkahs as we left Egypt?

One possible answer is that Ohel might sometimes refer to a Sukkah, and visa versa. This would be quite puzzling, however, given many detailed laws defining the structure of a Sukkah, with its temporary, permeable roof made with materials that grow from the ground, and so forth. A 'tent' is not described in that way, rather it is a structure with a slanted fabric roof held up with poles — disqualifying it as a Sukkah.

Another possible answer is that during the spring and summer months, the first six months of journeying from Egypt,
they resided in flimsy fabric tents, and when Tishrei and its
colder weather arrived, they fashioned stronger, more durable
structures with rigid walls: Sukkahs, booths. This would be the
reason why we celebrate the Yom Tov of Sukkos not in the
month of Nisan when they left Egypt, but in the time of the
year when Sukkahs were first used, half a year after leaving
Egypt, the seventh month of Tishrei, as will be explored.

Another interesting possibility regarding 'tents' or 'booths'
is what the Chayei Adam may be indicating when he writes
about the literal Sukkahs: בשעה שצרו על העיירות במלחמות סיחון ועוג
/ "(We sit in Sukkahs to commemorate) when they encircled
the cities during the battle of Sichon and Og" (*Shabbos u'Moadim*, 146). This would mean that sitting in a Sukkah we are reminded of when we sat in Sukkahs during the battles before
we entered Eretz Yisrael, the Land of Israel. Perhaps, beyond
the miracles that occurred while conquering these cities, there
was a miracle in the fact that we sat in booths. Normally, if an
army is attacking or being attacked, it shelters within fortified
barracks, while here, we sat in flimsy booths and yet were victorious.

This idea that the Sukkah is a remembrance of the wars with
Sichon and Og originates in the writings of the Rokeach, Rebbe Eliezer of Worms. These are his words: "There are commen-

taries (presently, no previous source of this idea is found) that say that when Klal Yisrael encircled Sichon and Og, and later (during the times of Yehoshua) the cities in Kena'an, then (during the battle) they sat in *Sukkahs* / booths, as it says in Shemuel (2, 11:11) "The Ark, Klal Yisrael, and Yehudah are dwelling in Sukkahs"... (such is the way of battle, for armies to shelter in booths)...for until Klal Yisrael conquered and settled the land of *Kena'an* / Canaan, which became Eretz Yisrael, it was still considered the process of 'leaving Egypt'. This occurred in the fortieth year after leaving Egypt. So we should not think, that we merely inherited the land from our ancestors, Avraham, Yitzchak and Yaakov, rather, we should know that when we left Egypt we waged war on these cities (and Hashem gave them) into the hands of Klal Yisrael" (ויש מפרשים כשצרו על ארץ האמורי

של סיחון ועוג ועל כרכים שבארץ כנען אז ישבו ישראל בסכות כמש"כ וארון וישראל ויהודה יושבים בסכות כי בשדה היה מסכך עליהן עד שכבשו רבת בני עמון כך ישראל עד שכבשו ארץ כנען זהו כי בסכות הושבתי את בנ"י כשצרים את האומות. וכל זמן שלא כבשו וחלקו קורא יציאת מצרים כמש"כ אשר הכה משה ובנ"י בצאתם ממצרים. והיא שנת הארבעים וזהו למען ידעו דורותיכם כי בסוכות. שלא יחשבו מאבתינו אברהם ויצחק ויעקב אנחנו יושבים בארץ אלא ידעו שיצאו ממצרים וצרו על הערים ונתנם ביד ישראל: *Hilchos Sukkos*, Siman 219. *Eliyahu Rabbah*, Orach Chayim, 625. See *Shu'T Chasam Sofer*, Orach Chayim, 185. ולא מצאתי פתר אלא עפ"י מ"ש הרוקח הובא בספר אלי' רבה ר"סי תרנ"ה. See also *Shu'T Toras Chesed*, Siman 35:2. *Derashos Chasam Sofer*, Sukkos, 5593).

In other words, we should not simply think that we inherited the Land peacefully and effortlessly, for sitting in booths on Sukkos is a reminder of the hardships of conquering the

Land and the marvelous miracles that Hashem performed for us that allowed us to settle the Land of Milk and Honey, completing our journey from Egypt.

There are tremendous *Chidushim* / innovative ideas present in these words of the Rokeach. For one, he is telling us that the Mitzvah to sit in Sukkahs (according to the opinion that we are to remember the booths that we sat in) was only given to Klal Yisrael at the end of their forty-year journey through the Desert (although they were apparently commanded years earlier to sit in Sukkahs, as recorded in the Book of *Vayikra*), and this refers to the Sukkahs of the encampment during the battles. In this way, we are also remembering the miracles of the battles of conquering Eretz Yisrael — an unexpected reason for sitting in the Sukkah.

Seemingly, this also helps us resolve the question of why a Sukkah is known to be a 'booth' and not a tent. In the Desert, they may have sat and journeyed in tents, but when they went to battle at the end of the Exodus process, they set up booths.

Some bigger questions are still not resolved, however. For example, why should we remember sitting in Sukkahs more than the miracles of the process of leaving Egypt and journeying to Eretz Yisrael?

Apparently, the Rokeach is saying that there were stages in the Exodus from Egypt, and the Exodus was not complete until stage two was completed. The journey began with the Exodus from Egypt, a momentous event celebrated on Pesach. The second stage of this journey was marked by entering and settling in the Land of Israel, and Sukkos is particularly connected to this second stage, as will be explored.

WHY WOULD WE NEED TO REMEMBER THE CLOUDS OF GLORY?

If we assume the opinion of Rebbe Eliezer, that on Sukkos we are celebrating the miraculous Clouds of Glory, this merely answers the first question of 'why' we are remembering and gratefully commemorating that miraculous protection and shade. But this leaves the second question unanswered: why officially commemorate this miracle and not the other miracles in the Desert? Many miracles occurred in the Desert. And perhaps a bigger question still applies to both opinions (that we are commemorating the booths or we are commemorating the Clouds of Glory): we were redeemed from Egypt during the month of Nisan, which is six months before Tishrei. Why are we celebrating Sukkos in the month of Tishrei at all? The Yom Tov of sitting in Sukkahs should seemingly have been established in Nisan; maybe on Pesach, we should be eating our Matzah in a Sukkah.

Let us begin exploring these questions with the writings of Rebbe Yaakov ben Asher (c.1269 to c.1343), who was one of the great systematic codifiers of *Halachah* / Law. He writes in

his magnum opus, the *Tur* (*Orach Chayim*, 625), that the festival of
Sukkos is not a commemoration of the miracle of the Clouds
of Glory, nor for that matter, days of remembering the booths
in and of themselves, rather, Sukkos is a festival of remembering *Yetzias Mitzrayim* / the Exodus from Egypt (This is also
the opinion of the Radbaz, *Metzudas Dovid*, Mitzvah 117). The purpose
of the Yom Tov is to remember going out of Egypt, and the
booths or Clouds of Glory are just a means by which we are
reminded. For if the Mitzvah of Sukkos is to remember the
miracle of the Clouds of Glory, why is there no Yom Tov for
the other miracles in the Desert, especially the *Mon* / Manna
and the *Be'er* / Well of Miriam (as the *Bach* asks, 625:2:1. The Alshich
on *Vayikra*, 23:33, asks the same). Thus, he reasons, the Mitzvah of
Sukkos for all generations is ידעו / "to know that Hashem took
us out of Egypt." And then perhaps our sitting in booths and
in the Clouds of Glory is only a secondary issue.

This, then, becomes a vital question: 'Why should we celebrate Sukkos in Tishrei, and not in Nissan, if it commemorates
Yetzias Mitzrayim?' And if Sukkos commemorates specifically
the Clouds and the booths, which we surely sat in for an extended period of time, why commemorate them in Tishrei?
Continues the Tur, "Now even though we did leave Egypt in
the month of Nisan, Hashem did not command us to make
a Sukkah in that time of year since it is in the (spring and)
summer, and it is common for people to make huts for shade
(in the warm months). If Hashem had done so, it would not
have been apparent that we made Sukkahs in fulfillment of the

Mitzvah of our Creator. Therefore, Hashem commanded us to make Sukkahs in the seventh month (Tishrei) which is in the rainy season, and when it is customary for people to leave their summer huts or gazebos and return inside their homes. However, we (visibly do the opposite and) leave our homes and dwell in our Sukkahs. Through this activity, we show that our dwelling in the Sukkah is in fulfillment of our King's command" (See also *Menoras haMaor*, Siman 148. Even Ezra, *Vayikra*, 23:43).[*]

The Even Ezra writes that the reason the Torah places Sukkos in Tishrei, and not in Nisan when Klal Yisrael left Egypt, is that Klal Yisrael did not rest in physical booths when they first left Egypt. When they first left Egypt, the Clouds of Glory protected them from the hot sun of spring and summer, and during those months they apparently did not need any other form of protection. Before winter began, however, they needed to create booths to protect themselves from the cold, and thus we commemorate these *Sukkahs* / booths in the month of Tishrei, before the onset of the winter (ואם ישאל שואל למה בתשרי זאת המצוה יש להשיב כי ענן ה' היה על המחנה יומם ומימות תשרי החלו לעשות סוכות בעבור הקור: Even Ezra, *Vayikra*, 23:43).

---

[*] In fact, Rabbeinu Tam rules that a Sukkah in which the rain is not able to enter, due to the density of the S'chach, is not Kosher — ור"ת פסק שאם עשאה עבה מאוד שאין המטר יכול לירד בה פסולה: *Tur*, Orach Chayim, 631 (Not Kosher even according to Torah law: *Pri Megadim*, Orach Chayim, 635. The Taz argues that it is only a ruling *mi-d'Rabanan* / from our Sages that it is not Kosher: Taz, *ibid.*, 635:2). See *Mordechai*, Sukkah, 1:732. *Hagahos Maimonios*, Rambam, *Hilchos Sukkah*, 5:9. Note Tosefos, *Sukkah*, 2a.

These meteorology-based reasons of the Even Ezra and Tur provide an answer to why Sukkos is not in Nisan, nor the spring or summer, but the question still remains why Sukkos is specifically in Tishrei. If we sit in a Sukkah during the rainy season to demonstrate that we are doing it for a Mitzvah, why not sit in the onset of winter rather than the fall, or in the depths of the winter, say in the month of Teves? One reasonable answer for this is that in bitter winter cold and precipitation, it would be *too* uncomfortable to sit in a Sukkah, and the Torah does not ask us to cause ourselves suffering or illness, we would be exempt from the Mitzvah. Then why not do it in Cheshvan, which may be rainy, but not yet too cold? Similarly, if the issue is that Bnei Yisrael built booths *before* the winter, then perhaps we should celebrate in Kislev, which is the last month of the fall, just before the official arrival of winter.

It could be argued (at least according to the Tur) that the reason Tishrei was chosen for Sukkos — as opposed to Cheshvan or Kislev, for example — is that Tishrei is the *beginning* of the fall rainy season. Therefore it is the perfect time to display the fact that we are moving out into our booths specifically as a Mitzvah: people naturally move from their gazebos into their homes at this time of year, while we are visibly moving from our homes out to our Sukkos. Later in the winter, no one is still moving from outdoors into their homes, so we would not be visibly displaying our devotion to the Mitzvos. Yet, fall 'officially' begins in the month of Elul,* and the truly transitional

---

* Although the fall months begin within the month of Elul, it could be argued that Tishrei was nonetheless chosen because as Chazal tell us, שילהי

month is later, in Cheshvan, so we still need to clarify why we do not celebrate Sukkos in Elul or Cheshvan.

Honestly, all of this might seem a little coincidental or even superficial; is it really possible that a seasonal weather pattern can push off the Yom Tov of Sukkos for six months, from Nissan to Tishrei? As everything can and should be understood on multiple levels, the real question is, what is the deeper, *intrinsic* reason that Sukkos is in the month of Tishrei? And why does Sukkos follow Yom Kippur and Rosh Hashanah, seemingly being part of the unfolding of the Yamim Noraim? And why does Sukkos begin specifically on the fifteenth of the month?

With regards to the other Yamim Tovim, the month when it should occur is not a question; for example, we celebrate the Yom Tov of Pesach and the Exodus from Egypt precisely on the date that we left Egypt. Sukkos seems unique in that the sitting in the Sukkah does not seem to be related to the particular date when it is celebrated. Furthermore, on Pesach there is a Mitzvah to eat Matzah because it is Pesach, the day we

---

דקייטא קשיא מקייטא / "The end of summer heat is more oppressive than the heat of the summer itself" (*Yuma*, 29a), and as Rashi notes (*ad loc*) this refers to the month of Elul. In this way, Tishrei is really the first cooler month of the year. And the reason that the 15th of Tishrei was chosen, and not the first day of Tishrei, is that the first day of the month is already a Yom Tov — Rosh Hashanah — so Sukkos, which has its own unique identity, needs to be later. Additionally, since the Torah establishes things in the 'middle' of their respective context (see *Chazon Ish*, Orach Chayim, Moed, 138:4), thus, the Torah establishes Sukkos in the middle of the first cooler month, when Klal Yisrael originally built their booths for protection from the oncoming winter winds, as well as move out of our homes while everyone else is moving indoors.

left Egypt and the celebration of our Exodus, and therefore we celebrate with eating Matzah or drinking four cups of wine, whereas on Sukkos this inherent timing does not seem to exist, as nothing historically significant seems to have happened on these specific days. From this we can derive that sitting in the Sukkah — performing the Mitzvah of Sukkos — is in fact what creates the Yom Tov of Sukkos (*Likutei Sichos* 22, Emor 2. Although, see the language of Tosefos, *Sukkah*, 46a, and the Rosh and Ran, *ad loc.*: ושמא כיון דסוכה מחמת חג קאתיא סברא הוא דזמן דידה אע"פ שבירך בחול פטור הוא אף בחג דזמן), but we still need to discover an intrinsic link between the Yom Tov of Sukkos and the month of Tishrei, and specifically the 15th day of Tishrei.

FREEDOM 'FROM' & FREEDOM 'TO':
The Two Yamim Tovim for the Exodus from Egypt

As the Tur explains, and as is obvious from the Torah's description, Sukkos is a Yom Tov to remember *Yetzias Mitzrayim* / the Exodus from Egypt. This actually raises a more fundamental question: why should there be a Yom Tov of Sukkos at all? If the essence of Sukkos is not the booths nor the Clouds of Glory, rather it is a remembrance of Yetzias Mitzrayim, why should there be *two* full seven-day Yamim Tovim — Pesach and Sukkos — established to remember Yetzias Mitzrayim? There are many Mitzvos that serve as a reminder of Yetzias Mitzrayim, as the Tur himself writes, but why are there two Yamim Tovim, and why isn't Pesach sufficient for the remembrance Yetzias Mitzrayim? If Pesach is not sufficient, in what way is it deficient, and if it is sufficient, could it be that Sukkos is in some sense superfluous, *Chas v'Shalom* / Heaven forbid?

It could be argued that the reason for the two is that Pesach focuses more on the more basic needs of our lives and Sukkos focuses on 'higher' needs. We remember Yetzias Mitzrayim on Pesach through the basic need of food; the Mitzvos unique to Pesach are eating the Pesach offering and eating the Matzah and the Maror. On Sukkos, we remember Yetzias Mitzrayim through the higher need of shelter; we celebrate the fact that we were protected and sheltered in our journey from Mitzrayim.

Yet, if there are two Yamim Tovim because Yetzias Mitzrayim involves a two-stage process, the two stages must be of a deeper issue than merely this hierarchy of physical needs, food, and shelter. An example of a two-stage process of redemption is that Pesach is connected with the miracles of the departure from Mitzrayim, whereas Sukkos is connected with the miracles in the Desert, as the Rambam writes (אמנם הדעת ב'פסח' הזכרת 'אותות מצרים' והתמדתה לדורות; אמנם הדעת ב'סוכות' להתמיד זכר 'אותות המדבר' לדורות *Moreh Nevuchim*, 3:43). Indeed, any genuine and lasting freedom entails two stages: 1) departing from the negativity, the restriction, captivity or oppression, and 2) owning, integrating and expressing the positive aspects of freedom. For his redemption to be complete, a slave must not only leave the situation and throw off the outer yoke of the master and their inner identity as a slave. He must also 'construct' his new status and dwell in it, integrate and feel his freedom — and behave as a free person.

There is 'freedom *from*'; freedom from oppression, slavery, and a negative situation, and there is 'freedom *to*'; freedom to choose a new, positive way of living, and to express your freedom.

The negation of a negative state — freedom *from* — only creates a context for the full attainment of a positive state — freedom *to*. Experiencing the first stage of freedom does not guarantee that the second stage will follow. There are plenty of examples of slaves and prisoners being physically freed from their oppressive circumstances but maintaining their identity as a victim; they never attained their freedom *to* live and express their freedom. Sadly, due to this partial redemption, many soon revert to their state of oppression and negativity.

Normally, the movement from stage one to stage two takes time. One needs to unlearn their identification as an oppressed person. A slave does not own his life, his master does; a slave cannot truly express himself, for he has no agency and no voice of his own. Owning your life means living with the recognition that you, and you alone, are responsible for your life and your happiness. Sadly, many who have been oppressed for years and then released, remained inwardly victimized, and as victims, they easily became perpetrators, *Chas veShalom* / Heaven forbid. It takes enormous perseverance and courage to build or rebuild one's mindset as a free, autonomous individual, and allow oneself to express this in thought, speech, and action. This is the significance of the Yom Tov of Sukkos.

As mentioned earlier, the Rokeach writes that a level of freedom was attained when Klal Yisrael left Egypt, but the *redemption* from Egypt was not complete until much later. In fact, it was not complete until we entered Eretz Yisrael, struggled for our sovereignty, and settled there, becoming a free people in our own land.

Pesach and Sukkos both celebrate our collective redemption from Egypt, yet Pesach celebrates our initial rescue from slavery and the dramatic birth of our nation, while Sukkos celebrates the completion of this redemption and our state of autonomy and self-actualization.

After Yetzias Mitzrayim, we experienced *Matan Torah* / the Giving of the Torah at Mount Sinai. Yet, we were not really ready to receive the Torah, and we needed to be 'forced' compelled to receive it: "And they stood *under* the Mount.' Rav Avdimi…said, 'This teaches that the Holy One, blessed be He, held the mountain over them like an (inverted) casket, and said to them, 'If you accept the Torah, good, and if not, this will be your burial'" (*Shabbos*, 88a).

Matan Torah compelled us to receive the Mitzvos, along with their paradigm of reward and punishment, accountability, and taking responsibility for our lives. Since we needed to be compelled 'from Above', it is clear that we were not yet ready to progress to the second stage of redemption, which involves *choosing* to live as free people. We were freed *from* our negative circumstances in Mitzrayim, but we were not yet free *to* live in positive freedom. In fact, a mere 40 days after Matan Torah, *Am Yisrael* / the nascent Nation of Israel created the Golden Calf, and many wished to go back to their old, self-alienating Egyptian habits, such as idol worship.

Creating the *Egel haZahav* / Golden Calf indicated that we did not yet absorb the message from Sinai and wished to live in a *Mitzri* / Egyptian mindset, which was by nature interwoven with idol worship.

We regressed. We were technically free, no longer literally slaves, but we had not yet chosen to commit to freedom, which means to serve HaKadosh Baruch Hu and to live with meaning, responsibility, and integrity.

Following the episode of the Egel haZahav, Moshe comes down the mountain and sees that not only are we regressing to a pre-Matan Torah state of consciousness and behavior, but we are doing so with joy and dancing, actually excited to let go of the Sinai revelation and experience. Moshe then smashes the *Luchos* / 'tablets' in which are engraved the essence of Torah. Some eighty days later, on the tenth of Tishrei, atonement is granted to Klal Yisrael and Moshe comes back down the Mountain for the second time, bringing to us the second set of Luchos. We are now ready to commit to them and live by them by choice.

What occurs between the smashing of the first Luchos and the giving of the second, eternally unbroken, Luchos is *Teshu-*

vah / returning to our purpose, taking responsibility for our actions, owning our lives, admitting our mistakes, and learning from them. We were able to recover our freedom by honestly observing ourselves and accepting upon ourselves a redeemed mode of consciousness and conduct. In other words, six months after leaving Egypt, we finally attained the second step of freedom, the freedom *to* choose Divine Instruction, *to* choose a life of higher values and higher accountability.

Every year on Pesach, we experience again an escape from the oppression and slavery of our inner Egypt — our addictions and our subjugation to our *Yetzer haRa* / inclination to negativity. Liberated from our constrictions and limitations, on Pesach we taste *Gadlus* / expansiveness, we taste what it means to truly live freely and authentically and live from a place of physical, emotional, mental and spiritual greatness (as explored in the volume, *The Month of Nisan* and in *The Haggadah: Pathways to Pesach and the Haggadah*).

In contrast to Pesach, on Sukkos we do not remember or make mention of our slavery and oppression; there is only joy. Sukkos is in fact called *Zeman Simchaseinu* / "the Time of Our Rejoicing." On Pesach night, we eat *Maror* / bitter herbs and say, "For what reason do we eat this Maror? Because the Egyptians embittered our ancestors in Egypt." We also eat Karpas dipped in salt water, a reminder of our tears as slaves. We recite the Haggadah over a broken piece of "poor man's bread." This is because Pesach is about 'freedom *from*'. We remember where we came from, and how we were taken out of that lowly state. On the night of Pesach, we declare, "We were slaves to Pharaoh in Egypt, but Hashem, our G-d, brought us out from there with a strong hand and an outstretched arm." We speak not only about our physical freedom, but our spiritual freedom, "In the beginning our fathers served idols; but now the Omnipresent One has brought us close to His service." Yet throughout the seven nights and days of Sukkos, we mention nothing about 'slavery', 'idol worship', 'bitterness', or 'tears'. We only celebrate the second dimension of Yetzias Mitzrayim, the stage of being an autonomous people who freely choose the path of Torah. Now it is not just that 'the Omnipresent brought us close to His service,' but that we ourselves are bringing ourselves close and serving Hashem out of love.

Each stage of our development is important. On Pesach, we are 'born' and spoon-fed the 'food of freedom' by our Divine Parent. On Shavuos, we become a Bar or Bas Mitzvah, 'compelled' to take up responsibilities. On Sukkos, we have reached true maturity; we celebrate our wedding (as will be explored in great detail), willfully joining our Chosen One, and rejoicing for seven days. On Sukkos, we move fearlessly and on our own power into a Sukkah, a temporary structure with very little 'Parental' protection — very little physical protection from the elements and potential intruders. In this mature level of freedom, we actively declare our commitment to our Beloved, and we take up our freedom to be ourselves and affirm that there is nothing external that can cause us to live in fear.

With these analogies for stages in our maturing process — birth and infancy, our Bar or Bas Mitzvah, and finally our wedding — we can also understand why the 'Season of our Rejoicing' is specifically the Yom Tov of Sukkos.

Very young children display unbridled joy and happiness because of their innocence and their freedom from dichotomies between how they feel and how they act. Sadly, as school children, they develop more self-awareness and social awareness. Later on, as adolescents, they begin to go through an uncomfortable sense of dichotomy between who they feel they are and who they want to be.

Say a young person is in a class where everyone is loud and boisterous yet they are more timid and shy. They want to be part of the group, but they are not comfortable being loud and boisterous, so they are torn between the social pressure to fit in and the discomfort of feeling like an outcast, and this produces anxiety. True happiness only comes with years of maturing, higher self-mastery, and autonomy. When we finally know and accept ourselves as we are, then we are able to consciously choose to marry and live with someone who complements us and makes us even more ourselves. This is authentic, deep happiness. And thus, Z'man Simchaseinu refers to the festival of Sukkos.

Pesach celebrates our being freed from oppression, while Sukkos celebrates that we are truly free in our maturity and self-actualization. This is why Sukkos follows Yom Kippur, the day of taking on responsibility for our lives and re-accepting the Torah. And this is why we need two full-fledged Yamim Tovim to remember Yetzias Mitzrayim: our liberation from Galus and our movement toward Geulah (In this way, Nisan corresponds to the *Avodah* / inner work of a Tzadik, whereas Tishrei, culminating in Sukkos, corresponds to the Avodah of the *Baal Teshuvah* / returnee, someone who truly takes full responsibility of his or her life: See *Haga'as Chochmas Shelomo*, Shulchan Aruch, Hilchos Rosh Hashanah, 592:8).

Another way of describing the sequence of the Shalosh Regalim, which will be discussed further on, is three stages in the development of Klal Yisrael: 1) Pesach celebrates our becoming a people, 2) Shavuos celebrates our becoming a people with a purpose, and 3) Sukkos celebrates our being a people with a purpose and with the Divine Protection that we need in order to fulfill that Purpose.

	PESACH	SHAVUOS	SUKKOS
CELEBRATION	Freedom from Galus	Giving of the Torah	Geulah and Settling Eretz Yisrael*
STAGE OF DEVELOPMENT	Becoming a people	Becoming a people with a purpose	Being a people with a purpose and with the Divine Protection to fulfill that Purpose

---

* The Torah speaks about Sukkos as when we enter the land and gather its produce — באספכם את־תבואת הארץ: *Vayikra*, 23:29. And the reason why the Navi (*Nechemya*, 8:17), speaks of the reentering to Eretz Yisrael and the celebration of Sukkos in the times of Ezra. ויעשו כל־הקהל השבים מן־השבי סכות / ויישבו בסכות כי לא־עשו מימי ישוע בן־נון כן בני ישראל עד היום ההוא "The whole community that returned from the captivity made Sukkos and dwelt in the Sukkos, as they have not done so from the days of Yehoshua" (when Klal Yisrael first entered in Eretz Yisrael). They of course celebrated Sukkos for all the years from the time of Yehoshua until the time of Ezra (*Erchin*, 32b), but there was a special emphasis during the time when we first settled the Land and when we returned. This also helps better understand the opinion that was explored, of the Rokeach, for the reason for Sukkos and why the idea of circling the Mizbe'ach of Sukkos is connected with the capturing of Yericho and the first entry into Eretz Yisrael: *Yerushalmi, Sukkah*, 4:3. Additionally, we celebrate Sukkos with the Arba Minim that grow in various environments within Eretz Yisrael, and we celebrate specifically with these Minim that are 'not under any Mazal' (*Seder haYom*, Kavanos haLulav. *Rosh Dovid* (Chidah), Emor. *Megaleh Amukos*, Sukkos, *V'Lekachtem*). The Arba Minim are like Eretz Yisrael as a whole, which is not under any Mazal, as the Ramban (on *Vayikra*, 18:25) writes: אבל ארץ ישראל אמצעות הישוב היא נחלת ה' מיוחדת לשמו לא נתן עליה מן המלאכים קצין שוטר ומושל בהנחילו אותה.

SUKKOS FOLLOWING YOM KIPPUR:
Hashem Protects Us Always, Even After We Fall

A question arises: why do we need to remember Yetzias Mitzrayim specifically through sitting in a Sukkah? There is clearly something unique about the fact that the Sukkah is a temporary structure, and that it is covered with S'chach such as cut branches from a tree. What is the significance of sitting in a temporary structure under the "shadow" of S'chach, and what is the relationship of S'chach with this second stage of freedom and Zeman Simchaseinu?

After offering verbatim the words of the Tur, the *Aruch haShulchan* (Orach Chayim, 625:5) writes that the reason Sukkos is in Tishrei and not in Nisan is that HaKadosh Baruch Hu wants to show us that even after we have sinned and strayed from the path of righteousness, justice, Torah, and Mitzvos, Hashem still protects us, and we rest in His *Tzeil* / shadow and are protected under His wings.

This is just like in the Desert, where, following Matan Torah (in Sivan), we sinned with the Golden Calf and then were forgiven and given the second set of Luchos on Yom Kippur. Then, on the day after Yom Kippur, we were commanded to create a *Mikdash* / a temporary Temple so that Hashem's Presence would rest there among us. This way, the Clouds of Glory would not depart from us. Similarly, HaKadosh Baruch Hu gave us the Mitzvah of Sukkos to reenact this for all generations: although we may have sinned through the prior year and not lived up to our full potential, nonetheless, on Yom Kippur, we align with Teshuvah, we receive atonement, and can begin with a clean slate. And as a sign that Teshuvah has been achieved, right after Yom Kippur we are commanded and invited to fashion a Sukkah, where we sit in the Tzeil and protection of HaKadosh Baruch Hu, as the verse says, "I delight to sit in His shade" (*Shir haShirim*, 2:3) which refers to Sukkos (*Zohar* 3, 255b). Hashem's love for us is unconditional and eternal; He watches over us, protects us from all hardship, and brings us to sit in His holy Tzeil.

This idea places Sukkos within the context of the High Holy Days; it follows Yom Kippur. It explains why we sit in the Tzeil and protection of HaKadosh Baruch Hu at this time of year.

The Sukkah is not merely a booth or temporary structure that is built because of the Mitzvah to build it, but it becomes an object of holiness itself, not just reserved for a Mitzvah but a sacred object in itself (*Sukkah*, 9a. *Beitza*, 30b. וקשה דמשמע הכא דמה שעצי סוכה אסורין היינו מטעם מוקצה ...לעיל קאמר מה חג לה' אף סוכה לה' אלמא דאסורין מדאורייתא ותירץ ר"ת דמה שאמר מה חג לשם אף סוכה לשם היינו לפי שיעור סוכה כגון ב' דפנות ושלישית אפי' טפח אבל אי עביד דפנות שלמות יותר משיעור סוכה לא נפיק מקרא ועל היותר קאמר שאסור מטעם מוקצה: Tosefos, *ibid.*).

When we are sitting in the Sukkah, we are literally sitting in Hashem's embrace, and in the canopy of the Clouds of Glory, the revealed Presence of the *Shechinah* / Indwelling Divine Presence. Throughout the year, we may have drifted and, G-d forbid, left the protection of the Clouds of Glory, but then on Rosh Hashanah we again awaken from our spiritual slumber, and on Yom Kippur we are washed clean, freed, and fully atoned. Then comes Sukkos and we once again bask in the Presence of HaKadosh Baruch Hu, fully embraced and fully accepted for who we are in the canopy of the Clouds of Glory.*

Sukkos is thus a celebration of 'return' — the returning of the Clouds of Glory once we have returned in Teshuvah. Sukkos is our return to wholeness, presence, and Divine space, after brokenness, after falling. The Chasidic Rebbes teach that when we enter the Sukkah, we are like a child who runs into the loving embrace of his or her mother (*Ma'or vaShemesh*, Rimzei Yom Beis Sukkos). When a child feels scared, vulnerable, or threatened, they run to their mother and hide beneath her dress. We too, consciously or not, feel we are in peril because of our previous actions, and the act of Teshuvah is running into the embrace of our אימא עילאה / *Ima Ila'ah* / Supernal Divine Mother. This occurs on Yom Kippur, which is connected with the *Sefirah* / Divine attribute of Binah, also referred to as *Ima*

---

*Interestingly, the Torah (Re'eh) describes the Yom Tovim of Pesach and Shavuos differently from Sukkos, in terms of their respective *Korbanos* / offerings. Speaking of the Pesach offerings, it says they should be done במקום אשר־יבחר ה' לשכן שמו שם / "in the place Hashem will choose to rest His name therein" (*Devarim*, 16:2). Speaking of Shavuos offerings, it says they should be done במקום אשר יבחר ה' אלקיך לשכן שמו שם / "In the place Hashem Your G-d will choose to rest His name therein" (16:11). Yet, when the Torah speaks of Sukkos offings, it says, במקום אשר־יבחר ה' / "In the place Hashem will choose," but omits לשכן שמו שם / "to rest therein." Why this omission? It is because, on a deeper level, the Ohr of Sukkos that is revealed as the Clouds of Glory is not limited to "that particular place" where Hashem chose to rest, i.e., in the Beis haMikdash, rather, when we build a Sukkah, Hashem's Presence rests there.

/ Mother. And then Sukkos comes along and we hide under the 'canopy' of her skirts, the holy Sukkah, the *Makifim* / 'surrounding lights' of Binah. There, in the loving presence of our Mother, we are protected from all negative influences and we are joyfully relieved.

Picture a child — lost, frightened, or perhaps having wandered off in a moment of anger — suddenly catching sight of their mother, arms wide open, waiting. Without hesitation, the child runs, heart pounding, tears flowing, and falls into her embrace. There, held close, every fear dissolves, and every hurt melts away. This is Yom Kippur — when every soul, no matter how far it has strayed, comes running back to its Divine Parent. And then comes Sukkos, when Heaven itself wraps us in an embrace. The Shechinah draws us near, holds us close, and whispers, "You are home. You are safe. I love you, forever." And in that embrace — in that shelter of eternal love — our hearts lift, our souls dance, and joy overflows.

In the Sukkah, we come to realize a gentle, wondrous truth, that there is nowhere to fall. No matter where we wander, no matter what path we tread, we are always cradled within Hashem's loving embrace. The walls of the Sukkah whisper to us: You are held. You are surrounded. You are safe. This is why the Mitzvah of Sukkah calls not only for sitting — but for *Da'as* — for conscious awareness, for deep knowing. For Da'as is Ta'anug, for when we open our hearts to truly feel this reality, when we awaken to the sweetness of being held by the Infinite, this knowing itself becomes the deepest Ta'anug — the purest pleasure. To know we are never alone, to feel there is nowhere to fall but into Hashem's arms, this is the joy of Sukkos. A joy not born from things going right, but from knowing we are forever wrapped in Divine love. In the words of a great Chasidic teacher: נודע שעיקר העבודה האלקות הוא בדעת כמו שאמר הכתוב דע את אלקי אביך ועבדהו והדעת הוא תענוג שעל ידי שעובד השם יתברך בדעת רחב נמשך לו תענוג בעבודתו מעולם התענוג / "It is known that the main spiritual work is of Da'as, as the Pasuk says, 'Know the Divinity of your father and serve Him.' And Da'as is *Ta'anug* / pleasure, because when one serves Hashem with expansive Da'as, pleasure is attracted to him in his Avodah from the World of Pleasure" (*Me'or Einayim*, Toldos).

WHY BEGIN SUKKOS ON THE FIFTEENTH OF THE MONTH?

Now we understand why Sukkos follows Yom Kippur, and why Sukkos is a full seven-day Yom Tov celebrating *Yetzias Mitzrayim* / the Going Out of Egypt and the sense of being free. What still demands an explanation is why, specifically, does Sukkos begin on the fifteenth, the midpoint of the month (besides the reason that the Torah always establishes constructs in the 'middle' [*Chazon Ish*, Orach Chayim, Moed, 138:4], and thus, *any* Yom Tov that is connected to a whole month begins in the middle of the month).

When Klal Yisrael fashioned the Golden Calf, the Clouds of Glory, which had enveloped them as they left Egypt, departed the camp.[*] The Clouds of Glory ascended on high

---

[*]*Targum*, Shir haShirim, 2:17. ובזעירות יומיא עבדו בני ישראל ית עגלא דדהבא ואסתלקו עֲנָנֵי יקרא די מטללין עליהון / "And in a few days, the Children of Israel made the

when they sinned, and they returned with the beginning of the building of the *Mishkan* / temporary Temple. The sequence of the narrative is as follows. Some 120 days after the sin of the Golden Calf, on Yom Kippur, the tenth day of Tishrei, atonement was granted as well as the second set of Luchos. The following morning, the eleventh day of Tishrei (*Shemos*, 35:1, Rashi), Moshe joyously gathered Klal Yisrael and informed them the Mitzvah of building the Mishkan and the need to start gathering the materials. Then the Torah tells us that Klal Yisrael began bringing "freewill offerings…morning after morning" (בבקר בבקר: *Shemos*, 36:3). On a deeper, non-literal level, this means they brought materials for the Mishkan on two mornings: the twelfth and the thirteenth of the month. On the fourteenth, the architects of the Mishkan had sorted out, weighed, and organized all the materials, and found that they

---

Golden Calf and the cloud of glory which had sheltered them was lifted." Although *Nechemyah*, 9:18-19, says, ואתה ברחמיך הרבים לא עזבתם במדבר את-עמוד העמן לא-סר מעליהם ביומם להנחתם בהדרך ואת-עמוד האש בלילה להאיר להם ואת-הדרך אשר ילכו-בה / "You, in Your abundant compassion, did not abandon them in the wilderness. The pillar of cloud did not depart from them to guide them on the way by day, nor the pillar of fire by night to give them light in the way they were to go," which seems to suggest that even after the sin, the Clouds of Glory did not depart. The Medrash says clearly as well — אלא אפלו באותה שעה לא זז מחבתן, לוה להן ע07011 כבוד ולא פסקו מהם המן והבאר: *Medrash Rabbah*, Bamidbar, 20:19 (see *Ta'ama d'Kra*, Nechemyah, ibid.). Yet, perhaps the Pasuk is talking about the clouds that guided them ("to guide them on the way by day, nor the pillar of fire by night to give them light in the way they were to go") as opposed to the 'Clouds of Glory', which were there simply for the *Kavod* / glory of Klal Yisrael. It seems that the *Aruch haShulchan*, quoted above, does not quote the teaching of the Gra precisely, because he brings, two Halachos prior, this Pasuk in Nechemyah and learns from it that the Clouds of Glory never departed. See also *Sefer haKuzari*, Ma'amar 1:97: ולא פסק המן לרדת למזונם, והענן לסוכך עליהם ועמוד האש להנחתם.

had more than enough. Thus, they began to build the Mishkan on the fifteenth,* whereupon the presence of the Clouds of Glory returned (*Pirush haGra*, Shir haShirim, 1:4. *Avodas haGershuni*, ibid., 3:4. Note Chida, *Nachal Kedumim*, Shemos, 32:25. See also *Derashos Chasam Sofer*, Shabbos Shuvah, 5595, where a similar idea as the Gra's is explained — but unlike the Gra, he does not say that the Clouds departed from Klal Yisrael, rather, that those who served the Golden Calf were ejected out of the Clouds of Glory).

In this way, constructing the Mishkan was the antidote for the sin of the Golden Calf, and on the Fifteenth of Tishrei, the Clouds of Glory returned amid great celebration, setting the beginning of the joyful celebration of Sukkos on the Fifteenth. And thus, the Clouds of Glory returned to us through our *Teshuvah* / return and inner *Avodah* / work. Through our desire to draw closer to Hashem and to let go of idol worship, we merited Yom Kippur, to be forgiven, and to be given the Mitzvah to build a physical space in which Hashem's Presence would rest in and among us (hence, women are exempt from the obligation to sit in a Sukkah, as women did not sin with the Golden Calf).

---

* Another question is, how could they have started to build the Mishkan on the fifteenth of the month, since the fifteenth is (or was to become) the first day of Yom Tov, and the *Halachah* / law is (*Shavuos*, 15b) that we would not be allowed to build the Mishkan or the Beis haMikdash on Yom Tov? There is an opinion that suggests that the prohibition of doing work on Yom Tov was only commanded *after* the building of the Mishkan was completed: *Teshuvas haRivash*, 96. The question nevertheless remains, since the fifteenth of the month that year was Shabbos, since Yom Kippur, the tenth of the month, was Monday, as Tosefos (*Baba Kama*, 82a) explains.

In a sense, not only did the Clouds of Glory return through our Avodah, but the Clouds of Glory were 'created', and made to settle close to us and surround us like a Sukkah, through our Avodah.

We thus revealed the Clouds of Glory during the first year of the Exodus narrative, and then again, during the times of the Mishkan. This revelation continued in the Beis haMikdash through the Avodah of Yom Kippur and Rosh Hashanah. Even today, the Clouds of Glory are generated through our Avodah of Yom Kippur and Rosh Hashanah.

TIMES OF THE BEIS HAMIKDASH

Once our journey through the Desert was complete, the Clouds of Glory that accompanied us through that journey departed. Yet, the Torah tells us, "You shall dwell in Sukkos seven days…in order that future generations may know that I made Bnei Yisrael live in Sukkos when I brought them out of the Land of Mitzrayim." According to one opinion, this is a reference to the Clouds of Glory, and therefore we create a Sukkah each year and remember the Clouds of Glory (In contrast to the Tur and the Bach, the Beis Yoseph maintains that the *Da'as* / awareness we need while sitting in the Sukkah is remembering specifically the Clouds of Glory that protected us in our journey through the Desert: Mechaber, *Orach Chayim*, 625. *Kaf haChayim*, 625:2. Since Da'as is essential to the Mitzvah, a Sukkah that is higher than *Esrim* / twenty Amos, with the S'chach above the height where we are naturally aware of it, is not Kosher: *Sukkah*, 2a. Twenty represents the world of *Keser* / Transcendence (as an allusion to this idea is that עשרים / *Esrim* in numerical value is 620, the same as the word כתר / *Keser*), which is beyond our grasp, beyond our Da'as, hence not Kosher: *Shushan Sodos*, Os 560).

From a deeper perspective, while sitting in the Sukkah, we are once again, on some level, sitting in the protection of Hashem's *Tzeil* / shadow, in the Clouds of Glory. In this way, the *S'chach* / covering, the permeable 'roof' which is the *Ikar* / main element of the Sukkah, embodies the Clouds of Glory, the protection of Hashem's Tzeil.

In the times of the Beis haMikdash, the highest, most exalted and sacred *Avodah* / service on Yom Kippur was the *Ketores* / incense (a special blend of eleven herbs and resins) offered in the Holy of Holies. Once a year, on Yom Kippur, the holiest day of the year, the *Cohen Gadol* / High Priest, potentially the holiest person alive, would enter the Holy of Holies, the holiest place on earth. Before entering, he would take a pan of burning coals in his right hand, and in his left a ladle filled with Ketores. Stepping into the Holy of Holies with great trepidation, he would gather the Ketores into his hand and place them over the coals. When an ענן / *Anan* / Cloud of the smoke of the Ketores would fill the Holy of Holies, he would gently back out of the room.

This Avodah of Ketores was performed by the Cohen Gadol in utter silence and stillness in the innermost sanctum. In contrast, the services in the Beis haMikdash that were done in the Outside Courtyard were performed with many Cohanim, with a backdrop of singing Levi'im and instrumental music played by Levi'im and *Yisraelim Meyuchasim* / confirmed Israelites — there were a lot of sounds and sights; animals, smoke, blood, billowing fire, and music. The service of the Ketores was a private Avodah. No other living being was present when the Cohen Gadol entered the Holy of Holies. Not even angels were allowed to enter, as it were (*Yerushalmi*, *Yuma*, 1:5). It was one person alone with the One Creator. Ketores literally means 'bonding'. This was a deeply intense moment of truth, of bonding with Hashem, with no sounds, sights, or even movements of angels.

As the smoke of the Ketores rose, it became like an ענן / *Anan* / cloud, a metaphorical manifestation of the ענני הכבוד / *Ananei haKavod* / Clouds of Glory.*

* In fact, through the forty years of the Desert, since the ענני הכבוד / Clouds of Glory hovered over them, similar to Yom Kippur, when the Torah says, that the Cohen Gadol cannot enter into the Holy of Holies, only on Yom Kippur, since כי בענן אראה על הכפרת / "For I appear in the cloud over the Kapores" (*Vayikra*, 16:3), thus, for the forty years Klal Yisrael was on a level of Yom Kippur (as the *Sefurno*, end of Emor writes). And for this reason, Aharon was able to perform the Avodah similar to Yom Kippur any day of the year and enter into the Holy of Holies: *Medrash Rabbah*, Vayikra, 21:6. *Meshech Chochmah*, Vayikra, 16:3. (The Mabit, *Beis Elokim*, Sha'ar haYesodos, 37, writes that in the Desert, Klal Yisrael did celebrate Sukkos, although the Rambam, in *Moreh Nevuchim*, 3:43, writes that in the Desert, Klal Yisrael did not perform the Mitzvah of Lulav and Esrog). The deeper reason for this is that throughout the 40-year journey, Klal Yisrael was on a level of Yom Kippur. Similarly, the Gemara tells us that when a person is learning Torah בעיוני / in-depth (as opposed to למיגרס / broad study and memorization) he may learn outside the Sukkah: *Sukkah*, 28b. On a simple level, this means that learning in depth demands a settled mind and that is difficult to maintain in a Sukkah, so he is exempt from learning in the Sukkah (כדי שתהא דעתו מיושבת עליו: Shulchan Aruch, Orach Chayim, 639:4. Rambam,

Through the Avodah of the Cohen Gadol in the Holy of Holies, the Cloud that rises up from that intimate, sacred space, flows upward and four days later settles back to earth becoming the S'chach, the embodiment of the Clouds of Glory (Mitteler Rebbe, *Ateres Rosh*, Yom haKippurim, Chap 2. Tzemach Tzedek, *Ohr haTorah*, Sukkos, p. 1,722. Rebbe Maharash, *Hemshech veKacha*, 84. *Sefer haMa'amarim Melukat*, Vol. 2, "BaSukkos Teish'vu", 4).

The S'chach of the Sukkah is in this way an embodiment of the cloud of Ketores — and the Clouds of Glory in which we dwell during the seven days of Sukkos. We sit and revel in the *Ohr* / light, the *Makifim* / surrounding, transcendent lights that have been unleashed by the intense Avodah of the holiest person, on the holiest day, in the holiest inner place.

THE AVODAH OF THESE DAYS

As everything that Hashem allows to occur has a deeper reason, קלקלתן תקנתן / "Their failure (the destruction of the Temple) is their remedy." Because of the collective 'failure' of Klal Yisrael in keeping the Beis haMikdash in existence with its physical Avodah of Ketores, every single one of us when we *Daven* / pray on Yom Kippur from the innermost recesses of our soul and psyche, come to embody the Cohen Gadol. We each have the immeasurable privilege and responsibility to perform the inner Avodah of the Ketores in the spiritual Holy

---

Hilchos Sukkah, 6:9). Yet the Baal Akeidah writes that when we learn Torah in depth, this itself is like sitting in Hashem's Sukkah: *Akeidas Yitzchak*, Sha'ar 67:122. Throughout our journey through the Desert, we were on this Yom-Kippur-level of consciousness and living, immersed in Torah.

of Holies on behalf of Klal Yisrael and the entire world.

As the day of Yom Kippur is unfolding, we become more and more disconnected from the externalities of this world and from our assumed identity. We squeeze and push ourselves in our *Tefilos* / prayers, we sweat in our Avodah, and we peel away more and more layers of self, until we arrive at the deepest core of our soul. Through our perseverance and perspiration, a metaphysical vapor, an *Ohr Makif* / encompassing light, flows outward from within us, much like the smoke of the cloud of incense that arose from the actual burning of the Ketores. This perspiration, 'vapor' or 'smoke' of our intense prayers rises from us and later descends as the S'chach of our Sukkah.

As Yom Kippur reaches its climactic peak, a sacred still-ness descends upon us — a silence so profound that it touches the deepest chambers of our soul. In this hallowed moment, we step beyond the clamor of existence and enter the hidden sanctuary within, that secret inner sanctum glimpsed but once a year. Like the Cohen Gadol in the Holy of Holies, we stand adorned not in garments, but in radiant, unblemished light. All layers of ego dissolve, the striving and tumult of life fade into nothingness, and we are left in pure, resplendent being. Motionless, yet luminous, we emanate the fragrance of our own inner holiness, a pristine purity untouched and eternal. The level of soul that is now revealed is one that is perpetually and forever in a state of *Ketores* / bonding and oneness with HaKadosh Baruch Hu, as in Aramaic, the word *Ketores* comes from a word meaning 'tied' and 'unified' (the Targum translates the

Pasuk ותקשר על-ידו שני / *"...And she tied a crimson thread on his hand"* (*Bereishis*, 38:28) as וקטרת על ידיה זהוריתא. In the language of the Zohar, בחד קטירא אתקטרנא בי' בקוב"ה / *"With one tie I am tied to HaKadosh Baruch Hu"*: *Zohar* 3, 288a).

Out of our acts of self-transcendence and Divine intimacy on Yom Kippur, a 'cloud', a Makif, fills us and projects outward, like the silent smoke of the Ketores. This 'glory' rises from within us and ascends on High. After some timeless moments, Yom Kippur comes to a conclusion. Descending gradually, we clothe ourselves in our individual personality again, and return to our homes with jubilation to 'eat our bread in joy'. Our Ketores continues to permeate the Heavens with a *Re'ach Nicho'ach* / pleasurable scent, for four days, corresponding to the four letters of the Transcendent Name of Hashem, the 'Yud-Hei-Vav-Hei'. Then we look up to find that the Cloud of *our* Glory has settled back down to us, and is now hovering lovingly over us in the form of the S'chach under which we sit, in the Heavenly embrace of the Sukkah, with the four walls corresponding to the higher Name of Hashem within which we are now presently sitting.

Just as the Teshuvah of Klal Yisrael in the Desert, which culminated on Yom Kippur, brought back the Clouds of Glory on the Fifteenth of Tishrei, our Teshuvah on Yom Kippur creates and draws down the spiritual Clouds of Glory on the Fifteenth of Tishrei, the first day of Sukkos.*

---

* The Medrash (*Bereishis Rabbah,* 48:10) teaches, (Hashem tells Avraham, when you welcomed your guests) "'You said (to them): "And recline beneath

SUKKOS: CHAPTER 1 | 49

Taking this idea even further, our process of Teshuvah is rooted in our earlier Avodah of Rosh Hashanah. The 'vapor' produced from the one hundred blasts of the Shofar on Rosh

---

the tree...." "By your life, I will repay your descendants in the wilderness," etc., as it is stated: "He spread a cloud like a curtain" (*Tehilim*, 105:39). That was in the wilderness. In the Land of Israel, from where is it derived? "You shall dwell in Sukkos for seven days" (*Vayikra*, 23:42). In the future, from where is it derived? It is as it is stated: "It will be a Shelter for shade by day'" (*Yeshayahu*, 4:6). In other words, in the merit of Avraham welcoming his guests and telling them to rest under the tree we merited the Mitzvah of Sukkos. In fact, Chazal say (*Rosh Hashanah*, 11a. See *P'nei Yehoshua*, ad loc) that this encounter with Avraham and the guests / angels occurred on Sukkos. The question is, if it is in the merit of Avraham saying "Rest under the tree," that we merited the Clouds of Glory and the Sukkah, why is a Sukkah under a tree not Kosher? For S'chach to be Kosher it needs to be something that grows from the ground, such as branches of a tree, but they need to be cut off from the tree. (Perhaps, when Avraham says, והשענו תחת העץ / "Rest under the tree," this must mean that the tree was already separated from its roots, and thus, Avraham is referring to a Sukkah, as that day was Sukkos, and so he is suggesting to them to sit in the Sukkah: *Ta'ama d'Kra*, Vayera. In fact, this is quite clear in another Medrash, והשענו תחת העץ, שעשה להם סכה / "'Rest under the tree,' means that he (Avraham) made for them a Sukkah": *Medrash Rabbah*, Bamidbar, 14:2). Moreover, the word *Sukkah*, says the Arizal, is numerically 91 (Sheim Hashem = 26, and Sheim Ado-noi = 65), which is the numerical value of the word *Ilan* / tree, so why not 'under a tree'? Of course, Chazal have a *Mesorah* / living tradition from Sinai that a Sukkah has to be under the sky and S'chach is only Kosher if it is no longer connected to the ground or the tree — but the question here is more a philosophical question. The Tree that Avraham tells the guests / angels to rest under is the *Eitz haChayim* / Tree of Life, as the Zohar teaches. The original Clouds of Glory, which are connected to the Tree of Life, were given to us in the Desert, but on Sukkos we celebrate the *return* of the Clouds of Glory, or at least the Clouds of Glory to come to us through our Teshuvah, our inner work on Rosh Hashanah and Yom Kippur. This is why we use a tree for the S'chach, and specifically one that is cut off from its natural source, for this symbolizes our participation, our return, and reconnection to our Source, to the Tree of Life (the S'chach), through Teshuvah.

Hashanah created a metaphysical cloud, and this became the S'chach of Sukkos. The מאה / one hundred blasts becomes האם / 'the Mother' (containing the same letters), referring to the loving embrace of the Sukkah (this idea will be explored in more depth later on).

We can feel the power of the Sukkah to the extent of the quantity and quality of Teshuvah that we accomplished, and the inward 'smoke' of the Avodah of Ketores that we generated within our inner Holy of holies, on Yom Kippur. Sukkos reveals outwardly what we accomplished inwardly on Yom Kippur. An individual who puts in the hard spiritual work of Yom Kippur senses the majesty of Hashem's enveloping embrace on Sukkos, and senses the reality of the Clouds of Glory. If a person doesn't sense this on Sukkos, they probably did not or could not 'burn Ketores' on Yom Kippur to their fullest ability. However, it is never too late — one can always do Teshuvah at any moment, even right now. One can always recreate a miniature Yom Kippur of Teshuvah, fill the Heavens with fragrance, and then enter the fully revealed Clouds of Glory, as if a Sukkah.

Sensing ourselves being enveloped in Clouds of Glory is feeling profound joy. The harder we have worked in Teshuvah, the more joy we can feel.

The joy we experience on Sukkos is a 'proof' that our Teshuvah, our deep, tear-soaked Avodah on Yom Kippur, has achieved its goal, and our Teshuvah was accepted on High (Sefas Emes, Hazinu). Now we begin life anew, with wonder, freshness, and overflowing happiness. Now we can joyfully 'draw water' from our inner wells of salvation.

ALL OF THE FIRST HALF OF TISHREI IS REVEALED IN SUKKOS

The Radbaz, the great *Posek* / Halachic ruler and Mekubal, a Rebbe of the Arizal (Rebbe Dovid ben Zimra, c.1479-1573), explains that there is significance in the fact that Sukkos begins on the fifteenth of the month, when the moon is full (*Metzudas Dovid*, Mitzvah 117). A full moon is the revelation of everything that has transpired during the first fourteen days of a given month. Whereas the first fourteen days of the month of Tishrei are characterized by concealed, inner illumination, on the full moon, this illumination is fully, outwardly revealed.

On Rosh Hashanah, the first day of the month, the moon is almost totally concealed from sight. "Blow a Shofar at the New Moon, בכסה / at the 'covered' time, for our Festival day" (*Tehillim*, 81:4). "What is a Festival Day in which the moon is 'covered'? This is Rosh Hashanah" (*Rosh Hashanah*, 8a-8b). On Yom Kippur, the tenth of the month, the moon is still not yet fully revealed. The Avodah of Rosh Hashanah, and that of the Ten Days of Teshuvah and Yom Kippur, are 'covered' or hidden within us, in quiet introspection. But when the Yom Tov of Sukkos arrives, we go out of the house and out of the Shul, and into the more public or open space of the Sukkah. Here, instead of the Avodah being one of seriousness and inwardness, it is one of externally expressed joy and even dancing. The more joy that we express on Sukkos, say the students of the holy Arizal, the more joy we will merit to experience throughout the entire coming year.*

On Sukkos, the joy we experience, the *Ohr* / light, and *Shefa* / flow that we feel, is an extension of the inner, reflective, more private Avodah we have achieved over the course of the first fourteen days of Tishrei.

THE 'VAPOR' OF THE SHOFAR
CREATES THE CLOUDS OF THE S'CHACH

As explored, the S'chach is produced by our inner Ketores of Yom Kippur, and yet it can also be traced back to an origin in the main Avodah of Rosh Hashanah, blowing the Shofar. The Arizal teaches that the one hundred blasts of the Shofar on Rosh Hashanah are projected outward, becoming the S'chach of the Sukkah. The word סכך / S'chach has a numerical value of 100 (Samech / 60, Chaf / 20, Final Chaf / 20 = 100. *Pri Eitz Chayim*, Sha'ar haSukkos. See also *Toras Levi Yitzchak*, p. 303), corresponding to the one hundred Shofar blasts.

---

* In the words of the Pele Yoetz: וצונו לשמח שמחה של מצוה והוא סימן טוב לכל השנה שכתבו גורי האר"י ז"ל, שמי שיהא שמח וטוב לב ולא יצטער כלל בחג הקדוש הזה, מבטח לו שתעלה לו שנה טובה ויהיה לעולם שמח: *Pele Yoetz*, 256. Note Rashi, *Devarim*, 16:15: והיית אך שמח: לפי פשוטו אין זה לשון צווי אלא לשון הבטחה / "'And you shall be only joyful...' In its literal meaning, this isn't the language of a commandment, but rather of a promise!" The Yom Tov liturgy uses the phrase, את ברכת מועדיך / "the blessing of the Yom Tov." Many have wondered about the intent of this blessing and where in the Torah it says that there is a special "blessing" for Yom Tov. The answer is the above Pasuk. Although "And you shall..." is usually used to convey a Mitzvah, but here, "And you shall be only happy," is not a Mitzvah, rather a 'blessing' — an affirmation and promise, as it were, that we *will* be only happy.

When we blow the Shofar, heat and moisture are projected through the breath of our mouths, coming from deep within our bodies. This 'vapor' is released into the ether, until it cumulates and forms a metaphysical cloud. This cloud is what eventually becomes the S'chach that we sit under on Sukkos.

MAKIF INTO PENIMI

On Rosh Hashanah, even on Yom Kippur and the days in between, we are doing the Avodah on a more inward level, as mentioned. This means we are producing more *Ohr Makif /* general light or *Makifim /* surrounding lights — 'clouds'. On Sukkos, we sit under these Makifim, yet we do so in the context of a defined, detailed, specific (meaning *Penimi /* within-the-physical-world) structure called a Sukkah.

On Rosh Hashanah and Yom Kippur, the 'Makifim' we create are a *general* desire to live our lives with the Presence of HaKadosh Baruch Hu. We declare our love for Hashem, but in a very general and abstract intangible way. This form of love later materializes as the Makifim, the surrounding Ohr of the S'chach of the Sukkah. Yet, the Sukkah itself is a meticulously measured and defined structure. This is the tangible *Kli /* vessel that receives the Makifim in a Penimi level (In this way, the Sukkah is also the *Malchus /* receptacle, as the Ramban seemingly teaches. See *Rikanti*, Emor. See also Shaloh, Sukkah, *Torah Ohr*, 6). While the main part of the Sukkah is the S'chach (Rashi, *Sukkah*, 2a, ועל שם הסכך קרויה סוכה), the walls of the Sukkah are sacred objects as well (*Sukkah*, 9a). Furthermore, S'chach without walls is not a Sukkah.

The well-defined structure of the walls of the Sukkah, and the space created inside them, represent a *Penimi* / inner light.

The S'chach is our Makif commitment, our general declaration, 'I love You, Hashem....' By sitting within the defined walls of the Sukkah, we say, '...And I am here; I am not going anywhere. I just want to be with You.' In response, Hashem stretches out His arms as 'the Higher Mother', and says, 'My precious child, I'm so glad you are here; I want to hold you tight.'

On Rosh Hashanah and Yom Kippur, we cry out from the depths of our soul 'I love You, Hashem.' But when we step into the Sukkah, it is as if we whisper something even deeper: 'I am ready not only to love You from afar, but to live with You — here, under one roof, in Your embrace — to share quiet moments together, without distraction, without distance.' And Hashem, like a loving Mother, answers: 'Thank you, My child. Yes — let these simple walls, these lines of the Sukkah, become our sacred space, the place where we internalize our commitment, where love becomes home, and devotion becomes life.'

After this initial 'dialogue' and Divine encounter on the first night of Sukkos, we progress to an even deeper, more integrated level of drawing Makifim into Penimi: waving the Lulav and Esrog. On the morning of the first day of Sukkos through the last day, we recite a blessing on the *Arba Minim* / Four Species, the *Lulav* / palm branch, two *Aravos* / willows, three or more *Hadasim* / myrtles, and an *Esrog* / a beautiful, unblemished citron fruit. This Mitzvah is preferably performed within the Sukkah, as the Arizal teaches.

There are many symbols encoded in this Mitzvah. In the Arba Minim, there are three 'lines', three upright branches that we take in our right hand, and we attach and tie these together in one bundle, one 'line'. Then we take the Esrog, which is shaped as a 'circle', and draw all four species together. The 'line' of the upright species is like an antenna that draws Light down from the S'chach, the Makifim, and then conducts this Light down into the 'feminine' Esrog. The Four Minim are lifted and then waved in the four directions, as well as, up and down, and then brought back to the place of the heart. These movements draw the pure Makifim created by our Avodah on Rosh Hashanah and Yom Kippur downwards and inwards into the deepest Penimi — our physical, human heart. The transcendent Light is now shining, not just in a spiritual 'cloud' that is beyond us or closely above us, nor in the defined space around us, but within ourselves and in our very bodies.

In this way, Sukkos is a most tangible revelation and consummation of all the effects of the effortful and emotional work we performed on Rosh Hashanah through Yom Kippur. Because these effects are *revealed*, they manifest as an Avodah of expressing *Simchah* / joy. Over the course of this time of joy, the Makifim that were generated from our inner work on the High Holy Days are integrated in ourselves and in the world, in a real, practical, and even physical way. This allows us to carry this illumination into the new year, and begin living life on a deeper level than ever before.

Rebbe Zusha of Anipoli once appeared in a dream to one of his students and said that the word סוכה / *Sukkah* is an acronym for ויאמר ה׳ סלחתי כדברך / "And Hashem said (to Moshe), 'I have pardoned, according to your words (of request)" (*Bamidbar*, 14:2). Sukkos is the culmination and the confirmation of Yom Kippur; our Teshuvah has been accepted, as well as our request to live on a deeper level in this coming year. The overflowing joy and lightness that we experience on Sukkos is not only a sense of relief following the more serious and effortful days of Rosh Hashanah and Yom Kippur, rather, this lightness arises from a deeper place within us — a place of sensing that we are forgiven.

A physical sensation of lightness often dawns upon people as Yom Kippur comes to a close, due to their unburdening and being forgiven. Negativity pulls us down, and makes us feel inwardly heavy, and even physically lethargic: כי עונתי עברו ראשי כמשא כבד יכבדו ממני / "For my iniquities have passed over my head (overwhelmed me); they are like a heavy burden, more than I can bear" (*Tehillim*, 38:5. See *Gittin*, 70a). Forgiveness lightens and strengthens us. As such, the sense of joy, elation, and lightness of being, is felt not merely because you did not eat and weigh your body down with food for twenty-five to twenty-six hours. Rather, it is a symptom of something deeper, that you have been freed of the psychological and spiritual weight of your past negativity. The joy that descends upon us on Sukkos is also a result of this sense of being forgiven, as Rashi writes דמי שנתכפר חטאו שמח / "A person whose transgressions have been forgiven feels joy" (*Menachos*, 20a). Sukkos is palpably the culmination and the confirmation that our deep inner work of Teshuvah has been accepted, and we have been transformed.

SUKKAH AS THE PLACE OF AYIN

Sukkos is also similar to a rite of passage, where one moves into a 'liminal' or transitional space so that one can then emerge renewed. This is similar to how the structure of a seed (Yesh) must disintegrate (become Ayin) before it germinates and gives rise to a new plant (a new Yesh). The disintegration of the negative Yesh of our past has progressed throughout the Ten Days of Awe, culminating on the first night of Sukkos, when we leave the security of our home and the old structures of our life, and enter a temporary shelter that is vulnerable and open to the elements. Now we sit in the liminal space of the Sukkah in a state of Ayin, while a new year and a new positive sense of identity is germinating within us, so that we can emerge from Tishrei reborn, as a new Yesh.

Through Rosh Hashanah and Yom Kippur as we get in touch with our real self, we experience real freedom and peace within ourselves, and we also experience a sense of peace with Hashem. This is an integration on all levels. As such, on Sukkos, we eat, drink, and even sleep all in a Mitzvah, a Divine cocoon, fully integrated, united, and at peace, fulfilling the prayer that we pray every day of the year: *U-fros Aleinu Sukkas Shelomecha* / "And spread over us the Sukkah of Your Peace."

Numerically, the word *Sukkah* is 91, which is also the value of the word אמן / *Amein* (parenthetically, the Names *Hashem/*26 and *Ado-noi/*65 together also equal 91). Sukkos is thus the confirmation, the אמן / *Amein*, to all our Avodah and experiences throughout the Days of Awe. As the *Chag haAsif* / Festival of the Harvest or 'Gathering', it is the focal point where we draw all of those experiences down and 'gather' them together. Klal Yisrael, too, is gathered under the Sukkah, and from this place of 'ingathering', we *Daven* / pray very powerfully and confidently that HaKadosh Baruch Hu will give us and all of Klal Yisrael a *Shanah Tovah uMesukah* / a happy, healthy, peaceful, sweet new year; may it be His Will!

Chapter 2

FROM 'ENGAGEMENT' TO 'MARRIAGE' AND BEYOND:
Sukkos as the Culmination of the High Holidays

As EXPLORED EARLIER, THERE ARE TWO FULL-WEEK SETS OF *YAMIM TOVIM* / HOLY DAYS EACH YEAR CELEBRATING THE EXODUS FROM MITZRAYIM: Pesach and Sukkos. Pesach is the essence of the month of Nisan, and Sukkos is the essence of the month of Tishrei.

In Nisan, the first month of the year, HaKadosh Baruch Hu is reaching out to us. This is a 'top-down' relationship: Hashem thrusts us out of Mitzrayim, lifts us out of constrictions and smallness, negativity and enslavement, gives us freedom, and reveals to us the Torah at Mount Sinai. We are like children, and our Parent, knowing what we need, 'imposes' redemption and guidance upon us from Above. We trust our loving Parent to do what is best for us, even when we have not earned it.

In Tishrei, by contrast, we assume more of a bottom-up relationship. We take the initiative to do Teshuvah, arise from below, and reach out to HaKadosh Baruch Hu. In this way, we ready ourselves to encounter the Divine, ultimately in a *Panim El Panim* / face-to-face relationship, as in a marriage. This final stage of our relationship with Hashem is illustrated by the symbol of Tishrei: a scale balanced between the two 'equal' sides, so to speak. Thus, the zodiac sign of the month is *Moznayim* / Libra, scales.

The progression of the Yamim Tovim of Tishrei is the deepening of this relationship. The more impersonal 'parental' relationship that began in Nisan stimulated in us a desire to be in a relationship, which becomes more and more intense in the month of Elul (as explored in the book, *The Month of Elul: Days of Introspection and Transformation*). This builds until Tishrei arrives and we experience our engagement, *Chupah* / wedding canopy, seven days of celebration, and finally, intimacy and moving 'together' into the world to create a dwelling place for the Divine in this world (In general, the unfolding of the Yamim Tovim is a progression towards *Sheleimus* / wholeness. In the words of the Ralag, כי בו המועדים היותר חזקים והיותר מיישרים אל השלמות: *Shemuel 1*, 8:1. See also *Metzudas Dovid*, ibid., 2).

In this way, during the course of Tishrei, we are orienting ourselves into a posture of a face-to-face encounter and relationship, the perfect balance of the scales. Within the Zohar, there is a book called ספרא דצניעותא / *Sifra d'Tzniusa* / the Hidden Book. It is a very dense, intricate, and mysterious text within the corpus of the Zohar, and found in the portion of Terumah. *Sifra d'Tzniusa* begins with these words: תאנא, ספרא דצניעותא, ספרא דשקיל במתקלא. תנא, דעד לא הוה מתקלא, לא הוה משגיחין אפין באפין / "We learned in the Hidden Book, a book that is weighed with a scale. We learned that until there was a scale there was no face-to-face providence…." This means that if a relationship has no 'balance', it cannot be 'face-to-face'.

On the original day of Rosh Hashanah, the first human being was created. Adam was actually created as two distinct human beings joined back-to-back. There was an imbalance between them, and they could not acknowledge one another face-to-face. Soon after, the Creator put them to sleep and 'surgically' separated them, and drew the female out of the male. As this process was encoded in the inception of Creation, this pattern repeats itself every year on Rosh Hashanah. The Creator is the 'male', as it were, and humanity is the 'female'. In the first moments of our relationship, we are not conscious of each other; we are in an *Achor b'Achor* / 'back-to-back' relationship. At some point, we 'fall asleep', or are 'anesthetized', and are separated apart. On Rosh Hashanah morning, with the blowing of the Shofar, we turn around and begin moving toward a balanced, *Panim-el-Panim* / face-to-face encounter (For an in-depth exploration of this topic, see *A Call to Majesty: The Mysteries of the Shofar & Rosh Hashanah*. In a back-to-back relationship, there are no stages of *Chibuk* / embracing, *Nishuk* / kissing, and *Yichud* / full unification, as it is a relationship that is already in a type of 'unity'. Only relationships that are face-to-face require these steps — אבל צריך שתדע כי בעוד ז"א ונוקביה אחור באחור אין צורך לזווגם על ידי חיבוק ונישוק משום דאז תרוייהו הוו חד גופא מחוברין אבל אחר שהוחזרו פנים בפנים שננסרו ונעשו שני גופים אז צריך להחזירן פנים בפנים על ידי חיבוק ונישוק לזווגם יחד: Arizal, *Sha'ar Ma'amorei* Rashbi, Naso).

From Rosh Hashanah forward, we are gradually leaving our 'Mitzrayim' of unconsciousness and spiritual immaturity, and expressing our commitment to our Beloved. We take responsibility for our lives (Rosh Hashanah), ask for forgiveness (Yom Kippur) and finally spend more than a week sitting with Hashem, devotedly enveloped by the Divine embrace of the Sukkah.

A balanced scale symbolizes a mature, responsible relationship between two 'partners', a face-to-face relationship. Only when Adam and Chavah are able to see and acknowledge each other, no longer back-to-back in an unhealthy 'fusion', as it were (*Eiruvin*, 18a), can Chavah (and Adam, as well) be called an עזר כנגדו / "a helper who stands opposite the other." In such an encounter, both partners recognize the other as their 'opposite', with their own mind and heart, and yet they choose to be with you in harmony, as a 'helper'. This is the definition of *Shalom Bayis* / 'domestic peace': a conscious, respectful harmonization of opposites. If partners do not recognize the 'opposite' or individual nature of the other, they cannot face each other and harmonize.

Through the Avodah, spiritual, mental, emotional, and inner work of Tishrei, we learn to stand up, be present, and with our own volition — without a mountain suspended above our heads — to do *Teshuvah* / to 'turn around' and face Hashem. Through the spiritual awakening of Teshuvah, we take responsibility for our unconsciousness and sincerely ask forgiveness from our Partner. We acknowledge the *Ein Sof* / Infinite Creator as 'opposite' us, and seek to rekindle a genuine, harmonious, face-to-face relationship with Him.

FROM BESULAH / VIRGO TO INTIMACY

Elul is the month that precedes Tishrei. Elul is the Mazal of *Besulah* / Virgo. During the thirty days of Elul, we prepare ourselves to meet our Divine Beloved,* reclaiming our purity so that we can once again face and experience HaKadosh Baruch Hu's Presence in an intimate way.

---

* We do so as 'the Captive Woman' in the Torah Portion of Ki Seitze, who weeps for her past and prepares herself for marriage for thirty days: "And she shall weep for her father and mother for *Yerech* / a moon or thirty days" (*Devarim*, 21:13). She is encouraged to weep and mourn for her lost family and culture, as she is about to take on a new journey in life: *Yevamos*, 48b. "The thirty days of Elul correspond to the thirty days of the captive woman": *Zohar Chadash*, Ki Seitze, 58b.

On Rosh Hashanah, we become engaged to HaKadosh Baruch Hu; on Yom Kippur, we are married; and on Sukkos, we celebrate seven days of *Sheva Berachos* / seven blessings. On the seventh day, Hoshana Rabbah, we participate in loving 'whispering' and *Neshikin* / kissing, and on Shemini Atzeres and Simchas Torah we finally attain intimacy and *Yichud* / full unification. In this culmination, we become so intimate, so unified in mind, heart, body, and spirit, that we are no longer looking 'at' each other, face-to-face, rather we look together outwards, as one. We face the same direction in joint aspiration and dreaming, looking at the new year that is beginning. We now understand what we need to do together as a 'couple' and co-creators.

IN GREATER DETAIL:
From Back-to-Back to Face-to-Face

On Rosh Hashanah Eve, there is a cosmic slumber, which allows for the great *Nesirah* / severing apart, separation to occur. To move from a position of back-to-back and meet face-to-face, there first needs to be a severance, as in the first narrative of the creation of Adam and Chavah. At first, "male and female He created them" — they are attached to each other, as it were, a masculine *Partzuf* / face or side, and a feminine Partzuf (*Eiruvin*, 18a). They are "back-to-back," unaware of each other. In the Torah's second narration of their creation, 'Adam' is put to sleep, and Hashem severs a part of Adam's 'side', namely his back 'side', and Chavah is drawn out as a separate individual.

In deep anesthetic sleep, the two are severed so that, once they heal, they can face each other as a true עֵזֶר כְּנֶגְדּוֹ / 'helper who stands opposite their partner'.

In the morning following this Rosh Hashanah Eve slumber, a Shofar is blown, representing the newly-formed human beings consciously coronating HaKadosh Baruch as the King of their universe. This Shofar blast is the very beginning of humanity's movement toward a face-to-face relationship with its Creator. We turn toward Hashem and anoint Him as our beloved *Adon* / Master; we stand to face Hashem and declare our commitment to Him. Feeling our deep soul connection, we promise to join Him in marriage.

Hashem is now *Karov* / near to us, close to each of us (*Rosh Hashanah*, 18a). It is a time when "the Source of Light is drawn to its sparks" (Mitteler Rebbe, *Derech Chayim*, p. 13d). We, the 'sparks', instinctively respond to the closeness of our Source by committing our lives to Him. This is why Rosh Hashanah is the time of the year in which we contemplate and judge our level of commitment to our Creator. The closeness that we are experiencing sweeps us into Divine judgment — evaluating what it means to be a human being and what it means to have *Bechirah* / free choice and not to live on autopilot. We need to contemplate what it means to be in a relationship with the Source of Light, so that we can be in an authentic, conscious, caring relationship with Him. The enormity of this responsibility and honor causes us to tremble in awe.

On the other hand, as we have already traversed the month of Elul and its thirty days of introspection, Teshuvah, return and reorientation toward our pure soul, we come to Rosh Hashanah with a certain confidence. We dress in our finest attire to Shul (quoted in *Tur*, Orach Chayim, 581. *Medrash Rabbah*, Vayikra, 29), and confidently declare, 'Hashem, I am Yours! Master of the universe, I am committed to our engagement and to living a life of true *Chayim* / life, connection, transcendence, and meaning, with You. I beseech You to inscribe me in the Book of Life, the book of *Olam haBa* / Eternal Intimacy. I am ready to live a more G-dly life, a life of deeper commitment to Torah and Mitzvos, a life where I am a walking *Kiddush Hashem* / sanctifying Your Name.'

Rosh Hashanah exudes a strong presence of Ohr Makif / 'general light' (or Makifim / 'surrounding lights'). We do not yet discuss the details, the specifics and technicalities of this Divine relationship, rather just the general commitment. This is much like when two people fall in love and are drawn to commit to marry simply out of their powerful bond. They follow their supra-rational impulse to commit to living together for the rest of their lives. They do not yet explore the details of their shared life, such as where they are going to live, or how they are going to divide up the responsibilities of finances, housework, and raising children. Those details are not important to them at this stage; they are simply wrapped up in their euphoric enthusiasm to marry each other.

WEDDING DAY: YOM KIPPUR

"'On the day of His wedding' — this is the giving of the Torah" (*Ta'anis*, 26b). Rashi clarifies: "This is the day that the Second *Luchos* / Tablets of the Torah were given — the day of Yom Kippur." Yom Kippur is the wedding day with our Creator, and the Luchos are our *Kesubah* / marriage contract. Because of this dynamic, it is also an opportune time to find a human spouse.*

Elul was a dramatization of the process of אני לדודי / *Ani l'Dodi* / "I am to my Beloved," in which we were working to get closer and closer to our Beloved. On Rosh Hashanah, our movement of *Ani l'Dodi* is even more pronounced, and we start sensing that ודודי לי / *v'Dodi Li* / "and my Beloved is to me," Hashem is coming close to us. Yom Kippur is the fortieth day and completion of this process which began on the first day of <u>Rosh Chodesh</u> Elul. The word לי / *Li* has a numerical value of

---

* The Mishnah, *Ta'anis*, 4:8, describes maidens, dressed in white, dancing in the vineyards to attract attention from the unmarried men. As it is a day of atonement and forgiveness, and a bride and groom are forgiven of their sins on their wedding day (*Yerushalmi*, *Bikurim*, 3:3), it was also deemed a day when one would find their destined spouse (*Yerushalmi*, *Ta'anis*, 4:11). When people are cleansed of sin, free of egoic consciousness, they can choose more accurately and clearly their befitting *Zivug* / spouse (this extends to all choices, and for this reason, certain Chasidic Rebbes would go to great efforts to choose an Esrog on Motzei Yom Kippur). Perhaps just knowing that one is forgiven creates the joy and clarity that allows one to recognize their future spouse. In the times of the Beis haMikdash, "A thread of crimson wool was tied to the door of the Beis haMikdash, and when the goat reached the wilderness the thread turned white": Mishnah, *Yuma*, 6:8. When it turned white, Klal Yisrael knew they were forgiven — and thus they danced wearing white garments. Once there was no longer a Beis haMikdash, this joyful custom was discontinued.

40, alluding to the moment in the first phase of the wedding ceremony, when the partners are formally committed by means of giving a ring and pronouncing the words, הרי את מקודשת לי / "Behold, you are betrothed to me."

Whereas on Rosh Hashanah we tell Hashem 'I am Yours, I am committed and dedicated,' on Yom Kippur Hashem tells us, 'Indeed, you are Mine, you are betrothed to Me. Come, let us celebrate our commitment.'

During the days of Rosh Hashanah through Yom Kippur, the Days of Awe, we feel inspired, spiritually aroused, filled with a passion for truth and connectivity, for a life of Olam haBa and understanding the depths of reality. For some, this experience can be vivid throughout all ten days. Others may feel this inspiration for a shorter period, perhaps even just five minutes out of these approximately two hundred and forty hours. Hopefully at some point during this intense period, we all shed a tear and felt the presence of depth, holiness, and connection.

It is helpful to watch for moments when you feel a deep connection with your soul, with HaKadosh Baruch Hu, with others, with community, with their ancestors, their sacred language and history, or the text of the Machzor. Relish in any experience of inspiration to live deeper and more connected to HaKadosh Baruch Hu, to others, and to the true goodness in life. Allow this mystical wedding day to come alive for you.

SUKKAH: THE CHUPAH & SHEVA BERACHOS

High inspiration is like a flame; it burns and flashes brightly for a few moments, but without wick and oil, it is soon extinguished. Such inspiration is an experience of an *Ohr Makif /* surrounding light, a general sense of illumination, yet there is not yet a wick and oil to hold this flame steady through time. Yes, we have made a commitment, and we are in love, and we even got married, but like all marriages, 'a wick and oil', real actions that ground and nurture the relationship, are necessary. Relationship with Hashem, too, takes work and practical steps of implementing and feeding our commitment. Therefore, after the conclusion of Yom Kippur, Hashem says, "It is wonderful that we are sanctified to each other, and that you are so inspired to be committed to Me, but let's wait four days before we call all the guests, the nations of the world" (on Sukkos we would bring offerings corresponding to the seventy nations of the world: *Sukkah*, 55b). Then, we can celebrate our seven days of *Sheva Berachos /* seven blessings, rejoicing under our Chupah, the Sukkah, together.

We wait four days to make sure our inspiration is authentically grounded in action. Sometimes people make grandiose romantic gestures in the spur of the moment, they feel excited and they act out their passion in the heat of the moment. Sadly, once the excitement and novelty wears off, they may feel trapped: 'What have I done? Now I see that I never wanted to be shackled to pleasing this person.' And so Hashem says, 'It's great that you are passionate and enthusiastic about Me; let's just wait a few days and see how you feel then.' Four days later, we enter the Chupah, still inspired by Yom Kippur, but now with *Yishuv haDa'a*s / a settled mind.

Four days after Yom Kippur, we enter the Yom Tov of Sukkos with Da'as, since to perform the Mitzvah of Sukkah we need Da'as, knowing what we are doing and why we are sitting there. Now the second phase of our wedding is complete with the *Sheva Berachos* / seven blessings under the Chupah, and we commence our seven days of feasting together with our family and guests.

In our intimate moments under the Sukkah, the four walls of the Sukkah become a Divine embrace. The Halachic minimum required for a Kosher Sukkah is two whole walls and a portion of a third, symbolically forming a chest and an arm that gather us in, plus a hand (the little of the third wall), holding us close in a *Chibuk* / hug. A Sukkah with four fall walls can be seen as a more passionate embrace, in which the arm and hand are wrapped completely around us.

To be intimate with another is to be fully present with them as they are, to be fully there for them. To do this, we also need a measure of transcendence and release of our own limited narratives and to be present with our own true nature. In this state of clarity, we can hold the entire story, the past, present, and future of the other person. Similarly, in the spiritual intimacy of Sukkos, we become like the Sukkah itself. We open ourselves to embrace the shared past and present and future of Klal Yisrael, and of all humanity.

We open our arms to the present, while affectionately remembering Rosh Hashanah and Yom Kippur, and holding our collective memory; how we went out of Egypt, and how Hashem sat us in tents and protected us with the Clouds of Glory. Even more than this, we embrace our redemptive future. Sukkah is connected with the word סכה / deeper seeing, seeing with *Ruach haKodesh* / holy intuition, as it were (*Kad haKemach*, Sukkah). Sitting under the stars in this holy atmosphere, we revel in a vision of the endless positivity of the future of the entire world.

By going out into the Sukkah, we are declaring and demonstrating in action, 'This year, I am ready to go wherever You, Hashem, want me to go — even into a "tent" in the cold — as long as I will be with You.' This is deeper than the inspiration of 'romance'; it is deeper than wanting to 'please' the other. This is a willingness to give of oneself, due to seeing that there is just *one self*. We recognize that we are inseparably united with *Ma'amireinu* / our 'Designated One', our Chosen One. This is true intimacy, openness, and presence.

HOSHANA RABBAH: NESHIKIN / KISSING

We have moved from a back-to-back relationship on the Eve of Rosh Hashanah, to a face-to-face relationship on Rosh Hashanah morning, to a point of total commitment, the day of our wedding, Yom Kippur. We then reached the Chupah and the Divine embrace of Sukkos. Now we arrive at the last day of Sukkos, the hidden and mysterious day of Hoshana Rabba. This day lifts us into the *Bechinah* / state of what the Arizal calls *Neshikin* / kissing.

After six days of Sukkos, embracing, and before the revelation of our total Yichud / unity on Shemini Atzeres, there is a level of Neshikin, in which the upper part of yourself is somewhat unified with the כנגדו, the Beloved Other 'opposite' you. This intimate connection on Hoshana Rabbah, occurring on the level of the mind, heart, and 'mouth' or speech, can lead to a blissful collapse into total unity. On this day, we multiply the intimate prayers of our mouth (*Hoshana Rabbah* literally means 'Abundant Prayers of *Save Us*'; there are customs of staying up all night in study or recitation of *Tehilim* / Psalms, and then lengthening the morning prayers with overflowing supplications punctuated with different forms of the word Hoshana), and give our heart and mind over in devotion to HaKadosh Baruch Hu.

One of the customs on Hoshana Rabbah is to "beat" the *Hoshanos* / a bundle of willow branches on the floor. The 'reasons' for this beating, besides that it is a Mitzvah (Yesod) or custom (Minhag) of the *Nevi'im* / Prophets, will be explored further on, when exploring the day of Hoshana Rabbah. Suffice it to say here, that when beaten on the floor, the leaves of the *Aravos* / willows release some moisture or 'vapor'. Furthermore, these leaves are shaped like lips (*Medrash Rabbah*, Vayikra, 30:14). In this way, slapping the willows on the ground is like 'kissing' the ground, and it also causes the 'lips' of the willow to 'kiss' one another.

SHEMINI ATZERES & SIMCHAS TORAH: YICHUD / ALONE WITH HAKADOSH BARUCH HU

After the seven days of Sukkos are concluded with the day of Neshikin, a day on a completely different level of Avodah / spiritual work comes into view: the eighth day, the day of Shemini Atzeres (In Israel, this is also the day of Simchas Torah). In the times of the Beis haMikdash, over the course of the seven days of Sukkos, we offered in total seventy bulls corresponding to the seventy nations of the world. On the day of Shemini Atzeres, we bring a single bull, corresponding to the singular Nation of Yisrael. Say our Sages (*Sukkah*, 55b), "This is a parable to a king of flesh and blood who said to his servants: 'Prepare me a great feast that will last for several days.' When the feast concluded, on the last day, he said to his beloved: 'Prepare me a small feast so that I can derive pleasure from you alone.'"

Intimacy demands complete privacy and aloneness with one's spouse (אביי באלי דידבי רבא באלי פרוחי / "Abaye would even drive away flies from around his bed and Rava would drive away gnats" — so that they would not engage in intimacy in their presence: *Niddah*, 17a). Shemini Atzeres is 'being secluded with Hashem'. It is a time when, as the Zohar (1, 64b) tells us, we are בלחודוי עם מלכא / "alone with the King." In another Medrash (*Tanchuma*, Pinchas, 16), a similar parable is offered in which after seven days of feasting, the King says to his beloved, נגלגל אני ואתה / "Let us roll (frolic), Me and you...." On this day, we playfully frolic alone with HaKadosh Baruch Hu in complete Yichud.

What began on Rosh Hashanah Eve — from the slumber and Nesirah / severing apart in order to turn face-to-face, to the engagement, commitment, marriage, Chupah, Sheva Berachos, embracing, and Neshikin — is now finally in a state of 'arrival'. This is the state of Zivug / coupling and Yichud / private unification.

Atzeres comes from the word *Atzor* / stop. This simply implies that we stop moving, as we have arrived. We were moving towards, and progressing forward to Yichud, now is the time of Yichud and we need to stop moving, becoming, and just be

According to Sefer Yetzirah, one of the most ancient oral texts we have, the month of Tishrei is connected with the sense of touch. In the world of deep and profound touch, Yichud or Zivug is a level of intimacy that demands an absence of separation and *Levushim* / Garments. Rather, the contact must be 'essence-to-essence' (*Kesuvos*, 48a. *Tikkunei Zohar*, Tikkun 66, 97b. *Ibid.*, Tikkun 58). For us to connect to the Yom Tov of Sukkos, there are certain Levushim or *Kelim* / vessels that the Torah tells us we need to use, for example, the *Arba Minim*, the Four Species. This is similar to Pesach, when, in order to connect with the inner quality of the day, we need to eat Matzah and Maror. There is normally a need for some sort of intermediary or tool, a vessel through which to 'grasp' the *Ohr* / light and the inner quality of a given Yom Tov. On Shemini Atzeres and Simchas Torah, we are no longer commanded to sit in the Sukkah, we no longer take the Lulav and Esrog in our hands; we do not have any special foods to eat with our mouth such as Matzah; there are no special vessels or garments needed; there is no special pattern of movement to perform. Without the Beis haMikdash, there is no 'unique' observance to be done on Shemini Atzeres. There is only a unique opportunity to *Atzor* / stop, to arrive and be still with our Source and Ultimate Destination. There is the unity of essence-to-essence, without any garments. (This is the deeper reason why the Arizal teaches (*Pri Eitz Chayim,* Sha'ar Mikra Kodesh. *Siddur Arizal*) that in the Berachah of "Mikadeish Yisrael v'haZ'manim," one should have in mind the Name of Hashem without any *Nekudos* / vowels. On these days, we are connecting to the Essence of Hashem's Name, beyond all expressions or 'vowels', as Nekudos are the 'Levushim' of the words of the Berachos: *Zohar Chadash,* Shir haShirim, 22:1. See *Sha'ar Yissachar,* Ma'amar Z'man Cheiruseinu, 8).

On Shemini Atzeres, there are also no Ushpizin / special spiritual guests that come to visit us. Each day throughout the seven days of Sukkos another Torah archetype comes to be with us, and a corresponding Divine Attribute. Avraham and Chesed / Kindness visit on the first day, Yitzchak and Gevurah / Power visit on the second day, and so forth. Shemini Atzeres has no such guests or Attributes, as it is a day of being with HaKadosh Baruch Hu essence-to-Essence, just אני ואתה / me and You, in a Yichud without any spiritual intermediary archetypes, attributes, or filters.

For this reason, as we celebrate the completion and the beginning of the new cycle of Torah reading on this day, we do not spend extra time 'studying' the wisdom of the Torah, rather we dance with a closed Torah scroll. The Torah itself is not seen as a 'garment' or separate vessel, as it is 'one' with HaKadosh Baruch Hu ("Three knots are knotted with each other, Hashem, the Torah, and the People of Israel": *Zohar* 3, 73a). Even study is an intermediary or interface separating us subtly from Torah itself. We embrace the Torah and dance with it without the *Levush* / 'garment' of *Seichel* / intellect; we are of one essence.

Simchas Torah is like the Yom Tov of Purim, when we attain the level of *Lo Yada* / 'not knowing', which is a kind of essential knowing, unrefracted by human intellect. We ecstatically celebrate the fact that Torah is inseparable from who we are, ingrained in the very substance of our being. We are so unified with Torah, that even without our intellectual supervision or our being mindful of our behavior, all our actions remain consistent with the morality, virtue, and holiness of the Torah (*Likutei Sichos,* Moadim, Sukkos, p. 138, note 26).

DANCING ON SUKKOS & SHEMINI ATZERES

Dancing is appropriate throughout all the days of Sukkos, as well. The Torah's term for Sukkos is a *Chag* / festival: שבעת ימים תחג לה׳ / for seven days you shall celebrate a *Chag* / festival for Hashem" (*ibid.*). Regarding this Pasuk, the Netziv (*Ha'amek Davar*, Devarim, 16:15) writes a great *Chidush* / novel interpretation: לשון תחוג משמע שמחה הבאה בריקודים ומחולות / "The word *Chag* suggests a joy that comes about through dancing," hence, we should dance on Sukkos. Indeed, in the times of the Beis haMikdash, there was a practice of Simchas Beis haShoeivah, in which thousands of people would gather in the courtyard of the Beis haMikdash and watch as the pious and the sages danced through the night accompanied by harps, lyres, cymbals, and trumpets. Today, many keep this custom of dancing on the nights of Sukkos, although now, everyone participates in the dancing.*

Dancing on Sukkos also relates to the Chupah and Sheva Berachos aspect of Sukkos — indeed, we dance in a way that is very similar to dancing at a wedding.

Shemini Atzeres and Simchas Torah feature dancing as a central form of Avodah. With great ecstasy, we grasp the Torah to our hearts as we dance in *Hakafos* / circles around the Bimah, the table where the Torah is read. On his walk home, after finishing Hakafos in his Shul, when the Arizal would hear singing and dancing in other Shuls, he would enter and dance along. Many communities would, and do, continue dancing into the early morning hours. Such is the holy Avodah of dancing on Shemini Atzeres and Simchas Torah.

---

* The word *Chag* / seasonal festival means something that is cyclical, as in *Chug* / circle, hence a circle dance. The *Tosefos Yom Tov* writes in the name of the Radak, on the Mishnah, *Rosh Hashanah*, 1:2, that תחג means 'You shall dance." The Gemara, *Chagigah*, 10b, says, 'ממאי דהאי וחגותם אותו חג לה / זביחה דלמא חוגו חגא קאמר רחמנא "How do we know that 'And you shall celebrate it as a *Chag* / festival to Hashem' (*Vayikra*, 23:41) is referring to an animal offering? Perhaps the Merciful One is simply saying, 'Celebrate a festival.' Regarding this, Tosefos (*ad loc*) writes, חוגו חגא — י"מ לשון מחולות / some say it means 'festival', and others say it means 'circle dances'.

As mentioned, a *Chag* / a festival is a cyclical event, as in *Chug* / circle. On every day of the Chag of Sukkos, the congregation processes in a circle holding the Lulav and Esrog, and at night many celebrate with circle dances. In many forms of dance, there are 'progressive' choreographic patterns of dancing forward towards a destination and retreating back again, and there are also patterns of dancing in circles. Circle dancing is not 'progressive', rather it is a kinesthetic depiction of centered presence, of the joy of having arrived, of the bliss of Yichud and unity.

In a circle dance, there is no hierarchy, no higher or lower, further or closer, leader or follower; everyone is in a 'balance', equidistant from the center, and everyone in the circle is face-to-face with the others. This symbolizes the Yichud of Shemini Atzeres, dancing face-to-face (to the extent humanly possible) with HaKadosh Baruch Hu, and dancing as one with the Divine Torah.

DANCING IN THE STREET

During the seven days of Sukkos we live enveloped by Hashem's embrace; we eat, drink, study Torah, *Farbreng* / sit in spiritual gatherings in the Sukkah. We have nowhere to go and nothing to do. By the time Shemini Atzeres / Simchas Torah arrives, we deeply know that our relationship with HaKadosh Baruch Hu is real and stable. This moves us to get up from this sitting position and dance. We receive the holy Torah scroll in our arms and dance — we are in love, our joy knows no bounds, for we have arrived. In this state of being, many leave the four

walls of the Shul and dance with the Torah in the streets, sharing our joy with the 'outer world'. Centuries ago, there was even
a custom to invite non-Jewish officials to the Shul on Simchas
Torah to celebrate (note *Zecharyah*, 14:16. והיה כל-הנותר מכל-הגוים הבאים
על-ירושלים ועלו מדי שנה בשנה להשתחות למלך ה צבא-ות ולחג את-חג הסכות). Our elation and songs of holiness reverberate outwards, illuminating
passersby and seemingly mundane concrete structures. When
a person is 'in love' or has just achieved dramatic success in life,
their enthusiasm can swell until they have the urge to shout it
out on the rooftops, to proclaim their joy to the entire universe,
to invite everyone into the celebration.

On Simchas Torah, we are so in love with Hashem that we
lose certain inhibitions, run out into the streets, and dance with
the Torah in front of passers-by. After having spent intimate
time with our Beloved for the seven days of *Sheva Berachos* /
seven days after marriage, marinating in a Divine embrace, we
are so permeated that our love spontaneously lifts us to our
feet and we find ourselves dancing for joy.

This love is no longer just Top-down, it is bottom-Up. After Yom Kippur, we rejoice in our having been forgiven, and
in having accepted upon ourselves the Second Luchos, which
embrace our humanity and our tendency to make mistakes,
and the *Torah she-b'Al Peh* / the 'bottom-Up' or 'Oral' aspect of
the Torah — the teachings welling up from the heart of deepest human inspiration and wisdom. We are thrilled with our
atonement and rebirth; our bodies and minds are now shining
with the blissful beauty of Torah, and our exuberance builds

until it becomes uncontainable. When we dance, it is as if we lift off from the earth; we defy gravity because our Teshuvah has unburdened us. We want everyone to know — not with any motive or showing off, but rather because we are tasting an *infinite joy.*

THE POSITION OF THE TORAH WHEN DANCING

Chazal inform husbands, "If your wife is short, bend down to whisper to her" (*Baba Metziya,* 59a). Both spouses need to try to be in a Panim el-Panim posture, and if one's partner is seemingly not yet 'on the same level', one should 'bend down' to connect face-to-face. Sometimes a face-to-face relationship forms between 'equals' who naturally see eye-to-eye in everything, and other times, one must 'lower' oneself or 'lift' oneself to their loved one's current state of being.

The Magid of Mezritch speaks of a father who gets on the floor to play with his child. This is the idea of lowering oneself to 'reach out' and encounter the other. One's love for the other makes them willing to descend to their beloved's level of understanding. Children are naturally, and in mystical terms, closer to the ground, and parents, out of their love, literally and figuratively bend down to communicate with them face-to-face.

The "Be'er Mayim Chayim," Reb Chayim of Tchernovitz, a student of the Maggid of Mezritch and the Maggid of Zlotchov, speaks of the various expressions of a parent's love for their child (*Be'er Mayim Chayim,* Parshas Naso). Sometimes, he says, you need to bend down to them, but sometimes you need to pick up the child and hold them so that their face is in front of your own and you can look straight into their eyes. This, too, is like a face-to-face relationship. There are also times when, in great joy, you lift your child above your head or put them on your shoulders; you make them a 'crown' above your head. The child becomes *your* crown.

It could be said that the same applies to Shemini Atzeres / Simchas Torah, when we dance with Hashem's Torah. On Shemini Atzeres / Simchas Torah, we dance holding the Torah, and become the 'legs' of the Torah. We lift the Torah and place it near our head, like a parent lifting a child up to an 'eye-to-eye relationship'. Some people, in their love and excitement, even lift the Torah above their heads. Of course, we cannot literally put the Torah on our shoulders, but in many Shuls, the custom is to take our children and put them on our shoulders while dancing with the Torah. This is a *Bechinah* / paradigm that is 'higher' than face-to-face, as it were, as the Torah 'crowns' us.

On Shemini Atzeres / Simchas Torah, when we finally attain the ultimate posture of face-to-face relationship, Zivug and Yichud, we may even reach a moment of 'lifting' our Beloved One, through His Torah, above our heads.

FROM BACK-TO-BACK, TO FACE-TO-FACE, TO PANIM ECHAD / 'ONE FACE', ONE VISION

Up until the present, the two possible paradigms of relationships were explored, back-to-back and the more mature form of face-to-face. Perhaps, there seems to be something even deeper.

There is a type of relationship that is back-to-back, this is similar to a child's relationship with a parent. The child is attached to the hip, existentially speaking, of the parent. Where the parent travels or moves, so do the young children.

This type of relationship can also be true of two physically, although not mentally / emotionally and spiritually, mature adults. For example, a person falls in love with another person because they feel overwhelmed in the other person's presence, and they are lost in the other.

Then there is the more mature, healthy, and desired relationship of face-to-face, of an עזר כנגדו; someone that is other than you, that chooses you, and you choose them. A person feels like an independent person, and yet, chooses to enter a relationship with another. This is the ideal, as the Torah shows us, expression and form of marriage. This is called a face-to-face relationship, both partners choose the partnership.

Having been married for a longer period of time, and this can be true of all relationships, the bond between the two becomes so unified that they start sharing the same views and outlooks on life and even the same dreams, hopes, and aspirations.

Imagine a younger couple sitting across from each other over a cup of tea and speaking about life, or just gazing at each other. This is a face-to-face encounter. Now, imagine a mature couple, having lived together and traversed many ups and downs together, sitting on a bench together, looking out in the same direction. In unison, they are looking back at their past, glimpsing the future on the horizon, or beholding their child's wedding. This is, in a sense, beyond the level of a face-to-face encounter. It is a unification of vision and perspective; there are two faces, but it is as if there is one person.

This is the full transformation of Adam and Chavah. On the day of Rosh Hashanah, they were initially created as one, but facing away from each other, unable to see or acknowledge the other. With the blast of the Shofar, they were separated so that they could gradually turn around and see the other, and 'find their soulmate' in each other. On Yom Kippur and Sukkos, they became, once again, one flesh, but this time sitting face-to-face, dreaming of their future together, and on Shemini Atzeres / Simchas Torah, they attained Yichud on every level of being. After Shemini Atzeres / Simchas Torah, they retain the essence of this oneness, finally sitting side-by-side, facing the same direction.

After the Yamim Tovim, we and HaKadosh Baruch Hu beyond even the *Bechinah* / level of 'two' lovingly facing each other. We finally reach the Bechinah of רצוננו / (our) will is רצונו / Hashem's will. Our desires and aspirations are in sync with Hashem's, our perspective is the same — and thus we are ready to go out into the world and fulfill HaKadosh Baruch Hu's desire for Creation. In this state of essential unity, we are able to transform the world into a holy, G-dly place, a place where Hashem's Presence is present and revealed, *Kein Yehi Ratzon /* So may it be His will, Amein.

Chapter 3
IMAGERY OF THE SUKKAH

THE SUKKAH STIRS THE SOUL AND AWAKENS THE IMAG-
INATION. THERE IS SOMETHING TIMELESS, ALMOST
OTHERWORLDLY, ABOUT STEPPING OUTSIDE THE walls
of our home and entering this fragile, holy space, its simple
walls embracing us, its roof of branches open to the sky. To
sit beneath its shade is itself a Mitzvah, an act that quiets the
mind and softens the heart. For generations, our sages, mystics,
and poets have been drawn to the Sukkah's gentle mystery,
finding within it endless symbols, images, and layers of meaning. What follows is a glimpse, a sampling of their timeless
reflections and sacred visions.

CLOUDS OF GLORY

The most primal image of sitting in the Sukkah is that it reminds us of our collective birth, the going out of Egypt, and the Clouds of Glory in which we traveled and were protected during our travels in the forty years in the Desert. We do not, however, celebrate this sacred history as 'his-story' or someone else's story, occurring in a distant past. Rather, we celebrate it as 'living memory,' moments of our collective past that are felt and enacted in the present. The days of Sukkos are "remembered and performed." The Arizal says this means that remembering these events causes us to 'perform' them and re-create them, as it were. By remembering the Exodus from Mitzrayim, we actively go out of our own personal and even collective 'Mitzrayims', our places of constriction, doubt, and smallness — and sit in our own Clouds of Glory.

THE CLOUDS OF GLORY PRODUCED FROM THE BREATH OF LOVE

On Sukkos, we recapture the spiritual experience of Yetzias Mitzrayim: אמר ה׳ זכרתי לך חסד נעוריך אהבת כלולתיך לכתך אחרי במדבר בארץ לא זרועה / "I remember, to your favor, the devotion of your youth, your love as a bride — how you followed Me in the wilderness in an uncultivated land" (*Yirmeyahu*, 2:2). Yom Tov is called a *Moed* / time, an appointment or 'date'. Indeed it is a time of celebrating our love relationship with Hashem.

The Sukkah is like the first tender stage of a relationship, when two souls find each other and quickly marry, not because of what they have, but because of who they are to each other. In those early days, they do not need a grand home or fine possessions. Even a small, simple space feels like a palace, because they are together. And this is what we say to Hashem on Sukkos, and what Hashem says to us in return: "I fondly remember those days when we sat together in that little hut, its walls swaying in the wind, its roof no more than a patchwork of branches. And yet, how beautiful it was! How precious! We had nothing, and yet we had everything. It was just us, lost in love, without a care in the world. That fragile Sukkah was our palace, our sanctuary, our special and forever place."

In this way, the Sukkah reminds us of our love for Hashem at the very beginning of our shared journey. It is this love, in fact, that produces the Cloud of Glory, as explained in the following story.

A secular scholar once asked the holy Ruzhiner, "What did the Sages mean when they said (*Ta'anis*, 9a) that the Clouds of Glory existed in the merit of Aharon?" The Ruzhiner responded with a beautiful image: "When two people love each other, the breath that leaves their mouths join as one; it becomes one breath. Aharon pursued peace and loved everyone, and naturally, the people loved him as well. Together, in their love for each other, their breath joined and created the Clouds of Glory." Love and unity — both between human beings and between us and HaKadosh Baruch Hu — create the Clouds of Glory, the Ohr that we dwell in throughout Sukkos.

Chazal say that if an *Ish* / man and an *Ishah* / woman merit, the *Shechinah* / Divine Presence rests between them; but if they do not merit, *Eish* / fire will consume them (איש ואשה זכו שכינה ביניהן לא זכו אש אוכלתן :Sotah, 17a). The words *Ish* and *Isha* are almost identical; the only difference is that in *Ish* the middle letter is Yud, and in *Isha*, the final letter is Hei. These two letters can be joined to form the Divine Name, meaning they are consciously making the Shechinah the 'third partner' in their union. However, if they ignore the Shechinah, the 'Yud and Hei', it departs, leaving in each word only the letters Aleph and Shin, which spell *Eish* / fire.

The Shechinah is the 'Cloud of Glory' produced through Klal Yisrael loving her 'Husband', HaKadosh Baruch Hu. Meteorological clouds retain droplets of water, while fire, by contrast, disperses droplets of water. Even if we have dispersed the Divine Presence in the past, our return to love reconstitutes this Cloud of Glory. The Second Luchos, too, represent the glory of Teshuvah, 'returning after falling away from love', and on Sukkos, we bask in their light, our breath joined with the Divine breath.

DIVINE HUG

As the Sukkah is the inner space of the Clouds of Glory, sitting in the Sukkah, even today, we are being embraced and experiencing, as it were, a Divine hug.

The *Halachic* / legal minimum enclosure for a Kosher Sukkah is two whole connected walls, plus a portion of a third wall. As explored, these elements make the Sukkah resemble a hug; the two whole walls are like an arm and a chest, and the portion of a third wall is like a hand bent at the wrist, which surrounds us in an embrace.*

In the Torah, *Sukkah* is usually spelled with three letters: סכה / Samach Chaf Hei. Graphically, these three letters hint to the three ways that a *Kosher* / 'Halachically valid' Sukkah can be built. The first letter, ס / Samech, refers to a Sukkah that is to-tally surrounded, meaning, one with four full walls. The second letter כ / Chaf, refers to a less stringent, albeit still Kosher Suk-kah, having only three full walls. The final letter, ה / Hei, refers to the bare minimum of walls required for a Kosher Sukkah, two walls and a small third wall (Chida, *Devash Lefi*, Ma'areches Samech. Alternatively, the Hei stands for the walls of the Sukkah. Samech is numerically 60, standing for the minimum amount of אצבעות / 'fingers' high that a Sukkah requires, 10 Tefachim, and a Tefach is the width of 6 fingers = 60. Chaf is 20, the maximum height of a Sukkah in Amos).

These three types of Sukkah are reflected as well in three types of hug (when visualizing these hugs using the letters Samech, Chaf,

---

and Hei, the right side of each letter can represent the Beloved's chest, and the other lines the Beloved's arms. A Dagesh dot in the space within the letter can represent the person who is 'hugged' by the Sukkah, with his or her face toward the right: (ה, כּ, פּ). The 'Samech' Sukkah depicts a full body hug, in which we are enwrapped, both of the Beloved's 'arms' completely encircling our back (ס). The 'Chaf' Sukkah is also a hug with both arms, but we are not completely enwrapped, as if the Beloved's hands are just holding our sides (כ). The 'Hei' Sukkah is a partial hug, as if with one arm holding our side and shoulder and the other hand placed politely on our back (ה).

This helps us understand why many pious individuals desire to have a full four-wall Sukkah, as they wish to experience being completely surrounded by the Divine embrace, powerfully hugged with the full contact of both the Beloved's right hand of *Chesed* / kindness and left hand of *Gevurah* / power.

The Chasidic Rebbes expand upon this image: when we enter the Sukkah, it is similar to a child who runs into the loving embrace of his or her mother (*Ma'or vaShemesh*, Rimzei Yom Beis Sukkos). Just as when a child feels scared or vulnerable, they run to their mother, and maybe even hide under her skirts, we too, consciously or not, feel in peril because of our previous actions, may may feel like we have lost our way, and the act of Teshuvah and Yom Kippur is when we return and run to hide under the skirt, as it were, and in the loving embrace of אימא עילאה / *Ima Ila'ah* / Supernal Divine 'Mother'. In Yiddish, there is a Chasidic saying, in the name of the Chidushei haRim: "We have a good Mother: She inflates us (with healthy esteem) on

Rosh Hashanah, cleans us up on Yom Kippur, and covers us on Sukkos."

Yom Kippur is connected with the *Sefirah* / Divine attribute of Binah, also referred to as *Ima* / Mother; on this day it is as if we are crying for our Mother. After Yom Kippur, we finally see our *Ima Ila'ah* / Supernal Divine Mother, with Her arms extended to us. We run to Her and rest in the 'Sukkah' of Her embrace. On Sukkos, we relish seven days dwelling in this nurturing atmosphere, shielded from any outside influence that wishes to harm us, until we are fully pacified and suffused with the light of Her Presence (the Sukkah is a manifestation of the *Makifim* / surroundings lights of Binah).

On Yom Kippur, we are like lost children returning home. On Sukkos, we open the door to our true home, the Shechinah embraces us and gently tells us, 'Everything is okay, you are home! I love you, and I will protect you." Our hearts soar in joy.

Even if we have fallen, Sukkos comes along and Hashem says, 'I will hold you.' The word סוכה / Sukkah, spelled with a Vav, is an acronym for four words: סומך ועוזר כל הנופלים / "Hashem supports and helps all those who fall" (*Bnei Yissaschar,* Tishrei, Ma'amar 10:4). To dwell in a Sukkah is to be held and lifted from our fallen state.

Whereas on Yom Kippur we turned to the Master of the Universe and pleaded, 'Please pick me up, I have fallen,' or 'Hold me and give me strength because I am falling,' on Sukkos, we settle into the Divine hug of the Sukkah until we come to the realization that there is really nowhere to fall. In this way, we train ourselves to have the abiding Binah, understanding that wherever we go we are always held in Hashem's loving embrace (וכמו ששמענו מהרבי מאיזביצא זצ״ל שכל נפש ישראל איך שנופל הוא נופל בחיקו של השי״ת. *Pri Tzadik*, Naso).

During the past year, we may have drifted, or G-d forbid even walked away from, the revealed Presence of the Shechinah. But then Rosh Hashanah arrives and we awaken from our spiritual slumber or stupor. With Yom Kippur, we are washed clean, freed, and fully atoned. Now comes Sukkos and we once again, we sit basking in the Presence of Hashem's light, consciously embraced, sensing deeply that we never actually left to begin with.

The full spelling of the word Sukkah has four Hebrew letters, סוכה.* The first letter ס / Samech of Sukkah, when spelled out is ס-מ-ך / Samech-Mem-Chaf, which has a numerical value of 120. The next letter ו / Vav when spelled out is ו-י-ו / Vav-Yud-Vav, numerically 22. The third letter Chaf, כ, is spelled כ-ף / Chaf-Pei, numerically 100.

---

* When *Sukkah* is spelled סכה without a Vav, it is because the Sukkah represents the Shechinah (see *Tikunei Zohar*, Tikun 21), and sometimes the Shechinah appears to be 'fallen' (as in סוכת דוד הנופלת / "the falling Sukkah of Dovid": *Amos*, 9:11), or in a state of 'lack', without the Vav. Vav (6) represents the revealed light of six higher Sefiros, Ze'ir Anpin. In *Birchas haLevanah* / the Blessing of the Moon (and in a sense all of our prayer requests, including those in the Shemoneh Esrei), we *Daven* / pray for the Shechinah to be 'filled' and revealed in its state of completion and fullness, like a סוכה, a full Sukkah.

The last letter ה / Hei is spelled ה-א / Hei-Aleph, numerically 6. The grand total of these values is 248, corresponding to the 248 'limbs' or parts of the body. When we enter a Sukkah, all of our body becomes enveloped by the embrace of the Sukkah. Our entire being is held in the arms of the Creator's infinite Love.

THE ARK THAT PROTECTS US

In the story of the Great Flood, the *Teivah* / Ark protected Noach and his family from the raging waters, giving them an oasis within the great chaos inundating their world, and ensuring the continuation of human civilization. We, too, live in a chaotic world, but what is our Teivah? It is the Sukkah (*Zohar* 3, 256a. Rebbe Maharash, *Hemshech VeKacha*, 95. *Sefer haMa'amarim Melukat*, Vol. 1, "B'Chag haAsif," Note 34). The Sukkah is our refuge from the mighty, raging waters of worry and doubt (*Torah Ohr*, Alter Rebbe, Noach). The world is flooded with self-alienating passions, unhealthy cravings, worries and uncertainties, and so HaKadosh Baruch Hu lovingly calls to us, 'Come sit with Me in My space and let go of all your inner chaos and worry!'

In this image, the Sukkah is a space that we 'enter'. Yet, on a deeper level, having already encountered a ritual 'death' on Yom Kippur (wearing white garments like shrouds, ceasing to eat, drink, and be intimate, etc.), we now fear nothing. We already sense that we are completely protected by HaKadosh Baruch Hu. The Sukkah is then not necessarily a space that we need to enter, rather, it is an outward manifestation of the state we are already in after the conclusion of Yom Kippur. After our spiritual *Avodah* / inner work on Yom Kippur, we are given the gift of physically sitting in the aura of the fearless confidence that we attained.

The word סוכה / Sukkah is related to the word נסיך / prince (*Bnei Yissaschar*, Tishrei, Ma'amar 10:5). Following our work on Yom Kippur, we sit in the Sukkah as a noble prince or princess, children and representatives of our beloved King, truly free and empowered, unafraid of the shallow temptations of the world. We are ready to go out after Sukkos into the world, into Hashem's Kingdom, prepared to right any wrongs and transform the darkness.

IMMERSION OF THE ENTIRE BODY

Rosh Hashanah, the 'head' of the year, is connected with our own head and 'mind'. On Rosh Hashanah, our mindset is of utmost importance (as explored in *A Call to Majesty*), on Yom Kippur, the essence of day reveals our 'soul' (as explored in *The Lightness of Being*), while Sukkos is our 'body' and our entire self, nothing remaining outside. On this festival, freedom from egoic fears, and the sense of protection in the Divine embrace, are not merely mental perceptions, nor subtle feelings in our soul; they are rather visceral bodily sensations. Hence, on Sukkos, as will be explored, there is a special emphasis on dancing and experiencing joy in the body.

In fact, the Mitzvah of Sukkah is unique in that it is a Mitzvah that we enter into with our entire body. This is similar to the Mitzvah of immersing in a Mikvah (*Likutei Sichos* 19, p. Hosafos.

Both Sukkah and Mikvah are Makif and connected to Binah). Yet, inside a Mikvah, when our body is underwater, we stop breathing and thus our bodily life is suspended, as it were. Within a Sukkah, however, we live and breathe, eating, drinking, sleeping, and celebrating with our bodies (The only other Mitzvah we enter fully would be settling the Land of Israel, insofar as the Ramban affirms that this is a positive Mitzvah, as alluded in the Pasuk, ויהי בשלם סוכו ומעונתו בציון: *Tehilim*, 76:3. See *Tehilos Eliyahu*, ad loc. Perhaps also the Mitzvah of R'iyah, appearing at the Beis haMikdash during the Shalosh Regalim, is a full body Mitzvah, yet, the Mitzvah of R'iyah is to appear with a Korban, Rambam, *Hilchos Chagigah*, 1:1; "And who comes to the Beis haMikdash on Yom Tov without bringing a burnt-offering has not only failed to perform a positive Mitzvah, but has violated a negative commandment").

There are three dimensions in Creation: *Olam* / 'world' or space, *Shanah* / 'year' or time, and *Nefesh* / 'soul' or conscious-ness. On Rosh Hashanah, the beginning of the new year, is a *Tikkun* / rectification of the dimension of 'year', and time in general. Yom Kippur is the day of atonement of soul, revealing our higher and innermost levels of soul, and Sukkos is the Tik-kun of space, of 'place' (Parenthetically, the rectification of conscious-ness needs to be in the center, between the other two Yamim Tovim, because without clear consciousness observing time and space, time and space have no clear definition). On Sukkos, with the rectification and ele-vation of physical space, we enter the Sukkah with our entire physical bodies, and all dimensions of our reality are illuminat-ed and perfected.

MORE SHADE THAN SUN

A Kosher Sukkah needs to have more shade from the S'chach than sunlight penetrating the inner space.

Sun is a metaphor for the parts of self that are clear, revealed, and conscious. Shade hints to the darker, shadowy parts of self that can lurk in the subconscious. On Sukkos, we need to enter fully into the Sukkah, not only our bodies but with all our inner parts, whether light or dark, conscious or subconscious. The ambiguities and uncertainties in life also need to be enclosed within the light of the Sukkah. Rebbe Bunim of Pshischa said that when we enter into a Sukkah, we enter with our boots and our *B'lateh* / mud. Even our most external layers of self, our 'boots', and even the dirt that they collect, are to be fully embraced.

Yom Kippur is the day of 'truth', the day we come clean before HaKadosh Baruch Hu, the day we come naked and vulnerable in front of our Maker, and say, here I am, this is me, and desire to change and be close to You. Through the inner *Avodah* / work of Yom Kippur, we bring Hashem 'two goats': one that represents our purity and is offered to Hashem in the Beis haMikdash, and one that represents our untamed 'shadows', which is led into the wilderness.

After Yom Kippur, we are no longer afraid of these darker parts of ourselves; we are no longer avoiding them, reacting to them or sweeping them under the rug. We are now comfortable with everything. In fact, we invite more 'shade' than 'sun' into the Sukkah; as we bring all of our shadows and 'sub-personalities' into this sacred space, they too are embraced, loved, held, until any negativity in them fades. Everything without exception can be transformed through the unending love and unconditional embrace of HaKadosh Baruch Hu.

'Shade' can also have an opposite connotation. There is a Sukkah above, in the upper worlds, and there is a Sukkah below on earth. Our Sukkah below is only a 'shadow' of that supernal Sukkah, but when we enter it we are entering into the shadow of the supernal Sukkah. Thus the shadow is our interface with higher Makifim and transcendent intimacy with Hashem.

BACK TO EDEN

In one way, the Sukkah is similar to the *Mikvah* / ritual pool, as we fully 'immerse' in the Sukkah. However, underwater in the Mikvah, we cannot breathe; it is as if we are not alive, as mentioned. In the Sukkah, not only do we breathe, but we come alive. In this way, the Sukkah is the womb of our Divine Mother, in which we gestate and are rebirthed.

Living inside our mother's womb is likened to living in Gan Eden, the place of our inception, our original purity and potential. Every year, we return to Gan Eden, to a place of perfection and unity made just for us, and there we truly come alive, immersed in motherly care and kindness. We emerge from the Sukkah into the new year, completely refreshed and renewed, with the urge to dance for joy.*

---

* Sukkah corresponds to Olam haBa, Pesach is connected with Eretz Yis-

TREE OF LIFE

A Sukkah is like Gan Eden, a glimmer of the World to Come, of that future state of unity and peace. When we perform the Mitzvah of dwelling in the Sukkah, we actively repair the disunity and chaos that spread throughout the world when the first human beings ate from 'the Tree of Knowledge of Good (mingled or 'unified' with) Evil'.

Chazal (*ibid.*), teach us that the identity of the Tree of Knowledge in the Garden of Eden was not clearly identified, so that later in history people would not say 'Look, there is the tree that brought death to the world." Other sages do speak about its identity, and some (*Ibid. Berachos,* 40a. *Sanhedrin,* 70a-b) cite a three way dispute about what the tree was: a grapevine, a fig tree, or a stalk of wheat, which grew like a tree (מתמרות היו כארזי ללבנון). Perhaps, as the Zohar writes (*Tikunei Zohar,* 107a), it was a tree that had all three fruits 'united as one'.

rael, and Shavuos with Torah. Olam haBa, Eretz Yisrael, and the Torah are the three great gifts given to Klal Yisrael: *Ya'aros Devash,* Derush 11. Note Rashi, *Yeshayahu,* 4:5-6. Rabbeinu Bachya, *Kad haKemach,* Sukkah. The Ritva writes, on Sukkah, 53a, the following regarding Simchas Beis haShoeivah — והוי יודע שכל השמחה היתיר' היתה בהלל ולהודות לה' על הטובה שעשה לישראל להשרות שכינתו בתוכנו וגם כנגד הע"ה הניתן לצדיקים / "And you should know, that the extra joy on Simchas Beis haShoeivah was with giving praise and thanks to Hashem for all the goodness and blessings that He bestowed on Klal Yisrael, to make dwell the Divine Presence amongst us, and also corresponding to the World to Come which is reserved from the rightcous." Indeed, "Some have a custom, upon leaving the Sukkah, of saying, יה"ר שנזכה לישב בסוכה של לויתן / 'May it be Your will that we merit to sit in the Sukkah of Leviyason (referring to the feast in the World to Come).'" Rama, *Orach Chayim,* 667. כל מי שמקיים מצות סוכה בעולם הזה הקדוש ברוך הוא מושיבו בסוכתו של עתיד הקדוש ברוך הוא לעשות סוכה לויתן: *Yalkut Shimoni,* Remez 653. לצדיקים מעורו של לויתן: *Baba Basra,* 75a.

The Medrash (*Medrash Rabbah*, Bereishis, 15:7) also has an opinion, ותרא האשה כי טוב העץ וגו', אמרת צא וראה איזהו אילן שעצו נאכל כפריו, ואין אתה מוצא אלא אתרוג / "And the woman saw that the tree / wood was good to eat." What tree is the wood, meaning the bark, eaten as the fruit? This we only find with an Esrog tree." If the fruit and the bark of the Tree of Knowledge tasted the same (*ibid.*: אילן שעצו נאכל כפריו), it represents a perfect state of 'oneness' in which outer and inner dimensions of reality reflect each other. Furthermore, the Esrog, the fruit which we hold in our hands on the non-Shabbos days of Sukkos, represents unity (the day of Shabbos is itself a manifestation of Divine Unity).

Elsewhere, the Medrash (*Pirkei d'Rebbe Eliezer* 13), writes, והנחש הלך ונגע באילן והאילן צווח ואמר רשע אל תגע בי שנ' (תהלים לו יב) אל תביאני רגל גאוה / "When the Snake went and touched the tree, the tree started crying out, saying: Wicked one! Do not touch me, as it is said, 'Let not the foot of arrogance come against me!'" Thus the tree resisted the disunity engendered by arrogance and greed. This sentence from Tehilim, אל תביאני רגל גאוה / "Let not the foot of pride come against me," is an acronym for the word Esrog. Thus, the Esrog, an expression of unity, is a tool we use on Sukkos to create a Tikkun for the Cheit Eitz haDa'as, and return to Eden and its state of integration and unification, in which all divisiveness is nullified, as diversity is integrated and harmonized.

Following the profound atonement, cleansing and soul-revelation of Yom Kippur, we have reclaimed our disparate 'sub-personalities' and different parts of our lives, and integrated and unified them. Then Sukkos comes and we take the Esrog of unity in our hands, together with the Lulav, Hadassim and Aravos, which all express oneness in multiplicity. We gesture with these four species in all six directions of space, and bring them toward the heart.

HOLY IMAGINATION

Coming on the heels of Rosh Hashanah, our collective birth, and from Yom Kippur, our rebirth, Sukkos is an opportune time to reclaim our positive imagination, of who we truly are and can be, and as a by-product, due away with the false perceptions of self, and the world of shallow and even negative fantasy.

Rabbeinu Bachya writes, כי לשון סוכה לשון ראייה, אמרו רז"ל למה נקרא שמה יסכה שסוכת ברוח הקדש / "The word *Sukkah* means 'seeing', as our Sages say, "Why was Sarah called יסכה / Yiskah? שסכתה / 'Because she saw' with Divine inspiration" (*Megilah*, 14b. *Kad haKemach*, Sukkah, 1. Maharal, *Gevuros Hashem*, 46). In other words, the Sukkah is connected to a type of higher seeing, Ruach haKodesh.

Similarly, the intermediary days of Sukkos were a time of *Simchas Beis haShoeivah* / Joy of the House of Water Drawing, in which they drew not only water but *Ruach haKodesh* / Divine inspiration and clarity (*Yerushalmi, Sukkah*, 5:1).

Merely sitting under the S'chach of the סכה / *Sukkah*, under the open sky and the stars, opens us up to be סכה /*Soche* / to see deeply, with Ruach haKodesh (*Bnei Yissaschar*, Tishrei, Ma'amar 10:1).

In numerical value, the word סכת / *Sukkos* (plural and without the Vav) is 480. This, says the Kav haYashar, is the same numerical value of the Name לילי-ת / *Lili-s*, a demonic force, representing the 'first' wife of Adam and the 'wife' of the *Samech Mem* / the archetype of all negative forces (Chazal call Sukkah a מצוה קלה / light Mitzvah: *Avodah Zarah*, 3a. קלה is 135, the same numerical as the name of the Samech Mem (סמא-ל), *Sam*/100, *E-l*/31, with its 4 letters: *Me'or Einayim*'). This feminine negative force is connected

---

* It is interesting to note that this Gemara (from *Avodah Zarah*, 3a) is a *Hemshech* / continuation of a previous Gemara: נכנסה לפניו מלכות רומי תחל / "The Roman Empire entered first before Him…" where the Romans appear before Hashem in Olam haBa wanting *Sechar* / a reward for supporting the performance of the Torah's Mitzvos in this world. Here, HaKadosh Baruch Hu suggests that the Romans try and see if they can keep the Mitzvah of Sukkos because it is "easy." In fact, they already had some form of waving a Lulav in their culture — branches that they would wave to claim their victory in battles, and they would also make booths during their times of celebration. Perhaps this is why Hashem chooses this Mitzvah, saying, 'Here, this should be easy for you, as you are familiar with this practice.' The *Seder haYom* from Rebbe Moshe ben Machir (16th Century, Tzfas) brings down that he heard that the reason the Torah chose the Four Species from among all other fruits or branches is that these four types are unique in that no 'force' has sway or influence over them. Thus, we are not afraid even of the Samech Mem, as we are holding up the banner of the King… עוד שמעתי כי

לכל אילן ואילן או עשב או ירק יש שר שולט עליו ואומר לו גדל וד' מינים אלו לא השליטם הקב"ה ביד שר ושוטר אלא כביכול מכחו ומהשגחתו הפרטית הם גדלים ולזה צוה לנו ליקח אלו הד' מינים מיוחדים לו בחג להראות לכל שעם ה' אלה והנה הנם בידו שאין להם פחד ואימ' משום בריה בעולם ואפילו לסמא"ל אין לו כח לשלוח יד בהם אחר שהם מצויינין ומסומנים בסימן של מלך: *Seder haYom*, Kavanos haLulav. See also *Rosh Dovid* (Chida), Parshas Emor. *Bnei Yissaschar*, Tishrei, 10:24. *Megaleh Amukos*, Sukkos, *U'Lekachtem*. The

with the world of fantasy, and it represents the inner fantasy of

---

Light of Sukkos nullifies the power of *Avodah Zarah* / idol worship, and all the 'planetary forces' of the universe, as can be seen from the Gemara, דבעי רחמי על יצר דעבודה זרה ובטליה ואגין זכותא עלייהו כי סוכה / And according to the other opinion, what does the Pasuk in Nechemya mean, where it says that those who returned to Eretz Yisrael in the times of Ezra and Nechemyah from captivity, "...made Sukkos, and dwelt in Sukkos, for since the days of Yehoshua, unto that day the children of Israel had not done so." Certainly, this Pasuk is not referring to actual Sukkos, rather, the Pasuk is saying that Ezra "prayed for mercy with regard to the evil inclination of idol worship and nullified it, and the merit protected them like a Sukkah": *Erchin*, 32b. See also *Rikanti*, Bamidbar, 14:9. אמנם בני ישראל אמרו...סר צלם ירמוז לשרי מעלה בצלו חמדתי וישבתי שאינו רק חלק ה' יתברך / "'Their protective shadow departed from them' — this refers to Supernal Princes (intermediary powers, as it were, of the nations who lived in Eretz Yisrael before Klal Yisrael settled there), Klal Yisrael however, proclaim, "In His shade relish and dwell," as we are only connected to Hashem Alone" (and do not rely on any intermediary forces). Or as Rabbeinu Bachya writes, *ibid.*, סר צלם מעליהם בזכות צל סכה, וה' שהוא צלן של ישראל אתנו. In general, the nations of the world are connected with the planetary influences, as just explained, and in particular to the sun (*Sukkah*, 29a: וגוים לחמה). More specifically, the Egyptian were predominantly sun worshipers (and idol worship in general is connected with the sun: *Sukkah*, 51b). On Sukkos, we need to sit in a Sukkah that has more shade (moon, reflected light, and on a deeper level, as just explained, the 'shade of Hashem') than sun. In this way, we symbolically push aside the Avodah Zarah of the sun and in general subscribing to the influence of planetary bodies, showing that "there is no *Mazal* / influence on Klal Yisrael," and we are, rather, sitting in the direct shade and canopy of haKadosh Baruch Hu. The Mechaber begins articulating the laws of Sukkos with the following: בסוכות תשבו שבעת ימים וגו' כי בסוכות הושבתי את בני ישראל הם ענני כבוד שהקיפם בהם לבל יכם שרב ושמש / "'In Sukkos you shall dwell for seven days etc....Because I protected you in Sukkos...' These refer to the Clouds of Glory who protected us from the intense heat and the sun of the desert": *Orach Chayim*, 625. This means literally, but also metaphorically, the Clouds of Glory, sitting in the Presence of the Divine, is our protection from being influenced by, or believing in, the (assumed) power of the sun, i.e., idol worship and planetary influences.

following desire with no consequences. In this way, sitting under the stars of the Sukkah gives us the *Koach* / ability to break free of all negative and shallow fantasies, and it opens us up to see correctly, with some measure of Ruach haKodesh. on any level, what is real and what is worth living for. Our perception is cleansed and we can see more clearly.

A reason why we may not see clearly, why our vision may be opaque or lacking in moral and spiritual clarity, is that the moral and spiritual atmosphere in which we live is itself clouded. On Sukkos we wave the Lulav and Esrog and we push aside these harmful (or clouded) winds (*Sukkah*, 37b). We thus purify our atmosphere of all physical, mental, emotional and spiritual pollutants; our psychic and spiritual environment is cleared of negative influences. Then, when we sit in a Sukkah, we see with great clarity.

Through the Lulav and Esrog, our *Makom* / space is refined and we become more susceptible to higher and deeper frequencies. When there is a purification of the *Avir* / atmosphere, higher more subtle frequencies do not get interrupted (Rebbe Chayim of Veloshin writes that his Rebbe, the Gra, was meritorious to receive a *Magid* to reveal to him Torah, but he felt that in exile, in *Chutz laAretz* / outside the Holy Land of Israel, the אויר / *Avir* / atmosphere is impure (גזרו על גושה ועל אוירה: *Gitin*, 8b), and thus any true message from Above, by the time it filters through the Avir of Chutz laAretz, becomes muddied and tangled with falsehood: Hakdamah, *Sifra deTzniusa*, Pirush haGra).

Sukkos is all about *Makifim* / surrounding, transcendent Lights. We all have a *Penimi* / internal, intimate perception and reality, what we know now and what we perceive presently. This is called our 'being'. We also have a *Makif* / transcendent, distant dream, what we hope to know and embody in the future. This is called our 'becoming'. During Rosh Hashanah and Yom Kippur, our 'being' became solidified and confirmed. When Sukkos comes, we connect to the world of 'becoming', that of higher visions, dreams and aspirations. 'Holy imagination' has replaced any negative or shallow fantasy, or self-serving imagination focussed on immediate gratification.

Besides the cleansing of the *Avir* / atmosphere, another reason we can receive real clarity of vision, and even glimpse Ruach haKodesh, is that Sukkos is a time of the *Yichud* / unification between 'Hashem', the Infinitely Transcendent aspect of HaKadosh Baruch Hu symbolized by the Four-Letter Name (Yud, Hei, Vav, Hei = 26), and the Imminent Divine Presence, symbolized by the Name Ado-noi (Aleph, Dalet, Nun, Yud = 65). Together, these Names equal 91, which is the same numerical value as the word *Sukkah* (Samech/60, Vav/6, Chaf/20, Hei/5 = 91 (*Sheim miShemuel,* Sukkos, 5678). Certain 'angelic' realities arise from the Name Ado-noi, while human souls originate in the Name of Hashem. When there is an inner Yichud between these two Names, then the Ruach haKodesh carried by the angels becomes revealed to us, in the world of souls (*Bnei Yissaschar,* Tishrei Ma'amar 10:2).

A Sukkah has four walls, expressing the four letters of the Name 'Hashem', the Transcendent, Infinite One, and the four letters of the Name Ado-noi, the One Who is Imminent within finitude. With finite human action, we build a Sukkah with four walls — a finite container, yet, one that manifests the Four Letters of the Name 'Hashem', a space where "Infinity" does and can reside. Similarly, in our own Avodah, the defined 'canvas' of our life is a finite form, yet our infinite dreams and transcendent visions can take hold there.

Our present reality is our Penimi, while our visions, dreams and aspirations are our Makifim / surrounding lights, as it were. Following Yom Kippur, we are no longer bogged down nor oppressed by our negative baggage, as we have gone through a process of deep internal cleansing. Now, within the pristine Makifim of the Sukkah, we are able to have healthy, positive visions, and to dream of a better life. Perhaps this is one reason that the Sukkah is outdoors, under the stars and the moon, the 'setting' for dreaming. Yet, there are also walls or 'borders' and 'structure' surrounding us, illustrating the fact that we are now able to draw dreams from the Makif, the realm of borderless possibilities, into the Pnim, the structures and borders of our everyday life in the coming year.

OLAM HAMALBUSH / WORLD OF POSSIBILITY

In the Sukkah, we sit under the S'chach, which represents a deeper realm called *Olam haMalbush* / the World of Garments. To explain briefly: Hashem, the Infinite One, creates the universe using the 22 letters of the Aleph Beis. The primordial sounds of the Aleph Beis are the vibrational building blocks, and precise combinations of these Divine sounds vibrate, forming, re-forming, and sustaining existence. Every movement of each existence in the world is a manifestation of corresponding spiritual movements and vibrations originating in the unmoving Oneness of the *Ohr Ein Sof* / Infinite Light. These vibrations or 'letters' are the very first movements rippling out from within the *Ohr Ein Sof* / Infinite Light.

The first revelation of the Divine 'desire to create' occurs in the *Olam haMalbush* / World of the Garment. This 'garment' is composed of the 231 possible Hebrew letter combinations. Since there are 22 basic letters in the Aleph Beis, combining each letter with another creates 462 combinations (22 letters x 21 letters = 462). Out of these 462, there are 231 possible 'forward combinations' of letters, also called *Panim* / face-combinations, such as Aleph-Beis, Aleph-Gimel, Aleph-Dalet, etc. — and 231 *Achor* / backward combinations, such as Beis-Aleph, Gimel-Aleph, Dalet-Aleph, and so forth.

Together, these primary letter-compounds are the supernal 'sound-bank' from which all vibration, energy, and matter are produced. This sound-bank houses both the potential to reveal the Infinite Light and the potential to manifest the finite vessel of Creation, the recipient of that revelation.

Olam haMalbush is, in a subtle sense, the world in which we sit on Sukkos. Sitting under the S'chach means being present within 'the world of all possible combinations', our own pure potential. We are sitting embraced by the Infinite creativity of HaKadosh Baruch Hu, as it were, in which everything is possible. In this embrace, we are given the ability to recreate ourselves anew, to find new approaches to our challenges, and to root ourselves and our coming year in a new, healthy, holy space. As such, the walls of the Sukkah are an embodiment of 'what is', and the S'chach is 'what could be'; the eventual unfolding and possibility.*

---

* Rabbeinu Bachya writes, ויש בבנין הסוכה רמז וזכרון שני העולמות העוה"ז והעוה"ב, העוה"ז הוא שהסוכה יש לה ג' דפנות רמז לבנין העוה"ז שיש לו שלשה דפנות מזרח ומערב ודרום כי צפון אין לו דופן...העוה"ז כי יש צורך מוכרח להיות גובה הסוכה למעוט עשרה טפחים זהו ששנינו ושאינה גבוהה י' טפחים פסולה... ונמצאת למד כי החלל הזה עשרה טפחים והסכך למעלה מעשרה, ובפירוש אמרו העוה"ב נברא ביו"ד / There is, in the structure of the Sukkah, a hint and reminder of the two worlds: haOlam haZeh / this world, and haOlam haBa / the World to Come. A (basic) Sukkah has three walls, which hints to Olam haZeh, which is constructed of three 'walls', east west, and south, for the north does not have a 'wall'. The height of the Sukkah must be at least ten handbreadths high; the Mishnah tells us that if it is not ten Tefachim, it is invalid… This teaches us that this space is Yud (10) high, and the S'chach is above the Yud (10), and the interpretation given is that haOlam haBa was created with the letter Yud: *Kad haKemach*, Sukkah, 1. This world, Olam haZeh, is connected with the Name Ado-noi, whereas Olam haBa is connected with the Name Yud-Hei-Vav-Hei (*Pesachim*, 50a). The Sukkah combines these two realities, Olam haZeh and Olam haBa, as the Zohar teaches: בסוכה, דאיהו כ"ו ה"ס דאיהי יאהדונה"י / "in a Sukkah" — (the inner letters of the word סוכה / *Sukkah*) Chaf-Vav / ו"כ are the numerical value of the Name י-ה-ו-ה (Yud-Hei-Vav-Hei = 26). The outer letters of the word *Sukkah*, Samech-Hei / ס"ה, have a value of 65, and this is the numerical value of the Name Ado-Noi, אדנ"י (Aleph, Dalet, Nun, Yud = 65). Combined, these two Names spell יאהדונה"י, the Name of Unity: *Tikunei Zohar*, Tikkun, 69. p. 107b. On the human level, this means when we enter the Sukkah we unify our pure potential with our present reality. (Note *Pri Eitz Chayim*, Sha'ar haSukkos, 3: סוד הסוכה כי סוכה גי' כ"ו ה"ס, והם הויה אדני. והנה רוחב הסוכה ד' ומשהו, נגד ד' אותיות השם. The question upon this statement is that the width of a Sukkah needs to be 7 Tefachim, not 4. Perhaps the Arizal means the 4 walls, but then what does ומשהו mean?).

BEIS HAMIKDASH & ERADICATING AMALEK

Another beautiful image of the Sukkah is that it is our personal miniature Beis haMikdash (וסכה היא במקום בית המקדש מעט: *Kav haYashar*, 95. *Sheim miShemuel*, Sukkos, Year 5681. *Kehilas Yaakov* (Kluger), Derush 24. Thus, the allusion in the Pasuk, ויהי בשלם סוכו ומעונתו בציון: *Tehilim*, 76:3). Just as Klal Yisrael was told of the Mitzvah to build the Mishkan on the day after Yom Kippur, today we begin to build, or at least speak about building, our Sukkah, our own sacred space, right after Yom Kippur. Also, prior to building the Mishkan and Beis haMikdash, Klal Yisrael needed to eradicate Amalek (this was done by Yehoshua in the Desert, and by King Shaul before initiating the Beis haMikdash that began to be assembled by King Dovid). Today, we must do the same on an inward level. Before we build our Beis haMikdash, our Sukkah, we must ensure that our inner Amalek is nullified. This means that the schism between our mind and heart, and between what we know and how we feel, must be dissolved through the joy of the heart as we emerge from Yom Kippur into *Zeman Simchaseinu* / the Season of our Joy.

SUKKAH AS A CHUPAH: THE JOY OF RECONNECTING

Finding something that was lost brings one great joy. For example, say your routine is to wake up in the morning, take your keys, start the car, and drive your children to school. If one day you wake up in the morning, and you realize your keys are missing, and everyone goes around frantically looking for the keys, there is some level of distress. But the moment you find them, there is great elation.

Or imagine catching up with a dear friend who you have not seen in years, and feeling your joy of reconnection. On Sukkos, we celebrate going under the Chupah, as it were, with HaKadosh Baruch Hu, having sadly been estranged, even if subtly, from our Beloved. As we go through the process of Te-shuvah culminating on Yom Kippur, we become reunited with our Loved One, and now we sit joyfully under the Chupah, the Sukkah. We experience the thrilling joy of rediscovering and rekindling our old love, as it were.

After Rosh Hashanah and Yom Kippur, once we have re-solved to recommit ourselves to *Kedushah* / holiness and *Dev-eikus* / unity with Hashem, we can enter this joyous 'wedding celebration' of intimacy. We, the Bride, have cleansed ourselves through the process of Yom Kippur, we are ready to enter into the Chupah with our Groom and rejoice in each other for the seven days of Sheva Berachos.

A Chupah hovers over a bride and groom as they enter into a covenant of mutual commitment and exclusivity. The Rad-baz, a teacher of the Arizal, explains that in this image, the Name 'Hashem' is the *Chasan* / Groom, and the Name Ado-noi is the *Kallah* / Bride (*Metzudas Dovid*, Mitzvah 117). The Suk-kah thus enacts the unity between the Name of Hashem and the Name Ado-noi* (On a deeper level, it is for this reason, the Radbaz

---

* Sukkah, spelled with a Vav (סוכה) is numerically 91, the same numerical value as Hashem (26) and Ado-noi (65). This idea is brought down in nu-merous sources, for example, *Zohar* 3, 255b. *Tikunei Zohar*, Tikkun, 69. p. 107b. Maharil, *Hilchos Sukkah. Pri Eitz Chayim*, Sha'ar Chag haSukkos 4.

writes, that a human bride and groom are exempt from sitting in a Sukkah, as they themselves represent Hashem and Ado-noi).

'The Bride' is likened to moonlight, and thus, on the 15th day of the month, when there is a full moon, Sukkos begins, and we are ready to celebrate with the Groom.

Another outstanding image of the union between Bride and Groom on Sukkos, us and HaKadosh Baruch Hu, is in the Mitzvah of taking the Lulav and Esrog. The *Lulav* / palm

---

Kav haYashar, 95. The trouble is that in the Torah and all of Tanach, the word Sukkah is always spelled without a Vav, as in סכה, which numerically is 85 (בסכת ישבו כל-האזרח בישראל ימים שבעת תשבו בסכת: Vayikra, 23:42. The Torah does use a Vav in the phrase הסכות חג: *ibid.*, 34. *Ibid.*, 43, but that is the second Vav, which implies many Sukkos, but it does not say, הסוכות חג. Note, *Tehillim*, 76:3). The word Sukkah is always spelled with a Vav in Chazal, meaning, by the Sages in the Mishnah and Gemara. We learn; הזה כעולם לא דלת באלף ונקרא הי ביוד נכתב הזה, העולם הבא. העולם / "This world is not like the world to come, in this world, the Name of Hashem is spelled Yud-Hei-Vav-Hei (numerically 26), but pronounced as Ado-noi (65)": *Pesachim*, 50a. In other words, there is a *Kesiv* / how the Name of Hashem is spelled (as in Yud-Hei-Vav-Hei) and there is the *K'ri* / how it is read and pronounced verbally and orally, and that is as *Ado-noi*. The difference between the Kesiv and K'ri is also the difference between the *Torah she-b'Kesav* / Written Torah, and the oral tradition of Torah, how it is read. The word *Sukkah* is spelled סכה in the Torah, but since there are no vowels specified in a Torah scroll, these letters could be read as *Sacha* or with other vowels. Yet, the oral tradition nevertheless guides us to read סכה as סוכה / **S**ukkah, with a Vav. (Thus, the word סוכה is כו, the inner letters (26), covered over by סה, the outer, revealed letters (65), as the oral tradition reveals what is hidden). The name of Hashem as spelled and yet how it is pronounced today is the unity between the two dimensions of the Torah and the Names of Hashem, the written and expressed. Hence, the numerical value of Sukkah, with a Vav, as 91 reflects this *Yichud* / Unity.

branch, shaped like a line, is symbolic of the masculine and the Sefirah of Yesod — the Groom. The rounded shape of the Esrog represents the feminine and the Sefirah of Malchus — the Bride. In the Mitzvah, we need to hold these two species together, enacting their unification.

Chapter 4

SUKKAH AS A PLACE OF ESSENCE-TO-ESSENCE ENCOUNTER

GENERALLY SPEAKING, WE ALL POSSESS FIVE SENSES: AUDITORY, OPTICAL, TACTILE, OLFACTORY, AND GUSTATORY. Yet, *Sefer Yetzirah*, the ancient "Book of Formation" discusses twelve experiential categories, expanding the concept of 'senses' to include elements such as 'sleep' and 'laughter'. These twelve senses are associated with the twelve months of the year. The *Chush* / sense connected with the month of Tishrei is *Tashmish* / 'coition' or intimacy between spouses, and more broadly speaking, the sense of touch.

'Intimacy' and 'touch' are experienced on a physical realm, but also, and even more profoundly can be experienced in spiritual realms as well, such as in the world of *Yichud* / unification with the Divine. The month of Tishrei and the *Yamim Tovim* / Holidays within this month express successive stages in our sense of Yichud with Hashem. Through the movement through the Yamim Tovim we are moving from potential estrangement to self-repair and 'beautification', to Divine engagement, wedding and intimacy and 'touch' with HaKadosh Baruch Hu, *Kaviyachol* / so-to-speak. This flow of stages begins with an 'upward' movement, from the human world 'below' toward the embrace and union with the Transcendent One, 'Above'.

During the preceding month of Elul, we embark on a path of self-reflection, repair, and Teshuvah for any mishaps or missed opportunities of the past year. This 'beautifies' our soul and refreshes our spiritual innocence, as we are resonating with the sign of the month, *Besulah* / Virgo. Once the month of Elul is over we are fully present, pure, and ready. The next step is Rosh Hashanah, in which we enter into our *Tenayim* / engagement ceremony, in which we, the Bride, make a formal commitment to our Divine 'Fiancé'. Everyone is stirred by the sounds of the Shofar, moved to call out to HaKadosh Baruch Hu, "I am Yours!"

Yom Kippur is our 'wedding day' (ביום חתונתו זה מתן תורה / "On the day of his wedding'; this is the giving of the Torah": *Ta'anis*, 26b. "(This means) the day that the Second Luchos were given, and that is Yom Kippur": Rashi, *ad loc*). After declaring our commitment on Rosh Hashanah, on Yom Kippur we call out from the depths of our heart, 'I love You, Hashem, I want to be with You, I want to feel Your Presence every moment!' We realize and actualize our 'oneness' with Hashem, our exclusive bond.

During Sukkos, we stay within the embrace of our wedding canopy, the Sukkah, and we celebrate for seven days of *Sheva Berachos* / seven days of 'Seven Blessings', rejoicing with the Groom and Bride. Sukkos culminates with full *Yichud* / intimacy on Shemini Atzeres / Simchas Torah.

The wobbly, temporary, insubstantial nature of the Sukkah calls forth our total *Bitachon* / trust. We realize that things that seem substantial and permanent are *not* fitting receptacles of our Bitachon, rather only the Ultimate Source and Giver of Life is a fitting 'object' of trust. This is why Sukkos is so joyful, as a state of joy is commensurate with one's level of Bitachon, and Sukkos is essentially an awakening of Emunah and Bitachon.[*]

---

[*] Bitachon brings true joy (*Chovos haLevavos*, Sha'ar haBitachon, Hakdamah), and Sukkos is all about Bitachon. In the words of one of the last great teachers of Torah in Spain who lived through the expulsion, Rebbe Yitzchak Arama, כי זה מה שיורה הוראה שלמה על שיהי' עקר היותו על החסיה והבטחון / בצל סכתו של הקב"ה בכל מעשיו ועסקיו יותר ממה שיבטח בעצמו ולא בטוב מזלו "For this (majority of shade over sunlight in the Sukkah) is a complete teaching on the principle of our being under the protection and security of the shade of the Sukkah of HaKadosh Baruch Hu in all our actions and dealings — even more than we trust in ourselves and our (personal) good fortune": *Akeidas Yitzchak*, Sha'ar 67:8, 13. Rebbe Yitzchak Abuhav, an earlier Spanish Rabbi and Mekubal writes, אבל ישים בטחונו במי שאמר והיה העולם כי לו לבדו היכולת...ולו לבדו המחסה והמסתור כדכתיב והבוטח בה' חסד יסובבנו / "But one should put his trust in 'the One who spoke and the world came into being', be-

We come to see that our life itself is like a Sukkah; 'wobbly', temporary and insubstantial. This drives us to cling to the one and only substantial reality there is: *Elokim Chayim* / the Living G-d. Indeed, a deeper reason why Sukkos is seven days is to stimulate the recognition that ימי־שנותינו בהם שבעים שנה / "The span of our life is seventy years" (*Tehilim*, 90:10), each day of Sukkos reflecting another decade of our lives (*Tur Berekes*, Hilchos Sukkos, 625). As the days pass, we are stimulated again and again to run into the embrace of the immortal Divine Presence, the timeless Beloved One who radiates in the inner space of the Sukkah. And this is where we take refuge and dwell.

UNITY WITHOUT GARMENTS OR VESSELS

As explored, the Sukkah is a manifestation of ימינו תחבקני / "His right hand embraces me," as the walls of the Sukkah surround us like a Divine hug. When we build the Sukkah, we do so according to the instructions of the Torah, symbolizing our resolve, commitment and desire to live a G-dly life, a life infused with meaning and purpose, in intimacy with HaKadosh Baruch Hu. Having prepared it in this way, then שם שמים / the Name of Hashem comes upon the Sukkah (*Sukkah*, 9a). We create the vessel, the physical space of the Sukkah, and then Hashem's Presence rests upon the Sukkah and we become enveloped within the Divine embrace.

---

cause He alone has the ability...and He alone is the shelter and hiding place (refuge), as written, 'Whoever trusts in Hashem, grace will surround him'": *Menoras haMaor*, Ner 3, Kelal 4, 6:1.

Genuine encounters demand presence and focus, and certainly if they are as deep as intimacy with a spouse. They require being fully in the present, without your mind wandering, G-d forbid, to other people, to other subjects, or to an unrelated past or future (וע"כ אמרו ז"ל לעולם יקדש אדם את עצמו בשעת תשמיש, וקדושה זו היא טהרת המחשבה שלא יחשוב באשה אחרת ולא בדברים אחרים רק באשתו / "Therefore our Sages say, a person shall sanctify himself when being intimate with his spouse, and this sanctity is the purity of thoughts, not thinking of any other woman or anything else, thinking only of his wife": *Rabbeinu Bachya*, Bereishis, 30:38).

The spiritual intimacy of Sukkos transcends and includes all time, bringing us into presence, and into the present moment, the eternal moment that is now and includes all of time. We rest in the embrace, the love of our Beloved, affectionately remembering Rosh Hashanah and Yom Kippur, our passionate declarations of commitment, and the days leading up to our wedding. We blissfully celebrate our shared eternal present moment, even while excitedly dreaming of our future together.

From the state of 'embrace' we move to that of 'Yichud'. The Divine *Chibuk* / embrace of Sukkos culminates in deep *Zivug* / intimacy, and *Yichud* / unity between Klal Yisrael and HaKadosh Baruch Hu. Marital intimacy is a state of presence that unifies the partners "as one flesh." As such, our Sages tell us that physical intimacy should be performed with no separation or intervening *Levushim* or 'garments'. It should be *Etzem el Etzem* / essence-to-essence, body-to-body, an encounter in which the sense of touch is most pronounced (*Tikkunei Zohar*,

שארה זו קרוב בשר שלא ינהג בה מנהג פרסיים שמשמשין מטותיהן בלבושיהן ... .Tikkun 58 / "*She'era* refers to closeness האומר אי אפשי אלא אני בבגדי והיא בבגדה יוציא ונותן כתובה
of flesh, which teaches that he should not treat her in the manner of Persians, who have conjugal relations in their clothes...: *Kesuvos*, 48a. ואף על פי שעושה כן / "even if he wants to do so for the purpose of modesty": *Shitah Me-kubetzes*, as loc. Ritzva, *ad loc*. See also *Beis Yoseph*, Even haEzer, 76:21:1. As an aside, the dancing customary during the days of Simchas Beis haShoeivah and then on Simchas Torah, is a fully embodied practice. It is not by nature ethereal, cerebral nor otherwise detached from the body. Dancing is touch; whether stamping with your feet on the ground, as is the custom for many, or lightly gliding, this type of activity is connected with the sense of this month, the sense of touch).

In an essence-to-essence encounter, there is no form of intermediary or intervening Levushim. When this deepest form of 'oneness' is performed "in the right time, with the correct intention," it can be the holiest of acts (*Igeres Kodesh*, attributed to the Ramban, Chap. 2. Instead of it being merely a *Cherpah* / disgrace, in the language of other Rishonim. Rambam, *Moreh Nevuchim*, 3:8. *Sefer haChinuch*, Mitzvah 117). And for this act to be a full unification, it needs to be direct, without any intermediaries.

The Gemara says there is a glimmer of the World to Come in three experiences: Shabbos, sunshine, and physical intimacy (*Berachos* 57b: שלשה מעין העולם הבא, אלו הן: שבת, שמש, ותשמיש. In the end, the Gemara says, *Tashmish* means תשמיש נקבים. Yet, a *Hava Amina* / 'informed perspective' in Torah *is* Torah). Each of these can be an experience of essence-to-essence Yichud, for they are forms of essence-to-essence unity without intervening Levushim. On

Sukkos, as well, we go beyond the world of Levushim in our intimacy with Hashem.

Every Mitzvah is an opportunity to connect, on a revealed level. Every Mitzvah opens us up to life, consciously and with awareness is Divine space, and every Mitzvah is an invitation for intimacy with the Giver of the Mitzvah. However, the Mitzvah of Sukkah is unique in that we actually enter into the object, and do so without any item in hand, without any intermediary Levushim or vessels. As our body enters the Sukkah, we are subsumed within the Mitzvah — there is no longer a Mitzvah-object separate from ourselves. Encompassed by Hashem's embrace, we are subsumed in Hashem, in complete unity.

All Mitzvos of physical action have a particular physical item through which the Mitzvah is performed. For example, on Rosh Hashanah, we hold a Shofar in our hand and blow it, and on Pesach, we hold Matzah and eat it. The physical object allows us to connect to the Giver of Mitzvos, the Source of Life, and participate in revealing the *Ohr* / Light that is shining during those Holy Days. The Mitzvah of Sukkah is unique; although it demands an action in relation to a certain structure, we do not hold the Mitzvah of Sukkah with our hands, nor do we blow it or eat it with our mouth. Rather, we enter it fully and 'live' there. Our whole self, the essence of what we are, merges with the essence of the Mitzvah.

WITHOUT THE 'VESSEL'
OF THE LULAV & ESROG

From another perspective, the Sukkah itself is a Levush or
Kli. Also, throughout the seven days of Sukkos, we wave the
Lulav and Esrog, which are 'garments' or 'vessels' of a Mitzvah.
Yet, on the eighth day (and the ninth day in the Diaspora),
the day of Shemini Atzeres / Simchas Torah, the peak of the
Yichud, we no longer wave the Lulav and Esrog. Technically,
we no longer need to sit in the 'vessel' of a Sukkah.

Shemini means 'the eighth day', and *Atzeres* means to 'stop',
to pause, as there is nothing for us to 'do' any longer. We simply
celebrate in Yichud with HaKadosh Baruch Hu and have no
need for a garment or vessel. We stop 'doing' and rest in a state
of 'being'. Hashem is declaring to us, "I love you how you are; I
don't need you to do anything for me. I love you for *being you*,
not merely for what you do." This is unconditional love and
honor. When we fully sense this unbridled, unconditional love,
our own innate love for HaKadosh Baruch Hu is awakened
and all we want to do, and can do, is dance (Infectious love draws
out dancing. The Rambam writes, השמחה שישמח אדם בעשית המצוה ובאהבת הא-ל
שצוה בהן. עבודה גדולה היא... וכל המגיס דעתו וחולק כבוד לעצמו ומתכבד בעיניו במקומות אלו
חוטא ושוטה... ואין הגדלה והכבוד אלא לשמח לפני ה' שנאמר דוד והמלך מפזז ומכרכר לפני ה
/ "The happiness with which a person should rejoice in the fulfillment of the
Mitzvos, and in the *love of Hashem* who commanded them, is a great service.
Whoever holds himself proud, giving himself honor, and acts haughtily in
such situations is a sinner and a fool...there is no greatness or honor other
than celebrating before Hashem, as it says "King Dovid was *dancing* wildly

and whistling before Hashem": Rambam, *Hilchos Lulav*, 8:15. Dance is an outward expression and therefore one that is (generally) done 'in front of' as in, "King Dovid was dancing...before Hashem" or "how does one dance in front of a *Kallah* / Bride": *Kesuvos*, 17a. Similarly, with regards to the seven days of Sukkos, the Torah says, ושמחתם לפני ה' אלקיכם שבעת ימים / "And rejoice before Hashem your G-d for seven days": *Vayikra*, 23:40. The highest, deepest level is to dance 'with' Hashem, as it were, on Shemini Atzeres / Simchas Torah, a time when אני ואתם נשמח ביחד / I and you celebrate *together*": *Yalkut Shimoni*, Emor).

Chapter 5
THE SUKKAH:
A PROTECTIVE & NURTURING SPACE

EVERY SOUL LONGS FOR A HOME. NOT SIMPLY A ROOF AND FOUR WALLS, BUT A SPACE THAT IS TRULY THEIR OWN. In this place, the heart can rest, the masks fall away, and we can simply be. There is a deep, instinctual yearning that in this vast world there should be a space that whispers to us, and us alone, *you belong here*.

Without such a place, something within us feels adrift, unanchored. A person without a home is not just missing comfort, they are missing a piece of themselves. For a home is more than shelter; it is where our inner world meets the outer world in peace. A person does not feel complete without a home, כל אדם שאין לו בית אינו אדם / "A man who does not have a home is not a man" (The Gemara says, כל אדם שאין לו קרקע אינו אדם / "A man who does not own land is not a man": *Yevamos*, 63a. Yet, Tosefos, *ad loc*, tells us this means a land to build a home, thus the above Chasidic saying: *Sichos Kodesh*, Miketz, 5718).

Different people see us through different lenses. To some, we are a parent; to others, a child. To some, a sibling, a friend, a teacher, a student, a leader, or a stranger passing by. Often, the roles we play in life become the names we carry — doctor, lawyer, entrepreneur, manager, artist. The world speaks to us in titles and labels, in images we create or expectations we inherit. But deep within each of us lives a quieter self — tender, un-adorned, untouched by roles or achievements. An I that simply is — beyond what we do, beyond how we appear, beyond how others define us. Sometimes, this innermost self longs for a place where it can rest. A space to exhale. A shelter to simply *be*.

The Sukkah is that place.

The Sukkah is a home not built by ego or accomplishment — but shaped by love. It is a Divine embrace woven from simplicity, humility, and grace. Within its walls, there is no need to impress, no need to perform. Here, we remember: You are not what you do. You are not what others see. You are beloved simply because you exist and the Beloved One Above created you.

In the Sukkah, we sit beneath the open sky, held by Hashem's presence, and we return to ourselves — whole, cherished, free.*

A TRANSITIONAL SPACE

From Elul through Rosh Hashanah and Yom Kippur there is a period of time dedicated to profound soul-excavation, seeking and finding our deeper selves. We are empowered to lay bare our deepest vulnerabilities and reveal our deepest

---

* Although they (the *Chachamim* / Sages) maintain that a person does not fulfill his obligation on the first day of Sukkos with the Lulav of another person, still, he can fulfill his obligation with the Sukkah of another, as it is written: 'All the citizen' (singular) in Israel shall reside in Sukkos.' This teaches that all of the Jewish people are (a singular entity) fit to reside in one Sukkah": *Sukkah*, 27b. The Torah says, regarding a Sukkah, תעשה לך / "you shall make for yourself," which means that the Sukkah must belong to you; it must be your Sukkah. How is it possible for everyone to be an owner of, for example, a regular-sized Sukkah? If the value of one Sukkah were divided among all the Jewish people, no individual would have even a penny stake in it; therefore, no individual could be considered even a part-owner of the Sukkah, the only way possible would be if each person borrows from the other, as Rashi explains.

Now, although you can borrow a Sukkah and it becomes 'yours', the Sages maintain that you cannot borrow a Lulav, because a Lulav needs to be yours, as the Torah says, ולקחתם לכם / "You shall take for *yourselves*." So the question, with regards to both a Sukkah and a Lulav, the Torah says it needs to be 'yours', yet, a borrowed Sukkah is Kosher but not a borrowed Lulav. The answer is that when you borrow an object from a person, such as a Lulav, the owner is still the owner of the object and you are simply borrowing the *use* of the object. When you borrow a 'home' since the definition of a home is that it is '*your* home', meaning the 'use' of the home is based on the fact that it is your private space thus, when you borrow a home from a friend or borrow a Sukkah in this context, you are borrowing not merely the use of it, but the ownership — it is temporarily your 'place of residence': *Likutei Sichos*, 19, Chag haSukkos, 1. Any Sukkah that you are sitting in to perform the Mitzvah of Sukkah is like your home, your space, your Sukkah.

yearnings and aspirations. If we have worked to excavate and expose our real self, after Yom Kippur we need a secure place, a safe environment where we are comfortable with who we are, without masks and facades, titles, or a need for 'social currency'. Only once we have gained confidence in the newly rediscovered 'pure soul' that we have become, can we venture out into public arenas and bare our soul to the world. Sukkos is the transitional safe space and home that allows us to integrate and gain confidence in our new level of self-revelation before we transition into the world.

Entering the Sukkah, even for just a few moments, allows us to be enwrapped and absorbed within a sacred Mitzvah. Rather than locks or safety systems to deem us protected, when we settle ourselves within a Sukkah we feel protected, safe, and secure in its holy embrace. Indeed, the word *Sukkah* in Hebrew, סוכה, stands for סומך ועוזר כל הנופלים / assists and helps all those who fall (*Bnei Yissaschar*, Tishrei). Sukkah is Hashem's embrace of the totality of who we are, even when we fall. Our secrets and our private narratives are understood and accepted.

Under the gentle embrace of the Sukkah, we find solace and renewal. Its shelter cradles our spirits, fortifying our hearts for the journey ahead. As the days unfold, its quiet comfort whispers courage into our souls, encouraging us to step forward into the year with unwavering authenticity. We emerge, rooted in self-awareness, graced with acceptance, and emboldened by the pride of standing firmly in our truth.

Chapter 6
FROM THE SPACELESSNESS
OF YOM KIPPUR
TO THE SPACE OF SUKKOS

A SUKKAH IS A SACRED SPACE THAT WE ENTER WITH OUR ENTIRE SELVES, AS EXPLORED. IT IS OUR TRUE HOME, WHERE WE FEEL FULLY PROTECTED AND where all of our self is embraced. There, we are allowed to fully express ourselves in the most holy and authentic way. In order to understand this on a deeper level, we need to explore Sukkos as flowing from Yom Kippur.

THE NATURE OF YOM KIPPUR

Yom Kippur is a day of forgiveness; this is clear from the Torah. To understand the nature of this day in more detail, however, we should investigate its practices and customs, and the ways we are to engage with it. How should we 'enter' Yom Kippur — what mindset will allow us to align ourselves with this day?

On Yom Kippur, there is a custom to wear white, clean garments, and in particular a white *Kittel* / robe. The Rama writes, נהגו ללבוש בגדים לבנים ונקיים ביוה"כ דוגמת מלאכי השרת וכן נוהגין ללבוש הקיטל שהוא לבן ונקי גם הוא בגד מתים ועי"ז לב האדם נכנע ונשבר / "The custom is to wear white, clean clothes on Yom Kippur, like angels. And the custom is to wear the Kittel, which is white and clean. This is also the garment in which a person is buried, and thus (while wearing it) the heart of man is humbled and broken open" (*Shulchan Aruch*, Orach Chayim, 610:4).

In other words, there are two reasons for wearing white on Yom Kippur: a) it symbolizes 'angels', pure and clean of negativity and sin, and b) white is worn as a reminder of death, to stimulate remorse, and to humble a person's ego. These two reasons can also be seen as the two dominant themes and perspectives of Yom Kippur.

Similarly, the Shulchan Aruch writes (*Orach Chayim*, 610:4), נוהגים בכל מקום להרבו' נרות בבתי כנסיו ולהציע בגדים נאים בבית הכנסת / "We are accustomed in every place to increase candles in synagogues and spread (fine) fabrics in the synagogue." This suggests festivity, a time to decorate the place of prayer with lit candles and beautiful tapestries. Yet, on the other hand, the Rama writes that every person should light a "soul candle" that will burn throughout Yom Kippur: גם נר נשמה לאביו ולאמו שמת / "and also a candle for a mother or father who has passed away" (in the name of the *Kol Bo*, as Yom *Kippurim*, plural, is an atonement of both the living and those deceased). Lighting a candle for the souls of those who have passed already is slightly more 'morbid', and this reminds us of our own mortality. Again, this reinforces this dual dynamic of Yom Kippur: angelic transcendence and festivity, and awareness of death and our personal mortality.

There are other 'death awareness practices' connected to Yom Kippur, such as the general prohibitions of eating, drinking, washing, and refraining from physical intimacy, which can be understood as experiential symbols of death, or at least of letting go of the incessant need to 'feed' life. The pre-Yom Kippur custom of *Kaparos* / 'Atonements' over a live chicken, and slaughtering the bird in front of the person, is meant to be a startling encounter with our own death.

Similarly, the custom to immerse oneself in a Mikvah before Yom Kippur is a 'death practice'. Oxygen is essential to us and without breathing we cease to live. As long as we are fully submerged underwater, we cannot breathe and we lack this 'vital sign'. A deceased body is immersed in a Mikvah and then wrapped in white garment. Beginning with the Mincha prayer before Yom Kippur, we repeatedly pray the וידוי / the penitent prayer, the exact prayer one attempts to pray before passing

from the world (The Rama also writes ויש מקומות שנוהגין לילך על הקברות /
"There is also a custom to go visit a gravesite on Erev Yom Kippur": *Orach
Chayim*, 605:1). All of these ways of subtly mimicking death or
reminding us of death are meant to stimulate the kind of 'existential crisis' which leads people to rapid spiritual awakening
and heartfelt *Teshuvah* / returning or 'repentance'.

When we enter Yom Kippur, are we to think of ourselves
as angels, transcendent, beyond sin, clean and white, or should
we think about remorse and death? What will induce us into
the definitive Yom Kippur state of mind? The answer is both,
and the common denominator between them is the powerful
release of our egoic identity, with all its reactivity, negative conditioning, and self-limiting entanglements.

THE FEARLESSNESS,
FREEDOM & ELATION OF SUKKOS

When Yom Kippur has pushed us into acknowledging our
mortality and the transient nature of life, from that point forward we can live with greater fearlessness. When we release
our detrimental fear, sadness, and anxiety around dying, we
gain courage and can more fully embrace living.

Sukkos, which occurs on the fifteenth of the month, the full,
revealed moon, is the revelation of the inner qualities of Rosh
Hashanah and Yom Kippur. On Yom Kippur, we inwardly attained a measure of detachment and fearlessness. Sukkos then
reveals this fearless state more outwardly, empowering us to go

outside the comfort and security of our home to dwell in an impermanent structure, one that is open both above and below to the environment and whatever may come along. There, our inhibitions relax, and we dance, eat, and drink, free to live more deeply and with greater joy.

We embrace the fact that this life is nothing but a 'temporary structure', and yet we are at ease with this, surrounded by Infinite Light. With an understanding that the trivialities of the egoic world are empty and transient, we realize that there is, indeed, nothing to fear. All that is left is 'fear' or awe of Heaven. The shallow, silly pleasures and pursuits of this world are no longer alluring, and they cannot hold us in their grip. Our family and any observers out in the world witness how free, joyful, and fearless we are, sitting in the Sukkah, and all are drawn toward this Light.

AT THE END OF THE DAY...

Yom Kippur's 'death practices', such as wearing a white Kittel similar to burial shrouds, fasting, and other such Mitzvos and customs of the day, 'force' us to detach from everything temporary and connect ourselves firmly to the Eternal. We are also thrust toward achieving our Divine purpose and mission in this life. We feel the urgency of taking up our soul's commitment, to dedicating our life to truth and authentic Teshuvah.

At the end of the day, the only life worth pursuing is one of meaning and purpose.

THE FOOD PIPE, THE VESHET

The 365 negative commands of the Torah correspond to the 365 days of the year (*Makos*, 23b. *Tanchuma*, Ki Tetzei, 2). The Zohar (1, 170a), teaches that these 365 prohibitive Mitzvos correspond to the sinews, main veins, and arteries (or passageways) of the body. The Mitzvah of Yom Kippur is connected with the passageway of the קנה / *Kaneh* / 'windpipe' or trachea (See *Entziklopedia Talmudis*, 1, Eivarim, p. 115, regarding the 248 body parts. There is a critical letter by Rebbe Isser Zalman Meltzer regarding this entry).

There are two 'pipes' or passageways through which we receive fuel from the outside world into the body: the trachea, through which we inhale oxygen, and the ושט / *Veshet* / 'food pipe', or esophagus, through which we ingest nutrients.

The Zohar associates the windpipe with the World to Come and Yaakov, "the man who dwelled in tents" of Torah study. The food pipe is associated with 'this world', and Eisav the hunter, the man of the field (*Zohar* 3, 231b). By definition, the food pipe is connected with the world of death and aggression, for it promotes the survival of the most 'egoic' layer of self, the body. To eat we need to cut off another life, whether a fruit or an animal. Even when we eat something that has already been cut from or fallen off of its source of life, the act of eating cuts it away from existence. With the grinding of the teeth and processing of the stomach, the food is broken down more and more until it completely loses its form. In this way, life feeds off death, and the Veshet is an essential feature of this paradigm. In contrast, the windpipe merely brings in life-giving oxygen and releases carbon dioxide. This process is more peaceful and gentle, and it is more about 'sharing' than 'taking'.

As the primary function of the food pipe is to 'take from life', it brings a spiritual danger of becoming a gateway to acts of real selfishness, and perhaps even to evil. For this reason, the וושט / Veshet has the real potential to host and strengthen the שטן / Satan, who is also the *Yetzer haRa* / 'evil inclination' and the *Malach haMaves* / Angel of Death. When a person overeats or over-indulges in acts of taking from this world, the Veshet is vulnerable to the influence of the Satan. 'Eating bread' is a metaphor for indulging in any physical, bodily pleasure. Pursuing these for their own sake, one can end up in a bottomless pit, in which the fulfillment of a desire leads to an even greater desire, *ad infinitum*. Chasing evasive and fleeting satisfaction, one sinks lower and lower into the empty abyss of the שטן, the Yetzer haRa. Ultimately, in this way, one can draw himself into the world of the Malach haMaves, of depression, hopelessness, and death, Heaven forbid.

שטן is related to the word שטות / *Sh'tus* / foolishness (*Shaloh, Sha'ar haOsyos*, Os Kuf, Kedushas haAchilah, 232), which refers to the temptations of the fleeting moment. Momentary 'satisfaction', if it can be called satisfaction at all, is what causes a person to sink further and further from his or her true self and foolishly become enmeshed in the Yetzer haRa and the Angel of Death. Indeed, as the Rambam emphasizes, overeating can lead to health issues that shorten one's life. Overeating is also a metaphor for other materialistic indulgences and compulsions which often fool people into making detrimental choices in life.

Shin and Tes (ט,ש), the common letters in שטן and ושט, and the difference between the words is the Vavs (וו) of ושט / *Veshet* and the final Nun (ן) of שטן. These letters, ו and ן, are very similar, the only difference being that the ן extends further down, descending below the baseline. Through obsessive overeating, says the Zohar (*ibid*. See also Shaloh, *ibid*.), the ו descends and the *Veshet* becomes 'Satanic', embodying the dark, empty world of depravity, insatiable desire, and death-like stagnation.

MOVING THE LIFE-FORCE: IN AND OUT

We are actually meant to take from life, to 'eat', and we are not asked to deny our physical and psychological needs. Yet we need to 'eat' in a balanced way. To live fully, we need to consume fuel and resources, to work in this world, and to 'take' what we need. We are designed to engage in marital relations, have children, provide for them, and thus consume elements of the world with the power of our 'Veshet'. Yet, it is important for our mental, emotional and spiritual wellbeing to create balance in our lives and the world around us. To create balance as we receive from life, we need to give even more back to life.

If taking becomes dominant and we begin to become possessed by a desire to have more and more, we sink lower and lower, rendering our 'Vav' as a 'Final Nun'. A 'Vav' naturally descends, but it stays above the baseline, within the borders of healthy egoic needs and a life balanced by giving back. A 'Final Nun' descends below the baseline of what is healthy, degrading our lower instincts in an attempt to satisfy what is essentially bottomless desire. If we follow this path, we fail to give back to life, and we stoop lower and lower into greed until we hit rock bottom and stop falling, but then we also stop feeling period, and end up massively depressed, hopeless, and dead.

STARVE AND YOU WILL BE SATIATED

"Rav Yochanan said, 'A man has a small organ (used for physical intimacy), if he starves it (does not overindulge), it is satiated. If, however, he satiates it (and overindulges), it 'starves', and desires more" (*Sukkah*, 52b).

Physical desire is rooted in the world of 'incompleteness' and is by nature insatiable. In fact, the more one tries to satisfy and pacify a physical desire, the more he ends up feeling like he is 'starving', and lacking fulfillment. Attempting to fill a sense of lack with an object only creates more lust, in a loop or 'self-fulfilling prophecy' of ever-greater lack. Stuffing emptiness creates greater emptiness, because every time a desire is satisfied, the 'vessel' of that desire expands. As the vessel expands, so too does the 'empty space' within it, triggering a craving for more extreme means of filling it, and more desperate feelings of emptiness and dissatisfaction.

Such is the nature of *Olam haZeh* / this world, the realm where the Veshet is dominant and the "hunter, Eisav" rules supreme. We have to be vigilant that the healthy 'taking' of our Veshet does not become imbalanced and fall below the line into the superficiality and despondency of the outer world, nor further, into the abyss of Satan, the Yetzer haRa, and ultimately the Angel of Death.

YOM KIPPUR AS ANGELIC, LIGHT, AIR — THE DAY OF THE WINDPIPE

Two of the most fundamental and elementary desires of the body are to eat — to sustain oneself and *survive* — and to procreate, to perpetuate oneself and *thrive*. These basic desires are found in animals as well as humans, and in fact in all forms of life. Throughout Yom Kippur, however, we have no connection to these pursuits, nor to the actual Veshet for that matter, as we do not eat or drink. Anything related to procreation is irrelevant to us on this day, and we do not feed any physical cravings. As a reflection of this idea, the word השטן / 'the Satan' is numerically 364, as the Satan has sway during 364 days of the year, excluding the 365th day, which is Yom Kippur (*Yuma*, 20a).

Yom Kippur is the day of the *Kaneh* / 'windpipe', when we are nourished only by breathing and speaking words of prayer and Torah. Yom Kippur is thus the day of *Ruach* / spirit or 'wind', and of *Neshamah* / soul — which comes from the word *Neshimah* / breath. We demonstrate that we do not essentially rely on food, rather, we live off breath and spirit. The Arizal teaches (*Eitz Chayim*, Yom Kippur) that on Yom Kippur, Malchus, which is also a code word for our reality, receives its food directly from Binah, which is called the *Hevel haElyon* / the Supernal Breath.

On Yom Kippur, we are like angels who exist without food, drink, or procreation. We don the white garments to symbolize that we are as pure as angels, following our immersion in the life-purifying Mikvah. We are transcendent and bright.

Angels are 'creatures of the wind', weightless and unburdened by the gravitational pull and burden of sin and negativity ("For my iniquities have overwhelmed me; they are like a heavy burden": *Tehilim*, 38:5). We are released from all burdens on Yom Kippur and fly upwards like angels. Many even have the custom of standing as much as possible while praying on Yom Kippur, in an angelic posture, upright and reaching upwards.

Many people feel physically lighter on Yom Kippur, as if they are subtly floating above the world. During the later hours of Yom Kippur, this feeling can become more and more vivid. We are untethered from the Veshet and food, from their downward pull, and from anything that can make us feel heavy or degraded in our life. This can create a sense of elation, fearlessness, and freedom.

It can be said that we do not 'fast' on Yom Kippur at all, rather, we are 'free' from food, from drink, and from intimacy. During these 25-26 hours, we are liberated from the *Bechinah* /paradigm of the Veshet and we soar beyond its influence.

We begin Yom Kippur with the Kol Nidrei service, the 'Annulment of Vows', which is a way of letting go of stifling, outdated commitments, conditions, and attachments. Similarly, the tractate that deals with the laws and practice of Yom Kippur, *Yuma* / 'The Day' (as it is "the one unique day" within the 365 days of the year), begins this way: "Seven days prior to Yom Kippur, the *Cohen Gadol* / the High Priest would be removed from his home" (*Yuma*, 1:1). The same Mishnah teaches us that in order for the Cohen Gadol to serve on Yom Kippur he had to be married and his wife had to be alive. And yet, as Yom Kippur approaches, he is removed from his wife and from his home. After his service on Yom Kippur, he would return to his home in great joy. He is married, but 'separated', meaning detached, from his wife, home, and family life. A Cohen Gadol thus needs to be a family man in general, yet, to prepare for Yom Kippur, he also needs to transcend that lifestyle and become free from his identity as a worldly person. Throughout the year, he is grounded in the world of the Veshet, but on Yom Kippur, he is completely a person of the Kaneh, as free as the whirling wind, a person of *Ruach* / spirit and *Neshamah* / soul, floating upon the Supernal Breath.

As we pass through the gate of Kol Nidrei, we too are untied and released from the world of physicality and the weight of the needs of the ego. Like the angelic Cohen Gadol, we rise into the higher realms of purity and light.

On Yom Kippur, we ask HaKadosh Baruch Hu for סליחה / forgiveness. The root of the word סליחה is, perhaps, לח / dampness, moisture. Having hardened into negative patterns of behavior, stuck in habitual actions that pull us down and make us spiritually parched, we ask Hashem to moisten us, to soften us with the pure dew of Heaven. All sin and negativity that can cling to our mind and body from our past, slide off us, and we can start over again, clean and weightless. On Yom Kippur, we are atoned and we begin anew, perfectly pure, like a freshly laundered white garment.

Yom Kippur is not about is not about 'refraining' from eating, rather it is flying beyond the paradigm of eating. The physical anchor of food is irrelevant to us. It is simply not an issue on this day; we are nourished by the Supernal Breath alone.

SUKKOS AS A TIKKUN AND GROUNDING FOR THE YOM KIPPUR EXPERIENCE

On Yom Kippur, we release ourselves into the Divine *Ayin* / emptiness, free from the influence of the *Veshet* / esophagus and all its associated *Yeshus* / limited being, and attachment to physicality.

We orbit beyond the biosphere of the 'animal self'. We are fed by the Ruach haKodesh, 'breathed' by HaKadosh Hu.

In this way, we taste the state described by Shelomo haMelech at the beginning of the *Book of Koheles*: הבל הבלים אמר קהלת הבל הבלים הכל הבל / "*Hevel Havalim* — 'Emptiness of emptinesses', says Koheles; emptiness of emptinesses, everything is empty" (1:2). Some have translated *Havalim* as 'futilities'.

However, Shelomo haMelech most certainly did not descend into a sense of 'futility' when faced with the transient nature of existence. Indeed, he asserts the opposite when concludes the book with the words, סוף דבר הכל נשמע את־האלקים ירא ואת־מצותיו שמור כי־זה כל־האדם / "The sum of the matter, when all is said and done: revere Hashem and observe His commandments, for this is all of human existence" (*Koheles*, 12:13). Without embracing the whole message of Shlomo haMelech and its profound spiritual instruction, a person who has recognized the emptiness of this world (the seven "Havalim" in the previous verse, corresponds to 'this world': *Zohar* 1, 146b. There are seven mentions because the world of Havalim was created in seven days, through the seven lower Sefiros) may end up in a vacuum of meaninglessness and purposelessness with no desire for anything, even for spirituality, meaning, purpose, Torah, or Mitzvos.

Despite these risks, standing in *Hevel Havalim* for the twenty-five to twenty-six hours of Yom Kippur is essential in order to allow a deep unbinding from negativity. It allows everything external to our souls, and outside of our deeper purpose, to fall away. There can be a spiritual danger if this 'Hevel' mode dominates our consciousness for longer than necessary. It is paradoxically possible to 'attach' to detachment and lose a sense of purpose and value altogether. Some people are driven by repressed or unresolved psychological issues to become so swept up in *Ayin* / nothingness that they get stuck in dissociation and lose their footing in this created world.

Without being able to say, סוף דבר הכל נשמע / "The sum of the matter, when all is said and done, is: revere Hashem, observe the Mitzvos," a person can get lost in the abyss of emptiness or bliss. It is possible to sense that הכל הבל / 'everything is nothing', and erroneously take this as the ultimate truth, losing their relationships, drives, yearnings, and dreams. Even the liberating experience of Yom Kippur may leave an individual feeling as if the rug has been pulled from under his feet, and he has nowhere to land. He may feel enchantingly elated, lofty, and airy, but shortly afterward, he may begin to feel out of place in this world.

Speaking of the entry into the Holy of Holies by the Cohen Gadol on Yom Kippur, the Torah says, וכל אדם לא יהיה באהל מועד / "And there shall be no אדם / man in the Tent of Meeting when he goes in to make atonement in the holy place…" (Vayikra, 16:17). Asks the Medrash (Medrash Rabbah, Vayikra, 21:12), וכהן גדול לא אדם היה / "Was not the High Priest a man?" With an intense immersion in our inner holy of holies, or a 'zooming out' into pure consciousness, it is possible for us to sense, at least temporarily, that we are not a human being, we are just 'being' itself.

The Medrash also recounts that when the Cohen Gadol would enter the Holy of Holies, he would be transformed; his face would burn like flames, and he would take on the appearance of an angel (בשעה שהיה רוח הקדש שרוי עליו היו פניו בוערות כלפידים עליו, הדא הוא דכתיב כי שפתי כהן ישמרו דעת וגו': Vayikra Rabba, 21. See also Moed Katan, 17a). After many hours in Shul, fasting, singing, and praying in fiery ecstasy, it is possible to feel as if our body has turned into light.

In any case, at the peak of the Yom Kippur service, the Cohen Gadol was no longer identified as an ordinary אדם / human being. The *Tzurah* / form of a person with failings had been shed. As he entered the Holy of Holies, he also entered his own inner space of transcendence and lost all attachment to external forms. His nature as a separate individual being was transcended, and he existed as a pure, transparent angel, as it were. Today, we all take the place of the Cohen Gadol in our Yom Kippur davening. We enter into our deepest inner space, the 'Holy of Holies' of our soul, and shed all our externalities. This is the state of Teshuvah, letting go of everything.

It can be difficult for a person to return from such an exalted experience, and when they do, they can experience a heightened sense of chaos and confusion. Thus the word *Teshuvah* has the letters that spell *Tohu* / chaos and *Vohu* / confusion or bewilderment.

On Yom Kippur, the Cohen Gadol would enter into the Holy of Holies. Today, when there is no Cohen Gadol, *we* are the Cohen Gadol, entering into our own inner Holy of Holies, the deepest level of our own consciousness. The *Yerushalmi* asks a question: "The Torah says, 'No man should be there when he enters the Holy of Holies.' But isn't the Cohen Gadol himself a man?!" And the answer is that when he enters the Holy of Holies, the Cohen Gadol strips himself of his identity, even from his *Tzuras Adam* / human form. When we enter our inner Holy of Holies, we too need to let go of our identity, such as, 'I'm the child of so-and-so, I'm the spouse of so-and-so, I'm the parent and so-and-so; this is my job, this is my status, this is what I do in this world.' Yom Kippur says, 'Strip yourself of all those things; let go of *everything* and enter into a place where you are formless and completely submerged in Divinity.'

Deleting our personal identity and form even temporarily may sound cruel and inhumane, but actually, this is why Yom Kippur is called the world of pure pleasure. The deepest pleasure in life is when we experience an absence of self, such as in a moment of awe, a state of creative flow, or intimacy. Still, it can feel unsettling to lose the crutch of personal identity and distinction for more than a few moments. Teshuvah can be chaotic and confusing, the seeming chaos as we are letting go of everything and trying to start life anew.

After the Teshuvah of Kippur, we feel lighter, emptier and freer, but we are still lacking groundedness in our human identity, and this is when a sense of even deeper confusion and chaos may come up. When we truly let go of everything, then who are we? In this fluid, unhinged, untangled, transparency of self, we can be left feeling like we are floating in the air with no anchor.

This is yet another reason why Sukkos follows right after Yom Kippur. "(After Yom Kippur,) the entire nation is busy doing Mitzvos; one person is busy building his Sukkah, and another is busy arranging his Lulav...." (*Medrash Rabbah*, Vayikra, 30:7). These days of intensive Mitzvos, including sitting in the

---

* The Rama writes, והמדקדקים מתחילים מיד במוצאי יו"ה בעשיית הסוכה כדי לצאת ממצוה אל מצוה / "The meticulous ones begin immediately at the close of Yom Kippur to build the Sukkah, so they can go from one Mitzvah to another Mitzvah": *Shulchan Aruch*, Orach Chayim, 624:5. And ומצוה לתקן הסוכה מיד לאחר יו"כ דמצוה הבאה לידו אל יחמיצנה / "It is a Mitzvah to begin building the Sukkah immediately after Yom Kippur. For if a Mitzvah that comes to one's hands, one should not delay performing it": *Ibid.*, 625. Indeed, *building* the Sukkah is a Mitzvah — אין החטבה מצוה אלא עשיית הסוכה: Rashi, *Makos*, 8a. *Sheiltos*, V'Zos haBerachah, Sheilta 169. Note, Mishnah, *Shavuos*, 29a. *Shu't Avnei Nezer*, Orach Chayim, 459. Whereas the Rambam rules, וכל מצוה שיש אחר עשיתה צווי אחר אינו מברך אלא בשעה שעושה הצווי האחרון. כיצד. העושה סכה או לולב או שופר או ציצית או תפלין או מזוזה אינו מברך בשעת עשיה אשר קדשנו במצותיו וצונו לעשות סכה או לולב או לכתב תפלין מפני שיש אחר עשיתו צווי אחר. ואימתי מברך שישב בסכה / "When, however, there is another commandment that follows the performance of a particular Mitzvah, the blessing should not be recited until the other Mitzvah is performed. What is implied? When a person makes a Sukkah.... he should not recite a blessing at the time he made it, saying, 'Who has sanctified us with His commandments and commanded us to make a Sukkah'...because there is another commandment that follows this action. When is the blessing recited? When one sits in the Sukkah": *Hilchos Berachos*, 12:8. This is as the *Bavli*, *Sukkah* 46a, teaches: העושה סוכה לעצמו, אומר ברוך שהחיינו וקיימנו...נכנס לישב בה אומר אשר קדשנו במצוותיו וצונו לישב בסוכה. Although, see *Yerushalmi*, *Berachos*, 9:3, which holds that we recite אשר קדשנו במצותיו / "...who commanded us with His Mitzvos, and commanded us to make a Sukkah," upon building the Sukkah. It seems that even according to the *Bavli* there is a Mitzvah in the actual building of the Sukkah as well, only it is not גמר מצוה / the completion of the Mitzvah (Alter Rebbe, *Shulchan Aruch*, Orach Chayim, 641:1). Or as the Rambam writes, *ibid.*, וכל מצוה שיש אחר עשיתה צווי אחר אינו מברך אלא בשעה שעושה הצווי האחרון. כיצד. העושה סכה: *Likutei Sichos*, 17, p. 188. Note 56. According to the Rambam, a person needs to say a Berachah each time they enter the Sukkah, and do so standing — כל זמן שיכנס לישב בסכה כל שבעה מברך קדם שישב: *Hilchos Sukkah*, 6:12. Yet, the Rambam rules (as the Gemara, *ibid.*) that Shehechiyanu should be recited when building the Sukkah, for example: כל מצוה שהיא מזמן לזמן כגון שופר וסכה ...מברך עליה בשעת עשיתה שהחיינו. ואם לא ברך על סכה... שהחינו בשעת עשיה מברך עליהן שהחינו בשעה שיצא ידי חובתו בהן / "(As with) very Mitzvah that comes

Sukkah for a whole week, ground our realization of the 'emptiness' of self by forging positive connections with the world. These reverent physical actions ensure that our illumination on Yom Kippur is not fleeting nor unsettling, rather transformative and tangible.

Sukkos completes Yom Kippur, anchoring the experience of transcendence, rooting and giving tangible form to the formlessness experienced on that day. Sukkos gives us back some *Yesh* / personal 'existence' to rebalance us after we have gone to an extreme in holy detachment and dissolution of ego in Ayin.

On Sukkos, we feel settled again. We sit in a Sukkah כי בסכות הושבתי / "because in Sukkos I (Hashem) sat you." The word הושבתי / *Hoshavti* is related to the word *Yishuv* / settle, as in, Hashem "shall settle my soul" (*Tehilim*, 23:42. Ha*Kesav v'ha*Kabalah, ibid.). When we enter into a Sukkah we become settled and grounded.

ENTERING HASHEM'S SPACE

In Modern Hebrew, another word for 'settle' is להתמקם / to 'place oneself' or settle into a place and get comfortable, and it comes from the word מקום / *Makom* / 'place' or space. On Sukkos, it is as if HaKadosh Baruch Hu carves out a Makom

around at a specific time during the year, such as Shofar and Sukkah... one recites the Shehechiyanu when making it (here referring specifically to the Sukkah), and if one did not say this blessing when making it, then he may recite the Shehechiyanu when he is fulfilling his obligation (meaning, when he is sitting in the Sukkah on Sukkos)."

for us to settle into within this transient, temporal, and shaky world. It is as if Hashem says to us, 'You feel emptied and untangled from your old ego-driven identity; well done! And now, if because of that emptying you cannot find your place in the world, if the world feels unstable and you lack footing, come settle into My Sacred Space, a place that I have carved out for you, and begin to rediscover yourself (כשם שחל שם שמים על

החגיגה כך חל שם שמים על הסוכה: *Sukkah*, 9a. This includes the walls as well — עצי

סכה אסורין כל שמונת ימי החג בין עצי דפנות בין עצי סכך: Rambam, *Hilchos Sukkah*, 6:15. See also Meiri, *Sukkah*, 9a. At least the walls that are essential to Sukkah: Tosefos, *Sukkah*, 9a. Tosefos, *Beitza*, 30b. The Rosh, *Sukkah*, 1:13, however, argues. And it is not even Muktzah *mi-d'Rabanan*: *Beis Yoseph*, Orach Chayim, 238. See *Taz*, ibid., 1).

'Come into the Sukkah,' says the Master of the Universe. 'Here's a safe transitional place to get your feet on the ground again. In this nurturing space, let us start to put you back together — but in a way that is more joyful, whole, and purposeful than ever before.'

Within this temporary structure, we find the ability to reconstruct our sense of self and carve out a new space for ourselves in this world. After seven or eight days, we can then re-enter the permanent structure of our home, completely renewed and empowered.

Lasting growth occurs gradually, through various progressive stages. First, we need to develop a desire for change by becoming aware of the detriment of our old ways (as in the self-reflection of Elul). Then we need to make a radical leap and commit to an entirely new paradigm of living (as in proclaiming Hashem as our King on Rosh Hashanah). After this, we still need to detach completely from our old way of being (as on Yom Kippur when we become a *Luftmensch* / an 'air person', uplifted, sky-like, transcendent, and aloof). Finally, we must ground our transformation in physicality and ensure that it is practical and lasting. Thus the Torah says, 'Build a Sukkah, settle temporarily into a physical yet porous structure, where air moves in and out. Here you can land softly and gradually begin to find yourself and your footing.

When we are in an 'angelic' state of airy-ness and lightness, having lost personal boundaries, we cannot transition immediately into the conventional world of blunt boundaries, solid walls, and a limiting roof. To move from our old *Yesh* / 'ego-based' self-definition to a new way of existing, we had to pass through an undefined state, a 'highly sensitive' or even 'vulnerable' state of *Ayin* / 'non-existence', as it were, and relinquish our old self. However, it is equally necessary to 'return' to a new state of Yesh, to ground our new spiritual level in healthy definitions in the actual world.

If we were to stay in a transcendent state, we might remain ambitionless, with no sense of time or functional identity. Therefore, the 'stage' of Sukkos is required in order to reintroduce ourselves to 'selfhood' — to re-embody as a 'conventional self' with positive and holy ambitions, dreams, and desires. In the carved-out Divine space of the Sukkah, we feel accepted for who we are in the moment, embraced in our transpersonal 'limitlessness' and sensitivity, protected and shielded from the world of harsh separations by Hashem's hug. And it is here where we begin to recalibrate and reconfigure, to eat and drink and reinhabit the gravitational field of personal life, with all its self-definitions, hopes for the future and interpersonal relationships.

FINDING OUR SPACE

The Creator of all time and space is the מקומו של עולם / *Mekomo Shel Olam* / the 'Place' of the World (*Medrash Rabbah*, Bereishis, 68:9). Hashem is the Essential Context and Backdrop, the 'Meta-space' that holds all space. Yet, this is not just an Impersonal Transcendent Space, rather it is a Space that adapts, with absolute precision, to who we are, forming a unique space in the world that fits us perfectly.

And so, after falling and the process of Teshuvah, which culminates on Yom Kippur, Hashem says, to us, come into the embrace of My Divine Space so you can find your personal space in the world. For indeed, אין לך דבר שאין לו מקום / "There is nothing that has not its place" (*Avos*, 4:3). Everything and everyone has their unique *Makom* / space to exist, and to function and express themselves in their own particular way (מקום הניחו לי אבותי להתגדר בו / my ancestors left me Makom / room / space through which to achieve prominence" *Chullin*, 7a). HaKadosh Baruch Hu carves out a specific space within Himself, so-to-speak, where we can regain our bearings, and be 'reborn' into a holy and wholesome new life.

FROM DEEP ALIENATION TO A SENSE OF BEING AT HOME

Sadly, a person who has lost his or her way, and is straying from the path of authenticity, justice, healthy spirituality, and righteousness, can feel that the presence of the Mekomo shel Olam is stifling, overwhelming or burdensome, and generally too demanding. In their despondency, it is as if they want to push Hashem away. Someone who feels strongly pulled to commit adultery, for example, might in their heart, 'cry out' to the Master of the Universe, and say: "Please G-d, step aside. Give me some room to be human. I need some space to breathe. It is too difficult to live with the constant awareness of Your Presence. I need space" (הנואף אומר, סלק עצמך, ותן לי מקום לשעה, הדבר, קשה עד מאד: *Yalkut Shimoni*, Naso, 705).

But of course, it is not at all true that he or she can find the real satisfaction of love and companionship in a space of violation of boundaries, deceit, and destruction of commitment, a place devoid of the Divine Embrace. Only their true, authentic, deepest Makom, their Divinely given place within the space of the Mekomo Shel Olam, can be truly satisfying.

Our 'home', our actual and metaphorical place and space within Creation, is rooted in the *Kodesh haKodashim* / the Holy of Holies (The Kodesh haKodashim is the Makom from which הושתת העולם / the world itself emerged and extended: *Yuma*, 54b. The place of the Beis haMikdash is exact — המזבח מקומו מכון ביותר / "The place of the Altar is very precise": Rambam, *Hilchos Beis haBechirah*, 2:1. And this essential space is the Makom of our collective birth — אדם ממקום כפרתו נברא / "Man was created in the place of his (future) atonement": *ibid.*, 2. *Medrash Rabbah*, Bereishis, 14:8. It is thus 'where we belong', both communally and individually). A highly alienated person is not aware of where he is or where he is going. He thinks he is seeking things and ideas that are fundamentally outside of himself; he does not realize that the place he is really seeking is his 'Holy of Holies' within. He yearns for the sense of belonging that can only come from being in the Makom from which he originates, his 'birthplace', as it were. This is a place of great holiness, purity, integration, and wholeness.

Yom Kippur is this 'Holy of Holies' as manifest within the fabric of time. On Yom Kippur, each of us, in our own way and on our own level, touch into our true home, the sense of belonging in our soul's Makom, our Holy of Holies.

Yet, our state of perception on Yom Kippur, while freeing, is also airy, disembodied, abstract, or ungrounded. Therefore, we are given Sukkos as well. The essential ingredient of the Sukkah, the S'chach, is spiritually created by the *Ketores* / incense or 'vapor' of our Avodah on Yom Kippur within our spiritual Holy of Holies. The 'airy' incense settles down to 'earth' as a physical material above our heads. The 'impersonal', ethereal Ketores congeals in real space and time and a personally tangible structure. We can *see* our Makom. Within the comfortable presence of its embrace, we become grounded. Our sense of belonging has become intimately real — there is no more pull to some other place. We feel vividly at home, deeply satisfied, resting in the place where we have always belonged.

After Yom Kippur, Hashem tells us all, just as Hashem told Moshe after the first Yom Kippur and the atonement for the sin of the Golden Calf, הנה מקום אתי / "You have a place with Me!" (*Shemos*, 33:21). One reason we read this portion on Shabbos Chol haMoed Sukkos is that it concludes with the idea of the Three Festivals, one of them being Sukkos. A deeper reason is that this portion includes Hashem's words to Moshe, "You have a place with Me." On Sukkos Hashem is calling us all to our place, calling us home: 'Here I have a place for you, carved out of the place where I originally formed you!' Rashi paraphrases this statement: יש מקום מוכן לי לצרכך...ומשם תראה מה שתראה / "Here is a place prepared by Me for your sake...*(and) from there you will see what you will see*" (*ibid.*). When we "see" the S'chach, we tangibly perceive our atonement; there is now 'room' for us in the world and a special place in the Heart of HaKadosh Baruch Hu. We have finally found and rediscovered our holy and integrated Makom, our most wholesome place within the world.

REBUILDING THE SELF

Sitting in the Sukkah under the vast sky, with the stars peeking through the S'chach, we feel our life is returning to us. A brief flight into *Hevel* / self-emptiness is radically freeing — but it is not 'our life', and Hevel is not meant to be a way of life. If it is adopted as a way of life, it quickly loses its liberative power and pulls one into the abyss, into a place of emptiness of all value and meaning. Soon, it seems as if there is no reason to exist. *Ye'ush* / 'giving up' or surrendering into depression can come from being mired in Yesh, but also from getting stuck in Hevel. And so, Sukkos comes along to bring us into a grounded structure where we can still glimpse the sky but we are not *in* the sky. We do not need to turn away from Ayin and the afterglow of our Hevel experience; in fact, in the Sukkah, we can derive great pleasure from its distant twinkle. However, to integrate the ecstatic emptiness and transcendent light of Yom Kippur into our life, we must come back to earth within a Sukkah. There, we find new space for our existence, and suddenly the joy of life returns — we now feel full of vision, vitality, and joy.

Sukkos is זמן שמחתינו / a time of our joy, in which we regain the joy of being. Sukkos is also חג האסיף / "the Festival of Ingathering," literally meaning the end of the harvest period. Inwardly, this phrase means 'the time of *self*-gathering', in which we collect and reintegrate our 'self' which we had transcended on Yom Kippur. This is joyful, as joy comes from finding ourselves and knowing ourselves.

S'CHACH AND THE WORLD OF INFINITE POSSIBILITY

In the sacred space of the Sukkah, we begin to resettle and return to life, and to fill our lives with positive, holy, and meaningful content in the present, and with dreams and yearnings for our future. As explored earlier, Sukkos is the space of *Olam haMalbush* / The World of the Garments, the world of all conceivable 'combinations' of all possibilities. Sitting under the S'chach we open ourselves to the infinite possibilities on our horizon. Basking in the Light of the *Ein Sof* / Infinite One, everything is possible if we so desire it. It is in this Divine embrace, and the sense of our Makom being within the Mekomo shel Olam, that we feel empowered to recreate ourselves anew, to find new, healthier, more wholesome, and authentic possibilities and spaces for ourselves in this world.

Our holy longings and dreams revealed to us on Sukkos, are built upon our self-transcendence and disentanglement on Yom Kippur, in concert with our becoming grounded in the Sukkah. The Creator associated our soul with a particular body, a set of genes, an environment and social context. Due to this, we understand that the Divine objective for us is not to live like *Luftmenschen* / 'air people', in the world of the wind, with no attachment to this world, to ambitions, desires and dreams. Rather, we are meant to be grounded in the presence of this world while simultaneously remaining *Hecher* / 'higher', above it. Our ultimate embodied purpose is not to live like angels, as we do on Yom Kippur. It is to be anchored in and engaged with this physical world, and yet with a healthy measure of detachment from the outcome of our sincere actions, and untangled enough to live without fear and apprehension about our personal and collective future.

Achieving this paradoxical posture of being in the world but above it, engaged yet unattached, dreaming of potential futures yet fully present in the now, gives us great power. It allows us to transform this world into a place of peace and justice, of righteousness and charity, of holiness and Divinity. Beginning with the space of the four walls around us, we can saturate the world with Torah, Mitzvos, and reverence for the Creator of all of life.

JOY & MOVEMENT / GROWTH

From another vantage point, Sukkos can be viewed as the antidote to the potential *Kelipah* / 'husk' or destructive side effect that may arise from immersing in the transcendent light of Yom Kippur. Yom Kippur is a day of the soul and of letting go of the trivialities and dramas of life, and physical or 'animal self' activities such as eating, drinking, intimacy, and so forth. Such radical letting go, and such elevation of consciousness, can lead a person to let go of the animal self and worldly personality altogether. It can cause one to give up on their life dreams. This detrimental side of transcendence can lead to depression and a stubborn sense of nihilism.

Remaining too long, whether literally in time, or figuratively in consciousness, in any transitional state of *Hevel* / breath, air, wind, can lead a person to think, 'Why strive? Why have ambitions? Everything is vanity; who cares about the future? In fact, who cares about anything at all?'

Sukkos is a time of *Simchah* / joy and happiness. The word שמח / *Sameach* / happy is similar to the word צמח / *Tzemach* / 'sprout' or plant (the letters Shin and Tzadik are interchangeable. For example, יצחק is spelled ישחק in *Tehilim*, 105:9). Our joy returns to us when we are once again invested in sprouting and growing, when we are planted in the earth, reaching upward toward our ambitions and our life's purpose, flowering in our talents and bearing fruit in our inner qualities.

NIGHT OF THE TZEIL & 'MORE SHADE THAN SUN'

On the night of Hoshana Rabbah, the final day of Sukkos, a person's צל / *Tzeil* / shadow has 'predictive' power. The Zohar teaches (*Zohar* 1, 220a. *Zohar* 2, 142b) that a person can tell by looking at his Tzeil in the moonlight of this night — or lack of shadow — what kind of year he is going to have and if he will live through the year. If a shadow is seen, then life will continue, if no shadow is seen, G-d forbid, the person may not live through the year, literally or figuratively.

On the other hand, the Rama, in his gloss to *Shulchan Aruch* / "The Code of Jewish Law," quotes this idea, yet he writes, ויש מי שכתב שאין לדקדק בזה כדי שלא ליתרע מזליה גם כי רבים אינם מבינים העניין על בוריו ויותר טוב להיות תמים ולא לחקור עתידות / "There is one who writes not to be concerned with this so as not to upset one's *Mazal* / fortune, and also because many do not understand this matter fully. It is better to be simple-hearted and not to investigate the future." In other words, most people do not really know what to look for, and attempting will just cause them to think negative, depressing thoughts, which will just worsen their Mazal. As one's Mazal is dependent on their mindset, and if one thinks he is in bad circumstances, he will draw toward himself bad circumstances. If you think you have bad Mazal, you will indeed have bad Mazal.

In any case, whether one looks at their Tzeil or not, the night of Hoshana Rabbah is the 'night of the Tzeil', so we need a deeper way of understanding this phenomenon. One deeper understanding is that if you can see your shadow, your dreams, and your inner world, you are truly 'alive', full of life, and will continue in this coming year to be full of life. If you cannot see your shadow, then you are a bit deadened to your inner life and future, *Chas veShalom* / Heaven forfend.

More broadly, this teaches us that on Sukkos we need to sit in a Sukkah where צלתה מרובה מחמתה / "the Tzeil from the S'chach is more prevalent than the sunshine that comes through the S'chach." Sun represents the world of predictability and inevitability, as it rises and sets in the same way each day. The sun is always full in the sky even when it is behind clouds. It is always the same. For this reason, "There is nothing new under the sun" (*Koheles,* 1:9. Hence, when there is intense sunlight, those who are energetically connected with the sun tend to leave the Sukkah: *Avodah Zarah,* 3a). On Sukkos, we need to relax into the pleasurable sense of sitting in Hashem's shade: בצלו חמדתי וישבתי / "I delight to sit in His shade" (*Shir haShirim,* 2:3). We need to sit in a 'cloud' of subtle bliss, in inner flexibility and the 'shadows' of imagination and openness to unknown possibilities — rather than in the 'cloudless' belief in the static, empirical or inevitable patterns of life.

Sukkos is a time of recreating the self, and on these shadow-speckled days and moonlit nights, dreaming is essential.[*]

THE SHADOW / SUBCONSCIOUS LEVELS OF SELF

On an inner level, צל / 'shadow' refers to our subconscious mind, our innermost dreams (Indeed, Tzeil can refer to something positive or negative: See *Tur Berekes*, Hilchos Sukkah, Siman 626). On Sukkos, we need to sit in this deep realm of imagination and reveal our subconscious dreams, envisioning and building up a healthy and holy *Tzurah* / image of self. This innermost Tzurah that we build and envision for ourselves, on the deepest level, will be a reflection of the צלא דמהימנותא / 'Shadow of Faith', which is an epithet of the Sukkah (*Zohar* 3, 103a). The self that we are re-creating or revealing is composed of complete faith in HaKadosh Baruch Hu, and complete faith in ourselves. Our faith in the Creator is expressed in our faith in Creation and in humanity as a whole, and yet the foundation of all faith is faith

---

[*] A Sukkah is a manifestation of the attribute of Malchus, as the Rikanti writes in Parshas Emor, in the name of the Ramban. See also Shaloh, Sukkah, *Torah Ohr*, 6. It is a temporary, transient structure, as Malchus which "has nothing of its own." Sukkah is called a מצוה קלה / "light Mitzvah" because לית ביה חסרון כיס / "Performing it involves no monetary loss": *Avodah Zarah*, 3a. "A light Mitzvah" also indicates the Sukkah's connection to Malchus. Rebbe Yaakov Sekili, *Toras haMinchah*, Derasha 3 (although, he speaks about the element of Malchus that does not lack anything). The state of the 'Sukkah' of Malchus is thus always in flux; sometimes it is in a state of *Sukkas haNofeles* / "the Fallen Sukkah," and sometimes as *Sukkas Shaleim* / "a complete Sukkah" and not associated with any 'loss'. As the vessel of the Sukkah "has nothing of its own," it gives us the opportunity to fill its 'empty space', and fill our own inner empty spaces with aspirations and hopes.

in ourselves, faith in our potential, our dreams, and aspirations. True *Emunas Hashem* / faith in Hashem brings with it *Emunas Atzmo* / faith in oneself.

This new empowered, faith-driven *Tzurah* / form of self, emanates from within the emptiness of form and attachment that is attained on Yom Kippur, from within the 'transcendence' and 'death' of Yom Kippur.* Sitting in a Sukkah for seven days, we are carving out a new space for ourselves. We are sitting in the infinite expanse of the World of Malbush, and now it is clear to us that everything is possible. We are unified with the Infinite One and hence we too are 'infinite', as it were.

Through our journey from Elul and Rosh Hashanah until now, we have been radically transformed and rebirthed. And now, through the days of Sukkos, we have been dwelling in the *Ohr Makifim* / Surrounding Light within the cosmic Sukkah in the upper World of Malbush, the realm of infinite possibilities, dreaming of our hopes and aspirations for the coming year.

---

* If someone does not see his friend for one year, upon a reunion he should recite, ברוך מחיה המתים / "Blessed is the One who resurrects the dead": *Berachos*, 58b. This is because, as the Maharsha explains, having gone through Rosh Hashanah and Yom Kippur, a time of judgment for life or death, it is as if one has been resurrected from the dead (וע"כ אומר ברוך מחיה מתים שניצול מדין מיתה בר"ה ויוה"כ). This is the ruling of the Shulchan Aruch, *Orach Chayim*, 225.

Now, on the night of Hoshana Rabbah, the night of the צל /
Tzeil, we need to go out and 'check our Tzeil' (although not literally, as the Rama rules) — to observe whether we have built up our
dreams and hopes for the coming year and years appropriately.
If we cannot see our Tzeil on this night, if it is not defined and
clearly revealed, then it is as if we are 'dead', in the sense of not
having defined and clear hopes and ambitions for the future.
To be human is to dream. Without dreams, we remain trapped
in our past, as if dead, stagnant, and devoid of all hope. Without dreams, it is as if life itself has ceased.

If nothing has been developed over the course of the six
or seven days of Sukkos, and if sitting in the Sukkah has not
produced any new dreams and visions or built you up — if, to
the contrary, you still feel floaty, airy, detached, this means that
the transcendent feelings of Yom Kippur have left you in a void
and swallowed you in the abyss. It means that the 'death practices' of Yom Kippur have then left you in a transcendent atti-
tude and posture toward life, in an emptiness that has not been
integrated and grounded in the real world, the world where
Hashem created specifically to dwell.

As explored, there is a dark side, as it were, of transcendence. A sense of radical detachment can easily be taken out of
context until one feels estranged from life, ends up feeling the
abyss of emptiness, and ultimately, ends up 'dying', metaphorically. One's zest for life, drive for creative expression, self-improvement, and friendship can 'depart', Chas veShalom. Sadly,
in extreme cases, all of this can eventually lead to literal death.

If, after Yom Kippur, we do not let the days of Sukkos ground and nurture us with a positive *Tzurah* / form and posture of hope for the future, we may end up being swallowed up in the vast, luminous *Bitul* / self-nullification of Yom Kippur, and become alienated from our own self and life, G-d forbid.

To deepen this idea: the Torah describes a tragic tale of two children of Adam and Chavah, Kayin / "Cain" and Hevel / "Abel." Kayin, the farmer, feels inspired to bring an offering to his Creator, albeit, not from his best produce. Hevel, the shepherd, sees what his brother is doing, and he imitates him, bringing an offering from his possessions, but from the best of his animals. Hevel's offering is accepted On High whereas Kayin's offering is not. Overwhelmed by envy, jealousy, and sibling rivalry, Kayin kills Hevel.

Clearly, Kayin was responsible for the murder of his brother. Yet, from another perspective, Kayin "broke a broken vessel" (מנא תבירא תבר: *Baba Kama*, 26b). When Hevel saw what his brother initiated, his creativity in Divine service, he merely imitated what his brother did. In other words, Hevel was creatively and spiritually already dead when he was killed; his physical death was an outward manifestation of what had already occurred on the inside.

'Kayin' and 'Hevel' represent two kinds of root souls; each person has traits that correspond to one or the other of these primordial characters. People who have the soul-type of Hevel are more spiritual, cerebral, or artistic. Shepherds had the freedom to meditate as they wandered from place to place with their flocks, and they would become somewhat transcendent and detached from the world — much like we do on Yom Kippur. Hevel is a person of *Hevel* / air, lightness, breath, or inspiration. When Hevel-souls lose their creative inspiration and begin imitating others, it means they have stopped living authentically.

When he saw his brother bring a creative, original form of offering, Hevel was extremely disturbed. In a fit of jealousy, he gave up on his soul path of originality and abruptly became like an automaton: והבל הביא גם־הוא / "and Hevel, *he too* brought" (*Bereishis*, 4:4). He was merely repeating what his brother had done. While he did bring his most expensive possession for an offering, it was not brought sincerely, from his heart, not inspired by a love of life or a desire for spiritually serving the Creator of Life. He no longer saw his own value as a dreamer and innovator. At that point, he experienced an inner 'death'. In the language of the Gemara, גברא קטילא קטל / "he killed a dead person."

Whatever our soul type, if we do not 'filter' the bright light of Yom Kippur through the S'chach of the Sukkah, so to speak, our romance with earthly life, our vibrancy, our creativity, can become subtly deadened. In any case, after Yom Kippur, we need to let go of being an 'angel', and make sure we see the beautiful 'shadow' cast by our opaque earthly existence.

As such, on Hoshana Rabbah night we need to check: is our Tzeil observably vibrant and filled with wholesome desires? Are we inspired to express our authenticity, uniqueness, and creativity? Or have we not yet returned from our 'death practices' of Yom Kippur, and are now only 'imitating' others' aliveness, or feeding off their creativity?

If we still do not 'see our shadow', we have an opportunity on Hoshana Rabbah to *Chap Arein* / 'seize the moment'. The 'final sealing in the Book of Life' for the coming year takes place on this day. We can still begin to return to life, and dream of what we will accomplish in this lifetime.

THE UN-TYING THE LULAV

Although the Lulav is bound tightly for the first six days of Sukkos, on the seventh day, Hoshana Rabbah, we unbind (at least some of the) ties on the Lulav, as will be explored later on.

An untied Lulav shakes much more loosely and wildly when we shake it, and this can add to one's joy (*Levush*, Orach Chayim, 664). Within the context of the present discussion of rebuilding one's Tzurah, this practice can be understood as follows.

Sukkos follows Yom Kippur when we shed all *Tzurah* / form, immersed in the fluid waters of the Mikvah of HaKadosh Baruch Hu, the Transcendent Infinite One. We detach ourselves from all human strife, and from the basic human necessities such as food and drink. But then comes Sukkos, when, liberated from all negativities, anxieties, traumas, and anything that weighs us down, we are able to reboot and recreate ourselves as a healthy, holy, wholesome human being. This is what we are doing for the first six days of Sukkos. The upright, tightly bound Lulav represents us putting ourselves back into shape, holding ourselves together, and securing the new Tzurah that is emerging. As our new sense of self is emerging, it seems to become tighter and tighter, as it were. In place of Yom Kippur's fluidity, lightness of being, and letting go of Tzurah, on Sukkos we are reintegrating Tzurah, inhabiting a new form.

Then comes the seventh day of Sukkos, Hoshana Rabbah, when in the morning we are asked to remove ties from the Lulav, 'loosening the reins'. As the Lulav also symbolizes our upright spine, loosening the Lulav means opening up to more 'freestyle' movement. Once our sense of self and identity has been secured and congealed, once we have established a positive posture and a healthy Tzeil, we can now let go somewhat, and wave and shake with less restraint.

Only a person who is secure in his or her identity can afford to relax in this way. The more comfortable a person is with himself, the more he can take himself lightly. When a person is fighting to find who they are in this world, struggling to establish an identity, there is little room for flexibility or humor. A person with an unhealthy, fragile ego is not malleable enough to make light of himself. Only when, like an anchor, you are solidly rooted in yourself, there is room to shake and wave in all directions, to let loose without losing your center and core integrity. A healthy, holy Tzurah is more open and able to be released from imposed restraints.

From Hoshana Rabbah we glide into Shemini Atzeres / Simchas Torah, a time when we dance with the Holy Torah. It is because our identity is now so secure, we know so deeply who we are, our Teshuvah is so complete, our re-acceptance of Torah is so ingrained, and we are so grounded in our real dream and purpose of living, that we can jump and dance and lift off the physical ground. Like an unbound Lulav, we can freely move up and down and in all directions. Our identity is so completely unified with our soul, Torah, purpose, and mission, that we can now dance and move freely, effortlessly, and with ease, in all dimensions.

Chapter 7
THE LENIENCIES OF SUKKOS: EMBRACING ALL TYPES

ESACH AND SUKKOS ARE THE TWO SEVEN-DAY *YAMIM TOVIM* / HOLIDAYS IN THE TORAH, AND AS EXPLORED earlier, they both celebrate the Exodus from Egypt. Yet, there is a stark contrast between Pesach and Sukkos regarding the manner in which these two corresponding holidays are practiced. Whereas Pesach is filled with various Chumros, stringencies, Sukkos is almost the opposite. On Pesach, there are many collective and individual strict customs followed. Some Chumros the Jews of Ashkenaz accepted upon themselves, some Chumros developed within local communities and social groups, and then on top of that, some Chumros are family traditions. For instance, over generations, some families developed a custom to not eat processed foods on Pesach, and others to drink only wine that they made themselves.

Even within the Torah, there are special Chumros regarding Pesach that are not found with other Yamim Tovim (שאני חמץ שהחמירה בו תורה לעבור בבל יראה ובל ימצא החמירו חכמים לבדוק ולבערו :Tosefos, *Pesachim*, 2a). Perhaps one reason for all of this is that *Chametz* / 'leavened' products are prohibited even *b'MaShehu* / 'when there is a minuscule amount in a mixture', and therefore the laws of *Bitul* / nullification, say, of one minor ingredient within a certain dish, do not apply. But, whatever the reason may be, Pesach is filled with Chumros, while Sukkos does not have such Chumros, for example, around the structure of the Sukkah.

LENIENCIES IN THE STRUCTURE OF THE SUKKAH

A simple definition of a Sukkah is a four-walled structure covered fully with *S'chach* / materials that have grown from the ground but are now disconnected from the ground. For instance, cut branches, bamboo sticks, palm leaves, and so forth, are Kosher S'chach, whereas man-made objects and even natural substances that are formed into a 'vessel' or 'utensil', are not Kosher S'chach as these can become ritually impure. When these straightforward requirements are in place, other laws of Sukkos have various types of leniencies (Although, the *Ikar* / main element of the Sukkah is the S'chach and not the walls — וסוכה היינו סכך: Rashi, *Sukkah*, 2a. On Shabbos, for example, we need walls to surround a particular space in order to create a *Reshus haYachid* / private domain, whereas on Sukkos, there is no law that we need to sit in a place surrounded by walls, rather, that we need to sit under the S'chach that is held up and close to the walls — ויש לומר דלא דמי רשות שבת שהוא למנוע רגל רבים לסוכה דבעינן מחיצות to the walls

מגו דהויא דופן לענין סוכה, *Tosefos, Sukkah*, 4b. *Rashba*, Shabbos, 7b. סמוכות לסכך
Sukkah, 7a. Yet, conversely, because הויא דופן לענין שבת. איתיביה אביי ומי אמרינן מגו
Shabbos is about shutting out the Reshus haRabim, there are also leniencies
over Sukkah. See *Chidushei Rebbe Chayim haLevi*, Brisk, Rambam, Hilchos
Shabbos, 16:16).

THE LENIENCY OF DOFEN AKUMAH

Dofen Akumah / a bent or moved wall is one example of a
leniency. Normally, right near the top of the walls of the Sukkah is where one places the Kosher S'chach. Say, for instance, a
person places invalid S'chach near the top of one of the walls,
and this covers an area extending less than six feet (four Amos)
from the wall, at which point valid S'chach begins, we can view
the invalid S'chach as an 'extension of the wall' (even though it
is overhead in part of the Sukkah). It is as if the wall is 'bent';
it extends vertically and then horizontally, and the Sukkah is
Kosher to sit in — although one may not sit under the invalid
S'chach.

THE LENIENCIES OF GUD ASIK AND GUD ACHIS

Another example is the principle of *Gud Asik*, where walls
below the Sukkah's floor are considered as if they extend upward and form walls of the Sukkah. For example, if someone
has a flat roof above his home, and he wishes to erect a Sukkah
on the roof, using the principle of Gud Asik, he may place four
poles on the four corners of the roof and place S'chach above
that structure. Although this Sukkah has no walls, the walls of
the home below are considered as if they extend upwards and

surround the space of the Sukkah. This principle of 'extending walls', also applies in reverse, called *Gud Achis*, 'virtually' extending a wall downward.*

---

* A Sukkah that is higher than 20 Amos (about 30 feet) is not valid, says the very first Mishnah in Sukkah. Rabbah explains this Mishnah: the Torah says, "You shall sit in a Sukkah *so you shall know*, for all generations, that I sat you in Sukkos," and this means we need 'to know', to be aware that we are sitting in a Sukkah. Therefore, if it is up until 20 Amos high, a person is aware that he is residing in a Sukkah because his eyes naturally catch sight of the S'chach. However, if it is more than 20 Amos high, a person is not aware that he is residing in a Sukkah, because his eye does not involuntarily catch sight of the S'chach at that height, and in this sense, he does not "know" that he is in a Sukkah unless he makes a concerted effort to look. This idea, that a person's eyes do not naturally catch sight of something above 20 Amos only applies to a suspended object, but if there are walls higher than 20 Amos, then people *will* naturally notice the ceiling. As such, when the Mishnah says a person 'cannot see' S'chach over 20 Amos, it is talking about a Sukkah where there were not four complete walls, rather, the walls were fashioned using the principle of Gud Asik. For example, there were four small walls, each reaching a height of Ten Tefachim, which according to the lowest estimation is about 31.5 inches (Rebbe Chayim Na'ah), and then there was an empty space of over 19 plus Amos (approximately 29 feet), so using the principle of Gud Asik there are indeed proper, although undesirable 'walls' to the Sukkah, but since the eye does not catch objects above 20 Amos the Sukkah is invalid. But if there were actually walls going all the way up, maybe it would be a Kosher Sukkah. In other words, the case of the first and opening Mishnah in Sukkah is about a Sukkah that is not built with 4 proper walls, rather, a Sukkah that is built with the leniencies of Gud Asik. In the words the Meiri: ענין טעם זה הוא שצריך לדעתו שתהא הסוכה עשוי' בענין שיהא אדם מצוי לזכור ולהרגיש שתחת סכך הוא עומד והוא סובר שסתם סוכה אין דפנות מגיעות לסכך שהרי די לנו במחיצות עשרה מן הקרקע ומכשירין אותם מטעם גוד אסיק וא"כ עד עשרים אמה מרגיש בסכך של מעלה הימנו שאע"פ שיש אויר הרבה מפסיק בין הדפנות והסכך עד שאותו אויר היה ראוי לגרום לו שישכח ענין הסכך ושיהא העניו דומה לו כאלו עומד בחצר שאורה רב מ"מ הואיל ואין הסכך גבוה מעט והרי רואה קצות הסכך לשעתו ומרגיש אבל כל שגבוהה מעשרים אמה ואויר הרבה מפסיק בין דפנות לסכך אין הסכך נראה לו אא"כ משליך ראשו לאחוריו לישא עיניו למעלה ואין אדם מצוי בכך.

It seems that in the times of the Mishnah and Gemara, the structures of the Sukkos were built using a minimal amount of wood and a minimal number of walls. Perhaps this had to do with the poverty of the people, or the scarcity of resources to build Sukkos. If so, that is sufficient reason to derive this lenience. However, as in all Halachic thought, there must be, and must have been, a deeper reason. This is in stark contrast to Pesach when poverty is not taken into consideration. In fact, ואפלו עני שבישראל לא יאכל עד שיסב. ולא יפחתו לו מארבע כוסות של יין / "Even the poor should eat reclining and should also drink four cups of wine" (*Pesachim*, 99b). Therefore, it cannot be merely an issue of material poverty, for then the leniency should apply to Pesach as well, hence, we need to delve deeper into the nature of the leniencies of Sukkos to decipher the inner truth they are conveying.

LENIENCIES IN THE MATERIALS OF THE SUKKAH & THE DIVINE EMBRACE OF ALL

Another leniency in the structure of the Sukkah deals with theft. There is a principle that אין הקרקע נגזלת / "Land cannot be stolen," and therefore, theoretically, if someone enters another person's Sukkah uninvited and sits to eat there, he has fulfilled his obligation. Even though one can fulfill the Mitzvah of eating in a Sukkah this way, one should not endeavor *L'chatchilah* / beforehand to do so (מיהו לכתחלה לא ישב אדם בסוכת חבירו שלא מדעתו כל שכן אם דעתו לגזלה: Rama, *Orach Chayim*, 637:3).

Yet, the sages and the head of the Jewish community in Babylon, during the times of the Gemara, once sat in a Sukkah where the wood of the Sukkah was actually stolen:

"There was a certain old woman who came before Rav Nachman. She said to him: 'The Exilarch and all the sages in his house have been sitting in a stolen Sukkah.' (She claimed that the Exilarch's servants stole her wood and used it to build the Sukkah.) She screamed but Rav Nachman did not pay attention to her. She said to him: 'Even when a woman, whose father, Avraham Avinu, had 318 slaves, screams before you, you do not pay attention to her?' (She claimed that she should be treated with deference due to her lineage, and she wanted them to dismantle the Sukkah and give her back the stolen wood.) Rav Nachman said to the sages: 'This woman is just a screamer, and she only has rights to the monetary value of the wood (not the wood itself)'" (*Sukkah*, 31a).

Perhaps, technically, the Exilarch did not need to return the pieces of stolen wood to the woman, and the Sukkah was nonetheless Kosher, but why would they sit in such an ethically, morally, and spiritually troubling Sukkah, and even remain there when challenged? *

---

* Pesach is the first of the three Yamim Tovim. It represents the birth of Klal Yisrael and the birth of our relationship with HaKadosh Baruch Hu. As we progress and the relationship deepens moving from Pesach to Shavuos to Sukkos, we become more comfortable and unified, and we experience more Deveikus with Hashem. The more we feel and are connected, the less worry we feel about deviating and moving away from Hashem. Chumros represent the early stages in a relationship, when there are still uncertainties,

There is a similar tale that is told about the holy Baal Shem Tov:

When the Baal Shem Tov moved to Mezibuz, the rabbis of the community, who were antagonistic to the teachings of the Baal Shem Tov, came to visit the Baal Shem Tov in his Sukkah. Upon entering, they looked around and concluded that the broken-down Sukkah was not Kosher. The Baal Shem Tov insisted that despite its appearances, it was whole and Kosher, and debated with them, bringing many proofs, but it was to no avail. At some point, after much debate, the Baal Shem Tov rested his head on his arms and went into a deep trance. A few minutes later, the holy Baal Shem opened his hand, and in it was a piece of parchment that stated, "The Sukkah of the Baal Shem Tov is Kosher. Signed, the Archangel Metatron." Parenthetically, this piece of parchment was inherited by the grandson of the Baal Shem Tov, the holy Degel Machaneh

---

and therefore, there needs to be an extra measure of carefulness. Once a relationship is secure and there is deeper intimacy, there is more room for openness and relaxation — of course, within reason and honor. In the same way, our conscious relationship with HaKadosh Baruch Hu is at first more formal and structured, but as trust and closeness develop, the bond becomes more intrinsic and fluid — of course, still within the protective boundaries of accurate adherence to Halachah. Similarly, our connection to Hashem transitions from obligation and the Avodah of an *Eved* / servant (on Pesach we were liberated from slavery and Hashem says now, "You are My servants and not servants to servants") to the deeper level of relationship of *Ben* / child (our Father teaching us, His children, Torah on Shavuos), and even deeper to a loving 'Spousal' relationship and intimacy on Sukkos, as explored in great detail.

Ephrayim, and it was used as a remedy for those who were sick and broken, seeking wholeness and healing. Eventually, a few years later, it was lost.*

The metaphorically 'sick' and broken Sukkah of the Baal Shem Tov, which was declared in Heaven to be 'whole' and Kosher, became a source of healing for the sick.

Again this begs the question of why the Baal Shem Tov was sitting in a debatable Sukkah and not observing the most stringent, scrupulous standards for a Kosher Sukkah (In the Ge-

---

* Here is the way the story is told, quoted in the Baal Shem Tov, Torah, Suk-kos: רבינו הבעל שם טוב הקדוש זכותו יגן עלינו בעת שתקע אהלו של תורה בפה מעזבוש היה אז במחנינו רבנים גדולים מתנגדי הבעש"ט ז"ל, והלכו בחג הסוכות להבעש"ט, ואמרו אשר הסוכה של הבעש"ט אינה כשרה על פי דין תורה, והבעש"ט ז"ל התווכח עמהם אשר סוכתו הוא כשרה, והניח ראשו על ידו על איזה רגעים ואחר כך פתח את ידו ונמצא בה פתקא מחתיכת קלף, והיה כתוב בו, סוכה זו של הרב ישראל בעש"ט כשירה נאום מט"ט שר הפנים והפתקא הזאת נשאר בירושה אצל נכד הבעל שם טוב ז"ל, הוא הרב הקדוש מסדילקוב ז"ל, [בעל דגל מחנה אפרים], והיה כאשר נזדמן איזה חולה רחמנא ליצלן, והלכו לבעל הדגל ז"ל, ציוה להניח הפתקא תחת מראשותיו של החולה, וכאשר עשו כן נתרפא החולה תיכף, וכן היה שתי שנים, שהניחו הפתקא תחת הכר של כל חולה ר"ל ונתרפא, ובכל משך השתי שנים לא נעדר שום אדם שם בעיר, ואחר כך נזדמן שהניחו פעם אחת הפתקא אצל איזה חולה ונעלם הפתקא, ואמר בעל הדגל על זה, שנתגלה לו מן השמים שאין ניחא זאת, כי הילדים למות (אבות פרק ד') על כן התפלל על זה שיקח מאתו בחזרה הפתקא. Note that the Minchas Elazar writes that a Tzadik sometimes needs to be a little more lenient in their practice, so as not to disturb their state of Deveikus: *Divrei Torah*, Mahadura Kama, Os 30. See Yerushalmi, *Shabbos*, 6:5. See also, *Tzava'as haRivash*, 46; ואל ירבה בדקדוקים יתירים בכל דבר דבר שעושה שזה כוונת היצה"ר לעשות לאדם מורא שמא שמא אינו יוצא בדבר זה כדי 'להביא אותו לעצבות. ועצבות היא מניעה גדולה לעבודת הבורא ית / "A person who is just starting out in the service of Hashem should not be overly scrupulous and stringent about everything he does. For, the intention of the evil incli-nation is to make you depressed by causing you to fear that you have not fulfilled your obligations in every detail. However, depression is a terrible and destructive quality that obstructs a person from the service of Hashem, blessed is He and must be avoided."

mara, the Mitzvah of Sukkah is actually called a מצוה קלה / an easy Mitzvah: *Avodah Zarah,* 3a. Although, there it means 'an easy Mitzvah to fulfill', rather than 'a lenient Mitzvah'. In fact, the Ya'avetz brings down that the Mitzvah of Sukkah שקולה כנגד כל המצוות / "outweighs all (other) Mitzvos": *Migdal Oz,* Otzer haTov).

From all of the above, it seems that Sukkah is a Mitzvah in which leniencies are practiced and perhaps even celebrated.*

Perhaps the answer is that the Sukkah represents Hashem's embrace of each of us in a full-bodied hug, no matter our condition. Even the broken, the shattered, the lost, and the misguided are all able to sit under the canopy of the Sukkah. The loving Divine embrace embraces all of us and each of us. כל ישראל ראוים לישב בסוכה אחת / "It is fitting for all of Israel to sit in one Sukkah" (*Sukkos,* 27b: כל האזרח בישראל ישבו בסוכות מלמד שכל ישראל ראוים לישב בסוכה אחת / "'All the אזרח / *Ezrach* / 'citizen' (singular) in Israel shall reside in Sukkos.' This teaches that all of the Jewish people are (a singular entity) fit to reside in one Sukkah." Furthermore, אזרח / *Ezrach* comes from the word *Zarach* / זרח / illuminate, as every member of Klal Yisrael is an important person, part of one vast 'luminary').

Symbolically, the Sukkah is meant to embrace both the financially poor and those who are spiritually poor. Hashem's loving embrace embraces all,* including those who are finan-

---

* Additionally, in contrast to Pesach and Nisan, the month of Tishrei is all about 'collective space'. Pesach is connected with 'individual space'. Every day of Elul and Tishrei through the end of Sukkos, we recite multiple times, אחת שאלתי מאת ה' אותה אבקש שבתי בבית ה' כל-ימי חיי / "One thing I ask of Hashem, only that do I seek: to live in the house of Hashem all the days of

cially unable to fashion a full Sukkah with four full walls of wood, and those who, metaphorically, cannot muster up the spiritual strength to erect a minimally Kosher Sukkah. Just as even a minimally Kosher Sukkah is by nature *Shaleim* / whole, we are, no matter our condition, essentially whole. Knowing this is the essence of healing.

"The world is sustained on *Din* / Judgment, *Emes* / Truth and *Shalom* / Peace" (Mishnah, *Avos*, 1:18). Din is related to Rosh Hashanah, a time of judgment. Yom Kippur is a time of Emes when we strip away all external definitions of self and stand nakedly and honestly in front of Hashem. Standing in the deepest truth of who we are, our soul becomes revealed. Sukkos is Shalom (*Sefer haMa'amarim Melukat*, Vol. 1, "B'Chag haAsif," 3), a time of unity, when all of us together, and all of ourselves, can tangibly enter the Divine loving embrace. Sukkos is a time when Hashem calls to us, 'Come to me in your entirety; if you cannot find your space in the world I will carve out a sacred space for you where you can find yourself. But come, in any case; allow

my life": *Tehilim*, 27:4. Indeed, we spend most of our waking hours on Rosh Hashanah and Yom Kippur in 'the House of Hashem', in Shul. Similarly, on Sukkos, we say כל ישראל ראוים לישב בסוכה אחת / "It is fitting for all of Klal Yisrael to sit in one Sukkah": *Sukkos*, 27b. Pesach, by contrast, is all about our private space, our homes, as the Torah says, "You shall not find Chametz in your homes," and as the Mitzvah of Korban Pesach is שה לבית / *Seh laBayis* / "a lamb for each household" (*Shemos*, 12:3). In fact, the word בית / *Bayis* / home appears, in various forms, 13 times in the section where the Torah describes the offering of Pesach. Pesach is thus all about our 'personal *Bayis* / home', whereas Sukkos and Tishrei are about the inclusive בית ה' / House of Hashem," the 'collective space' that includes all.

yourself, and all of you — all of Klal Yisrael, from the greatest of sages to simple youngsters, from the wholly righteous to the mighty strugglers — to enter My Sukkah.'

This is the deeper reason for the leniencies of the Mitzvah of Sukkah, and why the sages of old and the Baal Shem Tov chose to sit in Sukkos that 'needed healing' to demonstrate that the holy Sukkah includes all types of people, even the seemingly broken and low. Similarly, in the Four Species that we wave on Sukkos, we include an *Aravah* / willow branch, representing the person who has neither 'taste' nor pleasurable 'aroma' — neither the savory effects of Torah study nor of Mitzvah performance.

Not only was this a form of demonstration on the part of the Sages and particularly the holy Baal Shem Tov, but this was also a way of identification. By constructing and sitting in a Sukkah that needed the leniencies of law to render it Kosher, the Baal Shem Tov was declaring to all the physically and spiritually broken people in his town — and around the world; I see you, I understand you, I know your struggles, and I feel your existential and spiritual pain, I feel you. But know this; you are not rejected, you are not alone, Hashem is always with you, Hashem is holding you up, lovingly embracing you, and waiting for you to come back home.

And despite any appearances to the contrary, you are essentially whole and perfectly 'Kosher'. Hashem has carved out a Makom, a sacred space, and a Divine embrace, for each of us, exactly as we are in this moment.*

PESACH NIGHT VS. SUKKOS

On Pesach night, at the Seder, we tell the 'wicked son', you should know, "If you had been there. You would never have been redeemed!" But on Sukkos, we tell all of Klal Yisrael, you are all welcome into the Sukkah — "It is fitting for *all* of Israel to sit in one great Sukkah;" we are *all* being redeemed.

The reason for this distinction is that the story of *Yetzias Mitzrayim* / the Going Out of Egypt and the celebration of Pesach are connected to our state prior to *Matan Torah* / the Giving of the Torah, prior to HaKadosh Baruch Hu choosing Klal Yisrael as a whole. Before the Exodus from Mitzrayim, our relationship with HaKadosh Baruch Hu was one that demanded our consent and choice. A proof of this is that those who did not desire to leave Mitzrayim did not leave, and ended up languishing and dying there. But after Matan Torah and the Divine *Bechirah* / choosing of Klal Yisrael, no Jew will be left behind.

---

* The S'chach of the Sukkah needs to be natural material that grew from the ground, but which has not yet been shaped in a way that it can receive *Tumah* / impurity. S'chach represents a realm where Tumah cannot reach (*Tola'as Yaakov*, Sod haSukkah). The walls of the Sukkah, on the other hand, can be of materials that do absorb Tumah, demonstrating that Hashem השכן אתם בתוך טמאתם / "abides with them amid their impurity": *Vayikra*, 16:16. See *Toras haMinchah*, Derashah 83. *Kad haKemach*, Sukkah.

Eventually all of Klal Yisrael "will be gathered one by one" (*Yeshayahu*, 27:12) by Hashem Himself, and each of us will return fully to our 'place', to who we truly are and where we truly belong. The full and complete Redemption of the *Klal* / collective will be the full redemption of each and every *Yachid* / individual.

WE EMBRACE ALL

In response to the Divine embrace, we need to show a similar openness and embracing of others, so that we can actualize the teaching, 'All of Klal Yisrael are worthy to sit in one vast, unified Sukkah.'

On Yom Kippur, we are purified from all our sins and negativity and freed from all trivial competitiveness and petty judgmentalism of others. We are no longer plagued by jealousy, envy, or any other negative state of consciousness that infringes upon our ability to be in *Achdus* / unity with others. By the completion of Yom Kippur, we have let go of all false identification, we have been forgiven and we have become a being of forgiveness; fluid, non-rigid, and open to joyously embrace all souls. We are already subtly entering the space of all-embracing, all-unifying brotherhood with Klal Yisrael.

Chapter 8

ENTERING THE DIVINE EMBRACE & THE JOY OF SIMCHAS BEIS HASHOEIVAH

BEGINNING PERHAPS SOME SIX TO SEVEN HUNDRED YEARS AGO IN GERMANY, A UNIQUE CUSTOM DEVELOPED AROUND THE HIGH HOLIDAYS: on Rosh Hashanah or the following days, we go out to a body of living water containing live fish and symbolically cast away our unwanted negative baggage, our sins. This custom is called *Tashlich /* 'casting away' (This originates in the Minhag Ashkenaz: Maharil, *Hilchos Rosh Hashanah*, 9. This Ashkenaz custom is quoted by the Rama — who codified many of the Minhagei Ashkenaz: Shulchan Aruch, *Orach Chayim*, 583:2. Note Rashi, *Shabbos*, 81b).

Rosh Hashanah is a time of *Din* / Divine judgment, and so we attempt to do all we can to bring an element of *Chesed* / loving-kindness into the equation of Din.

Every meaningful *Tefilah* / prayer is answered On High, though sometimes the answer remains elusive and transcendent of physical reality. At times, we do not feel the effects of our prayers, although real effects are resonating in realms beyond our conscious self. Even when we do not see the Divine Chesed that comes in response to our prayers, our prayers have cosmic effects, spiritually altering the roots of existence for the good. The special benefit of Tashlich is that it draws Chesed down in a *tangible* way.

A living body of water is a source or matrix of life, a tangible manifestation of Chesed, of giving. Water is like an answer to prayer, so-to-speak, there to bestow life and well-being upon countless creatures. Fish themselves also hint at Chesed — their eyes remain open at all times, and openness is a key element of giving. Standing near these manifestations and symbols of Chesed, we recite the Thirteen Divine Attributes of Compassion to invoke the Ultimate Source of kindness and arouse a Divine desire to shower us with blessings from Above.

At Tashlich, we 'take hold' of our negativities, and the devastating weight that presses us downward, and cast it all into the waters. This physical act inspires us to reflect inwardly, yet it also has a somatic healing effect as we unburden ourselves and envision the stress of our failings being 'empathetically' received by the water, covered over and washed away.

Rosh Hashanah is a time of cosmic and personal renewal. In the new reality that we are co-creating for ourselves, we may wish to put aside our old self-image, forget about it or even toss it away. Most often, for something to change from what it is to what it is meant to become, there needs to be a moment when it ceases being what it is. For example, a seed rots in the earth before it can offer new life and infertility precedes fertility. Standing by the water we look at the old, negative image of ourselves and let it slip into the depths.

A mere few days after Rosh Hashanah, the festival of Sukkos arrives, and the symbolism of water shifts from Chesed to *Simchah* / joy. In the times of the Beis haMikdash, during the holiday of Sukkos, a festive celebration with ecstatic dancing and lively music took place as the Cohanim went to draw water from the well to pour upon the altar the following day. Though in the Torah there is no clear source for this practice of the libation of the Mizbe'ach with water (*Ta'anis*, 2b), certainly for the joy that accompanied the drawing of the waters, our Sages (*Sukkah*, 50b) invoked the directive to do it from a Pasuk in Yeshayah, that says: "You shall draw water with joy, from the wells of salvation."

This celebration was called *Simchas Beis haShoeivah* / "the Joy of House of the Drawing of the Waters." The joy was so immense and overwhelming that it was said, "He who did not see the joy of Simchas Beis haShoeivah never saw joy in his life" (*Sukkah*, 51a). It was impossible for someone who never experienced this celebration to truly appreciate the depths of joy that are possible in this world. But why such joy? After all, it seems it involved a simple, almost mundane, act of drawing water. Chazal tell us that the reason for the pouring of the waters on the Mizbe'ach is that it will act as a type of offering: ומפני מה אמרה תורה נסכו מים בחג אמר הקדוש ברוך הוא נסכו לפני מים בחג, כדי שיתברכו לכם גשמי שנה / "And for what reason did the Torah say, 'Pour water on the festival of Sukkos?' The Holy One, Blessed be He, said, 'Pour water before Me on the festival, so that the rains of the year, which begin to fall in this season, will be blessed for you'" (*Rosh Hashanah,* 16a). The question remains, why does pouring water on the Mizbe'ach stimulate such tremendous joy?

WHY JOY?

The Rambam suggests that this special joyful celebration on the nights of Sukkos was added to the general joy that we need to experience of Sukkos. While we need to celebrate and be joyous on every Yom Tov, the Torah specifically tells us that on Sukkos, "We should be happy before Hashem (i.e., in the Beis haMikdash)…for seven days" (*Vayikra,* 23:40), and the Torah tells us this three times. In this way, the celebration of Simchas Beis HaShoeivah was an additional overflow of the joy of Sukkos. Furthermore, this celebration was not called the *Simchas Shoeivah* / 'joy of drawing the waters', but rather the Simchas *Beis*

haShoeivah, 'the joy experienced *in the House — of* Drawing',*
because the joy is specifically connected with the Beis haMikdash, and not so much with the actual drawing of the water.

Indeed, the sobriquet of Sukkos is *Z'man Simchaseinu* / a
time of our joy, therefore, as a result of the overarching theme
of joy during Sukkos, the joyfulness overflowed and inspired
the dancing and music during the drawing of the water. As
such, perhaps there was nothing inherent in the 'drawing of the
waters' itself that evoked joy, rather, it was the *Z'man*, the *time*
of the drawing of the water, and the *place*, the Beis haMikdash.
The waters were drawn in the evening, the appropriate time to
celebrate the joy of Yom Tov in the Beis haMikdash.

Yet, as most commentators posit, as does Rashi, "All the joy
was there because of the *Nisuch haMayim* / Water Libation
(itself)" (*Sukkah*, 50b. Tosefos, *Shabbos*, 21a: דהואיל ולכבוד הקרבן היו עושין).

---

* *Likutei Sichos,* 17, Emor, 4. "The House of Drawing" is the place dedicated
to the celebration: ובית השואבה שם המקום שהיו מתקנין לשמחה: Rambam, *Pirush
haMishnayos*, Sukkah, 5:1. The Rambam clearly writes that it was a joy connected to the Yom Tov of Sukkos — אף על פי שכל המועדות מצוה לשמח בהן. בחג
הסכות היתה במקדש יום שמחה יתרה שנאמר ושמחתם לפני ה' אלהיכם שבעת ימים / "Even
though on all the holidays we need to be joyous, on Sukkos in the Mikdash,
there was *more* joy, as it says, "And you should be happy before Hashem…
for seven days": *Hilchos Lulav*, 8:11. Note *Ritva*, Sukkah, 53a: והוי יודע שכל
השמחה היתיר' היתה בהלל ולהודות לה' על הטובה שעשה לישראל להשרות שכינתו בתוכנו וגם
כנגד הע"ה. Since the joy of Simchas Beis haShoeivah is a direct outgrowth of
the Simchah of Yom Tov itself, it is understood that Simchas Beis haShoeivah is not a contradiction to the principle of "We do not mix one joy with
another" (*Moed Katan,* 8b) — it is *one* joy.

In other words, there is an intrinsic relationship between the drawing of the waters and the ecstatic elation that was expressed in that act.*

---

* Another explanation and reason for this major public event is *leHotzi mi-Da'as haMinim* / to uproot the opinion of the heretics. Since the idea of Nisuch haMayim is *Halachah leMoshe miSinai* and has no clear source in the Torah (*Ta'anis*, 2b), the *Minim* — those who believed only in *Torah she-b'Kesav* / Written Torah — asserted that we should not perform it. As the Mishnah says, ולמנסך אומר לו: הגבה ידך. שפעם אחד נסך אחד על גבי רגליו, ורגמוהו כל העם באתרוגיהן / "And the appointee says to the one pouring: 'Raise your hand,' so that his actions would be visible, since one time a *Tzaduki* / Sadducee intentionally poured the water on his feet, and in their rage all the people pelted him with their Esrogim'": *Sukkah*, 48b. Why did he pour on his feet? Rashi comments (*ibid.*), לפי שהצדוקין אין מודין בניסוך המים / "Because the Tzedukim did not believe in the Mitzvah of Nisuch haMayim." This is the reason the gathering of the water was done with great pomp, with loud blasts of the Shofar. Again, as the Mishnah says, ניסוך המים כיצד צלוחית של זהב מחזקת שלשה לוגים היה ממלא מן השילוח. הגיעו לשער המים, תקעו והריעו ותקעו / "Nisuch haMayim — how was it performed? One would fill a golden jug with a capacity of three Lug, with water from the Siloam pool. When those who went to bring the water reached the Gate of the Water leading to the Temple, they sounded a Tekiah, a Teruah, and a Tekiah." This is similar to the pomp and fanfare that was done with the Omer cutting. The Mishnah in *Menachos*, 65a, says, כל העיירות הסמוכות לשם מתכנסות לשם, כדי שיהא נקצר בעסק גדול, כיון שהחשיכה, אומר להן בא השמש אומר הין, בא השמש אומר הין, מגל זו אומר הין, מגל זו אומר הין, קופה זו אומר הין, קופה זו אומר הין, בשבת אומר להן שבת זו אמר הין, שבת זו אמר הין, אקצור והם אומרים לו קצור, אקצור והם אומרים לו קצור, שלש פעמים על כל דבר ודבר, והן אומרים לו הין הין הין, כל כך למה (לי) מפני הבייתוסים שהיו אומרים אין קצירת העומר במוצאי יו"ט / "How would they perform the cutting of the Omer? Emissaries of the court would emerge on the eve of the festival of Pesach and fashion the stalks of barley into sheaves while the stalks were still attached to the ground, so that it would be convenient to reap them. The residents of all the towns adjacent to the site of the harvest would assemble there, so that it would be harvested with great fanfare. Once it grew dark, the court emissary said to those assembled: 'Did the sun set?' The assembly said in response: 'Yes.' The emissary repeats: 'Did the sun set?' They again said: 'Yes.' The court emissary next said to those assembled: 'Shall I reap the sheaves with this sickle?' The assembly said in response: 'Yes.' The emissary repeats:

THE JOY OF FINDING WHAT WAS LOST

Although *Simchah* / joy is our natural state and it is who we really are, often we lose touch with ourselves and we find ourselves anxious, dispirited, and sad. We need practical methods to reclaim and re-attain our birthright of abiding joy.

'With this sickle?' The assembly says: 'Yes.' The court emissary to those assembled: 'Shall I place the gathered sheaves in this basket?' The assembly says in response: 'Yes.' The emissary repeats: 'In this basket?' The assembly says: 'Yes…Shall I cut the sheaves?' And they say to him in response: 'Cut!' The emissary repeats: 'Shall I cut the sheaves?' And they say to him: 'Cut!' The emissary asks three times with regard to each and every matter, and the assembly says to him: 'Yes, yes, yes!' Why do I need those involved to publicize each stage of the rite to that extent? It is due to the Boethusians (Tzedukim or Minim), as they deny the validity of the Oral Law and would say: 'There is no harvest of the Omer at the conclusion of the first Festival day of Pesach (unless it occurs at the conclusion of Shabbos)": *Sichos Kodesh*, Chag haSukkos, 5712. This of course addresses the fanfare, and also why *Chazal* / the Sages in particular were the ones dancing, but we still need to know why there was so much joy. There is another Gemara (*Baba Basra*, 115b-116a) that tells us that on the 24th of Teves (according to the version of the Rashbam), when a particular Halacha regarding inheritance was reestablished according to Chazal and the opinion of the Minim was uprooted, ואותו היום עשאוהו יום טוב / "…on that day (incidentally, centuries later, this date became the Yartzeit of the Alter Rebbe) they established a Yom Tov." Interestingly, the Alter Rebbe, in *Likutei Torah*, D'rushim Sukkos, pp. 79d-80d, explains in great length that *Nisuch HaMayim* / the libation of the waters is connected with the Sefirah of Chochmah, beyond the world of letters, the world of Binah, and thus connected with *Torah she-b'Al Peh* / the Oral aspect of Torah, the parts of Torah that, although, hidden within the Letters of Torah she-b'Kesav (as ליכא מידי דלא רמיזי באורייתא / "*everything* in Torah, not just Tanach, is alluded to within the Torah": note *Ta'anis*, 9a), is only revealed by Chazal. This explanation ties in directly to the overall *Peshat* / literal interpretation of the joy of Simchas *Beis haShoeivah*, the idea of the joy connected to Torah she-b'Al Peh.

One of the greatest experiences of joy is finding something that we lost, for example, reuniting with an old friend, or with a loved one returning from a long trip. Joy can surface when we resolve a conflict, or simply when we find our lost keys after much searching. Joy is drawn from righting a wrong, repairing something broken, or making whole something that was fragmented.

During Rosh Hashanah, in the Tashlich ceremony, we cast the hindering elements of self into the waters. We 'lost' those elements, as it were "in the depths of the sea where they will never be found." At that fragile state of our growth, that was beneficial, for to grow we need to go through a stage of complete *Havdalah* / severing from the old. Now, on Sukkos, we need a full, canopy-like embrace of what we are, a Sukkah that will indeed 'find', reintegrate, and include all our elements of self on a higher level of wholeness. We 'reunite' with our entire body and self, as everything is joyfully unified in the Sukkah.

The joy of Simchas Beis haShoeivah is the joy of finding what we have lost; retrieving the parts of ourselves that we released and cast into the water on Rosh Hashanah.

How do we traverse this gap between 'losing' parts of ourselves and joyfully 'finding' them again in the Sukkah two weeks later? What gives us the power to collect parts of self that previously we needed to let go of? The answer is the Ten Days of Teshuvah. In these days of introspection and opening our hearts to our Creator through 'higher Teshuvah,' returning out of Ahavah / love, who can remain unmoved to tears? These tears become the very instrument of our transformation.

If you are aware and conscious of the times, the Ten Days of Teshuvah, and you open up, expose all of yourself to yourself, and let it all come out, you will eventually find yourself crying. If not, declares the holy Arizal, this is a sign that "your soul is not complete." Something is still misaligned. Yet, having an awareness of your lack of inspiration can catapult you and even shake you out of your complacency and spiritual insensitivity. Either way, by the time we reach the climax of the Ten Days of Teshuvah at the end of Yom Kippur, our tears will have inspired a reorientation in our being to the extent that we can recollect and re-gather our lost parts and establish them within the new elevated context of our life. We have drawn the "depths of the sea" up to our eyes through loving Teshuvah.

Tears are a cleansing agent. The waters of our tears rinse and purify our hearts and ultimately allow for full transformation. Between the serious day of 'casting sins' into the water and the joyful day of 'drawing water from the wells of salvation', there are several days in which we can cleanse ourselves with tears. The *Mekubalim* / Kabbalists speak of the benefits of wiping one's face with the cleansing tears that one sheds in Teshuvah (*Yesod v'Shoresh haAvodah*, Sha'ar haKolel. *Zohar* 3, p. 75b). On Yom Kippur, this cleansing comes to a great crescendo, and then when we enter the Sukkah, we are finally home; we have arrived. We 'find' ourselves in an embrace of the totality of who we are. We are then strengthened and empowered to do a radical act of integration: to draw up and retrieve 'the lower waters' where our sins were cleansed and 'forgotten'. And with ecstatic joy, we pour these waters upon the Mizbe'ach.

TWO TYPES OF TEARS

Broadly speaking there are two types of tears. There are bitter tears of sadness, loss, and yearning, and there are tears of love, joy, and reunification. Avraham cried when Sarah passed away, but Yaakov cried when he first encountered his future wife, Rochel. Rebbe Akiva cried when he read the holy book of passion and longing, *Shir haShirim*. We may tremble and shed a tear of awe and yearning when the 'Book of Life and Death' is opened on 'Judgment Day', and we may shed a tear of boundless elation when we grasp the Torah and dance with it on Simchas Torah.

Through the Ten Days of Teshuvah culminating with Yom Kippur, the tears of wanting to return to come closer and re-unite with HaKadosh Baruch Hu are the 'salty' tears of yearning (מי עינים מלוחין, שבזמן שאדם בוכה: *Medrash Rabbah*, Bamidbar, 18:22). These are identified as the 'Lower Waters' which are crying to unite with the heavenly Upper Waters, having been separated from them on the Second Day of Creation (*Bereishis*, 1:7). Ultimately, the 'tears' of these Lower Waters become the salt which gives 'flavor' to the offerings upon the Mizbe'ach.

Once Sukkos comes about, the tears that may flow are tears of the joy of the sense of finding, reunification, and belonging. Sitting in the Sukkah we are present within the *Makifim*

/ surrounding lights of Binah, as explored earlier. The walls of the Sukkah are the Makifim, and the act of sitting and settling down in them is bringing the light of our Makifim, our self-transcendence, down into a place where it is tangible.

As we are sitting within these higher Lights we are resting within the warming and gentle embrace of the *Ima Ila'ah /* 'Supernal Mother.' Being engulfed within this sacred and protected space we may feel moved to tears of relief, like those of a child who has run back into the arms of his mother. The Baal Shem Tov says that just as a child runs away from danger and hides under his mother's skirts and is embraced, so we have run to higher Binah where we are embraced and surrounded by her Makifim. We let go in the arms of Love.

After the Higher and Lower Waters were separated on Day Two of Creation, the day of separation, the Lower Waters wept to return to supernal closeness with the Creator, until they were at last assured that they would be offered on the Mizbe'ach, as salt, and as Nisuch haMayim, the water libation, the pouring of the waters on the Mizbe'ach during Sukkos.*

---

* *Tikunei Zohar* 19b. Rashi, *Vayikra* 2:13. It is interesting to note that this teaching by the Rabbis is not found in Gemara nor Medrash, yet, seems to have been known, and thus quoted by Rashi and other Rishonim, as Ramban, and Rabbeinu Bachya, Vayikra ibid. Note *Ta'anis*, 25b. אמר רבי אלעזר כשמנסכין את המים בחג, תהום אומר לחבירו אבע מימיך, קול שני ריעים אני שומע. שנאמר תהום אל תהום קורא לקול צנוריך וגו׳ / "Rebbe Elazar said: When the water libation was poured during Sukkos, these waters of the deep say to the other waters of the deep: 'Let your water flow, as I hear the voices of two of our friends,' as it is stated: "Deep calls to deep at the sound of your channel." The deep calling to the deep are the two waters, the Upper and Lower Waters, as Rashi writes: מים עליונים ומים תחתונים.

Why was salt offered each day along with every offering, while water was poured on the Mizbe'ach only during Sukkos? Salt is more elevated, so to speak, as it is closer to the heat of the sun, the Source Above. The waters that were drawn for Nisuch Hamayim came from the depths of the well, deep in the earth, or even 'lower' than that, "the depths of the sea," as it were.

Teshuvah is akin to water, symbolizing the tears of our soul's deep yearning for Hashem Above. These spiritual tears have the power to draw up even the lowest waters of desire within us, transforming and elevating all our yearnings, including those we may have cast into the depths of the sea. Through Teshuvah, we return and reunify the lower waters with the upper waters. This process reflects the separation of lower and higher desires that occurred on the second day of creation. The lower desires, often associated with earthly and material pursuits, are reconnected with the higher desires, which align with our spiritual and Divine aspirations.[*]

---

[*] "Elokim said, 'Let there be an expanse in the midst of the water, that it may separate water from water...separated the water which was below... from the water which was above": *Bereishis*, 1:6-7. Chazal tell us that the tears of Teshuvah are connected with the depth of the abyss; עוברי אלו בני אדם שעוברין על רצונו של הקדוש ברוך הוא. עמק שמעמיקין להם גיהנם. הבכא שבוכין ומורידין דמעות כמעין של שיתין / "'Those who pass through' these are people who transgress the will of the Holy One, Blessed be He. 'Valley' indicates that their punishment is that Gehenam is deepened for them. 'Of weeping' and 'turn it into a water spring' indicates that they weep and make tears flow like a spring of the foundations [*Shitin*], meaning like a spring that descends to the foundations of the earth": *Eiruvin*, 19a. See *Tzafnas Paneach*, Rambam, *Hilchos Terumos*, p. 51).

The reunification of these waters through Teshuvah is symbolized by placing salt upon the offerings on the Mizbe'ach.
The salt represents the minerals present in water or tears, embodying our spiritual purification. This reunification is especially significant during Sukkos. During this festival, the lower
waters are drawn from the depths and brought up to the Beis
haMikdash above, where they are poured onto the Mizbe'ach
as 'upper waters'.

Inwardly, our personal Teshuvah produces 'salt', the bitter
tears of yearning that we shed on Rosh Hashanah and Yom
Kippur, which motivate us to draw up waters of even deeper
yearning from the lowest levels within us, and raise them up
until we can bring all our lower, fallen waters and desires up
to the level of 'Beis haMikdash', pouring them upon the 'Mizbe'ach', above. Then, our "sins have turned into merits"* (*Yuma*,
86b), and this is the great joy of reuniting and resolution.

Our sages say, אין שמחה כהתרת הספקות / "There is no joy like
the resolution of doubt" (*Metzudas Dovid*, Mishlei, 15:30. *Mishbetzos
Zahav*, Siman 682:1. As the Rama writes, וכבר כתב חכם אחד שלא טעם טעם שמחה
מי שלא טעם טעם התרת הספיקות השכליות / "One has not tasted the taste of joy until

---

* Just as there are ten days between Rosh Hashanah and Yom Kippur, there
are also ten days from Yom Kippur until Hoshana Rabbah, since on Hoshana Rabbah there is the final seal of our judgment on Yom Kippur: *Shaloh*,
Maseches Sukkah, Torah Ohr, Ayin. The first ten days are days of awe,
hence, Teshuvah of Yirah from below. The second ten days are days of love,
joy, and Divine embrace from Above, hence, *Teshuvah shel Ahavah* / returning closer and closer through love. Teshuvah of Ahavah is what transforms
negativity into merit (*Yuma*, 86b), judgment into unconditional acceptance,
and our lower states into higher states.

he tastes the resolution of intellectual doubts": *Toras haOlah*, 1:6. *Teshuvas haRama*, 5). The profound joy of Simchas Beis haShoeivah is the joy of finding what we had lost and forgotten and are now retrieving.

If you lose something that is not so precious,
finding it can be pleasant.

But if you lose a treasure, one deeply connected to you,

Say a part of yourself that you lost when you let go of your past in
Teshuvah —

Then, when you finally find and reclaim that lost part,
And recover the full spectrum of who you are,
And this reclaimed part is now cleansed, healthy, and sanctified,

This 'finding' is the greatest joy there is.

THE SPECIAL CELEBRATION OF
THE BAAL TESHUVAH

Among all holy days, only Simchas Beis haShoeivah emphasizes the concept of the Baal Teshuvah. Chazal tell us that the elderly pious and the sages among them, would dance during this great celebration, and some would say אשרי ילדותנו שלא ביישה את זקנותנו / "Happy is our youth (as we did not sin then), that did not embarrass our old age." Yet, another group would say, אשרי זקנותנו שכפרה את ילדותנו / "Happy is our old age that atoned for our youth," and this is the declaration of the Baal Teshuvah (*Sukkah*, 53a).

This unique celebration of being a Baal Teshuvah is in fact the whole point of Simchas Beis haShoeivah. It is the holy day of having returned, being reintegrated, and having found what we lost. On this day, we celebrate reuniting with our dejected, discarded parts, the lower self that we threw into the sea along with its negativity. During this Festival of Ingathering, we are drawing our lower waters up from the depths and placing them upon the Altar of the Beis haMikdash in miraculous wholeness and closeness to the Creator. Like a complete Baal Teshuvah, our past sins have transformed into merits!

LOWER WATERS

Chazal tell us (*Chagigah*, 14b; *Zohar* I, 26b; *Tikunei Zohar*, Tikun 40) that there were four sages who entered the *Pardes* / Orchard of Paradise by utilizing Divine Names (Rashi, Tosefos, *ad loc*). These four were Ben Azzai, Ben Zoma, Acher (Elisha ben Abuyah), and Rebbe Akiva. Rebbe Akiva instructed them prior to their ascension: "When you come to the place of pure marble stones, do not say, 'Water, water!'" The Gemara continues: "Ben Azzai gazed and died. Ben Zoma gazed and lost his sanity. Acher cut down the plantings (i.e., he became a heretic). Rebbe Akiva entered and exited in peace" (The *Bavli*, 14b, says "Rebbe Akiva *exited* in peace," and later it says he "ascended in peace and descended in peace" (*ibid.*, 15b). However, the *Yerushalmi*, in *Chagigah* 2:1, says he "entered and exited in peace"). What does "water" represent here, and what is "water-water"?

"Water" is desire (Rebbe Chayim Vital, *Sha'arei Kedushah*. *Tanya*, 1). Rebbe Akiva warned the other sages and instructed them:

'When you enter into the mystical experience, no matter how you perceive this inner reality, never say there are two *waters*. Do not make the mistake of thinking that there is a higher, nobler, Divine desire and a separate, lower human desire, which is lust and depravity. There is only One desire!'

At its core, all desire is a yearning to draw closer to Hashem. Even when it manifests as a craving for wealth, power, fame, or sensual pleasures, it reflects a deeper longing to connect, to feel, to be alive. On a deep level, our desire to be close to Hashem is a desire to be our true self, to be authentic and real, and through that reveal the *Kevod* / glory of Hashem in this world — although sometimes this essential desire is expressed in distorted ways.

In our own lives, the 'Lower Waters' represent our 'mundane' desires, which are vulnerable to distortion. And on Simchas Beis haShoeivah, we are drawing those Lower Waters, even those desires which we threw away, and we are bringing them "up" to Hashem, revealing that there is no essential separation between them and the Higher Waters. There is no "water-water," but rather a fundamental unity and wholeness pervading Hashem's Creation, and we are part of that. Sukkos is about bringing our whole self, *all* of us, into the Divine Sukkah.

Now, we stand elevated and whole, having reintegrated the parts of ourselves that we once pushed away during the Teshuvah process. This moment is one of immense joy, the profound joy of rediscovering what was lost and becoming truly complete once more.

Chapter 9
BEING HONORED, HELD & ESCORTED BY THE CLOUDS OF GLORY

I N LIFE, THERE ARE NECESSITIES AND THERE ARE ACCESSORIES; THERE ARE ESSENTIAL NEEDS THAT MUST BE MET FOR US TO SURVIVE AND THRIVE, AND THEN THERE ARE added blessings that make our lives more pleasant and enjoyable.

When Klal Yisrael left Egypt and began their forty-year journey through the harsh, hot desert on their way to the Promised Land, they needed food and water to survive. Anything else was extra. Three continuous miracles were provided during the journeys. The *Mon* / 'substance', meaning food, came in the merit of Moshe. The water, in the form of the Well of Miriam, came to them the merit of Miriam. The Clouds of Glory, which protected them from the elements, was received in the merit of Aharon. Whereas water and food are necessities for survival, the Clouds of Glory can be considered a luxury, an extra. They could have survived in the harsh conditions of the Desert even without the Clouds of Glory, but they certainly could not have survived without food and water. As such, on Sukkos, we are celebrating these Clouds of Glory, and not the necessities that Hashem provided us for our survival.*

CLOUDS OF GLORY & AVRAHAM

Chazal comment on the Pasuk, "And Hashem went in front of them" (*Shemos*, 13:21) with the following aphorism: "'In the way a person treats others that is the way Hashem will treat him.' Avraham escorted the angels, as it says, 'And Avraham went with them, to send them off'" (*Bereishis*, 18:16). Thus, Hashem ליוה / escorted (Avraham's) descendants for forty years in

---

* In the words of the Mabit, ואפשר לומר כי גם שהבאר והמן היו נסים מפורסמים לעין כל
והתמידו כל ארבעים שנה, כיון שהיה דבר הכרחי שא"א בלי מציאותם כלל לא הוקבע רמז להם,
אבל ענני כבוד שלא היה כל כך הכרחי כמו הם אלא כדי שלא יהיו בחורב ביום וקרח בלילה,
הוקבעו ימי החג רמז לענינם, כי גם בדבר שלא היה הכרחי כמאכל ומשתה עשה האל ית' נס
ופלא עמהם במדבר / "And one could say that the Well and the Mon, which were also 'public miracles' for all to see, and they even persisted the entire forty years, were *necessary*, for it would be impossible without their existence — and therefore no celebration to commemorate them was established. However, the Clouds of Glory were not as 'necessary', as they only (protected Klal Yisrael) from the (*discomfort* of) parching heat by day and cold by night, hence, the days of Sukkos were established to commemorate the Clouds, to show us that even something that was not as 'necessary' as food and water, Hashem performed a miracle and a wonder with these Clouds to protect us in our journey in the Desert": *Beis Elokim*, Sha'ar haYesodos, 37.

the Desert" (וה' הולך לפניהם. במדה שאדם מורד בה מורדין לו אברהם לו אברהם לוה מלאכי השרת)
דכתיב ואברהם הולך עמם לשלחם לפיכך ליוה הקב"ה את בניו ארבעים שנה במדבר: ללכת יומם
ולילה: *Mechilta* (d'Rashbi) Beshalach, 13:20).

Simply put, in addition to feeding his guests, which is a necessity and the definition of hosting, Avraham also escorted his guests. And in this merit, we were given the Clouds of Glory in the Desert. Hashem 'went the extra mile', as it were, not only feeding us but also going in front of us, much like Avraham did for his guests.*

---

* The Clouds of Glory appearing because of Avraham's great degree of self-lessness in greeting guests is also related to another Medrash, which con-nects the Clouds of Glory to the act of Avraham "standing over" his guests ready to serve them. *Medrash Rabbah*, Bereishis, 48:10 (See also *Tanchuma*, Vayikra 4), which teaches, אתה אמרת והשענו תחת העץ, חייך שאני פורע לבניך במדבר, שנאמר: פרש ענן למסך / "You said, 'And rest under the tree.' By your life! I will compensate your children in the Desert: "He spread a cloud for a cover" (*Tehilim*, 105:39). Or as the Gemara, says, בשכר שלשה זכו לשלשה בשכר חמאה וחלב זכו למן, בשכר והוא עומד עליהם זכו לעמוד הענן, בשכר יוקח נא מעט מים זכו לבארה של מרים / "In reward for three acts of hospitality that Avraham performed for the angels, his descendants merited three rewards. In reward for providing them with curd and milk, we merited the Mon; in reward for 'And he stood over them,' we merited the pillar of cloud; in reward for Avraham saying: 'Let now a little water be fetched,' we merited the Well of Miriam": *Baba Metziya*, 86b. In this way, the Well and the Mon came because Avraham gave the angels food and drink, while the Cloud of Glory came for his extra effort of standing over them, ready to serve. Although Chazal tell us that the Clouds of Glory came in honor of Aharon (*Ta'anis*, 9a), this is because in the merit of Avraham alone, the Clouds would have been temporary (because of the sin of the Golden Calf), but in the merit of Aharon we were engulfed in the Clouds of Glory (for the full) forty years in the Desert: *Maharsha*, Ta'anis, *ibid*. See also *Shaloh*, Maseches Pesachim, Matzah Ashirah, D'rush 2. Os 306-307, for an alternative way to reconcile these two Medrashim. In general, Sukkos is connected to Avraham, *Zohar Chadash*, Ki Sisa, 74b. The Three Yamim Tovim correspond to the three Avos (*Medrash Rabbah*, Shemos 31:2), the Ben Ish Chai writes that Avra-ham corresponds to Sukkos: תחלה בא אברהם אבינו וקיים עמוד גמילות חסדים וכנגד

WHAT YOU DO & HOW YOU DO IT

There are two components to an act of kindness: the act itself and the way in which it is carried out. If a hungry person is given a meal with reluctance or displeasure, the act may still technically be considered kind, as it fulfills the immediate need for food. However, the manner in which it is given can leave the recipient feeling embarrassed or insulted. This diminishes the kindness, rendering it less genuine — or in some cases, entirely negated. True kindness is not just about fulfilling needs, but also about doing so with warmth and compassion.

ACTING KIND & SHOWING HONOR

The manner in which you serve a guest is important, but even more so is the gesture of escorting them when they leave. After sharing a meal in your home, rising from your seat to walk your guest to the door, or even to the street, demonstrates the honor and respect you have for them, and it shows that you are honored to have received them in your home.

A desire to feed a hungry person stems from your kindness and compassion; escorting your guest after the meal goes beyond 'kindness'. By walking them to the door or even to the street, you demonstrate that they truly matter and that the opportunity to serve them was important to you. This gesture of

---

זה ניתן לנו חג הסוכות דעניינו הוא המשכת חסדים בסוכה ובלולב: *Ben Yehoyada,* Baba Kama, 50a. Although the Tur writes (Orach Chayim, 417) in the name of his brother, Rebbe Yehudah (who succeeded his father the Rosh) that Sukkos is equated with Yaakov, and Pesach with Avraham, as it says that for his cattle Yaakov fashioned Sukkos (*Bereishis,* 33:17). See, Shaloh, *Maseches Sukkah,* Ner Mitzvah, 53.

escorting is an expression of *Kavod* / honor, showing your deep respect and appreciation for their presence (In the words of the Maharal, ומי שאינו מלוה את האדם ואין נוהג בו כבוד ומניח אותו לצאת יחידי הרי מבטל את כבוד הצלם הזה / "And whoever does not escort a person, does not treat him with Kavod and lets him go out alone, cancels the Kavod of the Divine Image in him": *Nesivos Olam*, Nesiv Gemilus Chasadim, 5).

Greeting guests is part of הכנסת אורחים / *Hachnasas Orchim*, and escorting them as they leave is called לויה / *Liyavah* / 'escorting'. The Rambam writes, שכר הלויה מרבה מן הכל / "The reward for accompanying guests is greater than everything else" (*Hilchos Avel*, 14:2). Indeed, we learn of the positivity of escorting guests from Avraham, as the Rambam continues, והוא החק שחקקו אברהם אבינו ודרך החסד שנהג בה. מאכיל עוברי דרכים ומשקה אותן ומלוה אותן / "This is a statute which Avraham our Father instituted and the path of kindness which he would follow. He would feed wayfarers, provide them with drink, and accompany them (as they departed)."

It may be difficult to determine your host's inner feelings when they are serving you. Perhaps they are feeling kindness toward you or maybe not. However, if, after the 'obligatory' act of feeding you, your host 'goes the extra mile' and graciously escorts you to the door or to the street, it is a clear demonstration that they were honored and happy to host you.

After Hashem took us out of Egyptian slavery, He 'served' us food and drink in the Desert. This was, as it were, an 'obligatory kindness'. But then he also embraced and escorted us with the Clouds of Glory. This was beyond mere 'kindness', it was כבוד / *Kavod* / respect and honor, 'royal treatment'. Thus, they are called the *Ananei haKavod* / Clouds of Kavod, they are Hashem's Kavod but also ours (Chazal, in *Kidushin*, 32a, say, אפילו הרב שמחל על כבודו כבודו מחול שנאמר וה' הלך לפניהם יומם / "Even with regard to a teacher who forgoes his Kavod, his Kavod may be forgone, as it is stated, 'And Hashem went before them by day' (*Shemos*, 13:21)." In other words, Hashem forgoes, so to speak, His Kavod, in order to give *us* Kavod). This is why we celebrate the miracle of the Clouds of Glory and not the miracles of the Mon or the Well of Miriam. The latter were given to Klal Yisrael after they *asked* for food and water. The Clouds of Glory, on the other hand, were given out of honor, without being asked; out of pure, 'non-obligatory' Divine Kindness (*Kisei Dovid*).

If someone you love asks you, "Could you host me for a meal?" You will do whatever you can to provide them with food and drink. But when you honor them by walking them to the door, you do it without being asked. You do it out of honor, just to show how much you love and value them and to make their departure pleasant. Hashem likewise gives us the Clouds of Kavod, the Sukkah, as an act of Kavod, to show that He loves and values us, and that our journey through the Desert of the coming year should be pleasant (*Likutei Sichos*, 32, Emor, note 55. *Likutei Sichos*, 18, Chukas 3).

RESPECT VS. LOVE

Love does not necessarily equate to respect or honor (*Likutei Sichos*, 7, p. 342). In fact, respect can be deeper than love. While love can be about one's own feelings — "I" love you — 'respect' means setting oneself aside to give the other person space. Respect is about acknowledging the other's value and allowing them to exist fully and freely.

Love means '*I* love you'; respect means '*You* matter to me.' Respect comes from a greater level of selflessness. While the word *Kavod* is normally translated as 'honor', it is related to, and spelled the same as, the word *Kaved* / heavy (see *Targum Unkelus*, Shemos, 17:12, where the Targum translates the word, "heavy" as, "honor"). Accordingly, Kavod means to subscribe to the other person a great degree of importance or 'weight', meaning and honor. Real Kavod means to respect every facet of the other person; to seek out and appreciate the nuances of the Divine Image in every person we meet, and even to take every detail of their outer personality seriously. If I honor you, it means your experience carries weight: 'You matter to me.'

We celebrate Sukkos because the Sukkah, the Clouds of Glory, showed that beyond loving us and wanting to do kindness to us, Hashem *honors* us. Not only did Hashem show us respect by carving out for us a Makom, it was a *Makom Chashuv* / honorable, respected space in this world! In this way, we are celebrating our dignity, rejoicing in the honorable Divine Image placed within us. We dance with the realization that Hashem 'goes out of His way' to demonstrate to us how much we mean to Him, and He 'selflessly' accompanies us on our journeys, covering us with 'Clouds' of His very own Honor.

Chapter 10
HIGHER THAN ANGELS

A GREAT DEBATE OVER THE CENTURIES IS WHO IS 'HIGHER' OR GREATER IN SPIRITUAL STATURE, *NESHAMOS* / SOULS OR *MALACHIM* / ANGELS? The answer depends on perspective: is human potential taken into account, or just human behavior? A human being can choose freely, while angels transcend even the possibility of choosing the opposite of good (see for example, *Medrash Rabbah*, Bereishis, 78:1. *Even Ezra*, Bereishis, 1:1. *Sha'arei Kedushah*, Sha'ar 2). Humans can choose evil, or fail to choose the good, and as a result, fall into extremely low behavior. They can also potentially rise beyond the level of angels by activating their free choice and choosing goodness, life, holiness, and deeply noble behavior (*Nefesh haChayim*, 1:10). Sadly, though, some people do not activate their free choice, and instead, they go through life living impulsively and reactively.

To surrender your free choice is to surrender your potential to rise above the level of an angel.

An answer to the question also requires knowing whether we are viewing bodies or souls. If angels have some form of 'body' or *Yeshus* / material existence,* surely it is more subtle and refined than the coarse, 'lowly' body of humans. Yet, unlike angels, humans are essentially souls that are "part of the Divine, literally" (*Tanya*, 2). That speaks of a category which is higher

---

* The Rambam writes that angels are bodiless: *Hilchos Yesodei haTorah*, 2:3-8. *Moreh Nevuchim*, 1:49. See also *Sefer haIkarim*, Ma'amar 2:12. *Derech Hashem*, 1, 5:1. Hence, angels are identified with 'light' for their lack of any physical, tangible form. *Abarbanel*, Bereishis, 1:1. *Miflaos Elokim*, Ma'amar 3:3. Yet, other sources write that angels have some properties, such as refined fire: 'Pirush on the Rambam', *ibid.* Angels may also be composed of two of the four more ethereal elements, such as fire and wind: Ramban, *Toras haAdam*, Sha'ar haGemul. Alter Rebbe, *Torah Ohr*, Bereishis, 4b. *Likutei Torah*, VeZos haBerachah, p. 98a. Other sources write that angels are composed of refined water: Rebbe Matisyohu Delecreta, on *Sha'arei Orah*, p. 100-101. The Ramak writes that angels are composed of refined fire: *Pardes Rimonim*, Sha'ar 2:7. Yet, later on, he writes that angels are composed of all four elements, fire, wind, water and earth: Sha'ar 24:11. Rebbe Avraham Azulai, grandfather of the Chida, writes that angels are pure spirit, however, when they descend and appear in this dimensional universe they assume a body of fire and wind (or perhaps even bodies of subtle, refined, fire, wind, water and earth): *Chesed LeAvraham*, 1:28.

than 'higher' and 'lower'. As the soul is beyond the polarity of 'higher' and 'lower', it is unimpeded by lowliness and can be vested within a physical human body. Since the soul is rooted in the 'Highest of the High', it can shine into the 'lowest of the low', transform the human body, and rise to the highest reality, far beyond the static world of angels.

YOM KIPPUR: ANGELS — SUKKOS: SOULS IN BODIES

On Yom Kippur, we are like angels, for all the activities we do on Yom Kippur mimic angelic behavior (*Pirkei d'Rebbe Eliezer*, 46. Ramban, *Vayikra*, 16:8. Rosh, *Yuma*, Siman 24. Ya'avetz, *Toras Chesed*, Derush al Yom Kippur, p. 528. *Sefer haKuzari*, Ma'amar 3:5. *Drisha*, Orach Chayim, 606). On this day, we rest from acting to meet human bodily necessities. The fasting, and the other restrictions of the day, are not primarily intended to cause suffering to the body, but rather, to help us cease operating exclusively in the physical sphere, and ascend to an angelic state of functioning and consciousness. It is a day dedicated to achieving transcendence of the body and world. As we refrain from eating, drinking, and physical intimacy, we become lighter and lighter, less and less pulled by the 'gravity' of this world, and more and more ethereal and light, like angels.

To untangle ourselves from the trivialities of this world, and from mistakes and transgressions, we need to let go of attachments to our body and world on Yom Kippur. Sukkos, by contrast, the time of our joy and reintegration, is a time when we need to re-engage with normal bodily life.

Sukkah is a 'body-centered' Mitzvah, as are many Mitzvos, although unique to Sukkos is the fact that our entire body enters and participates in the Mitzvah.

In the Sukkah, we eat and drink, and maybe even sleep. These activities, eating, drinking, and resting, are necessary for virtually all physical creatures. In this way, we bring our basic physical needs into the embrace of the Sukkah. Sukkos is a celebration of 'souls in bodies'. While it is a spiritual, soulful holiday, it is celebrated through the meeting of physical needs.

BECHIRAH: DIVINE & OUR FREE CHOICE, IN THE BODY & IN THIS WORLD

Sukkos reveals the value of the body as the locus of the Divine *Bechirah* / choice. Hashem created this entire world for the purpose of forming the human body, which He chose to be the vessel of His revelation (*Tanya*, 49: ותכלית כל הצמצומים הוא כדי לברוא גוף האדם החומרי, ולאכפייא לסטרא אחרא, ולהיות יתרון האור מן החושך... כי זה תכלית השתלשלות העולמות). Here, in our physical bodies, we are 'co-creators' when we activate our own Bechirah and make a dwelling place for Hashem's revealed presence in this world. Appropriately, the MahariVeil, one of the last of the great Rishonim, writes that a person who performs the Mitzvah of Sukkah is as if he or she is a partner to HaKadosh Baruch in Creation (כתב מהרי"ו בתשוב' המקיים מצות סוכה כאלו נעשה שותף להקב"ה במעשה בראשית: *Ba'er Heitev*, Orach Chayim, 639, 10).

Through the process of Yom Kippur, we are purified and cleansed, so that we can make the correct choices. As soon as

Yom Kippur concludes, we choose to go out and begin building a holy Sukkah. Yom Kippur revealed our purity, and the
materials we will use to build the Sukkah are so pure they are
not even capable of receiving *Tumah* / impurity. Now we go
out of our homes and build a home for the Shechinah in this
world, for the Infinite Divine Presence to rest in this finite
physical reality.*

---

* In our own personal and inner life, we enact the idea of *Dirah beTachtonim*
/ 'drawing the Infinite Divine Presence down into finite reality' when our
Seichel, human intelligence becomes absorbed and unified with the Divine Intelligence of Hashem's Torah. Thus, the Halacha regarding learning
Torah with deep understanding and the Sukkah. Speaking about whether
a person should also sit in the Sukkah to learn Torah, the Gemara, *Sukkah*, 28b, says, אוכל ושותה ומטייל בסוכה ומשנן בסוכה. איני והאמר רבא מקרא ומתנא
במטללתא, ותנויי בר ממטללתא לא קשיא הא במגרס, הא בעיוני / "...One eats and
drinks and relaxes in the Sukkah, and studies Torah in the Sukkah. Is that
so? Didn't Rava say, 'Studying Torah and studying Mishna are undertaken
in the Sukkah, however, analytical study (must be undertaken) outside the
Sukkah?' But this is not a difficulty — the teaching that one studies in the
Sukkah is with regard to broad study. (Whereas the statement of Rava that
one should study outside the Sukkah) is with regard to study that is *b'Iyyun*
/ 'intensive' — detailed and deeply analytical study." As Rashi writes, this is
a *Din* / law of מצטער / 'one who is discomforted by or in the Sukkah': דמצטער
הוא ומצטער פטור מן הסוכה והאויר יפה לו להרחיב דעתו / "For he becomes uncomfortable (in b'Iyyun) and one who becomes uncomfortable is exempt at that
time from the obligation to sit in the Sukkah" (See also *Shulchan Aruch*,
Orach Chayim, 640:4). Therefore, if he wants or needs to, he is permitted to
study b'Iyyun outside the Sukkah. Yet the Akeidas Yitzchak writes (Sha'ar
67:8, Emor), that learning b'Iyyun outside of the Sukkah is not an issue
of exemption due to צער / discomfort, rather it is the opposite: אמנם לימוד
של עיון הותר (שם כ"ח.) לפי שהלמוד אשר על זה התואר הוא עצמו גופה של סוכה וטעמה
"However, when a person learns b'Iyyun, he is *allowed* to learn outside the
Sukkah, and the deeper reason for this is that this type of learning is the
essence of the Sukkah and the (actual) reason (for the Mitzvah)." In other
words, when a person is learning Torah b'Iyyun, completely intellectually engaged and absorbed, he is within the Sukkah of HaKadosh Baruch

The sacred space of the Sukkah is a mechanism for drawing Heaven, pure spirituality, down into the material plane.

GESHEM / RAIN / PHYSICALITY

It is for this reason that Sukkos is a time for the judgment of water (*Rosh Hashanah*, 1:2), and to draw down rain from the Heavens. In fact, all the Four Minim are connected to water and rain. אמר רבי אליעזר הואיל וארבעת מינין הללו אינן באין אלא לרצות על המים, וכשם שארבע מינין הללו אי אפשר בהם בלא מים כך אי אפשר לעולם בלא מים / "Rebbe Eliezer said: 'Since these Four Minim come only to offer appeasement for water (as they symbolize the rainfall of the coming year). And this symbolism is as follows: Just as these Four Minim cannot exist without water (they need water to grow), so too, the world cannot exist without water'" (*Ta'anis*, 2b). In particular, Sukkos is associated with a judgment for גשם / *Geshem* / rain. מאימתי מזכירין גבורות גשמים / "'From when do we begin mentioning Geshem (in prayer)?' asks the Mishnah. Rebbe Eliezer says, 'From the first day of Sukkos,' and Rebbe Yehoshua says, 'From the last day of Sukkos'" (*Ta'anis*, 1:1). In other words, during Sukkos, in the second blessing of the Amidah, we begin to recite — either on the first or last day — the passage, משיב הרוח ומוריד הגשם / "He makes the wind blow and the Geshem fall."

Hu — even when he is not sitting in a literal, physical Sukkah. Although note the words of the Ramak; "Certainly, a person is able to study on any given day. However, the times most conducive to deep understanding are during the long nights—from midnight onward—or on Shabbos...Likewise, during the days of Sukkos, while sitting in the Sukkah, there is great success in study. These hours I mention have been tried and proven by me, and I speak from experience." *Ohr Ne'erav*, 3, 1:11.

Our prayers for Geshem, specifically, begin on Sukkos. Rain has many names, as there are various types and seasons of rain. The two basic names for rain are Geshem and Matar. What is the difference between these two types of rain?

Rabbeinu Bachya (*Devarim*, 11:17) writes that the so-called 'lower waters', the natural waters, those of the ocean, are called Geshem, as Geshem comes from the word *Gashmiyus* / physicality. Geshem is exclusively a material phenomenon. The 'upper waters', the 'spiritual' waters of Heaven, are referred to by both names, Matar and Geshem. This is because Matar can be manifested as Geshem when it is drawn down.

On Sukkos, we draw blessings from the upper realms into the world of Gashmiyus.

RETURNING THE SPIRITUAL & DRAWING DOWN THE PHYSICAL

When the holy Baal Shem Tov would say the prayer משיב הרוח ומוריד הגשם / "He (literally) 'returns' the wind (the *Ruach* / spirit, the spirituality) and draws down the Geshem (the physicality)," he would gesture with his hands. When he said the words משיב הרוח / "Return the spirit," he would wave upwards. And when he said the words ומוריד הגשם / "and draws down the Geshem," he would moves his hand downwards. He was saying, 'Now, HaKadosh Baruch Hu, after our intense inner and deeper spiritual *Avodah* / work on the days of Rosh Hashanah and Yom Kippur, receive on High our prayers, our spirit, our

Ruach. And please draw blessings down into the Geshem, into the physical world.'

Now is the time to draw down to our lives the showers of blessings that we generated on Rosh Hashanah and Yom Kippur, life-giving waters which were stored in a hidden spiritual reservoir, Above.

(*Yehi Ratzon* / May it be Hashem's will)

להעביב ולהענין להריק ולהמטר...

מים אבים בם גיא לעטר —

...למוגג פני נשי בצחות לשם.

...To overcast the sky and make clouds, to empty them and cause rain to fall

— Water, with currents to adorn the valley

...to soften the surface of the earth with sparkling, gem-like drops.

(Excerpts from *Tefilas Geshem*, Musaf of Shemini Atzeres)

PART TWO:

THE FOUR SPECIES:
What They Represent
& Intentions for the Waving

Chapter 1

BEAUTIFUL FRUIT OF THE TREE: THE DEEPER MEANING OF THE FOUR SPECIES

ARBA MINIM: THE FOUR SPECIES

O N SUKKOS, THE TORAH TELLS US, "YOU SHALL TAKE...THE BEAUTIFUL FRUIT OF THE TREE (the Esrog or 'citron'), a palm branch (*Lulav*), myrtle branches (*Hadasim*) and willow branches (*Aravos*) from the stream, and rejoice before Hashem your G-d for seven days" (*Vayikra*, 23:40).[*]

---

[*] "Before Hashem," meaning in and around the Beis haMikdash, the Mitzvah is performed for seven days. Everywhere else, the Torah-based Mitzvah (or the 'separate' Mitzvah: Reb Chayim Stencil), is on the first day. Not the first day as in the *Kedushah* / holiness of Yom Tov, but rather, just the first day. אבל דברים שאינן מעיקר קדושת היום אלא שהן מצות הנוהגות באותו היום בלבד כגון כל הפסולין ביום טוב הראשון בלבד ואף אם לא תהיינה מצות הללו נוהגות ביום טוב שני אין כאן זלזול ליום טוב השני כלל כיון שאין המצות תלויות בעיקר קדושת היום כלל שהרי מצות נטילת לולב לא תלה הכתוב חיובו מחמת שהוא יום טוב אלא מחמת שהוא יום הראשון שנאמר ולקחתם לכם ביום הראשון / "Nevertheless, (these latter authorities argue,

Collectively, the Esrog, Lulav, Hadasim, and Aravos are called the Arba Minim, the 'Four Kinds' or Four Species. The latter three plants are neatly bundled together, this binding together is part and parcel of the actual Mitzvah itself,* and

---

this should not affect) matters that are not associated with the essence of the sanctity of the day, but are Mitzvos that are observed on that (first) day alone, such as all the factors that disqualify (any of the Four Species) on the first day alone. If (the stringencies associated with this Mitzvah) would not be observed on the second day, this would not be considered as demeaning the second day of the festival, for these Mitzvos are not dependent on the essence of the sanctity of the day at all. (The rationale is that) the Torah did not make the Mitzvah of taking the Lulav dependent on the fact that (the first day) is celebrated as a festival, but on the fact that it is the first (of the seven days of the festival), as it is written, "And on the first day, you shall take for yourselves...": Alter Rebbe, *Shulchan Aruch*, Orach Chayim, 649:21.

* The binding of the three together is part of the *Hidur Mitzvah* / the beautification of a Mitzvah (*Sukkah*, 11b. 33a), yet, it is not merely an additional Hidur — such as beautiful Sukkah or beautiful Sefer Torah, rather, a Hidur that is part of the Mitzvah itself, the beautification of how the Mitzvah itself is practiced. Tosefos, *Gittin*, 45b, writes that a women should not tie the Lulav, as women are exempt from the positive Mitzvah of Lulav: מכאן אומר ר"ת דאין אשה אוגדת לולב ועושה ציצית כיון דלא מיפקדה. But the question is, if tying the Lulav is only a Hidur of the Mitzvah not the Mitzvah itself, why can't a woman tie the Lulav? And the answer is that tying the Lulav with the other Minim is a Hidur *within* the actual practice of the Mitzvah itself, and women are not obligated in the Mitzvah: Note *Magen Avraham*, Orach Chayim, 649:8: משמע דלכתחל' לא יאגדנו עכו"ם כמ"ש סימן י"ד גבי נשים וכ"כ בהג"מ פ"א מה' ציצית בשם ר"ת וצ"ע דהא קי"ל לולב א"צ אגד וא"כ האגד אינו מן המצוה וע' בסוכה דף י"א ע"א ע"ב וצ"ל כיון שהוא נוי למצוה חשוב כמצוה עצמו. Note also Rambam, *Hilchos Lulav*, 7:6: מצוה מן המבחר לאגד לולב והדס וערבה / "The most desirable way of performing the Mitzvah is *to tie* the Lulav, Hadas and Aravah together." The Rambam does not use the language of Hidur, rather, מצוה מן המבחר / "The most *desirable* way of performing the Mitzvah": See *Sh'ut Avnei Nezer*, Orach Chayim, 433.

on each day of Sukkos (except Shabbos), we take them in our hands, make a blessing over them, and then, along with the Esrog, we wave or move them in a series of spatial directions.

Throughout the days of Sukkos, we follow the above Divine command and invitation. Yet, the question is what is the purpose and intention behind gathering these plants, besides of course being a Mitzvah, and more pointedly, how does the holding and waving of the Four Minim motivate us to "rejoice before Hashem"?

The Torah's Divine wisdom and Light comes to heal a deep existential wound that we all carry within. Despite the fact that *Ein Od Mil'vado* / there is nothing but Hashem, Hashem's Presence pervades all directions and dimensions, and Hashem is an indivisible Unity, One without a second, we feel ourselves thrust into a fractured world, where there is a discord between reality *as it is perceived*, and reality *as it is*. We feel this 'separation anxiety' on a deep level, at least subconsciously. Yet, despite all the conflict and resulting frustration, something deep inside us also always remembers and senses the ultimate Unity of it all. Often subtle, this recognition draws us toward piercing the veils and seeing beyond the appearance of separation. Our deepest desire is to experience spiritual intimacy with HaKadosh Baruch Hu, in every act and detail of our lives.

For seven days a year, we are given a tremendous gift. The Torah gives us the *Arba Minim* / 'Four Species', as tools that can empower us to fully pierce the veils in our lives, and remove all separation, negativity and obstacles to the perception of Divine Unity. With these tools, we can channel the consciousness of Unity into our mundane lives. We can make Divine intimacy a perpetual, lived experience.

However, in order to summon the full transformational power of the Arba Minim, we must be fully present while doing the Mitzvah. It is not just our bodies that perform the act of the Mitzvah, but our minds and hearts as well. Hence, the deepest type of Kavanah is one that we engage while actually performing the Mitzvah (*Igeres haRamaz*, Siman 6. *Shu'T Yoseph Ometz*, 44. See *Zohar*, Vayakhel, 213b, regarding Tefilah, ובעוד דפומיה ושפוותיה מרחשן, לביה יכוון). Kavanah is not just mental; it is eventually emotional as well, yet the more we intellectually understand the multiple layers of meaning in the Arba Minim and the *Na'anuim* / 'waving' ritual, the more of our heart and whole self will be involved in the Kavanah and the process of the act itself.

To properly explore the purpose and intention of waving the Arba Minim, we need to first understand why these four species in particular are chosen, and what each of them symbolizes, represents, and embodies.

The Torah itself only tells us to "take" these four species and rejoice, yet it offers no explicit reason for doing this. The truth is, we do not need graspable, rational, human reasons for the Mitzvos, for Mitzvos are rooted in the absolute simplicity of Hashem's Unity, and reasons suggest something extraneous to Unity. Reasons are movements towards a separate entity or subject. For example, if I am working for the 'reason' of making money, then the work is only a means to an end. In Unity, every 'means' is an end in itself. This is why the purpose and reason for a Mitzvah is the Mitzvah itself.

On the other hand, we are creations, not the Creator, and we live in a world of *perceptual* separation. In this world, our minds seek reasons for the acts that we do. Indeed, we are fashioned by our Creator to pursue meaning, to think and function in a binary mode, to make sense through reason and intuition, contrast and correspondence, physical form and mystical symbol, narratives of the past and dreams of the future. Therefore, while keeping Unity in mind, we also need to explore the ethical, philosophical and mystical reasons for the Mitzvos, including the Arba Minim. In the words of the Rambam, אף על פי שכל חקי התורה גזרות הם כמו שבארנו בסוף מעילה. ראוי להתבונן בהן וכל מה שאתה יכול לתן לו טעם תן לו טעם / "Although all of the laws of the Torah are decrees, as we explained… it is fit to meditate upon them and wherever it is possible to provide a reason, one should provide a reason" (*Hilchos Temurah*, 4:14). In other words, the reason we or anyone provides is not *the* reason for the Mitzvah, for in fact, Mitzvos are above reason. Rather, the reason is *a* reason, and one that may make sense to us relative to our experience of the world and our place in it.

We can organize all 'reasons' into four or five categories known by their acronym, PaRDeS: 1) *Peshat*, 'literal interpretation', 2) *Remez*, 'allegorical interpretation', 3) *Derush*, 'homiletic' meaning, 4) *Sod*, 'secret' or Kabbalistic meaning, and 5)

Sod shebe Sod, 'secret within the secret' also called the Neshamah of the meaning (*Emek haMelech*, Hakdamah), namely, the teachings of Chasidus.

Let us now discuss the *PaRDeS* of reasons behind gathering and "taking" the Four Species.

PESHAT / LITERAL INTERPRETATION

The Rambam writes, on a Peshat level, Sukkos is a joyous Yom Tov because it is the time of gathering produce from the fields (*Moreh Nevuchim*, 3:43) The Torah calls this festival *Chag ha-Asif*, the 'Festival of Gathering', or 'harvest festival', and explains, "After the gathering of your threshing floor and vat, you shall hold the Feast of Sukkos for seven days" (*Devarim*, 16:13).

Another Peshat level of interpretation is that we are commemorating the Sukkos or 'booths' that we sat in during our forty year journey through the Desert. The Torah says that we should sit in a Sukkah "...in order that your generations may know that I caused the Children of Israel to dwell in booths when I brought them out of the land of Egypt" (*Vayikra*, 23:43). According to a literal reading, we can say these Sukkos were either literal booths, or they were representations of the Clouds of Glory that protected Klal Yisrael on their journeys (*Sukkah*, 11b). Yet, the more prevalent interpretation is that Sukkos represent the miracle of the Clouds of Glory (Rashi, Ramban, *Vayikra*, 23:42-43), and specifically, as explored earlier, Sukkos celebrates the *return* of the Clouds of Glory following the episode of the Golden Calf — and hence the joy.

SEASONAL CONTEXT

While the primary Peshat reason for the Yom Tov is the historical narrative or the 'content' (recalling sitting in Clouds of Glory or in tents as we left Egypt and journeyed in the Desert), the reason can, as the Torah clearly establishes, also be understood within its particular seasonal and agriculture context. The seasonal context of Sukkos is that it is the time of harvesting and gathering produce from the fields. Fascinatingly, when the Torah first introduces us to the Yom Tov of Sukkos it speaks about it being a חג האסף / "celebration of ingathering" (*Shemos*, 23:16) and it does not mention Sukkos being associated with the Clouds of Glory until much later on (*Vayikra*, 23:41). Perhaps this is so because Sukkos is a celebration of the return of the Clouds of Glory that occurred following the episode with the Golden Calf (*Meshech Chochmah*, Shemos, ibid.), and the season is secondary. Either way, the seasonal reason needs to be understood in order to understand the Yom Tov of Sukkos. Once the seasonal content is layered with the historical content, the celebration of the Clouds of Glory, we can then understand the seasonal content within the context of the historical.

The deeper understanding of the seasonal phenomena is that on Sukkos, we 'gather' or assimilate into our lives all the inspiration and spiritual gains that we experienced during

Rosh Hashanah through Yom Kippur. Taking the enthusiasm and sense of commitment we experienced during those ten days, we now move deeper. On the Ten Days of Awe, we turn to Hashem and say, 'I love you Hashem, I want to live differently, I am committed to my relationship with You and to my spiritual development.' On Sukkos, we 'enter the Chupah' with Hashem, as explored earlier (The Maharal explains the gathering in terms of us returning to our Source — ויש לעולם חזרה ואסיפה, שאחר תכלית הכל העולם נאסף אל המקיים, שאין עמידה לעולם בעצמו, ונאסף אל המקיים, שבו נתלה...ואסיפה האחרונה עליונה הם גם כן ישראל [נאספים] תחת כנפי השכינה: *Gevuros Hashem*, 46)

The Rambam writes that Torah instructs us to gather these four types of vegetation in our hand because Sukkos is related to the seasonal gathering of vegetation from the fields; it is a harvest celebration. The reasons for these specific four plants are, 1) they are four species found throughout the entire Eretz Yisrael, 2) they are aesthetically pleasant, and 3) they do not wither quickly, so they are durable enough to remain intact for the duration of the seven day Yom Tov.

These four different species also originate from four basic natural environments and climates in Eretz Yisrael: the desert, the coast, the mountains and the rivers. The Lulav comes from the palm tree, which grows in the desert, and the Esrog fruit grows in the coastal plains. Hadasim come from myrtle trees, which grow in the mountainous regions, and the Aravos come from willow trees, which grow in riverbeds. Therefore, the context of the Four Species suggests that gathering them together symbolizes gathering and unifying all areas of the Holy Land

and specifically the Species that demonstrate the beauty of Eretz Yisrael (*Abarbanel*, Vayikra 23:39).

THE SEASON OF OUR JOY

The Torah says, "You shall take... the beautiful fruit of the tree, a palm branch, myrtle twigs, and willow...and rejoice before Hashem your G-d for seven days" (*Vayikra*, 23:40). Through this Pasuk, the Four Species are literally connected with "rejoicing before Hashem."

In an agricultural world, when the harvest arrives, one reaps the benefits of his hard labor and receives the produce that will be used throughout the winter months. It is, therefore, a naturally joyous time. The Chinuch writes that the Torah tells us to celebrate "before Hashem your G-d for seven days" (*Mitzvah*, 324), because instead of rejoicing in our physical abundance alone, as the season is a time of general rejoicing of abundance, we should take this time to thank and praise Hashem, the Source of all of life's blessings.* We are to direct our physical joy toward Hashem, and transform our natural joy of collecting the harvest into spiritual and elevated joy. According to the Chinuch, this is the Peshat of the reason that we take these physical plants in our hands during our spiritual service.

---

* "You shall make yourself a Sukkah... when you gather the harvest...." When a person gathers his harvest, he then feels empowered and completely in charge. Thus, the Torah says in these moments, go out in the Sukkah and realize that material success is temporary and that whatever we have comes from Hashem. Gratefully realizing that Hashem is sustaining us is a source of great joy.

Since the Lulav, Esrog, Hadasim, and Aravos are objects of a Mitzvah, they remind us to be joyful and thankful before the Creator, Who gave us the Mitzvah. Furthermore, they naturally bring joy to the beholder. In the words of the Chinuch: "All four species gladden the hearts of those who see them." Beyond being prevalent throughout the Land, durable, and aesthetically pleasing, they also inspire joy in those who behold them.

NATURE'S BOUNTY

Expanding on the seasonal context of Sukkos, a festival celebrating the wonders of nature, we hold the Four Species, which together express the full array of nature's splendor. This array is expressed through four different elemental categories: naturally occurring substances that 1) have both a beautiful aroma and a satisfying taste, 2) have a pleasant taste, but no aroma, 3) have a beautiful aroma but no taste, and 4) have neither an aroma nor a taste.

The first category is represented by the Esrog. There are some natural phenomena in our lives that do not require any human processing in order to extract their benefit. They come ready-made; we could call them 'transparent' or 'perfect'. 'Aromatic' alludes to anything that benefits life through spiritual beauty and abstract enjoyment, while 'tasty' alludes to anything that benefits us through more tangible forms of satisfaction or nourishment. The Esrog thus symbolizes all the things that Hashem gives us that are effortlessly and perfectly transparent to the Divine satisfaction. It embodies 'the world of transparency'.

The second category is represented by the Lulav, which contains a tasty or nourishing substance but has no striking 'aroma'. There are many natural phenomena that give us satisfaction in life, but have no outstanding beauty. We usually have to process these phenomena to extract their benefit, as is frequently the case with plants that are used for food. These embody 'the world of satisfaction'.

The third category is represented by the Hadasim, the myrtle twigs, which have a fragrant aroma but are inedible. Similarly, many natural phenomena benefit us simply by means of their beautiful appearance or delicate qualities, yet we would not 'take a bite out of them' as it were, nor would they satisfy our taste. These are expressions of 'the world of beauty'.

The fourth category is represented by the Aravos or willow branches, which contain no aroma and are inedible. These represent natural substances that provide only the raw materials and basic requirements of life, such as a physical place to live and utilitarian articles of clothing. They are of 'the world of utility'.

By gathering together these four elements in the form of the Arba Minim, we show gratitude and praise to Hashem for all of nature's gifts.

SPECIES	FORM OF BENEFIT / INDUCEMENT TO PRAISE
Esrog	*Transparency*
Lulav	*Satisfaction*
Hadasim	*Beauty*
Aravos	*Utility*

REMEZ: ALLEGORICAL INTERPRETATION

The shape of each of the Arba Minim alludes to a part of the human body, as the Medrash suggests (*Medrash Rabbah*, Emor 30:14. *Sefer haBahir*, 98). The round Esrog resembles the heart, the seat of emotion. The straight Lulav resembles the spine, which is understood as a channel carrying messages from the brain to the body, connecting the upper and lower dimensions of the body and consciousness (Lulav represents the spine, and thus there is a *Shedra* / spine in an actual Lulav: *Sukkah*, 30b). The leaves of the Hadasim are shaped like eyes, alluding to the faculty of sight. We bind three Hadasim to the Lulav, since eyes have three colors: the 'whites', red blood vessels, and the color of the irises (*Zohar* 3, 255b). The leaf of an Aravah looks like two lips, symbolizing the faculty of speech.

Binding and holding these four symbols together, and reciting a blessing over them, we invoke the unification of self that we are always aspiring to master. What we see with our eyes (what comes into us from the outside), and what we say (what goes out from inside ourselves) with our mouths and lips, should be consistent with the messages we receive from our higher, inner knowing, the mind, and then through our spine, as it were, our emotions, our heart, should be aroused accordingly.

We aspire that everything within us, our minds, hearts, and words, should be in harmony, and all directed upwards to the Unity Above. Therefore, when we recite the blessing and fulfill our obligation of performing the Mitzvah of the Four Minim, we hold them all together in a unity and then orient them upright, directing all our faculties towards the Divine Unity Above,* a "unity paralleling Unity."

---

* Yet, it is specifically through the straight, upward-pointing Lulav that all the Minim and all of self are directed and elevated Upward. When we stand up, pick up the Lulav and point it straight up, and then later wave the Lulav in six directions while it is pointing upwards, the other three Minim are elevated and with it, along with our entire self and the entire world. An allusion to this is in the words, אעלה בתמר / "Let me climb the palm." Literally translated, this means, 'I will be elevated (אעלה) through the palm, the Lulav (*Shir haShirim*, 7:9). Additionally, the letters of the word אעלה stand for אתרוג, ערבות, לולב, הדסים / Esrog, Aravos, Lulav, Hadasim (*Tikunei Zohar*, 13). The elevation occurs through the Lulav and that is why the blessing over the Four Minim is, על נטילת לולב / on the taking of the Lulav, but which literally means, on the Elevation of the Lulav, as the Avudaraham writes (ואחר כך נוטלין הלולב ומברכין עליו על נטילת לולב. נטילה היא כמו לקיחה שנאמר ולקחתם לכם ונטילה לשון חכמים הוא במקום לקיחה כדאמרי' נוטל אדם את לולבו. ועוד על שם שהוא מעלה ומוריד וכתיב וינטלם וינשאם כל ימי עולם ולכך אומר לשון נטילה שהיא הרם: *Avudraham*, Sukkos, Shemini Atzeres, 9). Additionally, the reason why we mention only the Lulav in the blessing over all the Four Minim is הואיל ומינו גבוה מכולן / "since it is taller than the rest": *Sukkos*, 35b. Although the Rambam writes, מברך תחלה על נטילת לולב הואיל וכלן סמוכין לו / "Before one takes them to perform the Mitzvah, he should recite the blessing on the taking the Lulav, for all the others are dependent upon it": *Hilchos Lulav*, 7:6. The *Lechem Mishnah* (ad loc) writes, ואולי יש לפרש דהיינו סמוכין לו כלומר שהוא מעולה מכלן / "Perhaps we can explain the Rambam himself to mean 'dependent' because it is higher (taller) than the rest." In any case, the point is that the Lulav is connected with height and elevation.

SPECIES	BODY PART	ELEMENT TO HARMONIZE
Hadasim	Eyes	*What is Seen*
Aravos	Lips	*What is Spoken*
Lulav	Spine	*Knowledge*
Esrog	Heart	*Emotion*

DERUSH: HOMILETICAL INTERPRETATION

Corresponding to the four categories of natural substances mentioned above, there are also four developmental stages among people in relation to Torah and Mitzvos (*ibid.*, 30:12. See also *Kli Yakar*, Vayikra, 23:40).

The nourishment of learning Torah develops and transforms the way we think, our internal reality, and our 'taste' becomes more refined and pure. The beautiful action-based practices of the Mitzvos develop and transform the way we act, which is our appearance or 'aroma'; our projection becomes refined and purified. Although a transformed mind ultimately transforms our actions, and actions can also reach inward and transform the mind. Still, generally, the focus of Torah is inner development, while the focus of Mitzvos and beneficial actions is outer development.

Some people have already transformed themselves inwardly through Torah knowledge, as well as outwardly through Mitzvos and acts of generosity. Like the Esrog, these people both 'taste' and 'look' good. They are notably transparent to the Divine Presence. They radiate a 'world of wholeness'.

Others are like a Lulav, they have the good 'taste' of higher knowledge, yet their external behavior and appearances are not so 'aromatic'. Their knowledge and deeds are not yet in sync with each other. Lulav is connected with the idea of Torah, as such, the three distinct letters within the word לולב / Lulav hints to the Torah. The Torah begins with the letter ב (as in בראשית), and concludes with the letter ל (as in ישראל), and the *Nevi'im* / Prophets begins with the letter ו (as in ויהי), the three distinct letters of the word לולב. These people evoke 'the world of Torah'.

Some people are like Hadasim in that their actions are beautiful, they are pleasant to be around, they do many Mitzvos, and yet they are empty of an inner life, devoid of Torah. Their minds and inner state have not yet been transformed; their 'taste' is not yet refined. These reveal 'the world of Mitzvos'.

Finally, there are some people who are like the Aravos, having no aroma or taste. They are 'raw material', ready to begin the path of self-transformation. They are currently expressing a 'world of lack', a need for decisive action.

When we take all four species, hold them together and recite the blessing, we realize we must bring together and unify all the different kinds of people to properly sing Hashem's praise. "(With regard to the) Four Minim, two of them produce fruit, and two of them (the Hadas and the Aravah) do not produce fruit. Those that produce fruit have a bond with those that do not produce fruit, and those that do not produce fruit have a bond with those that produce fruit. And a person does not fulfill his obligation until they are all bound together in a single bundle. And so too, when we fast and pray for acceptance, (we are not answered) until we are bound together in a single bundle" (*Menachos*, 27a). Our power comes from our unity, and so does our beauty.

The beauty of the One lies in the multiplicity of the Many. We can do this by judging each person according to his merits and finding the good points within every single person. Similarly, we must unify the different stages of development within ourselves, we must judge ourselves favorably and include every part of ourselves in our *Avodah* / inner work and Divine service, regardless of our apparent stage.

SPECIES	AREA OF TRANSFORMATION	STAGE OR AREA
Esrog	Both knowledge and action. Wholeness	*Both internal and external development*
Lulav	Knowledge, but not action. Torah	*Internal development predominates*
Hadasim	Action, but not knowledge. Mitzvos	*External development predominates*
Aravos	Neither knowledge nor action. Lack	*Neither; an undeveloped state*

SOD: SECRET / INNER INTERPRETATION

Rabbeinu Bachya writes that the Four Species embody the Name of Hashem, the Four letter name (*Rabbeinu Bachya*, Vayikra, 23:40). This parallels the teaching in the Medrash which says, "The Esrog is the Holy One…the Hadasim are the Holy One…the Lulav is the Holy One…the Aravos are the Holy One (*Medrash Rabbah*, Emor, 30:9). When we hold the Four Minim, we are holding in our hands, as it were, 'a part of Hashem' (פרי עץ הדר, זה הקדוש ברוך הוא …כפת תמרים, זה הקדוש ברוך הוא …וענף עץ עבת, זה הקדוש ברוך הוא …וערבי נחל, זה הקדוש ברוך הוא. Rashi, *Sukkah*, 36b, writes regarding a beautiful Esrog, דהא מצוה הדורה בעינן הואיל ומזכיר שם שמים עליו / "For a beautiful Mitzvah is required, since we mention Hashem's name upon it." Rashi cannot simply mean because we recite a blessing with Hashem's name upon the Esrog, since Hashem's name is recited upon all objects of Mitzvos, rather, perhaps Rashi is alluding to this idea, that the Name of Hashem 'literally' rests upon the Esrog, as the Four Minim 'embody' as it were, the Name of Hashem).

The Zohar explains (1, 202b), that the Four Minim correspond to the four letters of the Name of Hashem and thus to the Four Inner Worlds. These are the correspondences with the Four Worlds: The Esrog is the perfect and unified world of *Atzilus* / nearness. The Lulav is the world of *Beriah* / creation. The Hadasim are the world of *Yetzirah* / formation. The Aravos are the world of *Asiyah* / actualization.

The Arizal relates the Four Minim to the four letters of the Name of Hashem in more detail (*Sha'ar haKavanos*, Sukkos). The three Hadasim correspond to the letter Yud of Hashem's Name. Yud, as a word, is spelled with three letters: Yud-Vav-Dalet (ד-ו-י). These three letters in turn symbolize the Sefiros or attributes of *Chesed* / kindness, *Gevurah* / restriction, and

Tiferes / compassion.

The two branches of the Aravos correspond to the upper Hei of Hashem's Name. Hei is spelled with two letters Hei and a Hei (ה-ה). These two letters symbolize the attributes of *Netzach* / confidence and *Hod* / humility.

The long, straight Lulav corresponds to the long, straight letter Vav (ו). Both symbolize the attribute of *Yesod* / foundation and connection, and the *Duchra* / masculine quality of the Divine flow.*

---

* Rebbe Menachem Rikanti, writing a few hundred years before the Arizal, teaches that the Lulav embodies the quality of Tiferes, the three Hadasim are Chesed, Gevurah, and Yesod, the Esrog is Malchus and the Aravos are Netzach and Hod: *Ta'amei haMitzvos*. In the text, we are following the Arizal's understanding, which is similar to the Rikanti's, yet slightly different, for one, according to the Arizal, the Esrog is Malchus (Ateres) of Yesod, not Malchus itself (Yesod is the Sefirah that holds the previous five Sefiros and will transmit them to the receiver, Malchus. The Malchus of Yesod is how the idea exists within the *Mashpia* / giver, and takes form how it is going to be given over to the *Mekabel* / receiver, Malchus. This is Malchus as it is within Yesod. Since the Esrog is the Malchus, Ateres within Yesod, it is understood why in one place, the Zohar writes that the Esrog is Yesod: *Tikunei Zohar*, Hakdamah, 2,2. And in another place, the Zohar writes that the Esrog is Malchus: *ibid.*, Tikkun 21, p. 56b. *Zohar* 3, 256b. *Sha'ar Yissachar*, Ma'amar Mani Karva, 32:2). Additionally, the Pasuk says, "And you shall take to yourself פְּרִי עֵץ הָדָר כַּפֹּת תְּמָרִים וַעֲנַף עֵץ־עָבֹת וְעַרְבֵי־נַחַל." There are three words referring to the Esrog, פְּרִי עֵץ הָדָר, similar to the three letters in the letter Yud (which is always spelled Yud-Hei-Vav). There are two words referring to the Lulav, כַּפֹּת תְּמָרִים, similar to the two letters in the letter Hei (spelled Hei-Aleph, or Hei-Hei). There are three words referring to the Hadasim, וַעֲנַף עֵץ־עָבֹת, similar to the three letters in the letter Vav (Vav-Aleph [Yud] Vav). And there are two words referring to the Aravos, וְעַרְבֵי־נַחַל, similar to the two letters in the final Hei (Hei-Aleph or Hei-Hei): *Aderes Eliyahu*, Emor, 23:40. Likutim.

The Esrog corresponds to the final Hei (ה) of Hashem's Name, and thus it embodies the attribute of Malchus or 'kingship' and the feminine Divine Presence. It is for this reason the early *Mekubalim* / Kabbalists associate the Esrog with the feminine (*Sefer haBahir*, 172-173). Malchus, the feminine, receives from the masculine Yesod, above it. The Rikanti writes that the Esrog and Malchus also symbolize *K'neses Yisrael* / 'the Community of Israel', the ones who hold the presence of Hashem in the world, and the reality of the world today.

---

* The appearance of the Tree of Life is upside down — the Roots of the Tree above, cleaving to the Source of all Life, the Ein Sof, and gradually descending into the trunk and then the branches, where the branches finally bear fruit. Fruit is the end product of this process, hence it is 'Malchus'.

The Lulav, particularly, is what draws down *Duchra* / the masculine Transcendent Light into Malchus of the Esrog. Although the Hadasim and Aravos are also 'the masculine' the Yud and upper Hei, as explored, it is specifically the Lulav that reaches all the way up, and draws, through the spine, all the way down, that is the one who is the Duchra to the Esrog's Nukva. Hence, Chazal tell us (*Menachos*, 27a) that, among the Four Minim, only the Lulav and Esrog bear fruit. The Lulav comes from a date palm tree, a Tree that yields fruit, and the Esrog itself is a fruit. In other words, the Lulav is the tree that bears the fruit, the masculine that is unified with the feminine. Whereas the Hadasim and Aravos, corresponding to the inner, hidden letters in the Name of Hashem, the Nistaros/hidden, are somewhat transcendent, and thus, do not bear fruit. Although, technically, there are 'fruits' that grow on a *Hadasim* / myrtle branch, these are not considered full fruit, and thus their blessing is SheHakol, and not *Pri haEitz* / fruit from the tree: *Shibolei haLeket*, 160. *Shulchan Aruch*, Orach Chayim, 203:5 *Kaf haChayim*, ad loc: וכיון בני אסא אע"ג דבשלן והויין כפירות אינו מברך אלא שהכל) דאמרינן אינם עושים פירות הדס וערבה אינם עושים פירות שמע מינה דפירות בני אסא לאו פירות נינהו). It should be pointed out that a Lulav is Kosher even if it comes from a palm tree that does not yield fruit (as there are 'male' and 'female' trees, Rashi, *Pesachim*, 56a), since, it can be grafted with a palm tree that yields fruit. *Chazon Ish*, Kelayim, 2:18. Although, see *Chasam Sofer*, Sukkah, 34b.

More particularly, according to the Arizal, the Sefirah of Malchus referred to is the Malchus or 'crown' (*Ateres*) of Yesod; and they are two parts of a unified process. This is why the Torah calls the Esrog "the beautiful fruit of the *tree*" (Vayikra, 23:40), and not just the 'beautiful fruit'. And moreover, "the beautiful fruit of the *tree*" means, "a tree in which the taste of the tree (trunk) and the taste of the fruit are alike" (*Sukkah*, 35a), since the "tree" is Yesod, and the "fruit" is the Malchus of Yesod. It is the fruit (Malchus) of the Tree (Yesod) itself, and not a separate Malchus.* When we bring the Lulav and Esrog together in our hands, we are demonstrating and unifying Yesod with Malchus. We are joining the 'masculine' transcendence (Kudsha B'rich Hu), the deeper reality of '*Geulah* / redemption', with the 'feminine' immanence (Shechinah), the current and yet unredeemed state of the world.

SPECIES	LETTER OF DIVINE NAME	SEFIRAH / DIVINE ATTRIBUTE
Hadasim	Yud	Chesed / Gevurah / Tiferes
Aravos	Hei	Netzach / Hod
Lulav	Vav	Yesod
Esrog	Hei	Malchus of Yesod

These Four Minim correspond and embody the four letters of Name of Hashem, as mentioned. The Four letter Name is what channels Divine Infinite Light from total abstraction into our manifest word, from the point — miniscule space, beyond the Yud, and even beyond that as well, beyond all form, into the world of time and space. The movement and flow is from the tiny Yud into the horizontal and vertical expansive final Hei, and this material world. As such, we perform the Mitzvah by drawing together all the Four Minim, so that the Four Letters should be in a state of unity and so that we can draw down *Shefa* / Divine flow and blessings, from the Ultimate State of Unity Above into our (now) unified reality.

A very interesting source for the practice of holding all four Minim together while performing the *Na'anuim* / waving is from a dream of the Rikanti (*Rikanti*, Vayikra, 23:40. The Beis Yoseph quotes this dream as the source of the law, *Orach Chayim*, 651. Quoted also by the *Taz*, ibid.).

Rebbe Menachem Rikanti (1223-1290) an intellectual student of the Ramban, and a great Italian Mekubal and Posek, writes, "We need to place the Esrog with the other species (the Lulav, Hadasim and Aravos), not to separate them from the whole structure. This secret was revealed to me in a dream, on the eve of the first day of Sukkos as a pious man from Germany by the name of Rebbe Yitzchak stayed in my home. I saw in my dream that he was writing the Four-letter Name of Hashem but he was separating the final letter Hei from the first three letters. I asked him, 'What is this?' And he replied, 'This is what we do where I come from.' I rebuked him, and I proceeded to write the whole Name. Indeed, I was dumbfounded by what I saw, and did not understand. The next day, at the time of reciting the blessing on the Four Minim and waving them, I saw that he only shook the Lulav (and the Hadasim and Aravos attached to the Lulav) without the Esrog. And now I understand my dream" (צריך לסמוך האתרוג עם שאר המינים) שלא להפרידם מן הבניין, וסוד זה נגלה אלי בחלום בליל יום טוב הראשון של חג סוכות בהתאכסן אצלי חסיד אחד אשכנזי שמו ר' יצחק, ראיתי בחלום שהיה השם ביוד הא, והיה מרחיק ההא האחרונה מן הג' אותיות הראשונות ואמרתי לו: מה זה עשית. והשיב: כך נוהגים במקומנו, ואני מחויב בו, וכתבתי אותו שלם, ואשתוממם על המראה, ואין מבין. למחר בעת נטילת הלולב ראיתי שלא היה מנענע רק הלולב ומיניו בלתי אתרוג והבנתי פתרון חלומי. In this version of the story, the Esrog is the letter Hei in the Name of Hashem. The Maharil brings down the same story, but in the Maharil's version, the Esrog is the letter Yud: *Maharil*, Hilchos Lulav. According to the Arizal, the Esrog indeed corresponds to the letter Hei. Regarding the Esrog and the letter Yud see also *Ideres Eliyahu*, Emor, 23:40. *Nachalas Dovid, Derashos*, Derush 1).

This unifying act between Yesod and Malchus, *Duchra* / masculine and *Nukva* / feminine is connected with the teachings, earlier explored where the Lulav parallels the spine within the body, and is connected with the upright and lined-shaped letter Vav (ו), whereas the Esrog, Malchus, symbolizes Kneses Yisrael and is connected with the more shapely and vessel-like letter Hei (ה). And the dream indicated that these four need to be unified, as the Name of Hashem.[*]

---

[*] The question then becomes, if the point is for the Four Minim to be in unity, as in the Name of Hashem, then why not tie the Esrog together with the other three, which are bound together? The Gemara says that we do not tie the Esrog with the Lulav because of how the Pasuk is phrased — יכול יהא אתרוג עמהן באגודה אחת אמרת, וכי נאמר פרי עץ הדר וכפת תמרים והלא לא נאמר אלא כפת / "I might have thought that the Esrog should be bound with the other three species in one bundle. However, you could say, 'Does it say: The fruit of a beautiful tree — Esrog *and* branches of a date palm, the Lulav?' Doesn't it say only "branches of a date palm," without a conjunction?": *Sukkah*, 34b. *Sifra*, Emor, 16:7. This just tells us that it does not need to be tied together,b

the question posed is why not? What is the deeper reason?

Furthermore, not only are they not to be bound together, but they are not to be held in the same hand, rather, the Lulav in the right hand and the Esrog in the left hand, as the Gemara tells us לולב בימין ואתרוג בשמאל / "Lulav in the right hand and the Esrog in the left": *Sukkah*, 37b. *Shulchan Aruch*, Orach Chayim, 651:2. The word Lulav with the 4 letters is numerically 72, as the word Chesed (which is the right hand, *Tikkunei Zohar*, 17), and the Esrog, corresponding to the heart, on the left side, needs to be held in the left hand: *Zohar* 3, p. 256a. In fact, there is an opinion in the Rishonim that if you lift all Four Minim in one hand, you have not fulfilled your obligation: *Beis Yoseph*, Orach Chayim, 651, *Mishnah Berurah*, ibid., 15. Even when circling the Bimah when saying Hoshanos, one needs to be careful to hold the Lulav in the right hand, and the Esrog in the left: *Magen Avraham*, ibid., 6. Alter Rebbe, *Shulchan Aruch*, ibid., 13. *Chayim uV'rachah*, Os 186. *Elef haMegen*, 660:5. The Brisker Rav was also very careful about holding the Esrog in his left hand.

The Maggid of the Beis Yoseph asks this question — why the Esrog and the Lulav-bundle need to be separated, not tied together, and even held in the opposite hands: *Maggid Meisharim*, Emor, 29. See also *Yahel Ohr*, Likutim, Shemos, towards the end. In brief, the purpose of the days of Rosh Hashanah, Yom Kippur and Sukkos, is to create a deeper relationship between ourselves (Malchus) and HaKadosh Baruch Hu (Zeir Anpin, and beyond) in a posture of *Panim el Panim* / face-to-face. In order for this relationship to be genuinely conscious and close, it cannot be considered permanent or 'set in stone', since that would soon become a stagnant, unconscious back-to-back relationship. Rather, we need to choose and re-choose each day to become close. For this reason, the Esrog may not be tied to the Lulav; every day of Sukkos, we need to choose anew to draw the Esrog (Malchus) close to the Lulav (Zeir Anpin), so that they will be authentically Panim el Panim. Here are the words of the Maggid Meisharim: והא איכא למבעי כיון דכל מאי דאזלי בעלמא לאו איהו אלא איהו כדי לייחד ת"ת במלכות א"כ אמאי לא אגדינן לאתרוג עם ג' מינים וי"ל דהאי איהו ברזא דדו פרצופי נבראו ובתר הכי נסרה והעמידה כנגדו כי היכי דתתנהיר מיניה מה דלא הות מנהרא הכי מקדמ' דנא והכא נמי אי הוה אגדינן לאתרוג עם שאר מיניה לא הות מנהרא מיניה ולהכי לא אגדינן אלא מוקמינן.

The theme of the month is Binyan haMalchus. This refers to Hashem as a *Melech* / king rather than a *Moshel* / dictator. The former is a face-to-

The spine is also associated with the masculine power to procreate, drawing life-force from the mind into the lower parts of the body, and the ability to give seed (Tosefos, *Niddah*, 14a: עוד שמעתי כששוכב אפרקיד מתחמם השדרה ומחמת זה יתקשה האבר ויבא לידי קרי / "I also heard, that when a man lies on his back, the spine heats up, and because of that there can be a release of seed." See also Rashi, *Chulin*, 45b: תולדות האיש מן המוח היא באה שגיד הנשה של ירך וגיד הגוייה כולן מחוברין לחוט השדרה שהוא מתפצל ויוצא מתחת השדרה ונעשה גיד). The Arizal explains (*Pri Eitz Chayim*, Sha'ar haLulav, 3) that the Lulav is the spine and the letter Vav. Just as the spine connects to the head, the Lulav connects to the metaphysical 'location' of *Da'as* / knowledge or awareness, the 'middle column' of intellect in the mind. The seat of Da'as in a man's brain is the source of his *Zera* / seminal fluid (אין קישוי אלא לדעת / masculine intimacy is only possible with Da'as": *Yevamos*, 53b). By shaking and waving the Lulav and holding it close to the Esrog, we arouse the Divine 'seed' as it exists in the cosmic Da'as within the 'mind' of the Divine Masculine Attribute.

---

face relationship and the latter is a back-to-back relationship. There is no king without a people; not that it is necessarily a democracy, but there's an acceptance by the people, implying some form of choice, which implies some form of independence. A truly intimate relationship between people also requires freedom of choice, mutual acceptance, and a sense of two individuals coming together consciously. If the Esrog (Klal Yisrael) were to be bound to the other three Minim (HaKadosh Baruch Hu), it would be a blind 'fusion' without acceptance, individuality, or consciousness. This would evoke Hashem as a dictator and not a king, Chas v'Shalom. Throughout Tishrei, we are praying and intending to accept Hashem as our King — to have a conscious, intimate relationship with Him and to unify with Him out of our own free choice and individual agency. This is why we must draw the Esrog to the Lulav bundle each day anew.

From there, we draw it down the spine, until this spiritual Zera can be implanted in Malchus, the Divine Feminine Attribute. When we have facilitated this process, we will receive a 'birth' of blessings and abundance in our material and physical world.

SEVEN ITEMS & THE SEVEN SUPERNAL GUESTS

The three Hadasim, two Aravos, one Lulav, and one Esrog add up to seven items. The number seven corresponds to the seven days of Sukkos and the seven Ushpizin or spiritual 'guests' who visit our Sukkah over the course of the seven days Sukkos. The '*Ushpizin* / guests' who visit our Sukkah during Sukkos are Avraham, Yitzchak, Yaakov, Moshe, Aharon, Yoseph, and Dovid. These Ushpizin also correspond to the seven emotional *Sefiros* / Divine attributes or prisms through which the Infinite Light of the Creator is revealed in Creation. The three Hadasim correspond to the three *Avos* / Patriarchs, Avraham, Yitzchak, and Yaakov, who embody the qualities of Chesed, Gevurah, and Tiferes respectively. Avraham is Chesed, unlimited kindness and giving, Yitzchak is Gevurah, intense discipline and introversion, and Yaakov is Tiferes, blending 'giving' with balanced discipline (Hadasim correspond to the eyes, as explored earlier, and the Avos are the עיני העדה / 'eyes of our nation': *Pri Eitz Chayim*, Lulav, 3. The leaves of Hadasim grow in bunches of three. These are two eyes, and the third eye, rooted in Keser, called the 'open eye'. Note that the Medrash equates the Four Minim with the Avos and Yoseph, and the Four *Imahos* / Matriarchs: *Medrash Rabbah*, Vayikra, 30:10).

The two Aravos correspond to Moshe and Aharon, the greatest of all prophets and his spokesman, and prophecy is rooted in their respective Sefiros, Netzach and Hod. A prophet is someone who is a speaker, the voice of Hashem in this world (Rashi, *Shemos*, 7:1), and Aravos are connected with the lips (Arizal, *Sha'ar haPesukim*, Shemuel 5. *Rabbeinu Bachya*, Vayikra, 23:40: וערבי נחל הנצח וההוד הנקראים למודי ה' וערבה דומה לשפתים, שכן הנביאים כלם מקבלים הנבואה משם. Netzach and Hod are the source of Nevuah: *Zohar* 1, p. 183a. *Pardes Rimonim*, Sha'ar 23:14. See also *Tanya*, Igeres haKodesh, 19. Additionally, open lips represent speech, and closed lips silence. Moshe, who becomes the great speaker (healed of his speech impediment: *Medrash Rabba*, Devarim, 1. *Zohar* 2, 25a. *Agra d'Pirka*, 166) and verbally communicates the entire Torah to Klal Yisrael, is a person of open lips. Aharon, who practices silence (*Vayikra*, 10:3), is a person of closed lips, silence: *Sefas Emes*, Sukkos, 5654. Note the Medrash, *Pesikta d'Rebbe Kahana*, that equates the Esrog with Doniel, a type of prophet, and the other three last prophets, Chananya, Mishael, and Azarya: *Rabbeinu Manoach* on the Rambam, *Hilchos Lulav*, 7:6).

The Lulav corresponds to Yoseph, who embodies the focused energetic expression of Yesod. Yesod brings correction, balance, unification, and alignment to all the other Sefiros. Indeed, Yoseph brought correction and unity between his brothers, as well as between his brothers and his father, and he orchestrated a re-alignment of all the citizens of Egypt.

The Esrog corresponds to Dovid haMelech, Dovid the King, the expression of Malchus in this world (כיון שנמשח דוד זכה / בכתר מלכות. והרי המלכות לו ולבניו הזכרים עד עולם...לא תכרת המלוכה מזרע דוד לעולם "Once Dovid was anointed king, he acquired the crown of kingship. After-

wards, the kingship belonged to him and to his male descendents forever...
The monarchy would never be taken from the descendents of Dovid forever":
Rambam, *Hilchos Melachim,* 1:7). Malchus is feminine, the 'receiver'. For example, Dovid, who was originally apportioned only three hours to live, received a gift of seventy years of life from Adam (*Yalkut Shimoni*, Bereishis, Chapter 5, Remez 41).

Species	*Ushpizin* (the Seven Shepherds)	*Sefiros*
3 *Hadasim*	Avraham / Yitzchak / Yaakov	*Chesed / Gevurah / Tiferes*
2 *Aravos*	Moshe / Aaron	*Netzach / Hod*
1 *Lulav*	Yoseph	*Yesod*
1 *Esrog*	Dovid	*Malchus*

When we bring together the Lulav, Aravos, Hadasim, and the Esrog, we facilitate the alignment and joining of all these divergent energies.

SOD SHE-BESOD, SECRET WITHIN THE SECRET INTERPRETATION

The fifth level of interpretation of Torah, corresponding to the fifth level of soul, Yechidah, is the teaching of Chasidus. This is also called the *Razin deRazin* / Secret of the Secret (Mitteler Rebbe, *Imrei Binah,* Sha'ar Kerias Shema, 54), the place where the highest level of reality permeates and is revealed within the lowest level of realities.

In this way, Chasidus reveals how the highest and the lowest levels are intricately connected. And as such, the 'secret within the secret' is that there is 'no' secret. In the words of Rebbe Chayim Vital, "The *Peshat* / 'literal interpretation of Torah', and the Sod are one" (*P'si'osav Shel Avraham Avinu*, Os 62). Indeed, a true Peshat needs to be in total alignment with the ultimate Sod (Gra, *Even Sheleimah*, 8:21). As a student of the Baal Shem Tov puts it, כי באמת הפשוט והפנימיות הן בדרך א' / "For in truth, the simple and the innermost (meanings) are consistent" (*Me'or Einayim*, Shelach). The *Omek* / 'depth' of the Peshat is the Omek of the Sod.

From this perspective, not only are we creating a Yichud or 'unification' in the cosmic world by binding and taking the Lulav together with the Esrog, joining the Name of Hashem and thus affecting unity in all worlds, but on the Peshat and revealed level of existence, each of these four physical plants are already expressing profound unity within themselves (Alter Rebbe, *Sefer haMa'amarim*, 5568, p. 447. *Siddur*, Sha'ar haLulav, 264:4. Rebbe Maharash, *Hemshech V'Kacha*, 5637, 87. See the Rebbe, *Likutei Sichos*, 19, p. 358 at great length. *Likutei Sichos*, 29, Hoshana Rabbah).

Sukkos is called in the Torah חג האסיף / *Chag haAsif* / 'the holy day of ingathering', when, agriculturally speaking, the harvest is gathered and hence, it is a time when we gather together the Four Minim, which grow in four different climates. On a deeper level, not only do we enact a unification by gathering them together, but the fruit and branches themselves express unity.

The Lulav is a frond of palm leaves before they have opened out. *Lulav* is the Talmudic name, but the Torah itself calls the Lulav כפת תמרים / *Kapos Temarim*. תמרים / *Temarim* means 'palm leaves', and כפת / *Kapos* means 'bound together'. When we look at a Lulav, we see that under certain conditions it spreads open and divides into many leaves, but now it is in a unified state. The middle leaf of the Lulav, called the *Teyomes*, is a double leaf (like *Teom*, the word for 'twin' in the Torah), that needs to be attached as one in order for the Lulav to be a Kosher Lulav.

The Torah says that on Sukkos we should take a פרי עץ הדר / *Pri Eitz Hadar*, literally, a 'beautiful fruit of the tree' (*Vayikra*, 23:40). Our Sages say the word הדר / *Hadar* alludes to the fact that this fruit is שדר באילנו משנה לשנה / *sheDar b'Ilano miShanah l'Shanah* / "lives on its tree all year round" (*Sukkah*, 35a). The nature of the Esrog is to grow year round, which is very unusual for fruit, which for the most part is seasonal.* *Shanah* / year, comes from the word *Shinui* / change. A year is a full cycle of

---

* For this reason, generally, the principle regarding tithing is that אילן בתר חנטה / the tithing year of a tree follows the time of the formation of its fruit (as it grows from the rainy season), whereas the tithing of ירק בתר לקיטה / vegetables follows the time of their picking (as they grow as well from being watered). Yet, an Esrog, according to Rabban Gamliel, is similar to a vegetable regarding tithing, since it too grows with watering — דרכו לינדל על כל מים: Rashi, *Rosh Hashanah*, 14b. Note that water is called Hydor in Greek, very similar to the word Hadar. See, *Menachot*, 34b.

changing seasons. By growing all year round, the Esrog not only defies the changes, but more deeply, it grows throughout them all, drawing from all seasons and unifying all aspects of the year into one beautiful fruit.

Proper Hadasim have three leaves arranged in tiers of three. That is, there are three leaf clusters emanating out of the branch at the same level on the branch. This is another clear visual demonstration of the idea of unity. 'One' is a singularity, 'two' alludes to division and separation, and 'three' alludes to the possibility of unity.

Aravos grow in tight, unified clusters, which indicates that they may be used as part of the Four Minim. In a manner of speaking, Aravos grow like 'brothers', and 'brothers' is in fact their name in Talmudic terminology (*Shabbos*, 20a: מאי אח אמר רב אחוונא / "What does the word 'brother' refer to? Rav says it refers to a willow branch"). Parenthetically, the word *Aravos* has the same root as the word *Areiv* / 'blended together', another mode of unification.

Again, even on the surface of their appearance, all these four types reflect and embody a quality of unity, holding within them the 'secret' of unification.

Hashem Echad, Hashem is One, and the 'further' Creation is from the Creator, as it were, the more it moves away from unity into the realm of multiplicity and division. Yet, these Four

Minim express unity within their unique physical appearances and growth processes. This represents the deepest level of Divine Oneness: the Essential Unity that is not diminished by multiplicity.

Moreover, unlike all other natural forms of life and growth, which are under the influence of particular *Mazal* / angelic forces serving as conduits of the Infinite Creative force to create and enliven that particular form of life, these Four Minim are under the direct influence of HaKadosh Baruch Hu (*Tur Berekes* by Rebbe Chayim Cohen, a primary student of Rebbe Chayim Vital, Hilchos Sukkah, 651:2. *Seder haYom*, Seder Chag Sukkos. *Ohr haChamah*, Noach, 63b. *Megaleh Amukos*, Sukkos, U'lekachtem. *Bnei Yissaschar*, Tishrei, 10:24. כתבו בקבל" שעל אותן הד' מינים אין שולט עליהם שום שר (שיאמר לו גדל כנ"ל) כדרך שאר המינים רק הם גדלים בהשגחתו ית"ש: *Sha'ar Yissachar*, Ma'amar Mani Karva. See also *Rosh Dovid* (Chida), Parshas Emor, in the name of the *Toras Chacham*). As mentioned, the Four Minim embody the Name of Hashem, and so "The Esrog is *HaKadosh Baruch Hu* / the Holy One...the *Hadasim* are HaKadosh Baruch Hu...the Lulav is HaKadosh Baruch Hu...the Aravos are HaKadosh Baruch Hu."

As all of the Four Minim are direct conduits of the Presence of HaKadosh Baruch Hu, the Ultimate Unity, *Achdus haPashut* / Simple Oneness, Chazal tell us that they *are* (in a manner of speaking) HaKadosh Baruch Hu. For this reason, their natural processes of growth and development express unity, and even before being held together, they already embody Divine-like essential unity.

A COMBINED MAP OF THE *FOUR SPECIES*

	Esrog	*Lulav*	*Hadasim*	*Aravos*
Form of Benefit	Transparency	Satisfaction	Beauty	Utility
Area of Human Transfor-mation	Internal and External	Internal	External	Untransformed
Body	Heart	Spine	Eyes	Lips
Letter of the Divine Name	Hei	Vav	Yud	Hei
Sefirah	Malchus	Yesod	Chesed/Gevurah/ Tiferes	Netzach/Hod
Ushpiz / **Guest**	Dovid	Yoseph	Avraham/Yitzchak/ Yaakov	Moshe/Aaron

Chapter 2
UNITY IN MOTION:
INTENTION OF THE
NA'ANUIM / WAVINGS

I N ADDITION TO ALL THE ABOVE IMAGERY AND SYMBOLISM OF THE FOUR MINIM, THERE IS AN IDEA THAT THEY REP-RESENT WEAPONS OF BATTLE. The Lulav, in particular, is shaped as an upright sword or spear.

Our Sages tell us that once we pass through the period of judgment spanning Rosh Hashanah and Yom Kippur, on our mission to make truth and justice to prevail over falsehood and idolatry in this world, we proudly parade with our upright Lulav, showing everyone that we have been victorious in judgment (טלו לולביכם בידכם, שידעו הכל שאתם זכיתם בדין: *Tanchuma* Emor, 18. Other sources speak of both the Lulav and Esrog as demonstrating victory — אלא

במה שישראל יוצאין מלפני הקדוש ברוך הוא ולולביהן ואתרוגיהן בידן, אנו יודעין דישראל אינון נצוחיא: *Medrash Rabbah*, Vayikra, 30. *Yalkut Shimoni*, Vayikra, 651. *Medrash Tehillim*, 17. See also *Ha'amek Davar*, Vayikra, 23:43. Indeed, the reason we wave the Lulav during Hallel, where we express gratitude and thanksgiving, is as Tosefos explains, מנענעים משום דכתיב אז ירננו עצי היער מלפני ה' כי בא לשפוט את הארץ וכתיב בתריה הודו לה' כי טוב כי לעולם חסדו וכתיב נמי בתריה ואמרו הושיענו אלהי ישענו הושיעה נא ה'. / והיינו ירננו שמנענעים את הלולב ומשבחין בהודו ובאנא ה'. "And one waves the Lulav, since it says, 'Then all the trees of the forest will shout from joy in front of Hashem, who has come to dispense judgment upon the Land,' and then afterwards it says, 'Praise Hashem who is good, for His goodness is eternal' and then afterwards it says, 'You shall say, save us Hashem, our Salvation.' All of this means that we shall shout, wave the Lulav, and sing Hashem's praise, when expressing *Hodu* / thanksgiving and when crying out, 'Please, Hashem, save us'": Tosefos, *Sukkah*, 37b. In this way, the waving is connected with (positive) judgment. We are performing the Na'anuim, showing how the world is 'dancing' when Hashem is judging the world: See also *Aruch haShulchan*, Orach Chayim, 651:21).

In fact, the Zohar calls the Four Minim מאני קרבא / 'instruments of battle' (*Tikunei Zohar*, Tikkun 13, 29a), and the Ramchal, elaborates: "By waving the Lulav, we are holding up an emblem or weapon that disquiets our (spiritual and physical) enemies" (*Derech Hashem*, 4:7. רב אחא בר יעקב ממטי ליה ומייתי ליה, אמר, דין גירא בעיניה דסטנא / "When Rav Acha bar Yaakov would wave the Lulav, he would say: 'This is an arrow in the eye of Satan'": *Sukkah*, 38a). In other words, the Four Minim can be seen as instruments of war, of cutting away all destructive forces and negativity.

In general, there seem to be two basic 'reasons' for the Four Minim. One reason is to express the Unity of Hashem which is revealed in this world in the unity among people, unity within oneself, and unity within nature.* Another reason is a more aggressive image: the Four Minim serve to eradicate negativity and evil.

Having both these images in mind will allow us to further uncover the purpose and reason for the *Na'anuim* / the waving or shaking of the Four Minim, and to understand the *Kavanos* / intentions and meanings contemplated during the Na'anuim.

THE NA'ANUIM

The Gemara (*Sukkah*, 37b), says that we should wave the Arba Minim back and forth, and up and down. Today, the custom is to wave them in the four cardinal directions, plus up and down — six directions in total.

---

* The number seven symbolizes the natural world, and Sukkos is full of references to the number seven. For example, it is celebrated during the seventh month and it has seven days of Sukkos. On the last day of Sukkos, in the times of the Beis haMikdash, the Kohanim circled the altar seven times. There are seven items united in the Arba Minim bundle: one Lulav, one Esrog, three Hadasim and two Aravos. The Medrash (*Yalkut Shimoni*) writes that there are seven Mitzvos special to Sukkos: four for the Arba Minim, and one for the Sukkah, one for the Chagigah offering, and one for the practice of Simchah. The number of bull offerings were 70. Sukkos is thus about gathering in and uniting the natural world, and also uniting nature with Hashem — we take the elements of nature, and dedicate them to Hashem, as the *Chinuch* writes.

According to the Rambam, the Na'anuim are not a 'sidebar' of the Mitzvah, but rather an essential part of "taking the Lulav" and Esrog: "Once one (merely) lifts these four types…he has fulfilled his obligation, so long as he lifts them in the manner in which they grow (i.e., upright)…. (However,) the *proper* performance of the Mitzvah is to lift the bundle of the three species in one's right hand and the Esrog in the left, and then thrust them forward, bring them back, lift them upwards, and lower them, and wave the Lulav three times in every direction" (*Hilchos Lulav*, 7:9). Thus, the *L'chatchilah* / 'a priori' fulfillment of the Mitzvah is to perform Na'anuim (See Rosh on *Sukkah*, 3:33. Ritva, Ran, and the Meiri, *Sukkah*, 37b: ולא הוצרך להזכיר במשנה שבשעת הברכה צריך נענוע שקל וחומר הוא אם במקומות שבתוך ההלל צריך כל שכן בשעת הברכה שהוא עיקר. Although the Na'anuim are essential to the Mitzvah, the Rama writes that *B'dieved*, or 'after the fact', *any* form of waving is sufficient to fulfill the basic requirement of the Na'anuim — וכל הנענועים אינן מעכבין ובאיזה דרך שנענע יצא בדיעבד: *Orach Chayim*, 651:11. Tosefos, on the other hand, on *Sukkah*, 39, writes, דניענוע אינו אלא מכשירי מצוה בעלמא ולא מעכב. Although he also writes, המצוה לא נגמר עדיין לגמרי דבעי ניענוע. Note the Gemara, *Sukkah*, 42a and *Erchin*, 2b: קטן היודע לנענע חייב בלולב / "A child who knows how to 'wave' the Lulav (it does not say 'to hold the Lulav') is obligated to do so," which suggests that the Na'anuim are part of the Mitzvah. See *Chasam Sofer*, ad loc. See also *Chidushei haGriz* (Stencil), Erchin, ibid. *Likutei haGriz* 1, p. 20).

THE EFFECTS OF THE NA'ANUIM

The Gemara (*ibid.*) relates: "Rebbe Yochanan says, We wave them back and forth to (honor) Him who owns the four directions, and we wave up and down to (honor) Him who owns the Heavens and the earth. In the West (Eretz Yisrael, which is west of *Bavel* / Babylon), they learned: 'We wave them back and forth to counter harmful winds (from the four directions) and up and down to counter harmful dews.'"

These two opinions reveal a positive reason for the Na'anuim, and the negation of a negative reason. The first is to show the Oneness of Hashem which pervades all directions and dimensions — to declare Unity of the "Owner" of all creation. As the Chinuch writes, this means "remembering that Hashem is all of life." The second opinion is to 'negate negativity' by means of the Na'anuim; to nullify and destroy negative forces. This could also imply purifying the atmosphere of physical pollutants, and/or purifying the psychic and spiritual environment from negative influences.

REFINING OUR SPACE

When we shake and wave the Lulav in the six directions we are doing so within our extensive space and barometer. Our personal energy-field or 'soul' extends about six feet from our body, in every direction.* We live in our bodies, but our extend-

---

* Our Yechidah level of soul spreads out within our four Amos (approx 6 feet) around us: Mitteler Rebbe, *Imrei Binah,* Sha'ar Kerias Shema, 42. The Rebbe, Kuntres *Inyana shel Toras haChasidus*, 20. This is why של אמות ארבע / אדם קונות לו בכל מקום / "The area of four Amos around a person, his space, acquires from him any ownerless item that is resting there (which is like the power of his *Chatzer* / courtyard to do so, except even stronger — See *Beis Yoseph*, Choshen Mishpat, 268:6: פירוש דבעינן תרתי בחצר המשתמרת עומד בצד שדהו ושיאמר זכתה לי שדי. Although the Rashba writes, as quoted in *Beis Yoseph*, אבל הרשב"א חולק ואמר ה"ק מתניתין ואמר זכתה לי חצרי קנה לאו דוקא קנה דה"ה לא.

ed self, our *Ohr Makif* / surrounding light, as it were, spreads out around us, and that is our space.

For this reason, if we are open and hence susceptible to other people's negative perceptions and judgments of ourselves, and if we have spent time around such negative and pessimistic people, their energy-field can intermingle with our own and have a detrimental effect on us.

By waving the Lulav and Esrog in the six sectors of our extended field, we cleanse our immediate environment and create a protective wall around us to prevent negative forces from entering. This relates again to the earlier teaching, which equates holding up the Lulav to holding up a sword or spear, demonstrating our victory in that all negativity and harsh judgments have been cut away from our lives (Indeed, according to a Medrash, the Arba Minim correspond to the Four Exiles: Babylon, Persian, Greek, and Roman, and the victory over these four exiles: *Medrash Rabbasi*, Toldos).

Purifying and refining our six 'directions', our immediate space, our surrounding light, makes us lighter, untethering us from the gravity pull of materialism and ego, and thus creates

---

אמר כיון דעומד בצד שדהו ומשום סיפא נקטה וראייתו דכיון דארבע אמות דרבנן קונות אפילו
דהו בצד דעומד כיון דאורייתא חצרו ש"כ אמר לא :(Baba Metziya, 10a.) Not only are the objects in his four Amos his (Ramban, *Gittin*, 78a) but the actual four Amos themselves are his, as the opinion of the Ran in *Gittin*, ibid. (and seemingly, the Ritva, in his second answer): *Avnei Miluim*, Siman 30:5. *Shu'T Ri M'gash*, 106. All of the above implies that one's soul spreads out into his surrounding space.

a lightness of self, a joyfulness, and lightness of our feet, so to speak, and moves us to dance.

DANCING

Dancing, lifting the feet, is a natural expression of an elevated, refined world; defying gravity and leaping upwards. The nights of Sukkos are full of dancing, and generally, the entire joyful days of Sukkos are connected with the world of dancing.

Dancing is appropriate throughout all the days of Sukkos. As mentioned earlier, the Netziv (*Ha'amek Davar*, Devarim, 16:15) writes that since the language in the Torah regarding Sukkos is שבעת ימים תחג לה׳ / "Seven days it shall be a חג / *Chag* / festival to Hashem" (*ibid.*), he explains, לשון תחוג משמע שמחה הבאה בריקודים ומחולות / "The word *Chag* suggests a joy that comes about through dancing." In the times of the Beis haMikdash, there was a practice of Simchas Beis haShoeivah, where at night (besides the first night and the night of Shabbos), thousands of people would gather in the courtyard of the Beis haMikdash to watch as the pious and sages danced all night, accompanied by harps, lyres, cymbals, and trumpets. Today, many communities dance on these nights in the Shul or on the streets, with everyone participating in the dancing, not just the scholars and leaders. The Rebbe encouraged people to dance on each of these nights, and specifically in the streets, demonstrating that even the space outside of the *Reshus haYachid* / private domain, literally 'the Domain of the One', is also refined and elevated.

Through the Na'anuim, too, our entire personal space, and by extension, all of space itself, is refined and made lighter, nobler, and holier.

BACK AND FORTH

Essentially, the shaking and the waving of the Four Minim cleanses our space, rids it from negativity, and draws down positivity. It both counters harmful 'winds' and 'dews', and honors the One who owns the Heavens and the earth, drawing Hashem's Presence down into revelation within the 'space' of our lives.

To minimize the seeming contradiction between these two opinions, it is possible to say that the motions away from the body push negativity away from us, and the motions toward the body draw positivity and revelation of the Divine Presence toward us.* The outward movement negates the negativity of *Pirud* / duality and separation, while the inward movement affirms *Yichud* / Unity (Note *Avodas Yisrael*, Devarim, Sukkos). The act of drawing inwards brings this affirmation of Unity into your heart, internalizing and integrating Yichud into your way of seeing, feeling, and interacting with the world.

---

* The Arizal explains that through the *Holacha* / outward motion, we elevate the seven Chasadim (of the one Lulav, one Esrog, three Hadasim, and two Aravos). In this way, the five Chasadim (Chesed of Chesed, of Gevurah, of Tiferes, of Netzach, of Hod, plus the two general Chasadim) are elevated up to the Da'as within Tiferes (Zeir Anpin, which is Da'as in the Neshamah of Tiferes). And through the *Hova'ah* / inward motion, we are drawing these Chasadim into Malchus: *Sha'ar haKavanos*, Sukkos, Derush 5.

Furthermore, we bring the Arba Minim to our *Chazeh* / chest — to the same area that we tapped with our fist when we recited *Ashamnu* / the confessional prayers on Yom Kippur (*Hayom Yom,* 20th Tishrei). This act symbolizes the transformation of our heart, the seat of our subjective and ego-centric self. *Chazeh* comes from the word *Chozeh* / sees, since a person looking at himself only sees his body from the chest downwards. We draw positivity and Divine revelation into our hearts and into our *Chozeh,* into the way we choose to 'see' ourselves and the world around us.

As such, the two basic intentions are actually four. Within the intention of affirming Hashem's Unity, the outward movements push away the *Kelipah* / concealment that prevents us from being aware of Hashem's Unity in all directions, while the inward movement draws the recognition of Hashem's Unity into our lives.

Within the intention of purifying the atmosphere and its influences, the outward movement is pushing away negative influences, and the inward movement is pulling positive influences toward us.

DIRECTIONS

There are variations in the sequence of directions of the Na'anuim. The following is the Arizal's sequence. First, one waves the Arba Minim to the right, then to the left, then forward, up, down, and finally backward. The general custom of

Ashkenaz is different: forward, right, back, left, up, and down. No matter your custom, the intentions, Kavanos, and *Da'as* / conscious awareness detailed here can be integrated into your practice.

According to all customs, we begin by facing East. Each one of the six directions embodies one of the six emotional Sefiros or attributes. The right represents the quality of Chesed, giving and openness. Left is Gevurah, strength and restriction. Front is Tiferes, beauty and compassion. Back is Yesod, foundation and connectivity. Above is Netzach is victory and ambition. Below is Hod, devotion and humility. The center, being the person waving the Four Minim, is Malchus, royalty and receptiveness.[*]

South — Right — Chesed

North — Left — Gevurah

East — Front — Tiferes

Up — Netzach

Down — Hod

---

[*] The *Ben Yehoyada*, Sukkah, 37b, writes that the four directions are the four letters in the Name of Hashem. South (right, when facing east) is the letter Yud. North the upper Hei. East is the letter Vav and West is the final Hei. So when you face each direction you have in mind one of these letters. Up and Down is the Name of אהי״ה / Ehe'yeh (Binah), Up the letters י-ה / Yud-Hei, and down the letters א-ה / Aleph-Hei.

West — Back — Yesod

Center — Malchus

The seven emotional Sefiros are:

Chesed — kindness; love, openness

Gevurah — strength; inwardness, restriction

Tiferes — beauty; compassion

Netzach — victory; ambition

Hod — devotion; humility

Yesod — foundation; connectivity

Malchus — royalty; receptiveness

Chesed is the right column, giving and extending. On the left, is the restrictive column of Gevurah, strength, withholding and inwardness. Between Chesed and Gevurah is their middle column synthesis, the attribute of Tiferes, beauty and compassion. Tiferes represents giving with a sensitivity to the needs of the recipient, responding to how much the 'receiver' can and needs to receive. The latter is true compassion, which creates harmony and beauty, and it is the synthesis between unchecked giving and unchecked withholding.

The 'outer' implementing Sefiros begin on the expansive right column with the Netzach, victory and ambition. On the left column is Hod, devotion and humility. In the middle is the unifying agent, connecting the giver and the receiver — Yesod or 'foundation' and relationship.

Malchus or kingship is 'receptivity'. It is the vessel that receives from the preceding nine Sefiros.

SURROUNDING SPACE & INNER SPACE

When the six directions symbolize our 'surrounding space', our body represents our 'inner space'. The act of waving is a process of assimilating the six outer points into our inner self, or integrating the six Sefiros into Malchus.

'Surrounding space' is the idea of the *Ohr Makif* / Surrounding Light that is still beyond our immediate experience. The six-sided structure of the Sukkah also represents the Makif. Both dwelling in the Sukkah and waving the Four Minim are processes of bringing Makif down into Penimi, our inner reality. The entire festival of Sukkos helps us take all of the inspiration and commitment, and the glimpses of transcendence we have experienced on Rosh Hashanah and Yom Kippur, and bring them inside, into the tangible, practical details of life.

The S'chach is the Makif of the Sukkah, representing the 'steam' generated by our inspiration and perspiration, as it were, on Rosh Hashanah and Yom Kippur. The numerical value of the word *S'chach* is 100. The Arizal teaches that the S'chach is the Makif that we have created through the heartfelt cries that were pushed out into our environment as the 100 Shofar-blasts of Rosh Hashanah. This 'vapor' created through our exhalations and sighs in our prayers, as well as the Shofar blasts, rises up as a 'cloud' and becomes the S'chach of our Sukkah.

Similarly, as the Zohar writes and the Mitteler Rebbe explains, the S'chach is a materialization of the smoke of the *Ketores* / incense, which was burned by the *Cohen Gadol* / High Priest in the Innermost sanctuary, the Holy of Holies, on Yom Kippur (*Ateres Rosh*, Yom haKippurim, Chap 2. Tzemach Tzedek, *Ohr haTorah*, Sukkos, p. 1,722. Rebbe Maharash, *Hemshech V'Kacha*, 84). Today, when there is no actual Beis haMikdash, and no physical Cohen Gadol who is offering the Ketores, our own *Avodah* / inner work that we perform on Yom Kippur in the innermost chambers of our deepest truth and inner recesses of our soul is the service of Ketores. In the stillness and quietness of self, alone with HaKadosh Baruch Hu, and the 'smoke' or 'aroma' that we produced through our Teshuvah rises above in a transcendent column. On Sukkos, this spiritual 'aroma' descends back to us, hovering above us as our S'chach and embracing us as we enjoy food, drink, and community.

On Pesach, we perfect our 'inner space' as we clean our homes of all Chametz and then ingest the Matzah. On Sukkos, we perfect our outer space, as we 'cleanse' it with the Na'anuim, and envelop ourselves physically within the Mitzvah of Sukkah outdoors. The only other Mitzvah that we enter into physically is a *Mikvah* / ritual purification pool. Yet, when we immerse fully in a Mikvah, we are under water and must stop breathing. In that sense 'we' cease to exist in a Mikvah; it is not a place where we can live. By contrast, enveloped within the Mitzvah of Sukkah, our entire self is present. We 'live' there, fully participating in the human activities of breathing, eating, drinking, studying, conversing, and even sleeping.

Chazal tell us that with regard to the Esrog, every day of Sukkos is a separate day, since the Mitzvah of Lulav and Esrog is to be done anew each day. The Esrog thus represents Penimiyus or an inner, personal, and particular reality. With regard to dwelling in the Sukkah (since there is a Mitzvah to sit by day and by night), all of Sukkos is like "one long day" (התם, דמפסקו לילות מימים כל חד וחד יומא מצוה באפי נפשיה הוא. הכא, דלא מפסקו לילות מימים כולהו יומי כחדא יומא אריכתא דמי: *Beitzah*, 30b). The Sukkah, as a Makif, surrounds and includes all of the days of the Festival. Similarly, it symbolically surrounds all of Klal Yisrael, as "It is fitting that all of Klal Yisrael to dwell in a single Sukkah" (*Sukkah*, 27b). This is how all of Sukkos is כחדא יומא אריכתא דמי / "like one long day."

The Sukkah is our 'surrounding' light and awareness of the Oneness of Hashem and everything that this awareness entails and demands. Yet, it is also a light that still needs to be drawn down further into Penimiyus and be integrated. The Four Minim are like the antennae that receive this hovering Makif light and channel it all the way down into our consciousness, our Da'as, and then into our entire being. For this reason, many have the custom to recite the blessings over the Lulav and Esrog while standing in the Sukkah, symbolically and viscerally embodying the movement from the Makif to the Penimi, drawing down the Light and awareness from abstraction into our consciousness, into our hearts, into the way we see the world, and then into our words and actions.

DRAWING DOWN CHESED, LOVING-KINDNESS

Each time we wave the Lulav in one of the six directions, we move it in that direction three times 3 x 6 = 18 (י"ח). Eighteen / ח"י / *Chai* means life, as life and aliveness are defined by movement. On every day of Sukkos, we perform the waving sequence four times in total: once before Hallel, when we recite the blessings over the Lulav, and then three times during Hallel. Therefore, every day there are 4 x 18 wavings, equaling 72, which is the numerical value of the word *Chesed* / kindness, giving and expansiveness (*Zohar* 3, Pinchas, p. 256a).

According to the Arizal, the Na'anuim draw down the *Penimim* / inner aspects of *Chasadim* / Kindness, from Tiferes* into

---

* The Chasadim Penimim of Binah are drawn down in the four days between Yom Kippur and Sukkos. The Chasadim from the Makifim of Binah are drawn down with the Sukkah itself (In general, the Clouds of Glory are connected with Chesed/Chasadim, and to Aharon, the man of Chesed: *Sha'ar haKavanos*, Derush 4. Sukkos. *Pri Eitz Chayim*, Sha'ar haSukkos, 3. דא הוא עננא דאהרן, דאקרי יומם, דכתיב, יומם יצוה ה' חסדו *Zohar* 3, 103a. 191b). More specifically, the three times the word *Sukkos* appears in the Torah is for the three Makifim: the Makif over Ze'ir Anpin (Tiferes, the masculine), the Makif over Malchus (the feminine), and the Makif (of Binah) that surrounds them both. (Tiferes is associated with the Name Hashem / 26 and Malchus with the Name Ado-noi / 65 = 91, which together equal the word *Sukkah* = 91). These three Sukkos / Makifim also correspond to the three

our entire personal space, and through it to the entire world.

The seventy-two Na'anuim also contribute to the elevation of the world. The Zohar (*Tikkunei Zohar*, Tikkun 6) writes that they correlate to the seventy-two nations of the world. While there are seventy specific nations of the world, with regard to our collective journey toward the revelation of Moshiach, there are also two dominant prototypical nations: the nation of Yishmael and the nation of Eisav (Gra, *ad loc.*). These two are now mixed into the seventy specific nations. Our Na'anuim not only channel Chasadim into the world, they also break all the *Kelipos* / concealments of the world, gradually elevating all of human consciousness until all of Creation will recognize the Oneness of Hashem.

types of clouds that appeared in the Desert. The clouds that appeared after leaving Egypt, the *Anan* / cloud at Matan Torah (*Yuma*, 4b. Matan Torah is Tiferes: *Berachos*, 58a), and the Clouds of Glory that returned through Teshuvah (Binah). Perhaps these three are also related to the three reasons why, according to the Sages, a Sukkah that is over twenty Amos high is not Kosher: *Sukkah*, 2a-b.

The Chasadim Penimim of Tiferes are drawn down via the Lulav and Esrog. The Chasadim of the Makifim of Tiferes are drawn down through the *Hakafos* / circling the Bimah (Malchus) with the Lulav and Esrog. In other words, first the *Ohr Penimi* / inner light comes down and then the *Ohr Makif* / surrounding light. In every circumstance, an Ohr Penimi comes before an Ohr Makif (in the words of the Arizal, כי לעולם אור הפנימי נכנס קודם אור המקיף). This is similar to how, when one is building a house, he first builds the dwelling and then adds a wall around the courtyard for protection. All of this is done to help build *Malchus* / the vessel — ourselves in our relationship with HaKadosh Baruch Hu — so that as Malchus we can be complete, a full Partzuf, in full relationship with Hashem: *Sha'ar haKavanos*, Derush 3, Sukkos.

Many have the custom to recite the blessing over the Lulav and Esrog specifically in the Sukkah, prior to the *Shacharis* / morning service (*Sha'ar haKavanos*, Sukkos, Derush 1: והנה טוב הוא שאחר עלות השחר שהוא כבר יום קודם שתתפלל תטול הלולב בתוך הסוכה ותברך עליו. *Pri Eitz Chayim*, Sha'ar 29:3. *Tur Barekes*, Hilchos Sukkah, 651. See also *Yesod v'Shoresh haAvodah*, Sha'ar 11:14. *Siddur Ya'avetz*, Sukkah, recording this as the custom of his father, the Chacham Tzvi. Since the Lulav draws down the *Makif* / surrounding light of the Sukkah into the *Penimi* / internal reality, it is best to recite the blessing of the Lulav in the Sukkah: Alter Rebbe, *Siddur Im Dach*, Lulav. Meor Einayim, *Likutei Torah*, Sukkos. *Bikurei Yaakov*, Orach Chayim, 642:1).

Therefore, with the four times we shake the Lulav in Hallel, plus this initial shaking, there are five sets per day. Five sets times six directions per set equals thirty, corresponding to the minimum of thirty Shofar blasts that one needs to hear on Rosh Hashanah. The Shofar blasts shatter all concealments and sources of negativity, rectifying Chesed, and bringing life to the world. With the Na'anuim, we channel this rectified Chesed all the way down into our personal space and heart.

A DEEPER CORRESPONDENCE WITH THE INNER LIGHT OF CREATION

The Rikanti notes that we wave the Lulav and Esrog in six directions for six days (the seven days of Sukkos, minus Shabbos, when we do not wave them), and 6 x 6 = 36. We also kindle thirty-six lights throughout the eight nights of Chanukah (1+2+3+4+5+6+7+8=36). This illustrates the principle that every Rabbinic holiday is rooted in a Torah Holiday, and specifically that Chanukah is rooted in Sukkos.

The House of Shammai ruled that on the first day of Chanukah, eight lights are lit, and every night that number is reduced until the last day, when one light is lit. The House of Hillel ruled the opposite: on the first night, one light is kindled and one light is added each succeeding night, until there are eight. Hillel's ruling is based on the well-known dictum that in matters of holiness, we always need to increase. One reason for the ruling of Shammai is that the candles of Chanukah correspond to the bulls that were offered in the Beis haMikdash during Sukkos, which decreased each day. On the first day of Sukkos, thirteen bulls were offered, and each subsequent day there was one less. The House of Shammai saw Chanukah as a reflection or an extension of Sukkos (*Shabbos*, 21b).*

---

* The amount of *Parim* / bulls, offered incrementally, decreased day by day, whereas the amount of *Kevasim* / sheep, offered throughout Sukkos, remained unchanged, a fixed number each day. The decrease of bulls represents the decrease of the negative nations and their powers, whereas the sheep represents Klal Yisrael, the eternal and imperishable people: Rashi, *Bamidbar*, 29:18. Rabbeinu Bachya, *Kad haKemach*, Atzeres. (It is a decrease in the negative side of the seventy nations, and simultaneously the offering brings benefit for the nations as well: *Sukkah*, 55b). In general, a *Par* / bull represents Gevurah: *Zohar* 3, p. 179a. *Par* is 280 and alludes to Gevuros: *Sha'ar haKavanos*, Rosh Hashanah, Derush 7. White sheep represent Chesed: *Zohar* 3, 302b (ולא, ולא בעזים, ולא דרמז ליה אברהם בכבשות הצאן, האי חזי ותא). On Sukkos, there is a weakening (lessening) and thus a sweetening of Gevurah through Chesed, the Chasadim that are drawn down through the Mitzvos and practices of Sukkos. There were 98 Kevasim offered across Sukkos. Rashi explains that this corresponds to the 98 'curses' which are set forth in the Book of Devarim. Through these offerings, the curses are averted. In the middle of listing 98 curses that could

The thirty-six candles of Chanukah correspond to the thirty-six hours that Adam and Eve were enveloped in the light of Gan Eden — twelve hours of Friday, plus twenty-four hours of Shabbos. Thirty-six is also the number of times that the word *Ohr* / light appears in the Torah (*Sefer Rokeach*, Chanukah). By waving our Lulav and Esrog thirty-six times, we are transforming our mundane space into sacred space, a place where the pure light of Gan Eden, also known as the *Ohr haGanuz* / Hidden Light of Oneness experienced by Tzaddikim or enlightened souls, is revealed. The Na'anuim draw down and reveal this Divine Light, shielding and protecting us from all negative influences.

The word *Lulav* / לולב spells לו לב / *Lo Lev* / 'he has a heart'. Furthermore, the word לו / *Lo* is numerically 36. Thirty-six refers to the thirty-six hidden Tzaddikim in every generation (*Sukkah*, 45b), as the Lulav is connected to the Tzadikim (*Sefer haBahir*, 101), people who 'have a heart' and show extraordinary compassion to others. The Lulav reveals the inner Light of Creation, which is the Light within each one of us, our hidden perfection, our 'inner Tzadik'. Waving the Lulav in six directions for six days allows this inner Light to be fully revealed within our hearts, and to become a source of life, compassion, blessing, and *Shefa* / flow for ourselves and others.

---

befall us if we do not listen to the word of Hashem, the Torah provides a poignant reason, and according to the Arizal, an essential reason, for these curses: "Because you did not serve Hashem, your G-d, with joy and a glad heart." As such, the greatest Tikun to undo any possibility of the curses is to serve Hashem with joy, hence, the special emphasis on joy on Sukkos.

Numerically, the word Lulav is 68, which is the same value as the word *Chayim* / life.[*] The Lulav draws down for us, and for the entire world, life force, blessings and flow for the entire coming year.

A dried out Lulav, the Mishnah says, is unfit and not Kosher to be used on Sukkos, as it lacks beauty and appeal. The Yerushalmi (*Sukkah*, 3:1) says the reason a dried out Lulav is unfit is that "The dead cannot praise You, Hashem." In other words, a desiccated Lulav is 'dead', and we need life, and therefore such a Lulav is invalid. A Lulav is an expression of life and it draws down life.[**]

---

[*] *Sefer Rokeach*, 220. See also *Pesikta d'Rebbe Kahana*, 27:2. Note *Beis Yoseph*, Orach Chayim, 651:24: יש נוהגין שעושין פארות ערבה כמנין לולב. The three other Minim are also connected to Chayim, albeit not directly. *Hadas* is numerically 69, which is *Chayim* with the *Kolel* / addition of 1 for the word itself. Aravah is 277, which is Chayim (68) four times, plus the four letters of Aravah and the Kolel. Esrog is 610, and with the Kolel of the numbers and the Kolel of Esrog, it is 612 — nine times *Chayim* equals 612: *Imrei Pinchas*, Sukkos

[**] Note the Medrash, תכתב זאת לדור אחרון אלו הדורות הללו שהן נטוין למיתה. ועם נברא יהלל י"ה שעתיד הקדוש ברוך הוא לבראתו בריה חדשה. ומה עלינו [לעשות] ליקח לולב ואתרוג לקלס להקדוש ברוך הוא / "Write it down to the last generation (at the end of exile)" — this refers to the generation that is (spiritually speaking) dead. "And a (newly) created people will praise Hashem" — this means that Hashem will create us as new. And what should we do? We take a Lulav and Esrog and praise Hashem": *Yalkut Shimoni*, Vayikra, 651. The world of transgression and deceit is a world of death and deadness — "The wicked even during life are called dead": *Berachos*, 18b. Teshuvah is an act of recreation, of new 'self' and new life. Following Yom Kippur and Teshuvah, we now enter Sukkos as a new, refreshed, alive person, open to praising Hashem, as in, "The dead cannot praise You," and we praise Hashem by holding a Lulav, a symbol of life. A similar idea is expressed by the authors of *Tosefos*. וזהו שייסד הפייט הבוראים בריאה חדשה — צריך לאמרו אחר האוחז, דמיירי

The upright Lulav, as explored earlier, represents the *Shedra* / the spine, the vertebral column, which has eighteen vertebrae (*Berachos*, 28b. Anatomically speaking, there are five lumbar, twelve thoracic, and seven cervical vertebrae; a total of 24. Perhaps Chazal only counted the five lumbar, twelve thoracic, and one for the seven cervical), eighteen being the concept of Chai, Life. The eighteen movements performed in each set of Na'anuim allude to the word *Chai* / life, drawing down life to all of existence.[*]

בדין, ולפי המדרש נראה שאין לאומרו כי אם ביום הכפורים, דכתיב בספר תהלים ועם נברא יהלל י"ה, ומסיק על מי נאמר פסוק זה...על כל דור ודור נאמר שהם מתים בכל שנה במעשיהם הרעים, והקב"ה מחיה אותם ביום הכפורים, שמוחל להם עונותיו', ובוראי' בריא' חדש', וזהו ועם נברא יהלל י"ה: *Da'as Zekeinim*, Bamidbar, 29:2.

[*] Here is what the Zohar teaches: לולב דא צדיק. דדמי לחוט השדרה, דביה ח"י חוליין, לקבל ח"י נענועין דלולב. ואינון לקבל ח"י ברכאן דצלותא. לקבל שמנה עשר אזכרות, דהבו ליי בני אלים. לקבל שמנה עשר אזכרות דקריאת שמע. ונענוע לשית סיטרין, בחושבן ו'. תלת נענועין ח"י, אינון / "Lulav is the Tzadik (the attribute of Yesod), which is similar (in shape) to the spine, which has eighteen vertebrae in order to receive the eighteen Na'anuim of the Lulav, which in turn receives the eighteen Blessings of the Amidah (the fourth part of Shacharis), in order to receive the eighteen (times that the) Name of Hashem is mentioned in Chapter 29 of *Tehilim* (recited in the second part of Shacharis, the Pesukei d'Zimra). These receive the eighteen times that the Name of Hashem appears in the *Shema* (the third part of Shacharis). In each set of Na'anuim, we shake the Lulav in six directions, three times in each direction, thus 18 times": *Zohar*, 3, p. 255b. Also, in the first part of Shacharis there are eighteen *Birchos haShachar* / morning blessings, which have eighteen mentions of the Name of Hashem (beginning with *HaNosen laSechvi Vinah...* and concluding with Birchos haTorah). As there are a total of four sets of eighteen mentions of the Name of Hashem in the Davening, we perform the Na'anuim (the 18/*Chai* movements) four times in Hallel. The four sections of Shacharis culminating in the Amidah correspond to the four ascending inner worlds. After the Amidah, the Davening descends back through the four stages to the lowest world. We thus draw down life from the highest world into the lowest world.

Tenuah / movement is life. When we take a Lulav, a conduit of life-force, and wave it in the six directions, we are drawing aliveness, the power of vitality into all dimensions of life, especially into our *Lev* / heart. With joy, we channel the transcendent Divine life-force into our innermost self, the core of our heart (Alter Rebbe, *Likutei Torah*, Sukkos, 83c).

HOW TO PERFORM THE NA'ANUIM & THE KAVANOS

If you are waving the Arba Minim for the first time on any given weekday during Sukkos, the B'rachah is recited according to the following procedure:

1. Hold the Lulav bundle in your dominant hand. Before you pick up the Esrog, recite the blessing *Al Netilas Lulav*.

2. Then pick up the Esrog in your non-dominant hand and bring it together with the Lulav bundle. The top part of the Esrog touches the bottom part of the Lulav, and one or two of your fingers that cover the Esrog cover the place where they touch.

3. If this is also the first time you have performed the Mitzvah this year, recite the *Shehechiyanu*, joyfully celebrating the opportunity to fulfill this seasonal Mitzvah

1. Stand facing East. Keep the Esrog connected to the Lulav bundle throughout the set of Na'anuim, with fingers covering the point of connection.

2. While remaining facing East, move the bundle to the right, away from your body, and gently rustle the leaves of the Lulav as your arms extend as fully as is comfortable. Then draw the bundle inward, touching your heart with another gentle rustle. Repeat this two more times, extending your hands to the right and drawing them back inward to the heart.

3. In the same manner, extend your hands three times to the left, each time drawing them back to the heart.

4. Do the same directly in front of your body, toward the East.

5. Do the same upwards, raising your hands . Depending on where you are, be careful not to damage the tip of your Lulav on the ceiling or the S'chach.

6. Do the same downwards, lowering your hands to the level of your waist. There is no need to bend your body down. The tip of the Lulav should not be pointed towards the ground, as the Lulav should be upright throughout all of the movements.

7. Do the same behind you, twice by swiveling your body around part way and extending your hands toward (but not all the way to) the west, the space behind you, while keeping your feet pointed toward the east. On the third extension, your left foot swivels, allowing you to extend

your hands directly to the west. As you rustle the leaves on this last extension, open your top fingers of the hand holding the Esrog, revealing the place where it touches the Lulav bundle. As you swivel back to face east, bring the Four Minim back to your heart consciously and deeply internalize all of the directions and their qualities and intentions within your heart.

You have completed one full set of Na'anuim, making gestures with the Four Minim in six directions, three times consecutively in each direction, each time returning them to your heart.

As mentioned, there are two basic intentions in waving the Four Minim : a) honoring or revealing Hashem's Unity in all directions, and b) eliminating negative energies and influences in all directions. The outward gestures push away and eliminate what is not good, and the inward gestures draw in and absorb what is good.

KAVANAH 1:
HASHEM'S UNITY

In this Kavanah, you are declaring that Hashem's Presence fills all directions: 'Hashem's Presence is above me, below me, to the right, to the left, before me, and behind me.' Whenever the Lulav and Esrog are drawn back inward to touch your heart, you are declaring that Hashem's Presence is also dwelling within yourself, within your heart, mind and body, faculties and potentials.

Obviously, Hashem's Oneness encompasses all directions, and it is impossible to itemize or list the directions where Omnipresence can be found. The depth in this intention, however, is to explore our own realization of Oneness. Where, within our personal attributes or Sefiros, are we not yet acknowledging or trusting Hashem's Omnipresence? With the outward movement we can contemplate our lack of Unity-consciousness in specific areas of life, and with the inward movement, we can bring into awareness a greater revelation of Unity in relation to that area.

It is helpful to accompany the movements with a silent *Tefilah* / prayer or affirmation, such as the words suggested below. As a prayer, you could say, 'Hashem, help me push aside....' As an affirmation, you could say 'I push aside....'

Facing East, breathe, and settle your mind for a moment or two.

1. RIGHT / SOUTH (*CHESED* / חסד)

Outward movement: I push aside any 'concealment' involving my lack of recognition of Hashem's Hand in all my actions.

Inward movement: I draw to myself the awareness that Hashem is One; Hashem is present within all my actions.

2. LEFT / NORTH (*GEVURAH* / גבורה OR *DIN* / דין, HARSH JUDGMENT)

Outward movement: I push aside any 'concealment' involving my lack of recognition of Hashem's Presence within my 'harsh' experiences and states of contraction.

Inward movement: I draw to myself the awareness that Hashem is One; Hashem is present even in 'harsh judgment' and states of contraction.

3. FRONT / EAST (*TIFERES* / תפארת)

Outward movement: I push aside any 'concealment' involving my subtle belief that Hashem is not present before me, compassionately guiding me, helping me move forward in life.

Inward movement: I draw to myself the awareness that Hashem is One; Hashem's compassionate guidance is in everything I experience, leading me forward.

4. UP / ABOVE (*NETZACH* / נצח)

Upward movement: I push aside any 'concealment' involving my belief that I have reached my maximum spiritual ability.

Inward movement: I draw to myself the knowledge that Hashem is One; Hashem's Presence is above, always inviting me higher and higher, and opening greater spiritual, mental, emotional, and physical levels for me in the coming year.

5. DOWN / BELOW (*HOD* / הוד)

Downward movement: I push aside any 'concealment' involving my belief that in my 'lows' I am separate from Hashem.

Inward movement: I draw to myself the knowledge that Hashem is One; Hashem's Presence is my ground, even in my lowliness and lower states.

6. BACK / WEST (*YESOD* / יסוד)

Downward movement: I push aside any 'concealment' involving my belief in the existence of accidents or random events.

Inward movement: I draw to myself the knowledge that Hashem is One; Hashem's Presence is always backing me up; Divine Guidance is behind every experience and there are no accidents, only learning opportunities.

KAVANAH 2:

PUSHING ASIDE NEGATIVITY

With this Kavanah, we wave the Four Minim in order to disperse and eliminate negative 'winds' or influences. Again, we will correlate the directions with Sefiros and different areas of spiritual development. The inward and outward movements will again give us different angles on those areas of development.

Accompany the movements with a silent Tefilah or affirmation, such as the words suggested below. As a prayer, you could say, "Hashem help me push aside..." instead of "I push aside...."

Face East, breathe, and settle your mind for a moment or two.

1. RIGHT / SOUTH (*CHESED* / חסד)

Outward movement: I push aside my negative attachments and dependencies on false love. I push aside any negative fear of love or relationship.

Inward movement: I draw to myself the traits of positive love, openness, and generosity. I draw to myself loving relationships.

2. LEFT / NORTH (*GEVURAH* / גבורה)

Outward movement: I push aside my lack of boundaries and discipline, and excessive generosity. I push aside my negative judgments, and any inability to judge properly.

Inward movement: I draw to myself healthy self-control, and the ability to judge with loving kindness rather than anger. I bring in awareness of my positive power, strength, discipline, and also strictness and restraint when appropriate.

3. FRONT / EAST (*TIFERES* / תפארת)

Outward movement: I push aside negative 'integration' — my attachment to any objects or people in my life that deplete my physical, mental, emotional, or spiritual state of being.

Inward movement: I draw to myself positive integration and harmony, allowing me to observe everything and everyone with a holistic view, and to see the bigger picture.

4. UP / ABOVE (*NETZACH* / נצח)

Upward movement: I push aside lack of confidence, low self-esteem, or confusion regarding my abilities.

Inward movement: I draw to myself healthy self-esteem and confidence, and the ability to overcome all confusion, obstacles and hardships.

5. DOWN / BELOW (*HOD* / הוד)

Downward movement: I push aside my arrogance, insincerity, and ingratitude

Inward movement: I draw to myself the traits of humility, sincerity, and humble gratitude.

6. BACK / WEST (*YESOD* / יסוד)

Downward movement: I push aside my fear of the past; I also push aside all attachment to self-centered intimacy.

Inward movement: I draw to myself a state of unity with my whole self, and self-acceptance regarding both my past and my present. I draw to myself the ability to have only positive, selfless, holy intimacy.

PART THREE:

Hoshana Rabbah

Chapter 1

THE JUDGMENT OF WATER AND OUR PHYSICAL NEEDS

SUKKOS CULMINATES ON ITS SEVENTH AND FINAL DAY, WHAT TODAY WE CALL *HOSHANA RABBAH* / (THE DAY OF) GREAT SALVATION. HOSHANA RABBAH IS A unique and special day, rich with tradition and meaning. As the seventh day of Sukkos, it holds a dual significance, both as the culmination of the joyous Sukkos festival and as a day set apart for its own unique customs and spiritual significance. One of the earliest clear sources regarding this final day of Sukkos as a unique day, and one that stands out in its solemnity and focus on prayer, is the *Tur*, written in Toledo, Spain, by Rebbe Yaakov ben Asher (the Rosh). There, it is written, "On

Hoshana Rabbah, the custom is to add in reciting chapters of Tehilim (in Shacharis) as we do on Yom Tov and recite the longer Kedushah in Musaf and add some candles as we do on Yom Kippur. Why? Because on Sukkos, there is a judgment on water, and everything follows the end (and this day is the final day of Sukkos), and all of our life is dependent on water" (*Orach Chayim*, 664:1: ביום חמישי של חול המועד שהוא הושענא רבה נוהגין שמרבין מזמורים כמו בי"ט ואומר קדושה רבה במוסף ומרבים קצת בנרות כמו בי"ה. לפי שבחג נדונין על המים והכל הולך אחר החתום וכל חיי אדם תלויין במים. The *Bi'ur haGra* writes that there is a judgment on man with the water: שאז גמר דין של האדם גם כן עם המים. A slightly earlier source for this idea is found in the *Shibolei haLeket*, where it is written, ויום ערבה הוא יום חתימת הדין כיום הכפורים כדתנן ובחג נידונין על המים שבו היו מסיימין ניסוך המים: Seder Chag haSukkos, 371).

In other words, Hoshana Rabbah is like Yom Kippur, since life is dependent on water, and today is the 'final seal' on the judgment of water.*

---

* נאמר בשני "ונסכיהם", ונאמר בששי "ונסכיה", ונאמר בשביעי "כמשפטם" הרי Chazal tell us, מ"ם יו"ד מ"ם, הרי כאן מים מכאן רמז לניסוך המים מן התורה / "It is stated on the second day (of Sukkos) that one must offer 'their' libations (ונסכיהם), and it is stated on the sixth day, '...and its' libations (ונסכיה)'. On the seventh day it is stated (that they need to offer the offerings) 'according to their laws or judgments (כמשפטם)'. (These three words in Hebrew yield, at the end of each word, 'superfluous' letters): Mem (in ונסכיהם) Yud (in ונסכיה), and Mem (in כמשפטם), and these three 'superfluous' letters spell the word מים / *Mayim* / water. Hence, this is a Torah allusion to the Mitzvah of Nisuch haMayim, the water libation during the Yom Tov of Sukkos": *Ta'anis*, 2b. Since the final letter of *Mayim* is from the Pasuk of the seventh day, it shows a connection between water and the seventh day, i.e., Hoshana Rabbah. Moreover, the final Mem in the word Mayim is from the word משפטם / *Mishpatam*, which means law and judgement, as in a Mishpat — another allusion to Hoshana Rabbah being a day of judgement and specifically regarding water. Hoshana Rabbah is also the 'final seal' of judgment in general, and in this way, it is

In an agricultural society of the pre-modern era, and in the very hot climate of Eretz Yisrael, where we lived solely off the land and our very lives were dependent on rainfall, the dread and anxiety of entering the winter mounts is much more explainable. As the time of the Divine judgment of water for the coming year is being sealed and the fall and winter are looming before us, it is natural for us to want to say a few extra chapters in Tehilim, to *Daven* / pray a bit longer and create a miniature 'Yom Kippur' for ourselves. Praying for rain, we are praying for food and survival.

Today, with abundant packaged and canned foods, and with the technical advancements in water treatment, such as converting seawater into irrigation and even drinkable water, and extracting drinking water from humid ambient air, the need for rain does not seem as absolute or pressing. While rain is of course still important, it is now not as much of a life and death issue for many people.

---

the final culmination of the series of 'High Holy Days'. The word *Hoshana* / הושענא (spelled with a final Aleph) is comprised of the words הושע נא / *Hosha* / save, *Nun Aleph* / 'the number 51'. As such, Hoshana Rabbah means the salvation that comes on the 51st day, as Hoshana Rabbah is the 51st day from the entire High Holy Day season from the first day of Elul through the 21st day of Tishrei: *Bnei Yissaschar*, Tishrei, Ma'amar 12:3. The prophet says, אריה שאג מי לא יירא / "The *Aryeh* / lion roars; who does not tremble": *Amos* 3:8. The word אריה / *Aryeh* is an acronym for **E**lul, **R**osh Hashanah, **Y**om Kippur and **H**oshana Rabbah: *Shaloh*, Maseches Rosh Hashanah, 1. Hoshana Rabbah is the culmination of the days of judgment, and hence, days of 'trembling'.

Because our world is outwardly so different than that of our ancestors, and because Klal Yisrael is spread across the globe, not only in the arid climate of Eretz Yisrael, the overwhelming dread of a rainless season is no longer as much of a driving force in our prayers and practices. How, then, do we relate to Hoshana Rabbah today? First of all, we relate to the issue of rain in a more *Penimiyus* / inner way. But what do the words חיי אדם תלויין במים / "our lives are dependent on water," mean to us, today? And consequently, why is Hoshana Rabbah still such an intense day of prayer, like a miniature Yom Kippur?

'RAIN' MEANS PHYSICALITY

Geshem / גשם / rain is related to the word *Gashmiyus* / physicality (גשם, מלשון גשמות ודבר גופני: *Rabbeinu Bachya*, Devarim, 11:17). In this way, Hoshana Rabbah is considered the final drawing down of all our physical health and wealth for the entire coming year — although the absolutely final 'decree' for Geshem and physicality is on Shemini Atzeres.

The holy days of the month of Tishrei, from Rosh Hashanah through the Ten Days of Teshuvah culminating on Yom Kippur, and Sukkos, are an intensely spiritual period. On Rosh Hashanah and Yom Kippur, we pray all day, creating vessels to receive blessings. On Hoshana Rabbah and Shemini Atzeres, we are drawing down and absorbing all the spiritual dividends created through our spiritual work into the physical world.

Theoretically, we should begin mentioning *Geshem* / rain in the Amidah prayer on the first day of Sukkos, but because sitting in the rain on Sukkos is a negative omen and we are exempt from sitting in a Sukkah when it is raining,* we begin to remember rain on Shemini Atzeres, the day after we are obligated in the Mitzvah of Sukkah. On Hoshana Rabba, the

---

* The Rambam begins the laws of Sukkos with an explanation of the necessary dimensions of the Sukkah. In the first chapter he writes, שעור הסכה גבהה אין פחות מעשרה טפחים ולא יתר על עשרים אמה ורחבה אין פחות משבעה טפחים על שבעה טפחים (Chapter 4, *Hilchos Shofar, Sukkah*). In the next chapter (5), the Rambam explains the qualities of the S'chach: הסכך של סכה אינו כשר מכל דבר. אין מסככין אלא בדבר שגדולו מן הארץ שנעקר מן הארץ ואינו מקבל טמאה ואין ריחו רע ואינו נושר ואינו נובל תמיד. Then, in the next chapter (6), the he begins by explaining those who are exempt from sitting in a Sukkah, such as children or those who are sick, and that מצטער פטור מן הסכה / "One who is uncomfortable is exempt from sitting in a Sukkah": קטן...נשים ועבדים וקטנים פטורים מן הסכה. שאינו צריך לאמו שהוא [כבן חמש] כבן שש חיב בסכה מדברי סופרים כדי לחנכו במצות. חולים ומשמשיהן פטורים מן הסכה...מצטער פטור מן הסכה. From there, the Rambam continues: כיצד היא מצות הישיבה בסכה. שיהיה אוכל ושותה ודר בסכה. And then, after speaking about how to celebrate in the Sukkah, he writes, ירדו גשמים הרי זה נכנס לתוך הבית / "If it rains, one enters his home" (*Hilchos Sukkah*, 6:10). Seemingly, the idea of rain is not simply a *Din* / law in מצטער / 'being uncomfortable', as then the Rambam should have brought this Din regarding rain earlier, where he speaks about מצטער / being uncomfortable. Rather, ירדו גשמים / "if it rains," one has *another* reason not to sit in the Sukkah, and that is because when it rains "there *is no* Sukkah." This is a Din regarding the *Cheftza* / object, the Sukkah itself — as opposed to the general principle of מצטער, which is a Din regarding the *Gavra* / person who is exempt from sitting in the Sukkah. In the Shulchan Aruch, as well, the Din of מצטער is in *Orach Chayim*, Siman 640. The title of the Siman 640 (and some say that the Beis Yosef himself wrote these titles, and if he himself did not write them, they were written during his lifetime and he saw them) is מי הם הפטורים מישיבת סוכה / "Those who are exempt from sitting in the Sukkah." And in this Siman (640), the Mechaber, the Beis Yosef, does not mention that if it is raining one is exempt from sitting in the Sukkah; rather, the laws regarding rain are written earlier, in Siman 639 (the laws of ירדו גשמים are in Siman, 639:5-7). This fact again stresses that discomfort and rain are two separate ideas. When it rains, it is not that we are *Patur* פטור / 'exempt' from sitting the Sukkah; rather, when it is raining there is no Din of Sukkah.

final day of Sukkos, there is a final sealing of the blessings for rain, and then, on the next day, we start mentioning rain and continue to do so for the duration of the winter rainy season.

In the Amidah, the phrase mentioning rain is משיב הרוח ומוריד הגשם / "Who 'raises' the *Ruach* / wind and 'brings down' the *Geshem* / rain." In a literal sense, רוח / *Ruach* means 'spirit' and גשם / *Geshem* means 'physicality'. On Shemini Atzeres, when the Baal Shem Tov would recite these words, he would gesture upward with his hands when saying the words משיב הרוח / 'returns the Ruach', and he would gesture downward with his hands when saying the words מוריד הגשם / 'brings down the Geshem'. In this way, he was declaring that Hashem should raise the *Ruach* / spirituality, the prayers that we Davened on Rosh Hashanah and Yom Kippur, and lift them on High. Hashem should allow these spiritual 'arrows' to penetrate Heaven and open up the Gates Above, creating portals for the downflow of physical blessings so that humanity can receive them below. The Baal Shem Tov was praying, 'Receive our *Ruchniyus* / spirituality Above, and bring *Gashmiyus* / physicality down below. Hence, the Zohar teaches that the 'final, final' sealing of the judgment of Geshem is on Shemini Atzeres (*Zohar* 1, 220a. *Sh'ar HaKavanos*, Sukkos, Derush 6. *Pri Eitz Chayim*, Sha'ar haLulav, 5. *Siddur haArizal*, Yom Shemini Atzeres, Musaf. *Imrei No'am*, Moadim, Shemini Atzeres. Although, see Mahara m'Panu, *Asarah Ma'amaros*, Ma'amar Chikur Din, 26-27, where he suggests that there is a misprint in the Zohar). This means that the final seal on physical blessings for the coming year occurs on Shemini Atzeres (*Sha'ar Yissachar*, Ma'amar Z'man Simchaseinu, 1. *Sefer Chasidim*, 453).

SPIRITUAL BLESSINGS IN PHYSICAL FORM

In truth, all material blessings are but a Divine *Shefa* / flow that materializes in the physical realm. This supernal Divine flow, movement, and bestowal, when manifest in our realm of existence, show up as health, wealth, and all forms of physical success and sustenance.

"Rebbe Eliezer says, כל העולם כולו ממימי אוקיינוס הוא שותה / 'The entire world receives water from the waters of *Okyanus* / the lower waters, i.e., the ocean.' Rebbe Yehoshua says, כל העולם כולו ממים העליונים הוא שותה / 'All the world receives water from the Upper Waters'" (*Ta'anis*, 9b. Rebbe Eliezer is connected with the world of nature, and Rebbe Yehoshua with the world of miracles; thus their argument about when the physical world was created. Rebbe Eliezer says it was in Tishrei, the month of bringing physical blessings, while Rebbe Yehoshua says it was in the month of Nisan, the month of experiencing miracles: *Rosh Hashanah*, 11a).

The Medrash says (*Bereishis Rabbah*), Rebbe Yochanan's opinion is that rain comes from 'clouds' Above, and Reish Lakish's opinion is that rain comes from 'clouds' below (Rebbe Yochanan, the Tzadik (*Reshimos*, 12, Siman 11) the 'angel' (*Shabbos*, 112b), born with natural 'beauty' (*Baba Metziya*, 84a), speaks about the Above, Reish Lakish, the transformed bandit, the Baal Teshuvah (*ibid.*), speaks of the below). The Medrash *Pirkei d'Rebbe Eliezer* reconciles these opinions: "When we do the will of Hashem, we get our rain from the Upper Waters, but when we do not do the will of Hashem, we get our rain from the Lower Waters." ('Upper Waters' represent the

Above, the *Mashpia* / Giver, the Masculine Divine attribute, and 'Lower Waters' represent the below, the *Mekabel* / Receiver, the Divine Feminine attribute — המים העליונים זכרים והתחתונים נקבות / "The Higher Waters are masculine; the Lower Waters are feminine": *Yerushalmi, Berachos*, 9:2).

On a deeper level, this means that it is all a matter of our perception, our state of consciousness and the prism through which we see the world and engage with the world around us. We do not merely receive from life, from the outside in, rather, we project from the inside out, we contextualize and create as we interact with the world around us, in this way, we choose how we see and what it means to us. With regards to rain, and the blessings of life, when we are doing the will of Hashem, living a deeper and higher existence, one in which we are in constant dialogue with HaKadosh Baruch Hu, then we see through the veneer and sense Hashem's presence in everything of life. In this context, when it is raining and the world is being blessed, we sense the Upper Waters following down into the world and into our lives. Sadly, if we live a disconnected life, detached from the Living Presence of Hashem, all we see and experience is mechanical nature, natural phenomena, and when it rains it's simply raining, the opening of the lower waters, and it is just Gashmiyus.

LITERAL BOOTHS OR CLOUDS OF GLORY: DEPENDING ON ONE'S CONSCIOUSNESS

As explored, there are differing opinions regarding whether we are sitting in a Sukkah to remind us of the physical booths that we sat in, or the Clouds of Glory that accompanied us as we left Egypt. From a deeper level of insight and understanding, these opinions are not actually in conflict. They are, rather, perceptions within different states of consciousness.

The Chasam Sofer writes, "There are those who have refined and elevated their hearts and purified their bodies and mindset during these days…. For them, the Sukkah (today) is truly the Clouds of Glory…. For others, however, who have not refined themselves…the Sukkah is a literal booth that protects them from the elements" (יש אשר זיכו לבבם וטהרו גופם ורעיונם בימי הרחמים והרצון... ואצלם סוכה הוא בחינת ענני כבוד....ויש אשר לא רחצו...ולא זיכו נפשם... ואצלם בחינת סוכות ממש להצילם מזרם וממטר: Chasam Sofer, *D'rashos*, Drasha 53).

In other words, whether you sense you are sitting in the Clouds of Glory or in a commemorative booth depends on your refinement of mind and heart. The more refined one is, the more sensitive to Divine realities one becomes, and in this case, the more one can experience the Sukkah as the Divine Clouds of Glory. Of course, the Sukkah is also a physical structure with literal walls and S'chach. The question is whether your perception ends there, or if you have a sense of its deeper reality as well. While you are conscious that you are sitting in a physical booth, can you simultaneously tune into the world of spirit and recognize the subtle embrace of the Clouds of Glory and the Presence of Hashem holding you and protecting you?

YOUR GOODNESS REFLECTED IN THE BOUNTY OF THE EARTH

This ability to tune into the world of spirit extends to all aspects of life, as well. For instance, if you are observing the rain, you might see them as the 'lower waters', a natural or mechanical phenomenon. If so, you may see your life in general as mechanical and natural. Or you might see the rain as 'upper waters', as a manifestation of a supernatural life force. Then you may see your life in general as a miraculous *Shefa* / flow of Divine blessings from the *Elokim Chayim* / Living G-d.

Throughout the year, during the Amidah prayers, there is one blessing dedicated to the requests for physical sustenance and the request for rain. In this blessing, we say, "Bestow Blessings upon us Hashem…give rain and blessings upon the land and שבענו מטובך / satiate us from Your Goodness." Although some versions of the Siddur say ושבעינו מטובה / "and satiate us from *its* goodness," meaning 'from the goodness of the Land of Israel', there is also great depth in the version that says, "satiate us from *Your* Goodness." In any case, whenever we pray for physical sustenance and abundance, we can specify that we desire to recognize the blessings as Divine Bounty and spiritual fulfillment. When the land receives rain and produces goodness, indeed it is Divine Goodness reflected in this world.

This is the depth of this day's sealing of the *Din* / judgment of water and rain. Its pertinence today is no less than that of centuries ago, for it is also a judgment of our *relationship* with the material sustenance in our lives during the coming year. Will our relationship to material sustenance be utilitarian, mechanical, and natural — or will we sense within the 'lower waters' the presence of higher 'living waters', in a conscious relationship with HaKadosh Baruch Hu, sensing His Goodness within all the blessings of life?

Chapter 2
THE NIGHT OF WHISPERS

THERE IS SOMETHING HIDDEN AND MYSTERIOUS ABOUT HOSHANA RABBAH. TODAY, WE ALL KNOW THE OPEN SECRET THAT HOSHANA RABBAH IS A DAY OF JUDGMENT and the final seal of our judgment, but this was not well known centuries ago. Those who did know of this spoke of it in secret, in whispers.

The truth that Hoshana Rabbah is a *Yom Din* / day of judgment, and indeed the *G'mar haChasimah* / final sealing of the positive decree that will unfold during the year, was only revealed in the *Sod* / secret parts of the Torah, including the Zohar and other mystical writings (*Zohar* 2, 238a. *Zohar* 3, 31b. *Sefer haManhig*, Siman, 38. Rabbeinu Bachya, *Kad haKemach*, Aravah).

HOLDING PARADOX: SERIOUSNESS WITH JOY

It seems that one reason for the historical secrecy around the nature of this day is that most people cannot bear paradoxes, or two opposite feelings simultaneously. If you would have told people that Hoshana Rabbah is an extremely serious day of judgment, calling for introspection and intense prayer for salvation, it would impede their joy of Sukkos. They would not be able to fathom how this deep seriousness and great joy could coexist.

Being joyous on Yom Tov is a Mitzvah of the Torah, and Hoshana Rabbah is part of the Yom Tov of Sukkos. For some people, if they realize that it is a day of judgment, it may cause them to lessen their joy. Only those who are privy to the inner, more mystical teachings of Torah, those who can remain steady in the existential paradox of *Yesh* / existing and *Ayin* / not existing, can hold this day's experience of joyful seriousness. Perhaps this is why the teachings of the serious nature of Hoshana Rabbah were kept hidden.

Today, however, everyone knows that Hoshana Rabbah is a day of judgment. Ever since codifiers of Halacha such as the Beis Yoseph, the Rama, and the Magen Avraham, began quoting Kabbalistic sources and customs, the inner Hoshana Rabbah became known to those who do not follow a Kabbalistic path. Furthermore, certain customs of Hoshana Rabbahwhich reveal that it is a day of judgment were recorded in the *Shulchan Aruch* / Code of Jewish Law, for all to read. Nevertheless, people today may be less spiritually sensitive than in past generations, and knowing that Hoshana Rabbah is a day of judgment does not disturb their Simchas Yom Tov. While the average person's sense of Simchas Yom Tov is probably not as strong as it was centuries ago, neither is the average person's sense of awe and dread of judgment. Either way, the secret is out.

A LIVING, ORAL, BELOW-TO-ABOVE RELATIONSHIP

Another possible reason for the omission in the Torah and the Gemara of the judgment on Hoshana Rabbah is that the concept is meant to be part of the living oral transmission. The holy days of the month of Tishrei progress linearly, and they are characterized by movement from below to Above, meaning 'human-initiated' spiritual arousal. Our Avodah on these days entails arousing ourselves to Teshuvah, making efforts to elevate our lives toward Hashem.

Rosh Hashanah is the day of our collective birthday, which awakens, from below, our sense of responsibility to attain what it means to be a human being. Yom Kippur is a day of radical Teshuvah, generating great effort and resolve to rectify our own past, and to live more consciously and virtuously in the future.

On Yom Kippur, we follow Moshe Rabbeinu's example of making whole-hearted pleas to Hashem 'Above' for forgiveness, after the sin of the Golden Calf. As a result of that Avodah, on Yom Kippur, Klal Yisrael received atonement and the second set of Luchos 'from Above', however, even these Luchos were the handiwork of Moshe, below. Both the atonement and the Luchos came down to us as a response to our Teshuvah, to our demonstrations of sincere yearning to change and become closer to the Divine King.

Sukkos celebrates the transcendent Clouds of Glory, but specifically, the Clouds that return to us, created by our Teshuvah and self-elevation. Perhaps for this reason, at the culmination of Sukkos, there is an inordinate amount of *Minhagim* / customs, which have been created through the spiritual yearning, faith, and creativity of Klal Yisrael. In fact, the holy day of Simchas Torah, the culmination of all the festivals of Tishrei, is basically a massive Minhag, and it is celebrated with numerous Minhagim. Hoshana Rabbah, too, is full of evocative Minhagim, many of which acknowledge it as a day of Din, including lighting extra candles like for Yom Kippur, staying up at night reciting Tehilim and reading the Book of Devarim,*

---

* *Sefer Devarim*, in comparison to the first four books of the Torah, is like the 'oral' Torah within Torah. See Abarbenel on *Devarim*, Hakdamah. Maharal, *Tiferes Yisrael*, 43. Hence, the recitation of Devarim on the night of Hoshana Rabbah. Additionally, Devarim is like the 'seal' *Chosam* / ending of Torah, and tonight is the night of the *Chosam* / seal, and thus we recite or read Devarim. Also, Devarim is the fifth book of the Torah, and Tehilim, as well, has five books, so we recite them to nullify the five Gevuros. *Devarim* is also called משנה תורה / *Mishneh Torah*, and *Mishneh* has the numerical

eating Kreplach as on Erev Yom Kippur (the red meat in Kreplach represents Din and is surrounded by a white dumpling, representing the *Chesed* / kindness enveloping and sweetening our Din), immersing in the Mikvah before dawn, and wearing a pure white Kittel of self-transcendence like on Yom Kippur.

By contrast, Torah Law, and even Rabbinic laws that have been written down, are of a 'top-down' paradigm; we are directed to perform certain actions, and we follow. Minhagim, by contrast, are completely 'bottom-up'; we, Klal Yisrael, initiate practices in a desire to elevate our actions and consciousness toward HaKadosh Baruch Hu. Perhaps this is the reason that the aspect of judgment on Hoshana Rabbah is not stated clearly in Torah or Gemara. It is meant to remain a living oral tradition with a sense of humanity below rising up toward Hashem. Klal Yisrael, out of fervent joy and awe, *chose* to enter a final judgment before the Beloved.

In addition to the two possible reasons above, perhaps something deeper and sweeter is transpiring within the context of the progression from a face-to-face relationship with HaKadosh Baruch Hu, to marriage, to embrace and the hug on Sukkos, to the level of *Neshikin* / kissing on Hoshana Rabbah, as will be explored.

DAY OF JUDGEMENT

Yet, although it was once a secret holiday and now the secret

value of the three possible ways the Name Ehe'yeh can be spelled out, as will be explained further on.

is kind of out, the secret, the whisper of the day is public, still, the day still retains a sense of mystery, secrecy, and intimate whispers.

Hoshana Rabbah, as mentioned, is a *Yom Din* / day of judgment; it is the day of the *G'mar haChasimah* / final sealing for the new year. Hoshana Rabbah is in fact a חותם בתוך חותם / seal within a seal; a double seal (Arizal, *Sha'ar haKavanos*, Derushei Yom haKippurim, Derush 5. There is a *Remez* / allusion in the Torah to the fact that Hoshana Rabbah — pushed forward from Shemini Atzeres, since Shemini Atzeres is Yom Tov according to the Torah and not a time to say Tehilim, and so forth — is a day of Din like Rosh Hashanah and Yom Kippur. And that is that the Korbanos of Rosh Hashanah, Yom Kippur, and Shemini Atzeres, detailed in Parshas Pinchas, are all similar, thus linking all these days of Din). The final service of Yom Kippur was an official, outer seal, but in our yearning and 'arousal from below', we initiate an additional seal upon that seal, an inner, unasked, intimate seal and bond of love.

Hoshana Rabbah is a sealed, hidden day, despite being known to everyone at this point in history. In this sense, it is a 'double seal' — its hiddenness itself is sealed from view within a veneer of being 'known'.

It should be pointed out that while the clearly revealed sources for Hoshana Rabbah as a time of Din are found in the secret, hidden writings of the Torah, the idea is also hinted at in the *Yerushalmi* / the Jerusalem Talmud. On the Pasuk אותי יום יום ידרשון / "To be sure, they seek Me day by day" (*Yeshayahu*,

58:2), says the Yerushalmi, זו תקיעה וערבה / "This is the day of Tekiah (of the Shofar, meaning Rosh Hashanah) and Aravah (meaning Hoshana Rabbah)" (*Yerushalmi, Rosh Hashanah*, 4:8). On these two days, the young and old come to Shul to pray (*Pnei Moshe*, ad loc. Additionally, since it is the day of the final judgment of water, and since we need water to survive, it is a day of our final judgment as well, as explored previously).

BEATING THE ARAVAH

One of the customs on Hoshana Rabbah is to "beat" the *Hoshanos* / a bundle of (customarily five) willow branches on the floor. The Gemara (*Sukkah*, 44b) speaks about taking a willow branch and practice *Chavit* / חביט. Rashi (*ad loc.*) says this means waving it (לשון ניענוע). Yet, the Rambam understands the word *Chavit* to mean beat on the ground or a vessel (*Hilchos Lulav*, 7:22), and that is the way it is practiced today (Note that by hitting the Aravos on the ground, the Aravos "kiss," as it were, and the lips are 'sealed'. This symbolizes the fact that Hoshana Rabbah is the 'sealing', the G'mar haChasimah for the new year. Regarding the perspective that these 'sealed lips' are those of the adversaries of Klal Yisrael, see *Shaloh*, Maseches Sukkah. *Torah Ohr*, Os 75. Also alluding to the idea of a sealed, hidden day).

What is the meaning of this custom? Beating Aravos is a Mitzvah (*Yesod*) or custom (*Minhag*) of the Prophets (*Sukkah*, 44b), and one that is done as a *Zeicher* / remembrance for how it was done in the Beis haMikdash (*Sukkah*, 44a). Perhaps it is

---

* Today we take the Aravah on Hoshana Rabbah as a *Minhag Nevi'im* / custom of the Prophets (although it is not a *Takanah* / legal injunction of the Nevi'im), and as a זכר למקדש / *Zeicher l'Mikdash* / remembrance of

connected with the blessings of rain and water on Sukkos, and particularly on Hoshana Rabbah. We take a branch of what the Torah calls *Arvei Nachal* / river willows (although, technically,

---

מצות ערבה כיצד, מקום היה למטה מירושלים, ונקרא מוצא. יורדין the Beis haMikdash.
לשם ומלקטין משם מרביות של ערבה, ובאין וזוקפין אותן בצדי המזבח, וראשיהן כפופין על גבי
המזבח. תקעו והריעו ותקעו. בכל יום מקיפין את המזבח פעם אחת, ואומרים, אנא ה' הושיעה
נא, אנא ה' הצליחה נא. רבי יהודה אומר, אני והו הושיעה נא. ואותו היום מקיפין את המזבח שבע
פעמים / "How is the Mitzvah of Aravah fulfilled? There was a place below Yerushalayim called 'Motza'. They would descend there and gather willow branches (that were over 16 feet tall) from there. And they would come and stand them upright at the sides of the *Mizbe'ach* / Altar, and the tops of the branches would be inclined over the top of the Mizbe'ach. They then sounded a Tekiah, a simple uninterrupted blast, a Teruah, a broken sound and/or a series of short staccato blasts, and finally another Tekiah. Each day they would circle the Mizbe'ach one time and say, "Hashem, please save us! Hashem, please grant us success!" Rebbe Yehuda says that they would say, "*Ani V'Hu*, please save us." And on that day (Hoshana Rabbah, the seventh day of Sukkos), they would circle the Mizbe'ach seven times" (*Mishnah, Sukkah*, 4:5) Only the Cohanim would circle the Mizbe'ach — Rashi: אינה
מצוה לכל אדם אלא כהנים המקיפין בה את המזבח. Tosefos, *Sukkah*, 43b. See also, Orach Chayim, 660:2, *Taz*. Although other sources suggest that regular Yisraelim would also circle the Mizbe'ach: *Yalkut Shimoni*, Tehilim, 26, 703. *Ohr Zarua*, 2, 315. *Sefer Yirei'im*, Siman 422. *Ravy'ah*, Cheilek Beis, Hilchos Lulav, Siman 692. This seems to be the opinion of the Rambam as well, in *Hilchos Lulav*, 7:23 בכל יום ויום היו מקיפין את המזבח בלולביהן...וביום השביעי מקיפין
את המזבח שבע פעמים. וכבר נהגו ישראל בכל המקומות ...כדרך שהיו מקיפין את המזבח זכר
למקדש). *Minchas Chinuch*, Mitzvah 324:5. *Aruch l'Ner*, Sukkah 43b. In *Shu'T Ri Migash*, Siman 43, the question was asked, how can the regular Yis-raelim enter into the place of the Mizbe'ach? And he answers that Hakafah does not mean walking around the Mizbe'ach, as we do today on Hoshana Rabbah, rather, *Hakafah* means standing: see *ibid*. (Machon Yerushalayim, 5777) notes 1-3 for various other sources and ways to understand how a regular Yisrael could in fact 'circle' the Mizbe'ach). This practice is a הלכה
למשה מסיני / a law from Moshe: *Sukkah*, 44a. Today, on Hoshana Rabbah, we circle the Bimah with Aravos, and do so seven times as was done in the Beis haMikdash, — לולב דאית ליה עיקר מן התורה בגבולין עבדינן ליה שבעה זכר למקדש.
ערבה דלית לה עיקר מן התורה בגבולין לא עבדינן שבעה זכר למקדש *ibid.*

all willows are *acceptable*) because they grow near the river and need a large amount of water to survive. When these branches are beaten, they are said to release vapor or moisture from within. This symbolizes the hopeful release of the Upper and Lower waters that the Holy One will 'squeeze out' of Heaven so that rain will 'beat down' upon the earth and irrigate crops.

Furthermore, the Arizal teaches us that the word *Aravah* / willow is numerically 277, which is the same as the word זרע / *Zera* / seed (*Pri Eitz Chayim*. The Aravah is also analogous to Yoseph, as explained earlier, and Yoseph is the attribute of Yesod and thus connected with Zera, and thus Yoseph says, הא-לכם זרע / "Here is Zera for you": *Bereishis*, 47:23. As Aravah is connected with Zera, Hoshana Rabbah is an auspicious time to pray and receive a blessing for children).

Rain is Divine 'seed', so-to-speak, which impregnates the earth and all life below. In the language of Chazal, "Rain is the husband of the earth" (*Ta'anis*, 6b). Again the beating of the Aravah is a releasing of seed, and a symbolic enactment of the drawing down of rain and blessings for the coming.

Another possible reason can be offered and that is that the Aravah, the willow branch, represents the simpleton, the non-intellectual, and maybe the 'simple' person of Emunah and *Bitachon* / faith and trust (Rebbe Rayatz, *Sefer haMa'amarim*, 5710, Yom Tov Shel Rosh Hashanah, 1). As such, we take it in our hands, and with simple-hearted Emunah and Bitachon, 'beat' the earth to open up the opaqueness of this world of constriction and concealment (The Arizal in *Sha'ar haKavanos* explains that hitting the ground is to sweeten the Divine attribute of Din: See also *Zohar* 3, 31b-32a. This is called *Hamtakas haDin* / sweetening of judgment. There are five forms of Din or Gevurah, and so we take five branches. By hitting them on a hard surface, the leaves fall off and this represents the falling away, and expiration, of all harsh judgments).

As we leave the Sukkah at the conclusion of Sukkos and enter the larger world and the coming year, our custom with the Aravos demonstrates that with Emunah and Bitachon we can 'beat' or conquer, and ultimately transform, the world.

THE STAGE OF NESHIKIN / KISSING BEFORE YICHUD / INTIMACY

Within the great context of the unfolding holidays of Tishrei, the day of Hoshana Rabbah is the day of *Neshikim* / 'kissing' before the 'full intimacy' on Shemini Atzeres.

First, we need to turn around and stand face-to-face with Hashem and choose Him.* This is the first step in our Divine 'romance'. On Rosh Hashanah, we renew our engagement with HaKadosh Baruch Hu and openly declare, 'Hashem I am Yours!' Next comes Yom Kippur, the day of our cosmic wedding. On Sukkos, we celebrate our *Sheva Berachos* / seven days

---

* To turn from a position of back-to-back to a posture of face-to-face, there first needs to be a severing of the back-to-back fusion. On Rosh Hashanah Eve, there is a cosmic Divine slumber, which allows for this great *Nesirah* / severing and separation to occur. Following that night of slumber, in the morning, we blow the Shofar. The human being blowing the Shofar represents consciously choosing to coronate haKadosh Baruch as the Master of the universe. This is the very beginning process of turning toward a chosen face-to-face relationship with our Creator.

of blessing and rejoicing with a groom and bride. On Sukkos, we experience a Divine *Chibuk* / hug, a Divine embrace, the Sukkah itself is the Divine hug. On Hoshana Rabbah, we move from Chibuk to the *Bechinah* / level of *Neshikin* / kissing. All this is a prelude to the time of *Zivug* / coupling and *Yichud* / unity, just us and Hashem alone, on Shemini Atzeres. The *Aravah* / willow branch, particularly the leaves, are shaped and reminiscent of lips. In this way, the slapping of the willows on the ground is like "kissing" the ground, and it also causes the "lips" themselves of the willow to "kiss." This is the state and level of kissing before Yichud, which eventually will give birth to the new year, and a new and deeper me.

Indeed, the vapor or water that is released through the 'kissing' of the willows is similar to the saliva that is released in the human body through Neshikin just prior to Yichud. This is one step before the release of זרע / *Zera* / seed that will impregnate the new year with potential life (*Rok* / saliva and Zera are deeply connected. Thus for the performance of the Mitzvah of Chalitzah, the woman needs to spit in order to release her bond with her husband vis-à-vis his brother, instead of marrying him and having *Zera* / offspring: Arizal, *Sefer haLikutim*, Ki Tetzei).

In Neshikin, there are already beginning stages of the flow of *Mayin Duchrin* / masculine fluids and *Mayin Nukvin* / feminine fluids. These flows eventually lead to the planting of Zera, and the birth of the coming year, with all its blessings.

HOSHANA RABBAH AS A DAY OF JUDGMENT & HIDDEN / NIGHT CLOSENESS

Leil / the night of Hoshana Rabbah is a particularly serious and somber time (*Zohar* 1, 220a. *Zohar* 2, 142b).* On this night, there is some type of sealing of a person's fate', although, of course, Teshuvah can undo all decrees. To counter this strong energy of judgment, there is a custom to recite Tehilim and read the book of Devarim through the night.

---

* There is a tradition from the Geonim that the victory in the "final battle" of Gog uMagog will be on Sukkos. והכי אמר רב האי שמעתי מפי חכמים כי תחיית המתים / עתידה להיות בניסן ונצחת גוג ומגוג בתשרי / "And this is what Rav Hai Gaon says, I heard from the Sages that the resurrection of the dead will be in Nisan, and the victory of the war of Gog uMagog will be in Tishrei": *Tur*, Orach Chayim, 490. Parenthetically, this is not a war between Gog and Magog, rather, Gog is the king of the nation or land of Magog. The Arizal reveals that the victory will be on Hoshana Rabbah: *Pri Eitz Chayim*, Sha'ar ha-Lulav, 5. *Ateres Yehoshua*, Lech Lecha. The phrase גוג ומגוג / *Gog uMagog* is numerically 70, corresponding to the 70 Nations of the world: Arizal, *Sefer haLikutim*, Yechezkel, 38. *Likutei Torah*, Shemos. Over the course of the seven days of Sukkos, as explored, we elevated the 70 Nations of the world, and thus the elevated nations of the world are connected to Sukkos, as the Pasuk says, והיה כל-הנותר מכל-הגוים הבאים על-ירושלים ועלו מדי שנה בשנה להשתחות / למלך ה' צבאות ולחג את-חג הסכות / "All who survive of all those nations that came up against Yerushalayim shall make a pilgrimage year by year to bow low to Hashem and observe the festival of Sukkos": *Zecharyah*, 14:16. Whereas the arch negative forces of Eisav and Yishmael, who are Sam-El and Nachash, will be completely eradicated — ולא-יהיה שריד לבית עשו / and there will be no one left from the house of Eisav": *Ovadyah*, 1:18. Rabbeinu Bachya, *Kad haKemach*, Aravah: וההקפה שאנו עושין בזמן הזה הוא סימן ורמז לעתיד שתפול חומת ארם ויהיו כלים ואבודים מן העולם שכן התנבא דניאל על החיה הרביעית עד די קטילת חיותא אשא. והובד גשמה ויהיבת ליקידת Similarly with Yishmael: *Zohar* 2, 32a. *Zohar* 3, Pinchas, 146b. *Tikunei Zohar*, Tikkun, 21.

As explained earlier, an outstanding peculiarity of Hoshana Rabbah is its obscurity of revealed sources. The idea of judgment on Hoshana Rabbah is clearly delineated in the Zohar and hinted at in the Yerushalmi, but why didn't Chazal, the Sages of the Gemara, clearly teach this? Why leave room for the skeptical-minded to dismiss this notion of judgment; if judgment is so integral to Hoshana Rabbah, why not state so clearly?

Because of the very nature of Neshikin, a very private and quiet act of intimacy between lover and Beloved, it thus was (and is) a 'quietly whispered,' Yom Tov. In fact, when the Aravos are kissing each other, as it were, what a person notices first is the loud noise created by the clapping and beating of the Aravos. In this way, the noise is a distraction; external noise hides the *Bechinah* / level of Neshikim, as Neshikim is done in private and hidden away from view. It is a Yom Tov that is practiced openly — however its intimacy occurs in secret, hidden from the eyes of 'outside' observers.

Our Sages speak about a quiet time late at night when couples gently whisper to each other (*Berachos*, 3a. והשוכבים יחד מספרים זה עם זה: Rashi). This time of intimate whispering is when couples can transparently and vulnerably express what is bothering them and what they really want. There is no one else around, the doors are closed, and distractions are absent. The dark of night envelops them, creating a hiding place, where they can engage in the most genuine intimate dialogue and 'pillow talk'.

When Hashem wanted to speak with Yaakov, the sun un-expectedly set before its time (*Bereishis*, 28:11, Rashi. *Chulin*, 91b). Says the Medrash, this was so that Hashem could speak with Yaakov privately. To quote: משל לאוהבו של מלך שבא אצלו לפרקים, אמר המלך כיבו את הנרות כיבו את הפנסין שאני מבקש לדבר עם אוהבי בצנעה / "This is similar to a king who is visited by his beloved occa-sionally, and so he declares, 'Extinguish the lanterns, as I wish to converse with my beloved one in hiddenness, quietly, pri-vately'" (*Medrash Rabbah*, Bereishis, 68:10. As night is a time of hidden intimacy, Hashem even reveals Himself to Bilam during the hush of the night: *Medrash Rabbah*, ibid.).

Hoshana Rabbah in general is a time of Neshikin, but the sense of deep, quiet intimacy is most vivid late at night on Hoshana Rabbah. When we are reciting Tehilim (as is the cus-tom after midnight), Hashem, our Beloved, whispers to each one of us, 'Tell Me your deepest longings, deepest hurts, de-sires, ambitions, and hopes! I'm here for you!"

In these quiet moments of intimacy, we do not need to make any formal declarations or say any scripted words or long explanations. This is a time of deep, private understanding be-tween lovers, between us and HaKadosh Baruch Hu. This is the deeper reason why 'no one knows' about this special day; it is not publicized in the Torah nor even in the Gemara, and there are no 'formal' practices, only intimate *Minhagim* / cus-toms like between loving spouses. A couple does not publicize the intimate conversations they have together. On Hoshana Rabbah night, Hashem turns to His dearest and nearest and quietly whispers, 'Tell me, what do you really, *really* want? This is just between you and Me — don't be ashamed, I love you, I am yours — you can tell Me absolutely anything.'

Rav Shlomo Kluger writes (*Koheles Yaakov*, Derush 7) that on Rosh Hashanah and Yom Kippur, we do not ask for anything personal; our requests are always in the collective, we ask for all of the *Klal* / the whole, the community at large: "Remember *us* for life," "Inscribe *us* into the Book of Life," and so forth, always in the plural. This is so we will not be, as the Zohar (*Tikkunei Zohar*, Tikkun, 7) defines, like hungry dogs who bark, '*Hav-Hav!*' *Hav* in Aramaic, the language of the Zohar, means "Give!" If we are just asking, 'Give *me* this, give *me* that,' we sound like hungry dogs barking to be fed, and so, for this reason, we pray in the plural, for the collective, not for ourselves alone. We refrain from personal requests specifically in formal Tefilah when we are praying amid a crowd within a dictated time and setting. This kind of Tefilah is generally done during the day, when everything is 'revealed'. In the privacy of late night, however, there is no law dictating formal prayer, and no one else sees and no one is listening in. HaKadosh Baruch Hu beckons us into the Divine bedchamber and asks, 'My love, don't be shy, let us be totally open with each other and share our most personal feelings. Is there anything that you haven't been able to tell Me? I want to know what you, just you, want. Put aside everyone else; is there anything that is bothering you? What are your innermost dreams? (See also *Maharsha*, Berachos, 3a, on the Gemara that speaks about the late hour in the night, very early morning, as a time when spouses speak quietly to each other, הוא רמז האשה כ"י מספרת בתפלה

לבקש כל צרכה מבעלה שהוא הקב"ה / "This alludes to ourselves, the wife, who speaks words of prayer, asking for everything she needs from her husband, who is HaKadosh Baruch Hu").

This is the night of telling our unspoken hopes, aspirations, and innermost yearnings to our Beloved. And this is why it is a night shrouded in mystery and hiddenness. Everything is kept between us and Hashem. It is a time when we can be completely vulnerable and unashamed, holding nothing back, protected in the embrace of darkness, silence, and sacred confidentiality.

Chapter 3

SEEING YOUR SHADOW:
NIGHT OF DREAMS

O NE OF THE MORE MYSTICAL AND MYSTERIOUS
PRACTICES ON THE NIGHT OF HOSHANA RABBAH
IS RELATED TO TRYING TO SEE YOUR SHADOW IN
the moonlight.* The Zohar teaches (*Zohar* 1, 220a. *Zohar* 2, 142b)

---

* The moon is connected with the judgment of water, and today is the final day of judgment, and as explored earlier, the judgment of water is the
judgment of our livelihood. The Bach writes, ויש להם סימן בצל הלבנה ונראה בעיני
דמאחר שהלבנה מניע יסוד המים על כן ניתן בכחה ענין זה / "And we have a sign in the
shadow of the moonlight. And it seems to be, since the moon cycles affect
the tides of water, 'moving the elements of water', therefore moonlight has
this power to foresee the judgment of the water for the coming year": Bach,
Orach Chayim, 664:1.

and it is brought down by many early Rishonim — even some great Rabbis who lived prior to the revelation of the Zohar in the year 1290* — that on the night of Hoshana Rabbah, a person can tell by looking at their *Tzeil* / shadow in the moonlight or lack thereof, what kind of year he is going to have and if he will live through the year. This is because the shadow of a person is connected with their life force (*Kerisus*, 5b-6a).

According to this mystical practice, seeing your shadow would be a good sign, whereas if your shadow is not visible, it would mean that parts of your soul have already departed from you, and you will not live through the year (The *Mekubalim* / Kabbalists and mystics of the Rhinelands, the *Chasidei Ashkenaz* / Pious Ones of Germany, as they are called, speak of one attempting to see the shadow of his or her head and neck, and not the whole body: Rebbe Yehudah haChasid in his book, *Sefer Gimatriyos*, 171. The *Paneach Raza* (who quotes often from the Chasidei Ashkenaz) writes the same: *ibid*. See also *Sodei Razya*, by the Rokeach, p. 106**).

---

* כי בליל החותם לא יהיה צל לראש האיש אשר ימות בשנה ההיא: Ramban, *Bamidbar*, 14:9. Rikanti, *ibid*. *Sefer Tziyoni*, ibid. *Sefer Chasidim*, 1143. *Maor v'Shemesh*, Shelach, p. 48a. *Sefer Rokeach*, 221. *Chochmas haNefesh*, p. 366. *Kol Bo*, 52. *Sefer haEmunos*, Sha'ar 6:4. Kalev and Yehoshua tell Klal Yisrael that they should not be afraid to enter Eretz Yisrael and they have nothing to worry about because סר צלם מעליהם / "their protection has departed from them," Bamidbar, *ibid*. And as the *Paneach Razah* writes, מלמד שלא ראו צל צואריהם ביום הושענא רבה / "This teaches us, that they did not see the Tzeil around their necks on the day of Hoshana Rabbah."

** Other sources speak about the shadow of one's fingers representing his or her children. The Avudaraham also brings down exactly how this practice was done, although, he writes, we should not do it — ויש אנשים שנוהגין גם בליל הושענא רבא שכורכין עצמם בסדין ויוצאין למקום שמגיע אור הלבנה ופושטין מעליהם הסדין ונשארים ערומים ופושטין איבריהם ואצבעותיהן. אם מצא צלו שלם טוב הוא, ואם יחסר

It must be stressed that the Rama, the great codifier of law, although he is one who cites this practice, writes explicitly that today we should not pay attention to these matters. Most people do not know what to look for in the Tzeil, and a mistake in the procedure could cause a person to think negative thoughts and even further worsen his *Mazal* / fortune.* Hence, he writes, it is better to be simple hearted, not trying to peer into the future, rather living in the present (כתבו הראשונים ז"ל שיש סימן בצל הלבנה בליל הו"ר מה שיקרה לו או לקרוביו באותה השנה ויש מי שכתב שאין לדקדק בזה כדי שלא ליתרע מזליה גם כי רבים אינם מבינים העניין על בוריו ויותר טוב להיות תמים ולא לחקור העתידות מכאן אני אומ' שאין ראוי לנהוג מנהג :עתידות Shulchan Aruch, *Orach Chayim*, 664:1. זה: *Avudraham*, Sukkos, Hoshana Rabbah).

THE PROGRESSION & DEVELOPMENT OF SELF THROUGH TISHREI

What does this mean? As in every teaching of *Chazal* / our Sages, there are multiple layers in this idea, including a purely literal interpretation, a symbolic code, and a mystical revelation.

צל ראשו בנפשו הוא. ואם יחסר צל אחד מאצבעות ידיו סימן לאחד מקרוביו. ויד ימין סימן לבניו הזכרים, ויד שמאל סימן לנקבות...אני אום' שאין ראוי לנהוג מנהג זה :*Avudaraham*, Sukkos, Hoshana Rabbah.

* Besides the Tzeil departing the person on the night of Hoshana Rabbah, the sources also speak about the Tzeil departing the person thirty days before a person passes on: *Zohar* 1, p. 217b. 227a. *Likutei Torah* of the Arizal, Vayechi. *Pardes Rimonim*, Sha'ar 31:4. *Chesed LeAvraham*, 5:30. *Ma'amar haNefesh*, 2:9. *Ohr Hachayim*, Bereishis, 47:29. In other words, on the night of Hoshana Rabbah, the Tzeil could leave the person, but if he is destined to pass away after thirty days, the Tzeil will return and then disappear again thirty days before his death: *Pardes Rimonim*, ibid., p. 73b — 74a. *Sha'ar haKavanos*, Sukkos, 6. *Ma'avar Yabok*, Ma'amar 2:2, p. 201.

In the context of the unfolding and progressive days of Tishrei and its Yamim Tovim, this idea of seeing our Tzeil can be understood as follows.

Tishrei's holy days follow a sequence, designed to elevate and develop us, and each day builds on the previous one. On Yom Kippur, when "the essence of the day brings atonement," a person strips himself of all attachments to the world, attachments to status, money, position, beauty, and food. We let go of our social and personal self-definitions, and our very sense of a separate identity. The five prohibitions observed on Yom Kippur correspond to the five external points of identity by which people define themselves: their job or position, their economic status, their physical appearance, their inherited status or lineage, and their power or influence. On Yom Kippur, we rest and transcend these superficial definitions, and strip ourselves of these trivial senses of self. It is a day of transcending.

This is why the Cohen Gadol would "leave his home" seven days before Yom Kippur, saying goodbye to his wife and family, and go to the Beis haMikdash to perform his Yom Kippur service (*Mishnah, Yuma,* 1:1). He would leave his conventional life and personal identity, and enter a state of holiness and detachment beyond all attachments and definitions. We too, today enter into a 'Mikvah in time' during the twenty-six hours of Yom Kippur, a time when we are divested and transcendent of all sins, negativity, and all false perceptions of self and form. However, the rest of the year, we live in a world of duality and

Tzurah / form, and we need to dwell in a context of attachment and definition, albeit always remaining somewhat aloof. Accordingly, after the radical departure of Yom Kippur, we need to return to a context of identity and conventional life. Indeed, the greatest joy is in returning to the world and re-engaging life in healthier, more uplifted, and righteous ways. This is why the Cohen Gadol would return to his home and family amid tremendous celebration (*ibid.*, 7:4).

In the process of Teshuvah and letting go, a person could lose their footing altogether; 'Who am I now, what do I need to be doing?' If you have deeply let go of everything you were in the past, you may experience an identity crisis on some level. It is good to shed your limitations on Yom Kippur, but then you need to 'return home.'

Similar to the journey of Yom Kippur is that of a true Baal Teshuvah, someone who has radically changed his or her way of living and chosen to live a life dedicated to Torah and Mitzvos. Often, when someone sheds their old way of living and consciously enters the path of Torah, they can have an identity crisis. What is needed is a safe landing and healthy integration. Human beings cannot reside under the waters of a 'Mikvah'. We need to come out of the Mikvah and build our new life on solid ground, learning to experience Hashem's embrace within the 'four walls' of the conventional, human world. This is precisely, as explored earlier, the function of Sukkos after Yom Kippur.

SUKKOS AFTER YOM KIPPUR

Sukkos follows Yom Kippur because after being 'underwater' in the 'Mikvah' of Yom Kippur, HaKadosh Baruch Hu tells us, 'I am carving out for you a safe place under the canopy of My wings. Come into My space, come be embraced in the sacred space of Sukkah — and while you're here with Me, tell Me who you want to become and how you want to develop yourself. I know you do not want to go back to your previous way of being and you want to grow; I know you want to stay unhinged from your negative patterns of the past. So come, sit under the S'chach and find your true self. Come create a vision, a healthy and wholesome *Tzurah* / form, the new person that you want to become.'

Halachically, the purity that comes from immersing in a Mikvah comes not when one is underwater, but when one is *emerging* from the Mikvah (*Kesef Mishnah* on Rambam, *Hilchos Avos haTumah*, 6:16. *Tosefos*, Shabbos, 35a. See, however, *Pri Yitzchak*, 2:35. *Avnei Neizer*, Choshen Mishpat, Siman 72. *Devar Avraham*, Hashmatos, 2:15). The true measure of a successful Yom Kippur is not found in completely letting go and disappearing on the 'mountain top,' but in returning from there with healthy definitions, dreams, visions, and ambitions. We emerge from the Mikvah's waters of Bitul, transcending desires, to cultivate wholesome yearnings and aspirations. Now, we can pursue our goals without anxiety and tension. Our desires are no longer about rising 'above' others or being more successful than others—those are still connected to negativity. Instead, our new desires and our new Tzurah align with our higher intuition of why we were created. This intuition comes to us as we descend from Yom Kippur and settle back into 'self,' sitting in the Sukkah.

ENTERING A WORLD OF ALL POSSIBLE COMBINATIONS

S'chach is numerically 100, which indicates an inner world of transcendence. S'chach represents, as explored earlier, the loftiest of all worlds, the *Olam haMalbush* / the World of 'En-clothment' or Garments. This realm is like the motherboard of all Creation, a place of unlimited potential, a world in which all potential expressions can be revealed.

Olam haMalbush is the meta-root of all possible letter combinations, which in turn is the meta-root of all manifest reality. It is the medium through which Hashem, the Infinite Formless One, creates and is manifest within the world of form through the 22 letters of the Aleph Beis. By means of these primordial sounds or vibrations, Creation emerges and becomes physically manifest. The Aleph Beis is the array of vibrational building blocks of this and all worlds. Everything is created by a combination of Divine sounds, which continue to vibrate and sustain existence and all its details. The micro- and macro-movements of every entity in the world are manifestations of corresponding spiritual movements and vibrations emanating from the stillness and Oneness of the *Ohr Ein Sof* / Infinite Light. These vibrations or letters are the very first 'movements' rippling out from within the Ohr Ein Sof.

Olam haMalbush refers more specifically to the primary letter compounds, the supernal 'sound bank' from which all sound, vibration, frequency, light, energy, and matter eventually emerge. This sound bank houses the vital potential to reveal the Infinite Light and then the finite vessel of Creation.

Sitting in a Sukkah under the S'chach (and 'the Sukkah *is* the S'chach' — על שם הסכך קרויה סוכה: Rashi, *Sukkah*, 2a), we are sitting in the World of Malbush, where we are present within a world of 'all possible combinations'. We are sitting embraced by the Infinite creativity of HaKadosh Baruch Hu, as it were, in which everything is possible. In this embrace, we are given the ability to recreate ourselves anew, to find new possibilities, and to locate ourselves in a new, healthier, holier space in this world. As such, the Sukkah is an embodiment of both what is and what could be. It is the conduit for the constantly renewed manifestation of this world and of the 'World to Come', of the present reality and of the unbounded potential of reality.

Sitting in a Sukkah, we are basking in a place of pure potential, and here, Hashem is gently saying to us, 'Let us rewrite your story; tell Me the story you want to be written about in this coming year.' This is a 'joint effort', as it were, a partnership, because we have already come through Rosh Hashanah and Yom Kippur which developed our capacity for higher personal responsibility. Hashem could be the *Moshel* / Ruler of the universe without us, but Hashem asks us to participate so that Hashem can be the *Melech* / King, as "There is no king without a people." Hashem says, 'I don't just want to 'rule' over you; I want you to be a willing participant in my *Malchus* / Kingdom and Kingship.'

Rosh Hashanah celebrates the birth of mankind. To be human is to be responsible for our lives, not living at the effect of life, as merely a creation, but rather to be the 'cause' of our life, as a co-creator of life. Coming from Yom Kippur, where we have let go of everything, un-tying ourselves from all small and negative definitions, Hashem says, 'Tell Me who you want to become — *Na'aseh Adam* / "Let Us create a human...." What are your dreams and aspirations? Let Us, together, create *you*.

TZEIL: OUR PERFECT & WHOLE SELF

Prior to our souls descending into this material world, the Creator has a 'vision' for our lives. There is a Divine plan and storyline for our lives. Hashem sees, so to speak, that your unique soul would do well, and would reach its maximum potential, living in such-and-such area in the world, born to that family, with those siblings or lack thereof. There is something wonderful and magnificent that will be realized by you, and only you, with your specific set of genetic makeup, cultural conditioning, upbringing, financial status, and so forth. This is the way we existed (and still exist) within the perfect "imagination" of the Creator. In this perfect imagination of who we eventually will become, we are essentially perfect right now. In the perfect imagination of the Creator, there is an image of us living out our deepest physical, emotional, intellectual, and spiritual potentials.

Part of this pre-existent image of self is our entire self, soul, mind, and even some form of body. Just as we possess a physical form and body, a *Guf Gass* / dense material body, we possess, in a primordial way, a *Guf Dak* / ethereal subtle body (*Avodas ha-Kodesh*, 2:26. *Nishmas Chayim*, 1:13. Note Rashi, *Niddah*, 13b. *Avodah Zarah*, 5a). This ethereal body is our perfect image, our perfect self in the form that our Creator imagined us to be, before we were physically embodied (There are numerous names for the Guf Dak, such as *Chaluka d'Rabanan* / 'garment of sages' (*Zohar* 1, p. 66a. *Sha'arei Kedushah*, 1:1), *Malbush* / garb (*Seforno*, Kavanas haTorah), and *Tzelem* / image. *Nishmas Chayim*, 1:13).

Our primordial *Tzelem* / image or *Tzeil* / shadow is our perfect self, the story of our life the way the Creator envisions it and inscribes it in the Supernal Book of Life. Our *Avodah* / mental, emotional, and spiritual work in this world is to ensure that the story that we are telling, the life we are living, the book we are writing, is consistent with our Supernal image, prototype, and root.

On the night of the Tzeil — and deeply, on every night and in every moment of life — the Creator of all Life tells us, 'Let Us, together, create the best possible you.' We all originate in the *Tzeil* / Imagination, as it were, of HaKadosh Baruch Hu, in the Divine letters vibrating out from a place of infinite Divine Unity, wholeness, love, and light. Now, living in a body and world of duality and separation, we need to create, using our own Tzeil, our imagination, a beautiful life, a life story of harmony and deep consistency with the deepest Imagination of Hashem. Sitting in the Sukkah, we need to envision our-selves living fully and with presence, in the way Hashem imag-ined we would, according to our deepest potential, truly and authentically.

Let us now delve, in greater detail, into the nature of Tzeil and its relationship to Sukkos.

PLACE OF OUR COLLECTIVE & PERSONAL IMAGINATION

Throughout Sukkos, we sit under the *Tzeil* / shadow of the S'chach. We tap into the prophetic nature of the Sukkah and who we were as a people as we left Egypt and were protected by Hashem in literal booths and in the Clouds of Glory. We sit in the צְלָא דמהימנותא / "shadow of faith and hope," where we dream, hope, and feel what it means to be collectively pro-tected and embraced by HaKadosh Baruch Hu. As the Zohar teaches on the Pasuk, בצלו חמדתי וישבתי / "I delight to sit in His shade" (*Shir haShirim*, 2:3. *Zohar*, 3, 255b) — and on the Pasuk, אשר אמרנו בצלו נחיה בגוים / "...regarding Whom we said, 'He Whose shade we would live in while among the nations'" (*Eichah*, 4:20) — we need to imagine what it is for Klal Yisrael to sit together in the 'Divine shade'. And we need to visualize how life will be when the Sukkah will rise from its 'fallen' state and we will sit in the ultimate, eternal Sukkah — the collective vision and *Tikvah* / hope of Klal Yisrael.

The collective soul of Yisrael does not cancel out our indi-vidual existence or role, rather it includes us in our individuality. Our collective vision for the future needs to include our personal vision for ourselves as well. We need to find our individual story, dreams, and hopes within the collective vision of a redeemed Klal Yisrael and world. And we need to envision our own personal development, and the realization of our personal dreams, hopes, and imaginations within the context of the grand vision of creation.

On the final night and day of Sukkos, a time when there is a heightened sense of possibility for the completion of history and the *Acharis haYamim* / End of Days (as the tradition that the 'final battle' will take place on Hoshana Rabbah, *Tur*, Orach Chayim, 490. Arizal, *Sefer haLikutim*, Yechezkel, 38. *Likutei Torah*, Shemos), which is the hope of Klal Yisrael, and by extension all of humanity. As such, we need to make sure that our own personal Tzeil is strongly and prominently noticeable. We must uncover our true essence as an individual, and recognize who we have the potential to become. It is time to start living our hidden dreams, deepest hopes, and highest aspirations and embrace the profound inner yearnings of our heart.

MORE SHADE THAN SUN

For the seven days of Sukkos, we need to sit in a Sukkah that has צלתה מרובה מחמתה / more shade than sun, and this is why the walls cannot be so high that the walls are providing all the shade, not the S'chach (*Sukkah*, 2b).

"There is nothing *new* under the sun" (*Koheles*, 1:9). The sun represents predictability, inevitability, and routine; as it rises and sets in the same way each day. In our own lives, the sun represents predictability as well, the idea that who we are in the past will inevitably predict who we will be in the future. Under a 'direct sunlight' paradigm, there is no possibility for *Chidush* / newness, imagination, or dream, so-to-speak, and one lives on autopilot. On Sukkos, we need to spend time in a space where there is more *Tzilasa* / *Tzeil* / shade than the sun.

Shade is a metaphor for our subconscious mind; our dreams, our imaginations, and even more deeply, our inner 'prophecy', meaning our deepest spiritual premonition or intuition of who we really are. This is why the word *Sukkah* comes from the *Sacha* / 'seeing', as in שסוכת ברוח הקדש / "one who sees with *Ruach haKodesh* / Divine intuition" (Rabbeinu Bachya, *Kad haKemach*, Sukkah, 1. *Bnei Yissaschar*, Tishrei, Ma'amar 10:1. וכמו שקנו ישראל מעלת השכל בחג / *haShavuos*, קנו עוד מעלה עליונה בחג הסוכות, הוא רוח הקדש השורה עליהם / "And just as when on Shavuos Klal Yisrael acquired the ability of correct intelligence, on Sukkos, we acquired something even deeper, and that is Ruach haKodesh": *Gevuros Hashem*, 46). This is also why there is the celebration of Simchas Beis haShoeivah, the Joy of the House of Drawing, on Sukkos. It is called *Beis haShoeivah* / the House of Drawing, as they 'drew' Ruach haKodesh, Divine inspiration and clarity on those nights (Yerushalmi, *Sukkah*, 5:1).

For the seven days of Sukkos, we need to sit in a place of 'more Tzeil than sunlight', a place of deep and holy imagination where we 'dwell' more in hope than in memory, more in a place of who we can become than who we have been. More in the luminous shadows of the untold future, than in the 'already told' past. We need to sit in a place of 'more possibility than inevitability'.

Generally speaking, there are two fundamental Yamim Tovim of the year: the week-long celebration of Pesach and the week-long (plus an extra day or two) celebration of Sukkos. Pesach is about memory and the past, and in a way, creating a Tikkun for the past. Sukkos, as explored from various different angles, is about the future, imagining, and dreaming of a personal and collective redemption, and hence, a Tikkun for our imaginative foresight and our future.

On Sukkos we sit in a clear, sacred space of pure potential, the world of Malbush, and intuit how we are going to live out our true potential in the world. We let go of our 'sun' reality on Yom Kippur, but we were still floating, formless and spaceless. Now we enter back into space, into the shade of a holy structure, and share 'prophetic' visions of ourselves with the Master of the Universe.

For the seven days of Sukkos, Hashem is constantly telling us, 'My Name is resting upon the Sukkah; it is My space and I am entering into it with you. Together, we can co-write your new story, but first tell Me, what would you like that story to be about?'

At the end of Sukkos, on the night of Hoshana Rabba, as the days of Tishrei are reaching their climax, the night of the צל / *Tzeil*, we need to stand in the moonlight and see if we can observe our own 'shadow' and 'check our Tzeil.' We need to check and see if, during Sukkos, we have built up our dreams and hopes for the coming year. If you can observe your shadow, your positive dream of the future, it means you are going to live that out in the coming year. If, after seven days of sitting in the World of Possibility and holy imagination, you had zero intuition of your future, and you have no dreams or aspirations, then you have no Tzeil, then you are not going to 'live' this year, then you are not going into the year fully alive as an *Adam* / human being.

Adam has the same numeric value as the word *Mah* / מה / 'what?' This means that to be an Adam, a human being, is to ask questions. *Adam* also comes from the word *Adameh* / similar (or *Adamah* / earth), related to the word *Dimyon* / imagination. We are created in the Divine imagination, in the Tzeil of Hashem, and we, in turn, create our reality through the prism of our own imagination. Hence, if we lose touch with our Dimyon and stop dreaming, longing, and yearning, if we cease asking questions and probing deeper, we cease being fully human. We have no Tzeil and we are, on one level, dead. Without dreams we are stuck.

Yet, if Tishrei has slipped by you due to any reason, it is really never too late to begin again. There are favorable moments, but no exclusive moment in which we can tell Hashem whom we want to become. Your Creator, your Co-creator, is always waiting to hear your dreams and hopes, and to begin collaborating on a new story of you.

We are not merely *Homo Sapiens*; we are more accurately *Homo Imaginus.* To be human is to dream. We feel the essence of our humanity when we put to use our ability to reimagine our lives and our entire world. May we never cease to dream.

Chapter 4
UNBINDING THE LULAV

HOSHANA RABBAH IS SATURATED WITH VARIOUS CUSTOMS, AS MENTIONED, ONE OF THEM BEING THE PARTIAL UNBINDING OF THE SPINE OF THE Lulav. On the seventh day of Sukkos, Hoshana Rabbah, the contemporary custom, although not mentioned in the Gemara / Talmud, is to untie and undo some of the ties on the Lulav itself.

Besides the ties that bind the Lulav with the Hadasim and Aravos (or where they are placed together in woven palm leaf sockets), the Lulav itself is also bound together further up on the Lulav. The Torah tells us that on Sukkos (essentially on the first day), we need to take "the product of Hadar tree, כפת תמרים / branches of palm trees" (*Vayikra*, 23:40), meaning the Lulav branch. The term כפת also means 'bound', telling us that the leaves of the palm branch should not be open, rather they should still be naturally 'bound' together in a straight line, in their 'unified' state before they open in their maturing process. As such, to ensure that the leaves of the Lulav remain closed, we bind them together (In the words of our Sages כפות תמרים, כפת אם היה פרוד יכפתנו / "(Regarding the) branches (כפת) of palm trees: כפת (means 'bound', indicating that) if the leaves of the Lulav were spread, one should bind them": *Sukkah*, 32a).

In this way, the Lulav remains tied throughout the first six days of Sukkos, but on the seventh day, on Hoshana Rabbah, we should undo (at least some of the) ties, so that it should not be completely כפות / bound together.

WHY UNTIE THE LULAV?

The great German 13th Century scholar, and codifier of law and Ashkenaz customs, Rebbe Mordechai, known simply as 'the Mordechai', brings down in the name of earlier Rishonim that in the Torah, the phrase כפת תמרים / "branches of palm trees" is missing a Vav (כפת, not כפות). Vav is the number six, hence this omission tells us that for six days the Lulav should be tightly tied together, but on the seventh day, on Hoshana Rabbah, it should be untied, at least slightly (see *Tur, Beis Yoseph*, ibid., 664. See also an earlier Ashkenaz source, *Sefer Rokeach*, Siman 220).

One simple reason for untying the Lulav is so that it can be waved more freely, which can elicit greater feelings of joy (*Levush*, Orach Chayim, 664). The general reason for waving the Lulav on all the days of Sukkos is that it increases joy (שקבלה היתה בידם שאף בתוך ההלל היו מנענעים להתעוררות שמחה: Meiri, *Sukkah*, 37b), yet that is with a 'straight-laced', upright Lulav. When the Lulav is allowed to relax, move wildly, and rustle loudly, it mimics an ecstatic frenzy of joy.

Additionally, one of the purposes of waving the Lulav is to negate negativity, "(in the four directions) to counter harmful winds, and up and down to counter harmful dews", as explored earlier. Then, on the day of the "final seal," we unbind the Lulav and shake it more vigorously and get rid of all negativity in one final push (*Bach*, Orach Chayim, 664:2: וכיון שעכשיו הוא גמר החתימה למים מתירין אגודו כדי לנענע בו היטב).

A more symbolic reason relates to the fact that Hoshana Rabbah is the spiritual stage of *Neshikim* / 'kissing' before the Zivug and *Yichud* / unification of Shemini Atzeres. Just as a bride unbinds her braids and lets her hair down before the Chupah, the custom of the groom is to undo all of his ties, such as his shoelaces and belt. The Lulav is the image of a groom. On Hoshana Rabba, when we unbind the Lulav, 'he' is loosening his ties, representing a movement toward imminent Yichud (*Ohr haMeir*, Devarim).

IN THE SEQUENCE OF THE HOLIDAY

In the context of Sukkos following Yom Kippur, and both preceded by Rosh Hashanah, a deeper explanation of the unbinding of the Lulav is as follows.

The entire process and sequence of the holidays is about building a new healthy, wholesome, holy identity, that will participate in the coming new year with depth, mindfulness, and presence. Rosh Hashanah is our collective birthday, on Rosh Hashanah the new beginning of the new year, we are committed to do it differently, deeper, higher, this coming year. Rosh Hashanah is making a commitment, like getting engaged to our beloved, to do things differently. The comes Yom Kippur, the holy transcendent day of atonement, the day in which we let go, where we actively shed our entire negative *Tzurah* / form, and way of being in this world. To let go of all resentment, doubt, and lack of moral and spiritual clarity, we step into the proverbial 'Mikvah' of Yom Kippur, its atmosphere of transformative fluidity. Immersed in this cleansing 'space', in this bath of Hashem's formless Light, for twenty-six hours, where we surrender our attachments to everything mundane. We unhook ourselves from the basic 'ground' of human life, such as food, drink, and we ascend, weightless, swimming in the luminous waters of Infinity, with no form or context. We are free of all neediness and negativity, of all trauma, drama and despondency, of all anxieties and angers. Then we drift down, like a cloud of sweet incense, into the joyful days Sukkos. There we re-embody, re-create, re-imagine, and re-congeal in a wholesome and holy Tzurah.

We wave an upright and firmly tied Lulav for the first six days of Sukkos, ensuring that the leaves of the Lulav do not open. This firm, 'gathered' shape represents how we are putting ourselves back together into a healthy shape, after the 'shape-lessness' of Yom Kippur. Like the leaves of the Lulav, we become 'centered' and upright, strongly integrating the light of Yom Kippur into the world.

Once our new Tzurah is confirmed, once we know who we are and what we want to do in this world, we find ourselves in the decisive day of Hoshana Rabba, the 'Final Judgment'. Yet, we are then invited to untie and unbind the Lulav, letting the 'spine' of the Lulav, and of our body, relax and move a little more freely. This is because once our new identity is congealed, and we have a 'strong backbone', we let go a little bit. The free-flowing, rustling Lulav, represents an inner loosening of self, that can only come with a strong sense of who we really are.

The more comfortable a person is with himself, the more he can take himself lightly and even laugh at himself. A person who is struggling to find his space in this world has very little opportunity to 'let down', and enjoy a state of flexibility, lightness, and humor. Stubborn and inflexible individuals, whether intellectually or emotionally, often have fragile egos. They lack the malleability to make light of themselves and are not open enough to hear the perspectives of others. Only an anchored ship can thrash about without sinking. Only when you feel deeply rooted and on solid ground, can you afford yourself the luxury of allowing your joy to wave and shake more freely, without losing your center, your footing, and your core identity.[*]

Following Hoshana Rabbah come the ecstatic days of Shemini Atzeres / Simchas Torah, when we let loose even more and dance with abandon with the holy Torah. We are able to leap up and down, sway from side to side, and be inwardly and outwardly flexible, precisely because we have become so deeply rooted in the knowledge of who we are. In this culmination of the holy days of Tishrei, our identity is solidified and se-

---

[*] Here is a similar teaching from the Mei haShiloach, in another context. The Torah says, אם בחקתי תלכו / "If you walk with my *Chukim* / statutes...." Why does the Torah use the term 'walk' in relation to the term *Chukim*, which is a cognate of the word for 'engraved'? What does "if you walk with My engravings" mean? Says the Mei haShiloach: היינו כל זמן שלא נחקק ונקבע בלב האדם קדושת הש"י נקרא עומד, כי צריך לצמצם עצמו בכל עניונ ושלא להתפשט רצונו כי שב ואל תעשה עדיף, וכאשר יפנה האדם לד"ת עד שיחקקו בלבו ויקבעו בו, אז יוכל האדם להתפשט ולילך בכל ענינים שירצה כי ה' עמו / "As long as Hashem's statutes are not engraved and the holiness of Hashem, may He be Blessed, set into the heart of a person, it is (a phenomenon) called 'standing'. For one needs to concentrate himself in every area of life, for "It is better to sit and not act." But when a person applies himself to *Da'as Torah* until it is engraved in his heart and fully established in himself, then he can spread out and 'walk' in every area of life as desired, for Hashem is with him": *Mei haShiloach*, Bechukosai. In other words, when the Torah is you, not an 'addition' to who you are (like ink on paper), but rather ingrained and unified (like an engraving in stone), then you can flow and move about with ease.

cured, our Teshuvah is complete, our acceptance of Torah is so engraved. We are so grounded in our dream and purpose in life that we can jump and lift off the ground. Our identity is so completely unified with the Torah, that we can now move freely and with ease in all directions and dimensions, without veering off the path.

To dance is to defy gravity and heaviness. So too is unbinding the Lulav. When the Lulav is no longer pressed together into a mold, it rustles and 'flies about' freely through the air. After 'straightening up' and taking responsibility for our lives in the formal atmosphere of Rosh Hashanah, then rising and transcending the world like a straight column of incense smoke on Yom Kippur, and after building up a new healthy sense of a solid self on Sukkos — on Hoshana Rabbah, we unlock our spine, so to speak, and allow it to wave freely with joy. This freedom accumulates to the point that we leap and jump in ecstasy on Simchas Torah, and dance into the night with unbridled, uncontainable Simchah.

Chapter 5
THINKING BIG

HOSHANA RABBAH LITERALLY MEANS 'GREAT SALVA-
TION'.* WHY WAS IT GIVEN THIS NAME, AND WHAT,
EXACTLY, DOES 'GREAT' REFER TO?

---

* Hoshana Rabbah is the day of the year that the most offerings were offered
(maybe besides Erev Pesach). Hoshana Rabbah is the last day of Sukkos,
thus it was the last day that a person who made a *Neder* / vow to make an
offering could bring that offering without violating a prohibition. If someone promised to bring an offering, they needed to do so right away, but
when needed, they would not violate the prohibition of 'not delaying', until
the entire cycle of Pesach, Shavuos, and Sukkos had transpired. Hence,
Hoshana Rabbah was the last day available to bring these promised offerings, as Rebbe Eliezer of Worms explains in *Sefer Rokeach* (Hilchos Sukkos). As such, Hoshana Rabbah is a 'great' day, a day with a great number
of offerings. He also explains that the *Dibbur* / speech, as in taking a vow, a
Neder to bring an offering, is like *Matar* / rain (שדיבור נקרא מטר). Inwardly
this means that by keeping our words, the vows we initiate, our *Matar* /
rain, vapor / words, fulfills their purpose and irrigates. In this way, on Hos-

Rabbah, great, big, or abundant, obviously refers to the very 'great' salvation that we will experience, G-d willing soon, with the coming Final Redemption. The salvation itself will be abundant and great. Rabbah can also refer to the Great One, as in a salvation that will come from the Great Source of all Salvation. Rabbah can also refer to the recipient of the salvation, a 'great people', Klal Yisrael, who thinks big and performs acts of great self-sacrifice and spiritual beauty.

On Hoshana Rabbah, the Great One blesses us with great salvations. We, who are the co-creators of our realities, need to 'think big' on this day and ask and pray, and open ourselves to receive even greater blessings.

Rebbe Yisrael, the holy Ruziner, once offered a parable about thinking big and asking for great abundance:

Once, a mighty ruler, who was childless for many years, was blessed with a healthy son. Born in the lap of luxury, the child felt entitled to everything and was completely dependent on his parents. Knowing that one day his son would inherit the throne, he wanted him to become mature and independent. The king decided to send him away to a distant land so that he would learn independence and responsibility, and strengthen his character.

After a few years, the king sent a messenger to check up on his son. The messenger met with the young man and said, "Sire, your

nahah Rabbah, the day we fulfill our obligations and our 'waters' come to irrigate our practical life, we ask Hashem to draw down Divine Rain and *Shefa* / flow, and that it be a source of blessings in life.

father sends this message: 'I hope you did not forget that you are the son of the king and act accordingly!' And now, sire, being the son of a mighty ruler, I shall grant you any request; whatever you desire, you shall receive."

Sadly, having lived away from the kingdom for so long, and having immersed himself in such a different lifestyle, the fact that his father was the king did not fully register in his mind. He told the messenger, "I would like a new pair of boots."

In one moment, the young man could have changed his life; he could have asked to return home, to rejoin the kingdom, and been showered with all kinds of wealth. He could have asked for *Rabbah* / great and meaningful things, but, pathetically, he asked for *Katnus* / smallness, a triviality. On the day of Great Salvation, we need to ask the Great One for great things. We need to realize that we are children of the Supreme King, and think bigger — and then think even bigger than that.

Rebbe Naftali of Ropshitz used to tell the following story to demonstrate the inability of a person who lives 'small' to think 'big':

Once in Russia, there was a simple soldier who performed a heroic act in battle and saved the life of Nicholas I. When he was granted a private audience with the king, he was told that he could ask for anything and his wish would be granted. When he was brought in front of the king, he only requested that the king change his commanding officer, who had been tough on him.

Instead of seeking a promotion to become the commanding officer himself, or even to retire with wealth and luxuries, he chose to remain a simple soldier.

This poor soldier was operating within a limited identity. In his eyes, he was nothing more than a soldier of the lowest rank, who needed to follow orders and was not able to think of himself as capable of giving orders to others. He did not see himself as big enough to choose a life of relaxation and honor. Without the perspective and confidence to dream of bigger and better things for himself, he only sought to 'rearrange the furniture' within his rather pathetic life.

Some of us, sadly, get so used to our own mediocrity or fear of failure that we find it hard to accept a meaningful or important opportunity that is being presented to us. We might not even notice that it is being presented to us. Many have developed a psychological narrative in which they always lose. Either they shrink away from any risks, or they 'pre-determine' the outcome of their efforts before they even begin. This blinds them to any unexpected growth or blessings.

Hoshana Rabba, the Great One wishes to offer us a Great Salvation, we need to ensure that we have the confidence and determination to ask for Greatness and do so with Greatness.

BEING OPEN TO THE GREAT POSSIBILITIES

If one sets their sights so low that they cannot see an opportunity or blessing that may come their way, it is as if they are sitting in a disqualified Sukkah, one that is so tall that the S'chach is unnoticed and beyond their scope of vision. We need to sit under S'chach that is lovingly close to us and visible to us. And yet, by means of this 'close S'chach', we receive revelations of the immeasurably great, transcendent world of Makif, the world of Malbush, of inconceivably great potential — our potential. This allows us to imagine and see what is far beyond normal human sight. Sukkos 'clears the air' so that we can see the open expanse of all possibilities, and dream, and truly think big.

Hoshana Rabbah, at the culmination of this cleansed atmosphere, our seeing is now much higher and deeper, and we are open to true, infinite greatness and blessings.

If our bar has not been raised, and our scope of vision has not been expanded, then, sadly, we will continue to create and believe in our own limitations and narrow view of what is possible for us. If we have not allowed the Sukkah to instill in us some level of Ruach haKodesh, so to speak, we will have become entrapped in our small picture of life. It is similar to an elephant raised in captivity. When a chain is placed on the elephant's leg as a baby, then even years later, after the elephant has grown into a mighty animal, it still thinks it cannot detach from the chain. The poor elephant cannot even imagine the truth: it could easily break free with the slightest pull of its leg.

Another *Mashal* / parable describes this predicament:

A homeless man sitting on a park bench has just found a half-eaten hotdog in the trash and is about to have his lunch when he hears his name being called. He looks up from his meal and finds himself face-to-face with an old friend who was once his work partner. Dismayed at his condition, the friend begins asking him about his life. After a few minutes of talking, the old friend's heart opens and he offers the homeless man a job, along with a place to stay while he gets back on his feet.

Just at that moment, a cat climbs up on the park bench and starts sniffing at the hotdog. As they are talking about this amazing life-changing opportunity, all the homeless man can think about is shooing the cat away to save his hotdog. Finally, the cat makes a swipe, snatches the hotdog out of the man's hand, and runs away. Without thinking, the man jumps up and chases the cat through the park, winding this way and that between trees and bushes, running through puddles, and jumping over flower beds. The cat is too quick for him and eventually, he throws up his hands in despair and gives up. Just then he remembers, "Oh my G-d! My friend. The job! The apartment! What am I doing chasing after this cat for a half-eaten hotdog?!" He hurries back to the park bench, but by the time he arrives, his old friend is gone. The opportunity had passed.

Although this Mashal is a caricature, it points to the challenges and appetites that we all have, which exert control over us. Our attachment to immediate gratification can blind us and hold us back from making or accepting very beneficial changes in our lives. The homeless man's predicament symbolizes any challenge or unhealthy behavior or situation that you very much need to change. The 'hotdog' is whatever tiny or trivial benefits you receive while still in your situation or contraction of your true greatness. The man's friend represents the opportunity to leap out of that situation into a completely different reality. And the cat symbolizes the temptation or distraction that keeps you stuck in your behavioral patterns or smallness, not allowing you to remain present or receptive long enough to accept and commit to the direction that is ultimately best for you. The cat keeps *you* in the bag, so to speak.

As we are celebrating Sukkos, may we clarify our vision of our strengths, gifts and potentials, and may we begin to think bigger than we ever have before. In the shade of the S'chach, may we gaze in wonder at the greatness of our *Nefesh Elokis / Divine soul*, and have premonitions about how we will live up to this greatness as the year unfolds. Then, on Hoshana Rabbah, the day when the Great One wishes to grant us great salvations and blessings, we will already be empowered to shamelessly request unlimited blessings and success for ourselves and for Klal Yisrael. We will have the confidence to open ourselves and receive Hashem's limitless physical and spiritual gifts, and be double-sealed for an year of self-actualization, and of unprecedented, revealed goodness and deepest sweetness.

Chapter 6

THE SPECIAL QUALITY
OF THE ARAVAH

OSHANA RABBAHIS *YOM ARAVAH* / יום ערבה / THE DAY
OF THE *ARAVAH*, THE WILLOW BRANCH (*BERACHOS,* 34A.
SUKKAH, 43B).

In the times when the *Beis haMikdash* / Holy Temple was
standing upon the earth, Yom Aravah was practiced as the
Mishnah delineated: "How is the Mitzvah of the Aravah ful-
filled? There was a place below Yerushalayim, and it was called
Motza. They would descend there and gather willow branches.
And they would then come and stand them upright at the sides

of the *Mizbe'ach* / Altar, and the tops of the branches would be inclined over the top of the Mizbe'ach. They then sounded a Tekiah blast, a Teruah (broken) sound, and a Tekiah. Each day they would circle the Mizbe'ach one time and say: 'Hashem, please save us. Hashem, please grant us success'.... And on that day, the seventh day of Sukkos (Hoshana Rabba), they would circumambulate the Mizbe'ach seven times.... At the time of their departure at the end of the Yom Tov, what would they say? *Yofi L'cha, Mizbe'ach, Yofi L'cha Mizbe'ach!* / 'It is beautiful for you, Mizbe'ach; it is beautiful for you, Mizbe'ach...'" (Mishnah, *Sukkah*, 45a).

Today, without a physical, literal Beis haMikdash and Mizbe'ach, we practice as follows. We circumambulate the *Bimah* / the place where the Torah is read, with a person holding a Sefer Torah next to the Bimah. We make seven circles, reminiscent of the seven circles around the actual Mizbe'ach. During these circumambulations, we hold the Arba Minim. After the seven circuits, while reciting various Hoshanos prayers, we take a bundle of five Aravos, and we strike the ground five times.*

---

* The custom to take Aravos, even today, is so essential that when the calendar was established special consideration was taken to ensure that the day of Hoshana Rabbah does not fall out on Shabbos, as on Shabbos we would not be able to perform this practice. *Yerushalmi, Sukkah*, 4:1. Tosefos, *Sukkah*, 43b. The Rambam, however, writes that the calendar was set up in a way to align the true position of the sun and moon with the way we measure their rate of progress, and therefore, one day we establish Rosh Chodesh and one day we push off, so Tuesday is established, Wednesday not, and so forth, but this has nothing to do with consideration when Rosh Hashanah and Hoshana Rabbah fall out during the week: *Hilchos Kiddush haChodesh*, 7:7. ומפני מה אין קובעין בחשבון זה בימי אד"ו. לפי שהחשבון הזה הוא לקרוב הירח והשמש בהלוכה האמצעי לא במקום האמתי כמו שהודענו. לפיכך עשו יום קביעה ויום

In the times of the Beis haMikdash, they would adorn the Mizbe'ach with the Aravos and following the circling they would declare, "It is beautiful for you, Mizbe'ach; it is beautiful for you, Mizbe'ach." What is the beauty that the Aravah adds to the Mizbe'ach? What is so special about the Aravah? There are four species that are used throughout the days of Sukkos, the Lulav, Esrog, Hadasim, and Aravos, but it is only the Aravah that is singled out for this "beautification" of the Mizbe'ach, and only the Arava gets a special day all to itself, as it were. What is so unique about the Aravah, and what is the special symbolism of the Aravah that causes it to deserve its own special 'holy day'?

THE BEAUTY OF SIMPLICITY

Because the Aravah is not overflowing with an aroma, nor saturated with taste, it represents a type of raw simplicity and humility (Aravos are called the *Evyonim* / poor: *Pri Eitz Chayim*, Sha'ar Sod haPurim, 5). After six days celebrating all four Minim, but most prominently the tall and proud Lulav and the beautiful, fragrant Esrog, we come to recognize that humble simplicity has an outstanding value that is worth celebrating.

דחיה כדי לפגע ביום קבוץ האמתי. כיצד. בשלישי קובעין ברביעי דוחין. בחמישי קובעין בששי דוחין. בשבת קובעין אחד בשבת דוחין. בשני קובעין. The Ra'avad, upon this Rambam, writes harsh words: א"א מפני שהמחבר הזה מתגדר מאד ומתפאר בחכמה הזאת והוא בעיניו שהגיע לתכליתה ואני איני מאנשיה כי גם רבותי לא הגיעו אליה ע"כ לא נכנסתי בדבריו לבדוק אחריו. אך כשפגעתי בדבר הזה שכתב נפלא בעיני הפלא ופלא, ואם יהיה המולד בבגה"ז על הדרך האמצעי למה לא ידחה למחרתו אל המולד האמיתי. ולדבריו אין ראוי לקובעו לעולם ביום מולדו ומה חטא אד"ו שלא יהיה בו המולד לעולם באמיתי ולעולם ידחה ומה זכה בגה"ז שיהיה ולא ידחה. ואנו קבלנו דחיית אד"ו משום יום ערבה שלא יבא בשבת ומשום יוה"כ שלא יבא לא בערב שבת ולא במ"ש, ודחיית בד"ו משום אד"ו, והוא בעיני כמתעתע עכ"ל.

Sometimes it takes time and a cultivated sensitivity to recognize the true value of simplicity over 'louder' qualities. People are often attracted to beautiful appearances and luxurious 'fragrances' more than unassuming substance and authenticity. Having celebrated for six days, dancing and singing with the beautiful Minim and feasting in a beautifully decorated Sukkah, on the seventh day we turn abruptly to the Aravah and declare, 'Actually, humility and simplicity is most praiseworthy — now we will celebrate with you!'

Fascinatingly, while people are very careful and scrupulous that their Esrog, and to some extent the Lulav and Hadasim as well, should be of superior beauty and fulfill the most precise Halachic requirements, one's approach to the Aravah is almost the opposite.

In the Torah, Aravos are called *Arvei Nachal* / willows of the brook, however, in practice, willows that do not actually grow near a brook are also technically Kosher. According to Rashi (*Sukkah*, 33b), the superior level of observance is to take willow branches that actually grew near a brook (according to Tosefos, this is required: *Ibid.*, 34a), yet, the practical ruling is that one does not need to be scrupulous and try to find Aravos that grew by the water. In fact, in the final analysis, it is deemed better to use Aravos that *do not* grow by the water (Taz, *Orach Chayim*, 647:2: ו"ה טפי ניחא להראות חידוש וליקח אפי' שלא מן הנחל).

Why is there such a seeming discrepancy here between the Torah's literal description and the practical guidelines of our holy Sages? There is, of course, a Halachic reason for this (as the Taz explains), but from a deeper perspective, it is precisely because the Aravos express humility and simplicity. We take more 'humble and simple' Aravos, those that are not glorified by outstanding beauty, superior stringency, and not sourced in the very rare circumstances of soil that is next to an actual, natural brook of water.

BEAUTY IS IN UNITY

The root of the word Arava is ערב / *Arav*, similar to the word עירב / *Eirav* / mixing, blending. It is also related to the word ערב / *Areiv* / sweet, pleasing, as in וערבה לה מנחת יהודה / "And the offerings of Yehudah shall be pleasing to Hashem" (*Malachi*, 3:4. *Ohr haTorah*, Pinchas, 1, 107. *Likutei Sichos* 22, Emor 3).

The humble beauty or sweetness of the leaves of the Aravah lies in their nature to grow together in bundles. In this way, Aravos are like harmonious "brothers," as the Talmud refers to them (*Shabbos*, 20a: מאי אח אמר רב אחוונא / "What does the word 'brother' refer to? Rav says, it refers to a willow branch). The leaves of the Aravah have no smell or taste, but precisely because of its 'lack', the Aravah is able to be united and attached to the Lulav and Hadasim. Its 'egolessness', as it were, opens it to cleave to others, and that is its beauty: its humble unity with others (hence, on Hoshana Rabbah we welcome the *Ushpiz* / 'guest' of Dovid HaMelech, who is Malchus. The nature of Malchus is לית לה מגרמה כלום / "it has nothing of its own." Dovid haMelech's very life is borrowed from others. This type of simplicity is the mark of *Emunah Peshutah* / absolutely simple faith).

On its own, the Aravah has no beauty, nor taste or smell, yet this is precisely why it is able to mingle and 'blend' with the other Minim. Beauty comes from colors, sounds and dynamics that contrast yet harmonize or complement each other. The Aravah 'knows' that it is nothing without others, yet in the presence of the other three Minim, it both multiplies their magnificence, and becomes magnificent in its own right.

When you make yourself into a receptive, open, empty vessel, you have the space inside to be like an ערבה / *Aravah*, part of an ערב / *Eirev* / mixture, harmonizing, and sharing space with others. If you are like a blank, empty canvas, you can receive all colors and dynamics, and become beautiful in your own right. If you just think of yourself and your needs, you are just you, a separate individual. But if you are humble and self-empty like the humble Hillel, you can proclaim, "If I am here, everyone is here" (Sukkah, 53a). In other words, 'I am simply present and open, and as a result, I'm in harmony with everyone — and the best qualities of everyone are here, shining in me.'

Once, a man came to the Alter Rebbe and gave him a 'laundry list' of things he felt he needed from Hashem. The Rebbe asked him, 'When you wake up in the morning, do you ask yourself what you want to get out of life today, or do you ask yourself how you can use your *Kochos* / abilities for what Hashem wants of you today?' The latter is *Bitul* / self-transparency, the way of the Aravos.

The early Mekubalim reveal that Hoshana Rabbah is connected to a level of Heaven called Aravos (Rabbeinu Bachya, *Kad haKemach*, Aravah). Chazal speak of Seven Heavens, including the highest heaven, called Aravos — in this context, often translated as 'Clouds' or 'Heavens' (*Chagigah*, 12b). Hashem is called רכב בערבות / *Rochev Aravos* / Riding the Aravos. As the 'Rider' above even the highest heavenly realm, this Divine epithet means 'the Primal Cause of All Movement in the Seven Heavens and the earth' (*Tehilim*, 68:5. Radak).

Riding represents not only causing or guiding movement from above but also represents a type of closeness. Hashem says, 'I ride with those who are like Aravos, willow branches, empty of ego.' When we selflessly serve the Infinite One, who is higher than the Seventh Heaven, He 'rides' upon us finite human beings, as if on a chariot. Through this close contact, He lifts us up even beyond the world of Aravos, higher than the highest heavens.

A person who is like an egoless Aravah can unite and harmonize not only with other people but with the One Above, the Rider, the Primary Mover, who steers all events and manifestations. This person is like the *Shliach* / messenger of a majestic king, empty of their own will. Every movement of the messenger is unified with the will and being of the king alone. And this is the person's majesty, and their beauty (שלוחו של אדם כמותו / "One's Shaliach is like oneself": *Kiddushin*, 43a).

THIRSTY FOR MORE

The simplicity of the Aravah, its lack of outstanding fragrance and taste, represents a humble way of being receptive to others. 'Blending' with other people also means being open to their ideas, opinions, and ways of thinking. More than just being able to mingle with others, an 'Aravah person' has a genuine will and desire to connect with others, and a thirst to learn and grow from their experience and knowledge.

Aravos are called *Arvei Nachal* / willows of the brook, because that is their most natural habitat. Willow trees need to draw water continuously. This fact can be observed in our Arba Minim. The leaves of our Aravos shrivel and dry more quickly than our Hadasim or Lulav. They cannot sustain even a few days without some form of water or moisture. This need for water creates a deep 'desire' in the Aravah to seek water.

On Hoshana Rabbah, we take a bundle of five Aravos and declare that our desire, yearning and seeking are more valuable, in a way, than having everything we desire. As an Aravah-person, we may not yet have 'taste', 'fragrance' or great spiritual beauty in our own right, but we are seeking water, seeking life and growth, and seeking connection with others who will help us become spiritually tasteful and fragrant.

The 'greatness' of the Aravah is that it has a strong *Teshukah* / desire for water, which is a symbol of wisdom and unity (*Aravah* is numerically 277, the same as the word זרע / *Zera* / seed (as explored earlier), which comes from desire, and creates unity and growth).

Sages and philosophers throughout the ages have debated on which is more valuable, an actual achievement, or the desire to achieve itself (see *Ohr Hashem*, Ma'amar 3:2. *Mei Marom*, 1:136). Chazal tell us, גדולה שמושה של תורה יותר מלמודה / "Service of Torah is greater than studying it." This means serving a Torah scholar and spending time in their company is greater than learning Torah from them (*Berachos*, 7b).

On a deeper level, the act of Torah study is finite; we can only delve into a specific subject within a limited period of time. However, when a student with a genuine thirst for knowledge spends time in the company of a great scholar, it ignites an ever-growing passion and desire to learn. This Teshukah or yearning becomes boundless and infinite, driving the student to continually seek wisdom and deeper understanding (כי הלמוד הוא בגבול והתשוקה והתפלה הוא להש"י שהוא בלתי גבול: *Mei haShiloach* 1, Likutei haShas, Berachos).

In fact, this is the advantage that human beings have over all other creatures, even over angels: Teshukah / desire (*Tzidkas haTzadik*, 248: עיקר האדם הוא החשק שבלב שבו הוא יתרונו על המלאכים). Desires and inclinations, ambitions, passions, urges, and cravings are definitive of the human condition. This may sound like a disadvantage, however these energies have the power to animate people throughout their lives. Every yearning is ultimately a yearning for closeness with our Creator; when our cravings are revealed as deep spiritual desires, they can drive us to unlimited growth and the accomplishment of truly great deeds.

We can 'think big' and focus our desires upon more beneficial objects, but we cannot permanently free ourselves from desire itself. Even the desire to extinguish desire is a desire. What's more, without desire, the world would cease to function (*Sanhedrin*, 64a), and this tells us it is not the Creator's will that desire be killed.

In many ways, human beings resemble the Aravah — at times, we may lack pleasant fragrance and taste, and find ourselves depleted in Torah and Mitzvos, higher consciousness, and righteous actions. Yet, it is precisely because of this that we are filled with immense Teshukah, a yearning to return to our Source, to grow, and to become more. This longing propels us forward, inspiring us to seek deeper meaning and fulfillment in our lives.

We are alive and we are thirsty for the water of Torah wisdom, for growth in Mitzvos, for connection and Yichud with HaKadosh Baruch Hu, and for living in harmony with others.

Chapter 7

HOSHANA RABBAH &
THE NAME EHE'YEH

H OSHANA RABBAH IS THE 21ST DAY FROM ROSH HASHANAH,[*] THE CELEBRATION OF THE BIRTH OF MAN. THE MYSTICS AND SAGES TELL US THAT BE-ING THE 21ST DAY, Hoshana Rabbah is connected with *Sheim Ehe'yeh* / the Divine Name אהי"ה / *Ehe'yeh* / 'I-Will-Be', which has a numerical value of 21 (*Asarah Ma'amaros,* Ma'amar Chikur Din, 2:24).

---

[*] Rosh Hashanah is the moment of our collective creation, and sadly, the day Adam and Chavah ate from the Tree of Knowledge and disconnected ourselves from the Source of all Life. As a result, Adam and Chavah were asked, and we, their descendants, are continuously asked, *Ayekah* / 'What are you up to? What have you done?' This is the Divine invitation to Te-shuvah, the call to engage in the process of Tishrei. There are four letters in the word *Ayekah* (*Asara Ma'amaros,* Ma'amar Chikur Din, 24): Aleph / one, stands for the first day of Tishrei, Rosh Hashanah. Yud / 10, stands for the tenth day of Tishrei, Yom Kippur, and Chaf / 20 stands for Hoshana Rabbah, the twentieth day after the conclusion of Adam and Chavah's first day. The final letter in *Ayekah* is Hei / 5. On the original Tishrei, Hoshana Rabbahwas on *Hei* / the fifth day of the week, Thursday — twenty days after the conclusion of Adam and Chavah's first day.

As explored earlier, Hoshana Rabbah is the day of the final *Chosam* / חותם / 'seal' for the coming year, and as the holy Arizal explains, the numerical value of the word *Chosam* is 455, the value of Sheim Ehe'yeh, in all its possible spellings (*Chosam*, plus 1 the word itself, is 455: *Sha'ar Hakavanos*, Sukkos, Derush 7).*

---

* The Name Ehe'yeh is spelled אהי״ה / Aleph-Hei-Yud-Hei.

Aleph is always spelled Aleph/1, Lamed/30, Pei/80 = 111

And Yud is always spelled Yud/10, Vav/6, Dalet/4 = 20

111+20 = 131

The letter Hei can be spelled three ways:

Hei/5, Yud/10 = 15

Hei/5, Hei/5 = 10

Hei/5, Aleph/1 = 6

When Hei is spelled with a Yud, which represents Chochmah, the numeric value is 161:

Aleph/1, Lamed/30, Pei/80 = 111

Hei/5, Yud/10 = 15

Yud/10, Vav/6, Dalet/4 = 20

Hei/5, Yud/10 = 15

111+15+20+15 = 161

When Hei is spelled with a another Hei, which represents Binah, the numeric value is 151:

Aleph/1, Lamed/30, Pei/80 = 111

Hei/5, Hei/5 = 10

Yud/10, Vav/6, Dalet/4 =20

Hei/5, Hei/5 = 10

111+10+20+10 = 151

When Hei is spelled with an Aleph, which represents Da'as, the numeric value is 143:

Aleph/1, Lamed/30, Pei/80 = 111

Hei/5, Aleph /1 = 6

Yud/10, Vav/6, Dalet / 4 = 20

Hei/5, Aleph/1 = 6

111+6+20+6 = 143

The sum of these three permutations is **161+151+143 = 445**. The word חותם (Ches/8, Vav/6, Tav/400, Mem/40) plus the word itself is 445.

These three filled names in total are 445, but if you subtract the original 21 from all 3 names the total is 392, and adding 3 for the three names equals 395, the value of the word משנה / *Mishnah*. Mishnah means 'the second', as the main חותם is on Yom Kippur at Neilah (חותם of Yesod), and this is the חותם of Malchus, the 'second Chosam'. This is another reason (*Kaf haChayim*, Orach Chayim, 664:5) that we recite the Book of Devarim, also called *Mishneh Torah*.

The Chosam of Yom Kippur during Neilah is the *Chosam Penimi* / internal seal, the seal of Yesod. In Avodah, inner and spiritual work, Yesod is *Kedushah* / holiness, light untangled and unattached to negativity, which is the idea of Yom Kippur. On Hoshana Rabbah there is a *Chosam Chitzoni* / external seal, the seal of Malchus. In Avodah, Malchus is *Emunah* / faith in Hashem who believes in us, and thus Emunah is also faith in ourselves, who are created by Hashem.

Sheim Ehe'yeh first appears in the Torah to Moshe, at the burning bush. When Moshe first encounters a bush that is aflame yet not consumed, he approaches it and has an encounter with the Divine. There he is informed of his mission to liberate Klal Yisrael from Egypt. Moshe asks, "When they ask me what His Name is, what should I tell them?" (*Shemos*, 3:13). Moshe is asking for a revelation of the highest Name. The response he receives is, "Tell them *Ehe'yeh asher Ehe'yeh* sent you."

In English, many have translated this as 'I Am That I Am,' but the verb is in future tense, so it is more accurately translated as 'I Will Be What I Will Be.' A fundamental interpretation of this is, 'I will be with them now, in this hardship, and I will be with them in future hardships' (Rashi, *Shemos*, 3:14).

Ehe'yeh corresponds to the Sefirah of Keser, and refers to the inscrutable will *to be* the Divine "I," as it were, that is 'becoming', or coming into this world (The double expression *Ehe'yeh asher Ehe'yeh* refers to two levels within Keser. The first *Ehe-yeh* is *Ne'elam haElyon* / the concealed upper dimension of Keser, and the second *Ehe-yeh* is the revelation of Keser: *Zohar* 3, p.11a).

As the night of Hoshana Rabbah is the night of dreams, of potentials, of the Tzeil that we have created over Sukkos, it is appropriately connected with this highest Name of Hashem, the Name representing 'becoming' and pure potential, "I will be."

On this night, it matters not who you were, not even who you are now, as through the process of Rosh Hashanah, Yom Kippur, and the days of Sukkos, you have let go of your negative past, freed yourself from all old, stale, unworkable identities, and sat for six days in Hashem's canopy, in the Divine Tzeil. You have dreamed up a new possible you and now you are beginning your journey into the new year and new you. (Hence, as Rosh Hashanah is the 'head' of the year, and the beginning of the judgment, with the conclusion on Hoshana Rabbah, Rosh Hashanah is deeply related to dreams and the dreams on Rosh Hashanah are more powerful. Chazal say, שלשה צריכים רחמים מלך טוב, שנה טובה וחלום טוב / "Three matters require a plea for mercy to bring them about: A good king, a good year, and a good dream": *Berachos*, 55a. This refers specifically to Rosh Hashanah, the day the new year begins, when we crown Hashem as King, and when dreams are most often true visions. In the words of the *Maharsha*, ad loc., חלום דר"ה הוא היותר אמתי).

On the day when the Divine Name Ehe'yeh is revealed, we need to answer to ourselves and to HaKadosh Baruch Hu, as it were, 'Who are we becoming; what does our inner 'Ehe'yeh' compel us to be?'

HOSHANA RABBAH & THE NAME OF HASHEM

While Hoshana Rabbah is the 21st day of the month, 21 days after the creation of Adam and Chavah, it is also the 26th day after 'Day One' of Creation itself, which was on the 25th of the month of Elul. In this way, Hoshana Rabbah is connected not only with the Name of Ehe'yeh (21) but also the Name of Hashem (26), which is Yud/10, Hei/5, Vav/6, Hei/5 = 26 (*Kad haKemach*, Aravah. Note that the first three letters of 'Hashem', Yud-Hei-Vav, equal 21, and the Hei at the end brings it to 26).

Hoshana Rabbah is connected with Ehe'yeh on a revealed level, as anyone with a calendar can see that it is the 21st day of the month. Hoshana Rabbah's connection with the Name Hashem is on a subtler, more concealed, inner level. What does this imply?

POTENTIAL FUTURE OR FUTURE ALREADY NOW

HaVaYaH is the 'Essential' Divine Name and the source of all the other Names and Attributes (Rosh, end of *Yumah*, Siman 19). Both HaVaYaH and Ehe'yeh are permutations of the verb 'to be', yet the Name Ehe'yeh has a subtly different 'focus.'* This difference is illustrated by the letters that change between them: The Yud of HaVaYaH becomes the Aleph in Ehe'yeh, and the Vav of HaVaYaH becomes the Yud in Ehe'yeh:

---

* There is another difference between the Aleph of Ehe'yeh and the Yud of HaVaYaH. The first-person future-tense verb begins with an Aleph. The word שב / *Shev* means 'sit'; with an Aleph before Shev, אשב / *Eishev*, it means 'I will sit.' When one speaks of another person about to sit down, however, he says, ישב / *Yeishev* / 'He will sit.' Thus, when Hashem speaks about Himself (so to speak), Hashem says Ehe'yeh, but when we speak of Hashem or to Hashem, and when Hashem is speaking in terms of His relationship with us, it is Yud-Hei-Vav-Hei (*HaVaYaH*). In the words of the Rashbam (*Shemos*, 3:14), "He calls Himself Ehe'yeh and we call Him Yud-Hei-Vav-Hei."

HaVaYaH	Was-Is-Will-Be	**Yud**	Hei	**Vav**	Hei
Ehe'yeh	I Will Be	**Aleph**	Hei	**Yud**	Hei

The Aleph at the beginning of Ehe'yeh is what makes this Name a future tense verb, representing a yet unrealized future: 'I will Be.' The Yud at the beginning of HaVaYaH is what makes this Name an 'eternal present' tense verb, representing the future revealed in the now, as the 'eternal present' includes the future: 'Was-Is-Will Be' (Alter Rebbe, *Siddur Admur haZaken*, Kavanos haMikvah, p. 315).

Hoshana Rabbah is not only about one's 'becoming', one's potential self, the person they will be. It is not only about the Name of Ehe'yeh, meaning, 'On a revealed level, I am in my present state, in the potential of my future state.' Hoshana Rabbah is also about our hidden essential self. It is also about the Name of Hashem, the eternal present, which means the revelation of our future self in the present moment.

On a more *Penimiyus* / internal level, everything in the future is already present in the now, in a concealed state. It is just that within the unfolding nature of process and time, we are 'here', and arrive 'there'. In the inner, higher world, אין כוח חסר פועל / "A potential does not lack actuality." In this way, the deepest *Nekudah* / point within all time, the present moment included, is *Olam haBa* / the World to Come, the potential actuality, which is always already here and now.

All of this means that the way to demonstrate the Name of Hashem on Hoshana Rabbah and move forward, is not only to dream of the possible you, the person you desire to become or the way you dream of living in this coming year. It is also to start living this truth, living your dreams right now.*

If you wish to do something in the future, do it now. If you dream of becoming someone tomorrow, embody that person today.

---

* "Each day, they would circle the Mizbe'ach one time, and say…*Ani V'hu /* אני והו save us": *Sukkah,* 45a. What are these Divine Names? One interpretation of Rashi is that משבעים ושתים שמות הן …השם הראשון והו… ושם השלשים אני הוא ושבע / "These two Names are two of the Names of the seventy-two Names of Hashem. The first of the seventy-two names is והו / *V'Hu* and the thirty-seventh Name (the first Name of the second set of the thirty-six Names within the seventy-two Names), is אני / *Ani.*" (Just as there are seventy nations, and Yishmael and Eisav are the two archetypes, these Names of Hashem, Ani and V'Hu stand apart from the other seventy, and are perhaps the archetypes of the other seventy). *V'hu /* והו is the Sefirah of Tiferes (which also corresponds to the Name of Hashem), and אני / *Ani* is Malchus (Ramak, *Pardes Rimonim,* Sha'ar 23). Malchus is *Ani /* אני (I). Yesod is *Anochi /* אנכי ('I'). Tiferes is *Atah /* אתה (You). And Keser is *Hu /* הוא / (the hidden 'He'). As such, these two Names are a Yichud between Tiferes and Malchus, *potential and actual. V'hu* is phonetically connected with the level of *Hu,* Keser and hence there is a Yichud between Keser (the Name Ehe'yeh) Hashem, and life in this world, which is Malchus.

PART FOUR

SHEMINI ATZERES SIMCHAS TORAH

Chapter 1

שמיני עצרת החג
SHEMINI ATZERES, OUR FESTIVAL

HEMINI / EIGHTH REFERS TO THE EIGHTH DAY OF SUKKOS, YET, WITH REGARDS TO MANY ISSUES, IT IS CONSIDERED ITS OWN YOM TOV. Atzeres means a pause or a closing, as it is the closing Yom Tov of Sukkos, and also the closing day of the entire season of holidays. As such, there is also an Atzeres in Pesach, the closing day of Pesach. The entire 'Pesach season' comes to a close on Shavuos, and thus Chazal / our Sages call Shavuos Atzeres (Although it is not called *Atzeres* in the Torah — "The reason why the Torah itself does not refer to this day as an Atzeres may be the fact that shortly thereafter (after the giving of the Torah) all the accomplishments of this day were lost": *Sefurno*, Emor, 23:26).

Interestingly, when the Torah describes the final day of Pesach, the Torah says of the seventh day (of Pesach), עצרת לה׳ אלקיך / "an Atzeres to Hashem your G-d" (*Devarim*, 16:8). By contrast, when the Torah speaks about this day of Shemini Atzeres it says, ביום השמיני עצרת תהיה לכם / "On the eighth day (of Sukkos), Atzeres shall be for you" (*Bamidbar*, 29:35). Why is Shemini Atzeres a day Atzeres "to you", rather than an Atzeres "to Hashem your G-d"? What does it mean that this Atzeres is "to you"?

On all the other Yom Tovim throughout the year, we say in the liturgy, "Today is the *Chag* / holiday of Sukkos (חג הסוכות)," or "Today is the *Chag* / holiday of Matzos (חג המצות)." First we proclaim that it is a holy day and then which holy day it is. Yet, on the Yom Tov of Shemini Atzeres, we do not say, 'Today is the Chag of Atzeres (חג העצרת),' but rather, the reverse: עצרת החג הזה / "Today is (Shemini) *Atzeres the Chag*...." Why are these words reversed in order?

We need to understand what "Atzeres to you" means, and why we call this Yom Tov "the day of Atzeres that is a Chag," rather than the more conventional sequence of words as used to introduce all other Yamim Tovim.

OUR PAUSING CAUSES THE YOM TOV

Shemini Atzeres is unique in that it does not commemorate any historical narrative. There is nothing particularly distinct about the day of Shemini Atzeres other than being a Yom Tov. Moreover, we do not perform a special Mitzvah, such as eating

Matzah or waving the Four Minim, on this day. It is not a day of 'doing'.

On Sukkos, performing the Mitzvah of Sukkah 'makes' the Yom Tov. On Shemini Atzeres, our *Atzeres*, our 'stopping', resting, and gathering is itself the Chag and makes the Chag.* As such, on Shemini Atzeres, we say, "the day of Shemini Atzeres, the Chag," since the day and the celebration of 'stopping', 'non-doing', creates the Chag.

HISTORY AS THE PRESENT

Every Yom Tov throughout the calendar is not merely a celebration of things past or a marking of history, as in *'his*-story' — *someone else's* ancient story that we are remembering. Rather, on each Yom Tov we are celebrating an 'I-story', a story of our true self, our soul, and a meta-history, a living memory, sacred moments of the past that are felt in the present.

---

* This is also the reason why in Parshas Pinchas, which speaks about the offerings of each Yom Tov, the Torah calls Pesach, Shavuos, and Sukkos "a holy occasion," מקרא־קדש, and *therefore*, כל־מלאכת עבדה לא תעשו, "do not do any work": *Bamidbar*, 28:18. 28:25. 28:26. 29:1. 29:7. Yet, with regards to Shemini Atzeres, the Torah does not say מקרא־קדש / "a holy occasion," rather, it says, ביום השמיני עצרת תהיה לכם כל־מלאכת עבדה לא תעשו / "On the eighth day, there shall be a day of Atzeres to you, you shall not work at your occupations" (29:35). The reason is that Atzeres is not a 'sacred day on its own' upon which we should not do work; rather, through the act of *Atzeres*, pausing to be with Hashem for one more day, the day becomes a Yom Tov, a day when no mundane work shall be done: See *Likutei Sichos*, 33, Pinchas 3, pp. 176-185

The Megilah says that the day(s) of Purim are "remembered and performed." This is also true for all the other Yamim Tovim. By means of remembering those past events, we 'do' them, we re-enact them. For example, as we remember the miracles of the Exodus, or the sitting in the Clouds of Glory, or the Purim or Chanukah story, there is a recurrence of the setting and potential for those miracles, in the present. By performing special Mitzvos, such as kindling the Menorah, eating the Matzah and sitting in the Sukkah, we draw down the very same Divine flow that was revealed in the past and that inspired those miraculous events — into our world and our time. And the purpose of this is to inspire transformation now, and to reveal the very same kind of miracles today, in our life, in our story.

While this is true with every Yom Tov in general, it is applied in a very specific way on Shemini Atzeres, when there is no historical event being commemorated and there is no special Mitzvah. Shemini Atzeres is, and always was, about us simply encountering the Divine in the present moment: עצרת תהיה לכם / "...the day of Atzeres shall be *to you*." This is, by the Torah's explicit definition, each individual person's day. It is a celebration of ourselves in intimate personal dialogue with HaKadosh Baruch Hu. On this day, we do not need to describe our story using metaphors from past events and names other than our own. The 'event' celebrated by Shemini Atzeres is the one happening to us in the present. *We* are making this Yom Tov by 'stopping' and being close to Hashem.

Shemini Atzeres is the culmination of the entire high holiday season; what began in Elul reaches its crescendo on this final day. For fifty days since the First of Elul, we engaged in rebuilding ourselves for the coming year so that we can enter the new year from a higher and deeper way of living. We shed our negative past, our images of self that were holding us back, we took responsibility for ourselves, we sat for seven days in the Sukkah, dreaming ourselves into a new reality. Now that we have secured a healthy, holy sense of self, we can truly celebrate. There is such a strong sense of an 'us', and *our* story of rectified selfhood in relationship with HaKadosh Baruch Hu, we can now celebrate *ourselves*.

In the comfort of knowing who we are, and knowing with Whom we are in dialogue, a powerful sense of joy and ease arises. Hence, on Shemini Atzeres there is no longer a Mitzvah to eat in a Sukkah or Shake the Lulav and Esrog; rather, just to be, *Atzor* / stop, and rejoice.* This is the pinnacle of a relationship, where spouses find pure contentment and joy simply by being in each other's presence. There is no need for grand ges-

---

* The Torah says, והיית אך שמח / "And you shall be only joyful...": *Devarim*, 16:15. Upon this, Chazal say that the word אך / "only" comes to include (that there is a Mitzvah) to evening of the last day of Sukkos, i.e., Shemini Atzeres/Simchas Torah: *Sukkah*, 48a. But the question is, the word אך only comes to limit, as an exclusion (for example, *Eruvin*, 105a, Rashi, כלומר אכין ורקין מיעוטין), so why does it function as an inclusion in this Pasuk? It is because here, the Torah is saying that on the night (day) of Shemini Atzeres/Simchas Torah, we need to be "only" happy, excluding all other Mitzvos that we do throughout Sukkos. It includes this day in joy, but excludes all other activities — today there is no special Mitzvah, there is only Simchah.

tures or outings, to do something or be somewhere, to experience happiness; their company alone brings unparalleled joy.

The joy of Shemini Atzeres is the joy *being*, being ourselves in relationship to the Ultimate Self. This is a subtle, internal type of joy. It is a joy that comes by ceasing to feel a need to move and 'do', a joy of arriving, of finally stopping. This gives the Yom Tov a dominant sense of inwardness, except perhaps during the Hakafos (See the Rebbe's Ma'amar, *Lehavin Inyan Shemini Atzeres*, 5714. *Sichos Kodesh*, Leil Simchas Torah, 5744).

DANCING AS AN ACT OF OFFERING SPACE TO OTHERS

The more we feel comfortable and at ease with being ourselves, the more free we feel to get up and dance.

In Eretz Yisrael, the Land of Israel, Simchas Torah is on the day of Shemini Atzeres itself, and dancing permeates the day. In the Diaspora, many have the custom to dance with the Torah on the evening of Shemini Atzeres as well as on the following day which is designated as Simchas Torah. In any case, dancing is an integral way of celebrating Shemini Atzeres and Simchas Torah. The Rebbe Rashab (Rebbe Shalom DovBer of Chabad), would say, "One must truly cherish the 48 hours of Shemini Atzeres and Simchas Torah; at every moment one can draw treasures in buckets and barrels, both materially and spiritually. This is accomplished through dancing" (Rebbe Rayatz, *Sefer haMa'amarim*, 5711, p. 79). Dancing is connected with the essence of this Yom Tov.

Dancing is an act of defying gravity, leaping upwards, flying higher.

'Dance' is called רקד / *Rakad*, similar to the word מרקד / *Meraked* / sifting, which is a prohibited act on Shabbos, exemplified by removing debris from flour (*Shabbos*, 73b). When a person dances, say the Chasidic Rebbes (*Likutei haRim*, Likutim, Nesu'in, p. 166), they can do it in such a way that they can experience *Hispashtus* / a removal of their material bodily consciousness, creating a transcendent, out-of-body experience. In dance, one can use the body itself to transcend the 'debris' of over-identification with the body. Dancing is thus a practice of letting go of your rigid, defined space and inhibition of movement. We even give room to others to enter our space, as each dancer grasps the hand or shoulders of their neighbor, or bumps into others when the circle becomes crowded.

The traditional Chasidic dance, as defined by the Baal Shem Tov and his students, is a circle dance. While the dancers hold hands and turn in a circle, they also repeatedly move in and out from the center to the periphery. Moving in, they gather close together near the middle of the circle, and moving outward to the circumference of the circle they stretch away from each other, back and forth. As the Alter Rebbe writes, this 'choreography' is specifically connected with the unique joy of Shemini Atzeres / Simchas Torah (In the words of the Alter Rebbe, speaking about the dancing on Simchas Torah, כמו ע"ד משל שמרקדים במחול שמתרחק האחד מחבירו וחוזר ומתקרב והריחוק הוא סיבת הקירוב / "It is like in a circle dance where one moves away from his partner and then returns and comes close — the distance is the reason for the (subsequent) closeness": *Likutei Torah*, Shemini Atzeres, 86c).

In this form of dancing, we hold our own space for a moment when we are on the periphery, and then when we press toward the center of the circle we allow others to enter our personal space. This teaches us in a kinesthetic and tangible way that we can welcome people into our space when we feel confident and secure in holding our individual space. The repetitive in-and-out movement of the circle builds this ability to be both independent and close to others.

PAUSING & BEING PRESENT IN THE MOMENT

On the Shabbos of Sukkos, many have the custom of reading the Book of Koheles, which acutely demonstrates the transient nature of life and nature, the fickleness of life, and the vanity of it all: "Utter emptiness, utter emptiness, all is empty...."

Koheles expands on this insight: "A generation goes and another generation comes," "The sun rises, and the sun sets," "a time for being born, and a time for dying," "a time for planting and a time for uprooting the planted," "a time for weeping and a time for laughing," "a time for wailing and a time for dancing...." Everything is part of a great, timeless circle dance. Everything ventures out and then returns home, separates and unifies, differentiates and equalizes, ceaselessly turning, and turning again.

Paradoxically, we too, in turn, also progress through a linear, temporal dimension of life as well: "The sum of the matter is this, when all is said and *done*: revere Hashem and observe His commandments, for that is the entirety of man. And he *will* stand judgment…" (*Koheles*, 12:13-14). At the end of the progression of past to future, all of the Divine-infused consciousness and action that we have cultivated will be revealed in its glory and fullness. In this culmination of our journey, we will see our utter fullness, as well as the emptiness of all the fleeting vanities and trivialities to which we had been attached.

In a linear paradigm of time, we have a past, present and future. Yesterday we were 'there', today we are 'here', and tomorrow we will be 'somewhere else'. Everything fluctuates and is in continuous movement. This is true on physical, emotional, mental and spiritual levels. Maybe I was happy long ago in the past, and now I experience apprehension for the future, but the cyclical nature of reality, which is is replicated throughout all the cosmos, can also prompt us to focus more on the present moment, and to be 'empty' of our past and future, just full of joy in the ever present now.

Throughout all of Sukkos, and all the more so on Simchas Torah, we embody the world of circles, of Hakafos. As we dance and turn, we reconnect with the beautiful, majestic, unfolding of the present moment as it emerges from the Divine *Ayin* / Emptiness — and this triggers ecstatic lightness and unbridled, unconditional Simchah.

On Shemini Atzeres / Simchas Torah, the day(s) of 'stopping', we also 'move' with great dynamism; we are independent and we are welcoming, empty and full; we transcend the body *with* the body, we are serenely empty and we are overflowing with exuberant aliveness and joy; we are stillness dancing.

Chapter 2

TIME FOUND &
HAVING ARRIVED HOME

Regarding the eighth day of Sukkos, called עצרת / Atzeres, Rashi says: "The word עצרת is derived from the root *Atzar* / עצר / 'hold back' or stop, as in, 'I, Hashem, am keeping you here with Me for one more day.' This is similar to the case of a king who invited his children to a banquet for a certain number of days. When the time arrived for them to take their departure he said, 'Children, I beg of you, stay one day more with me; קשה עלי פרידתכם / it is so hard for me to part with you'" (Rashi, *Vayikra*, 23:36. See also, *Sukkah*, 55b. The word קשה is numerically 405, as the Names Hashem / 26, Sha'dai / 314, and Ado-noi / 65, are Names connected with *Zivug* / unity (*Sotah*, 2a), hence their connection to Shemini Atzeres).

'From My perspective,' declares our beloved Divine King, 'I am always with you. However, from your vantage point, you perceive yourselves as leaving Me. Indeed, as you depart and separate, each returning to your own homes and places, you are "separating" from Me' (*Likutei Sichos* 2, Shemini Atzeres / Simchas Torah, p. 433).

In this way, Shemini Atzeres is the day when Hashem says, 'It is difficult for Me to see you depart after all the intimate holy days we have shared together! It is also difficult for Me to see you, My children, depart from each other, after seeing you forgiving each other, befriending each other, gathering together, and growing together, in precious harmony for so many days. So please stay with Me here, in the atmosphere of Yom Tov, for one more day!'

The question is, how will one more day together alleviate the pain of departing? It seems only to postpone the departure.

'Found time is always precious.' Imagine you are on a four-day vacation, and on the night that you are scheduled to return home and to your job, your boss calls and says, 'We don't need you tomorrow at work, take another day off.' It is just one more day, nonetheless, it brings a special type of joy. This is the joy of Shemini Atzeres. Hashem says to us, 'Take another day off, it's on Me! Stay with Me for another day of our intimate spiritual vacation. It's hard for me to see you go; please let's be together one more day.'

All other days of Yom Tov are set forth as official days of encountering Hashem during historical moments on the calendar. Shemini Atzeres is not the commemoration of a historic event in the past; it does not appear on 'the calendar of historical moments', so it is not part of the 'originally planned vacation'. With the addition of Shemini Atzeres, both we and HaKadosh Baruch Hu, as it were, feel elated with the extra day together.

THE ADVANTAGE OF BEING AT HOME & ON VACATION

For all the excitement and magic of traveling and vacationing, there is still nothing like coming home again, eating your own food and sleeping in your own bed. There is a deep comfort that comes with familiarity. Shemini Atzeres is the best of both worlds. We move from the Sukkah back into our home, and yet, we are still on our spiritual vacation, even while at home.

Regarding the extra joy of Shemini Atzeres, the Rambam writes that Shemini Atzeres comes to complete the joy of Sukkos, since on Sukkos we were not able to fully enjoy the holidays as we were sitting outdoors and not living comfortably in our homes. Now that we leave our temporary dwelling and find refuge from the elements indoors, we can truly relax and celebrate (אבל צאתנו מסוכות למועד שני רצוני לומר שמיני עצרת, הוא להשלים בו מן

השמחות מה שאי אפשר לעשותו בסוכות אלא בבתים הרחבים ובבנינים: *Moreh Nevuchim,*
3:43. Note Targum Yonasan: ביומא תמינאה כנישין תהוון חדוא מן מטילכון לבתיכון כנישת
חדוא ויומא טבא / "On the eighth day, gathering into one's home should be done
with joy. When you enter your home it shall be a day of joy and a Yom Tov":
Bamidbar, 29:35).

Our joy on Shemini Atzeres is more penetrating and abundant because we are finally home. In fact, when Shemini
Atzeres is defined as רגל בפני עצמו / 'a festival day on its own', it
also means that on Shemini Atzeres we do not sit in a Sukkah,
but rather return to 'our own' home (*Sukkah,* 48a. Says Rashi, רגל בפני
עצמו, שאין יושבין בסוכה (Although, see also Rashi, *Yuma,* 3a. *Rosh Hashanah,*
4b. *Chagigah,* 17a). As the Targum, *ibid.,* writes, ביומא תמינאה כנישין תהוון חדוא
מן מטילכון לבתיכון. Some communities sit, as Chabad does, in a Sukkah on
Shemini Atzeres; others recite Kiddush in a Sukkah, but not because of an
obligation of the day).

On a deeper level, the joy of coming home is not merely the
joy of no longer being on the move, and the relief of resting
from travel and movement, rather, more inwardly, it is the profound joy of having 'arrived'. After working hard to get somewhere, whether physically, mentally, emotionally, or spiritually,
when we finally have a breakthrough, the sensation of having
arrived brings us immense joy.

Home is Presence

Home is Being

Home is Arriving.

On Shemini Atzeres we come Home.[*]

Besides being a *Regel* / festival day 'in its own right', Shemini Atzeres is still part of Sukkos, the time of 'spiritual vacation'
and 'travel', and transcends our regular activities and self-per-
ception. We still have a sense of radiant sacred time and the
delicious Divine embrace — yet now, all this is present within
the context of the comfort and familiarity of our own home.

---

[*] This is especially true if we view our time outdoors, in the Sukkah, as a type
of exile for the purpose of atonement. The Medrash teaches, למה אנו עושין
סוכה אחר יום הכפורים [לומר לך שכן] אתה מוצא בראש השנה יושב הקדוש ברוך הוא בדין על
באי העולם וביום הכפורים הוא חותם את הדין שמא יצא דינן של ישראל לגלות ועל ידי כן עשוין
סוכה וגולין מבתיהן לסוכה והקדוש ברוך הוא מעלה עליהן כאלו גלו לבבל *Yalkut Shimoni,*
Emor, Remez, 653. See *Eliyah Rabbah,* Orach Chayim, 625: איתא במדרש אמר
ר' אליעזר למה אנו עושין סוכות אחר יום כיפור אלא שמא יצא דינינו ביום כיפור לגלות לכן אנו
עושין סוכה וגולין מבתיהם לסוכה / "It is brought in the Medrash: Rebbe Eliezer
said, 'Why do we make Sukkos after Yom Kippur? Insofar as our judgment
on Yom Kippur is to be exiled, we make a Sukkah and exile ourselves from
our homes to the Sukkah." See also *Sha'arei Teshuvah,* ibid. In the words of
Rebbe Yonason Eibshutz, והנה יעצה לנו התורה בסוכות שהוא סוף ימי תשובה לקבל
על עצמנו גלות ולהיות כל העולם נחשב בעינינו כתוהו וכצלו *Ya'aros Devash* 1, Derush,
6. Or as the Pele Yoetz writes on *Sukkah,* 256: "והיא העומדת לאדם לכפר במקום
גלות / and the Sukkah stands for the person to atone in the place of exile."
Additionally, Sukkos is called *Rishon Hu l'Cheshbon Avonos* / "the first day
(of the year) for accounting of sins" *Tanchuma,* Emor, 22:1. Having come
from Yom Kippur and being busy in building the Sukkah and buying the
Four Species, we are so involved in Mitzvos that there is no time to sin.
Thus Sukkos is the time to complete our Teshuvah.

Throughout our journey through Tishrei, we have been moving upward and inward in stages of closeness to our Beloved, until we reached a place where we can be intimate with HaKadosh Baruch Hu in a very real and meaningful way. We have elevated our lives into a *Panim-el-Panim* / face-to-Face with our Creator. At the peak of this spiritual mountain, we abruptly move from the Sukkah into our home, bringing all the rarified purity, beauty, joy and freedom indoors with us. The highest levels of consciousness are suddenly integrated with our home, the primary structure of our mundane life. Our inner work has been done and we have come full circle. We have arrived.

Shemini Atzeres, the Eighth Day, is of the supernatural world and paradigm of eight — beyond, yet including, the natural cycle of seven. It is at once 'above time' and 'within time'. For this reason, it can hold the paradox of movement and arrival; being outside our familiar place and constructs, and yet being settled, at home.

MOVEMENT WITHIN A WORLD BEYOND MOVEMENT: A PLACE OF ARRIVING

Speaking of Shemini Atzeres, our Sages tell us that this eighth day of Sukkos is similar to a grand seven-day party thrown by a king for all his subjects. After the seventh day, all the other subjects leave, and the king says to his chosen beloved one, 'We have already fulfilled our obligation towards our subjects, now let us, just me and you, celebrate together!' In the words of the Medrash, נגלגל אני ואתה / "Let us frolic (literally 'roll') together, me and you" (*Bamidbar Rabbah*, 21:24: משל למלך שעשה

סעודה שבעת ימים וזימן כל בני שבמדינה בשבעת ימי המשתה כיון שעברו שבעת ימי המשתה אמר לאוהבו כבר יצאנו ידינו מכל בני המדינה נגלגל אני).

What does the word נגלגל / *Nigalgel* / 'frolic' mean in the context of this Yom Tov?

A *Gal* / גל is a wave, a rising movement. Normally, when we speak of movement, it is a movement for the purpose of getting somewhere, as in, a person moves from point A to get to point B. *Ni-gal-gel* contains a 'doubling' of the word *Gal*. When a word is doubled in Hebrew, it means 'a wave *for the purpose of a wave*', a movement for the purpose of that movement itself. This movement is not to get somewhere, but rather, simply to move, enjoying the movement itself. On this Yom Tov, we spend time together with Hashem just for the purpose of spending time together.

On a deep level, *Gal-Gal* means movement without movement, a movement within the stillness of already having arrived. We are simply frolicking and playing with HaKadosh Baruch Hu, as it were, sensing that our work and goals have already been accomplished, yet still feeling empowered to move forward. There is a sense of joyful excitement, of traveling, coupled with the ease of beingness and stillness.

On this day, our sense of having arrived at home means that we are beyond the world of movement, process, and progress, and even focused inner work and growth. Our only *Avodah* / work is to 'play', to עצר / *Atzor* / stop climbing and just to frolic joyfully in the intimate embrace of HaKadosh Baruch Hu. The Mitzvah act of the day is to 'not-do', to do beyond doing.

At the end of the progression of the Yamim Tovim we are connected with the 'end of progression' the *Acharis haYamim* / End of Days, the goal and reward of all history, the state of arrival and redemption after all the hard work that Klal Yisrael has done throughout the entire process of time.

We move from the seven days of Sukkos, during which we sat in the embrace of the Seven Heavens, to being in the paradox of 'eight', at home in this world and yet, at the same time, in the highest of heavens. Shemini Atzeres / Simchas Torah is Heaven on Earth.

This is a time when we are "to You Alone" (לְךָ לְבַדְּךָ: *Mishlei*, 5:17. *Medrash Rabbah*, Shemos, 15:23. *Sefer haMa'amarim Melukat*, Vol. 1, p. 363), a day when אני ואתם נשמח ביחד / "I and you shall celebrate together" (*Yalkut Shimoni*, Emor). Unlike the previous days of Sukkos, when we celebrated "in front of Hashem" — as it says, ושמחתם לפני ה' אלקיכם שבעת ימים / "And rejoice *before Hashem your G-d* for seven days" (*Vayikra*, 23:40) — today we celebrate ביחד / together, joined as one, as it were. We are not 'in front of', rather 'with'. One this day, ישראל ומלכא בלחודוהי / "Yisrael and the King are alone" (*Zohar* 3, 34a. *Ohr haTorah*, Shemini Atzeres, p. 2,149).

When we find ourselves alone with the King, nestled in the inner chambers of deepest Unity, we can present our heart's desires to the King, and our wishes will surely be fulfilled. As the holy Zohar beautifully expresses, "In this profound joy, the King is alone with us... and whatever we wish to ask, we are granted" (*Zohar* 3, 32a: ...ובההוא חדוותא לא משתכחי במלכא אלא ישראל בלחודייהו (כל מה דבעי שאיל, ויהיב ליה).

Megilas Esther portrays an intimate moment between the King and Queen Esther: ויאמר המלך לאסתר גם ביום השני במשתה היין מה־שאלתך אסתר המלכה ותנתן לך / "The King said to Esther on the second day, during the feast of wine, 'What do you request Esther, and I will give it to you!'" Says the illustrious sage and Mekubal, the Rebbe of the Beis Yoseph, Rebbe Yoseph Tai-tazak, "the second day the day of the feast of wine" refers to the second day after Hoshana Rabbah — the day of Simchas Torah (*Kaf haKetores*, Tehilim, 116). This day is like Hoshana Rabbah, 'the night of whispers', as explored earlier, when the King of the Universe whispers to us, 'Please tell me what you truly want,' and the flow of Divine abundance is completely open to us. However, on Shemini Atzeres / Simchas Torah, our request is not transmitted via somber recitations of Tehilim and extra supplications, rather simply through our overflowing joy. In our pure Simchah and intimacy, completely at home with our Beloved, even whispers are hardly necessary. In our oneness, the Beloved simply looks at us with the sweetest 'smile', and knows exactly what we need. We spontaneously receive everything we ever wanted: just to frolic affectionately with our Friend, our Infinite-Intimate Only One, the Source of All Blessings.

THE JOY OF BEING 'IN THE RIGHT PLACE'

To be at home is to be exquisitely comfortable in your place, knowing that here is where you are meant to be. Much anxiety, discomfort, frustration, and disempowerment can come from not knowing your own *Makom* / place, whether socially, professionally, or spiritually, let alone geographically. עז וחדוה במקומו / "Strength and joy are in *Mekomo* / His place" (*Divrei haYamim*, 1, 16:27. *Chagigah*, 5b). This Pasuk applies to us as well: when we come to dwell in our true *Makom* / place, we feel strength and joy, a sense of purpose, aliveness, alertness, presence, and empowerment. This is the joy of being.

Our *Avodah* / inner work during Sukkos is to find our place, to discover our space within the Divine space, within the transient and temporary space of the Sukkah. On Shemini Atzeres, we are literally returning home. Having found our place out in the world, we can now appreciate our place, our home-base, like never before. We are fully present within the deeper joy of being in the right place, exactly where we are meant to be.

Shavuos is the *Atzeres* / culmination / absorption of Pesach, much as Shemini Atzeres is the Atzeres of Sukkos and by extension the entire progression of high holidays, Rosh Hashanah and Yom Kippur as well. Yet, Shavuos is fifty days after Pesach, whereas Shemini Atzeres is the day after Sukkos. Says the Medrash, "Shemini Atzeres theoretically should be fifty days after Sukkos, just as Shavuos, the Atzeres of Pesach, is fifty days after Pesach.* It is only that Hashem said, 'Winter is coming and it will be difficult for them to travel from their homes and come here (six weeks later, back to the Beis haMikdash in Yerushalayim), so since they are already here, let them celebrate (this Atzeres) right now'" (*Tanchuma*, Pinchas 15). On a deeper level, the Medrash is saying that on Shemini Atzeres we do not need to 'travel' to Yerushalayim, our collective home, as we do for the three Yamim Tovim, Pesach, Shavuos and Sukkos. This is because on Shemini Atzeres / Simchas Torah we are 'there already'.

---

* Shavuos is seven weeks after Pesach. This represents the fact that in order to properly 'absorb' the Light and freedom of Pesach, be cleansed from the impurities of 'Egypt', and receive the Torah on Shavuos, we need to cleanse ourselves for forty-nine days, seven times seven. This is much like the seven 'clean days' after menstruation, before intimacy. *Zohar* 3, 97a. Similarly, on Shemini Atzeres / Simchas Torah we celebrate the absorption of the Second Luchos (given on Yom Kippur) and the Torah she-b'Al Peh, which comes after attaining freedom from the *Yetzer haRa* / negative inclination on Yom Kippur. Despite the fact that Shemini Atzeres / Simchas Torah 'should' have been seven weeks after Sukkos, we celebrate it immediately following Sukkos. Part of the reason for this — in addition to the reason just mentioned — is that the Avodah of Yom Kippur is Teshuvah and on Sukkos, we celebrate the Clouds of Glory that were generated specifically through our Teshuvah (the Clouds of Glory being a manifestation of the Ketores, as explored earlier). The world of Teshuvah was created 'before' Creation (*Pesachim*, 54a), beyond Creation, beyond time. As Teshuvah is beyond time, it can be accomplished in one moment (*Zohar* 1, 129a); transformation is instantaneous, and we do not need to wait seven full weeks to cleanse and transform. On the deepest level, Teshuvah is instantaneous because it is really the revelation and awareness that we are 'already there', 'already whole' and 'already home'.

We are already in Yerushalayim, the home of Klal Yisrael, even in our house or apartment, wherever it may be (Note Chasam Sofer, *Derashos* 2, p. 236). This is the radical shift in awareness we make on Shemini Atzeres / Simchas Torah: we realize we are essentially always in our true Makom.

Chapter 3
LAUGHTER & TRANSCENDENCE

Near the end of *Sefer Mishlei* / The Book of Proverbs, it says, עז־והדר לבושה ותשחק ליום אחרון / *Oz*, 'power', and *Hadar*, 'splendor', are Her garments, and she laughs on the last day" (*Mishlei*, 31:25). *Oz* refers to the 'powerful' day of Rosh Hashanah, the day of Divine Judgment, when we are allotted our empowerment and blessings for the coming year. *Hadar* refers to the splendorous days of Sukkos. On Sukkos, we hold a *Pri Eitz Hadar* / fruit of a tree of beauty, which is the Esrog. "She" refers to Klal Yisrael, and "laughs on the last day" refers to Shemini Atzeres / Simchas Torah, 'the time of our joy' — and the 'last (holy) day' of Tishrei (*Pirush haGra*, ad loc.).

Laughter is intrinsically connected with this final day in this long progression of Yamim Tovim. It is brought down in the talks of the Rebbe Rayatz that on Simchas Torah, Chasidim would find things to make them laugh.

As explored, the entire process of the Tishrei holy days is to reach a state of *Zivug* / unity, 'coupling' with HaKadosh Baruch Hu by the time Shemini Atzeres arrives. To enter this state of intimacy, there are two preliminary stages, the great sage Rav teaches us: שח ושחק / to speak with love, and to create a sense of lightness and laughter (רב כהנא על, גנא תותיה פורייה דרב. שמעיה דשח ושחק ועשה צרכיו: *Berachos*, 62a).

Rosh Hashanah and Yom Kippur, and to some extent Sukkos as well, are all about 'speaking'. Most of these days are spent in Davening; praying to, and lovingly communicating with, Hashem. In fact, we recite an entire *Machzor* / special prayer book, on Rosh Hashanah and on Yom Kippur. Now, having said all that was needed to be said, we can finally enter the world of laughter and become ready for deep intimacy.

A DAY / TIME BEYOND WORK OR LEVUSHIM / GARMENTS

Throughout the days of Tishrei, we interacted with many *Levushim* / garments or intermediaries such as the Shofar, the Lulav and Esrog and the Sukkah, through which we connected with the Divine. Specific practices and interfaces helped us connect with the power of these days. Those were days of עז־והדר לבושה / "Strength and splendor are her garments."

Garments reveal something of a person by means of conceal-ment. On Shemini Atzeres we no longer need the conceal-ment of an interface; we find ourselves beyond all *Levushim /* vessels, 'methods', and practices, and we spontaneously "laugh on the last day." This laughter comes from a sudden awareness of pure presence, of openly revealed 'being' — and a realization that despite all our hard work to get 'here', we were paradoxi-cally always 'here'. Humorously, even in all our striving, we are never not here.

LAUGHTER AS RELEASE

Laughter is triggered by the stark incongruity between an expectation and the actual scenario or outcome. For example, we expect a person to be held up by the chair he is sitting on, and when they are not, it can trigger a comedic release within us. The more inconsistent and unexpected the punchline, the funnier the joke.

Our brains are hardwired to observe, interpret, and make sense of our three-dimensional reality. Observing the world in sequence, one image after the next, one sound after the next, our brains are conditioned to process information linearly and rationally; 'one plus one equals two' seems to be iron-clad wis-dom. When a seemingly indelible pattern is broken, when we see that in this case perhaps 'one plus one' does not equal two in a certain context, the brain's capacity to process is suspended and the tension of cognitive dissonance is discharged through laughter.

We expect certain patterns in *Avodah* / inner work and character development: we assume we need to move one step at a time, incrementally and linearly. We believe that serving our Creator conforms to the world of process and progress, and that the more work and effort we put into the journey, the more successful we will be. This is our perception of the linear progression of the Yamim Tovim, as well. Then, when the final Yom Tov day comes, we are invited to 'stop', as we have arrived at the goal, the 'end of days', the world of reward and *Tachlis* / ultimate purpose. After all the hard work throughout the month, and really throughout the entire exile, we are told, 'And now you are Home! There's nothing more to do and nowhere to go. This is the grand, cosmic 'joke' of Creation; it does not make sense to the rational mind that we can let go of effortfully reaching toward self-improvement and an elusive future redemption.

After all the work and progress, throughout the month and throughout the year, we are told on Shemini Atzeres that we do not need to do anything, for whatever we are looking for is already right here. We hear that all we need to do is open our eyes and behold the utterly unexpected, almost unbelievable truth: our 'little me' is, right now and right here, in total Divine intimacy and union! And this is why she, Klal Yisrael, "laughs on the final day."

YITZCHAK / LAUGHTER IS 'OUR FATHER'

In the times of Moshiach, we will call Yitzchak, specifically, "our father" (*Shabbos*, 89b). The name Yitzchak means laughter and indeed he was named because of laughter. Avraham, his father, embodied the Avodah of Chesed, a mode of spiritual work characterized by a movement of light from above to below; drawing Hashem's Light down into the world of apparent darkness, in order to reveal more and more light within the world. Yitzchak, on the other hand, was the embodiment of Gevurah, characterized by a movement of light from below to above. Yitzchak dug wells; his Avodah was to reveal the depths of holiness concealed within the darkness, for within the dark recesses of the earth there are already living waters, wellsprings of life and Divine Light (*Torah Ohr*, Toldos).

Both 'drawing Light down into darkness' and 'revealing Light within darkness' suggest a dichotomy between Light and darkness. But the great cosmic punchline of creation is that there never was a real dichotomy, because darkness never ultimately existed in its own right. If you dig deeper and deeper into any form of darkness, whether inwardly into your subconscious mind or outwardly into worldly negativity, you will in the end always strike 'living waters', Divine aliveness, flow, and Light.

At the end of time, this will be the punchline to all of human history. We will laugh at the awesome awareness that darkness never had any real existence; it was only a temporary concealment of the ever-present Light of Hashem.

Laughter comes about when you are shown that what you thought was true is not. Naturally, we think that this physical world is separate from its Source, even though the Creator has revealed the fact that *Ein Od Milvado* / "There is nothing but Hashem" (*Devarim*, 4:35). When the cognitive dissonance between our thoughts and the true status of the physical world will be resolved, all experiences will be seen for what they already always were: refractions of the Infinite Light of Hashem radiating within a finite hue. And so, Yitzchak, laughter, will be our 'father', our source of identity and our wellspring of inspiration.

THE AVODAH BEYOND AVODAH

After all the Avodah and hard spiritual labor of drawing Light into the darkness, gradually refining Galus, it is revealed that Hashem's Light is right here; there is nothing to do and nowhere to go.

That future time when "She will laugh at the end of days" is essentially always here in the depths of the present moment. One who can penetrate this mystery can have a liberating laugh at their sense of mortality. One who presently tastes *Olam haBa* / the Coming World can laugh about *Olam haZeh* / this world, because they see how all pain and suffering, all hardships and concealments, will be effortlessly flipped to joy and redemption (*Meor Einayim* on *Berachos*, 31a. *Beis Yaakov*, Toldos, 13:1). They can laugh because ultimately all concealment will be shown to be part of the process of revelation. The *Tzimtzum* / constriction of the Infinite Light itself will be *Ya'ir* / illuminated. Not only will there be a disclosure of Hashem's Infinite light within this world of Tzimtzum, the 'Tzimtzum itself will shine.' Conceal-ment will paradoxically reveal the Infinite Presence of Hashem within the apparent void.

This is the inner *Ohr* / illumination and awareness that we taste on Shemini Atzeres / Simchas Torah. Recognizing this is an 'Avodah beyond Avodah', a dynamism revealed within restful *Atzor* / 'stillness', presence revealed within process.

It should be clear that in order for us to attain the *Geulah Kelalis* / collective, historical redemption, or even to attain a *Geulah Peratis* / an authentic 'personal liberation', we need to labor through a process of becoming, journeying, striving, of yearning, hoping, and growing. We need to arrive at the peak of the mountain before we realize that the peak is wherever we stand. This is because redemption is only revealed through contrast with exile; light cannot be perceived without any con-trast with darkness.

The Torah itself is written with 'black fire' upon 'white fire' (*Medrash Rabbah*, Devarim, 3:12. *Medrash Rabbah*, Shir haShirim, 5:11. *Tanchuma*, Bereishis, 1), 'black fire' refers to Torah that is revealed to us in our dualistic world, in the black ink letters of the Torah delineating how we ought to live and practice life, the Mitz-vos. 'White fire' refers to the parchment or the transcendental white light that surrounds and fills the open spaces of the let-ters. In order to access this white fire beyond Avodah, we must engage with the black fire, the Avodah of righting our wrongs and elevating ourselves.

SIMCHAS TORAH AND THE WHITE FIRE

On Simchas Torah, we connect and are connected with the white fire of the Torah, the Ohr beyond intellectual and spiritual exertion. For this reason, we dance with the Torah on Simchas Torah, rather than celebrate the Torah by learning more Torah. And this is the reason we dance with a wrapped Torah as opposed to an open Torah which can be read and intellectually deciphered and understood. We are connecting with the Essence of the Torah, beyond the letters and words, beyond intellectualism, beyond learning, and even beyond efforts to perform Mitzvos, as it were.

On the level of black fire of Torah, some are more learned and others are less learned. On the level of the transcendent white fire of the Torah, all of us, whether a scholar or not, whether behaving righteously (or not yet), we are directly connected and bound to the holy Torah.

At the time we left Egypt, there were 600,000 men, paralleling the 600,000 'root' souls of Klal Yisrael. Yet, there were many more than that in Klal Yisrael who left Mitzrayim, and throughout history, countless souls have been embodied. All of these millions of souls are 'combinations' of the 600,000 root souls. Our Sages say that just as there are 600,000 'root' souls, there are 600,000 'root' letters in the Torah.

If one actually counts the letters of the Torah, one will discover that there are much less than 600,000; in fact there are only about 304,800 letters in the Torah. Yet, 600,000 does not need to refer to the literal black letters; just as there are many combinations of souls, there are many 'sub-letters' or combinations of root letters.

One way to unpack these sub-letters, and potentially count them, is to take notice of the 'white fire letters', the hidden letter-like forms and empty spaces that subtly appear within and around the black letters. For example, if you relax your gaze for a moment, you can clearly see a white letter Chaf (כ) nestled within the letter Pei (פ). Another way to see sub-letters is to notice the presence of 'small letters' forming each regular letter. For example, there are two Yuds (י) and a Vav (ו) within the letter Aleph; a Yud above, a Yud below, and a tilted Vav in the middle (א).

Yet another way of enumerating the 600,000 root letters is by counting the Yuds in each letter. For example, Aleph has two Yuds, Gimel (ג) has one, and Shin has three (ש). Also, the *Milu'im* / 'fillings' of letters could be counted, meaning spelling out their names. For example, *Aleph* is spelled Aleph, Lamed, Pei. The Milu'im of the *Targum* / Aramaic translations of the letters could also be counted as sub-letters (See *Chesed l'Avraham*, 2. *Pri Tzadik*, Shemos. *P'nei Yehoshua*, Kidushin, 30a. *Likutei Torah*, Behar, 43d. Although counting the Milu'im of every regular letter in the Torah would admittedly produce many more than 600,000 letters).

Our root soul, who we are in our essence, is intrinsically one with the White Fire of the Torah, no matter our level of scholarship or conscious engagement with the Black Fire of the Torah. The word ישראל / Yisrael is an acronym for יש שישים ריבוא אותיות לתורה / "There are 600,000 letters (again, meaning sub-letters) in the Torah" (*Zohar Chadash*, Shir haShirim). This means that every soul is rooted in a letter, or 'sub-letter', of the Torah (*Megaleh Amukos. P'nei Yehoshua*, ibid.).

On Simchas Torah, everyone dances with the Torah, not only the scholars and sages and the pious ones who were already dancing on the nights of Simchas Beis haShoeivah. We dance with a wrapped, closed Torah scroll, which hides the black letters, so to speak, leaving only the hidden 'white fire' with which everyone is connected.

A person may think, 'What do I have to do with Hashem's Torah? I'm far from understanding it; I'm estranged from it. I practice very little — and even that, I barely hold onto when push comes to shove. I wish I could learn Torah, but I don't know much Hebrew and the concepts are difficult to understand....' Simchas Torah comes and an intuitive sense spontaneously bubbles up: 'I just want to grab the Torah scroll and dance with it! I and the Torah are one!' This is a true intuition; the root of who you are and the root of the Torah are forever and inseparably one.

For those who sadly live their lives in disconnection or estrangement from the beauty, wisdom and wholeness of a life of Torah observance, this oneness may seem unreal, like a joke. Yet, even so, the joke has a punchline, an unexpected resolution: no matter one's state, no matter how far one has wandered, one is always connected with and at home in the Divine Torah, indelibly inscribed as one of its revealed or hidden letters.

On Simchas Torah, the ultimate resolution and punchline to all riddles and jokes is revealed, for on this Final Day, we suddenly see all our deeper wholeness and connection that had been concealed to us.

In Hebrew, the word for laughter is שחוק / *S'chok*. This word has a numerical value of 414, the same as the term, אור אין סוף / *Ohr Ein Sof* / Infinite Light (*Ohr haTorah*, Beha'alosecha, p. 331a. See also the Mahara M'panu, *5550, Likutim.* Alternatively, שחוק equals twice the word אור / *Ohr*: Arizal, *Sha'ar haMitzvos*, Vayelech). Sometimes the ability to laugh is what allows us to transcend our limited, confined perceptions and conceptions of our lives. If we always focus on limited, linear, strict definitions of reality, as if 'law and order' is the only valid paradigm in life, our relationship with Torah may sadly feel a bit dim and alienating. When we laugh, we open our minds and hearts to a broader view of reality; we glimpse flashes and sparks of the Infinite Light, and we have intuitions of Infinite Truth. We sense a connection with a wisdom that is much deeper than our limited personal perceptions; we feel a profound and unwavering unity with Hashem's Infinite Torah.

Laughing at the End of Time / ותשחק ליום אחרון is also a laugher of overcoming our own 'final day' — our mortality. Joy and laughter reveal our intimate bond, our ultimate oneness, with the Source of All Life, and connect us to the world of immortality, the 'end' of all concealment and separation, the world of *Chayim Nitzchiyim* / eternal life.

Laughter is a foretaste of the complete and final Redemption. In the holy words of Sarah Imeinu, צחק עשה לי אלקים כל־ השמע יצחק־לי / "Elokim (constriction) has made laughter for me; whoever hears (understands) will laugh for me..." (*Bereishis*, 21:6). It is as if she is saying, 'When the great, meta-historical joke is deeply heard; when the total expansiveness of my people's Redemption is fully understood as the product of the contraction of their exile, the entire cosmos will burst out in cathartic laughter for us, and unbelievable joy.'

Chapter 4

SASON & SIMCHAH: JOY OF BEING & JOY OF MOVEMENT

I n *Eretz Yisrael* / the Land of Israel, Shemini Atzeres and Simchas Torah are on the same day. In the Diaspora, there are two days of Yom Tov, and the second day of the Yom Tov of Shemini Atzeres is dedicated to the celebration of *Simchas Torah* / the Joy of Torah. Sukkos is an eight-day Yom Tov — seven days of Sukkos, plus the eighth day of Shemini Atzeres, yet, in the diaspora, there are nine days of Sukkos, and the added day has its own name, *Simchas Torah.*

WHY THE ADDED DAY IN THE DIASPORA?

The first day of Sukkos must be on the fifteenth of Tishrei, the midpoint of the month. Months follow the lunar cycle, and in the times of the Beis haMikdash, the beginning of the new monthly cycle was established when two witnesses came to the High Court and testified that they had seen the new moon.

A lunar cycle is twenty-eight days, however, because of its interaction with the solar cycle and from our vantage point on planet earth, it usually takes approximately twenty-nine and a half days after the previous new moon for the current new moon to be revealed to the eye. Since the new moon is only visible after twenty-nine days, and even then it might not be immediately seen, months can have either twenty-nine or thirty days.

If, on the thirtieth day of a month, two witnesses came forward and properly testified that they saw the new moon, then the High Court would declare *Mekudash, Mekudash* / "Sanctified, sanctified," and that day would become Rosh Chodesh, the first day of the new month. As a result, the previous month would be retroactively defined as a twenty-nine day month. If no witnesses came forward on the thirtieth day of the month (or if it came later in the afternoon), then the High Court would establish the following day as the first day of the new month, and the previous month would have had thirty days.

After the High Court had established the new month, only those close enough to Yerushalayim would know when the new month had begun. This is because messengers would be sent out to notify all the Jewish communities around the world of the day when Rosh Chodesh had occurred. In those times, there were no reliable means of communication other than traveling by foot or by animal, and for those who lived further than a fifteen-day route from Yerushalayim (or even less, due to not being able to travel on Shabbos and Yom Kippur, Rashi, *Rosh Hashanah*, 21a), the timing of the fifteenth day, the beginning of Sukkos, would be uncertain. Since the distant communities could not have been informed that the previous month had been only twenty-nine days, the day that they might assume to be the fifteenth, based on their own observations of the moon, could in fact be the fourteenth.

Our Sages ruled that such a community should celebrate the first two days of Sukkos on *both* days: on the day they assumed to be the fifteenth, and on the day they assumed to be the sixteenth of the month, which might in fact have really been the fifteenth. Since one of the two days would be the actual fifteenth day of the month, the actual day of Sukkos, the distant communities would fulfill the Mitzvos of Sukkos on the correct day. As for the inevitable outcome of celebrating one of the two days of Sukkos on the wrong day, a *Safek* / doubt regarding a *Mitzvah d'Oraysa* / Torah-based Mitzvah should be approached with stringency; it is better to celebrate a Yom Tov on the wrong day than to not celebrate it on the right day. The same logic applies to the eighth day of Sukkos, which potentially, is really only the seventh day, and therefore, we need to celebrate two days.

This is the historical and Halachic reason that holidays are observed for two days in locations outside of Eretz Yisrael, where it would have taken longer than fifteen days for messengers to arrive. Today, there have been numerous advances in calendrical science, we know exactly when the new month is, and we no longer establish new months through witnesses. Yet, we still celebrate Yom Tov in the Diaspora with two days, since it was a universal practice of our ancestors — it is a *Minhag* / custom (the idea of Simchas Torah being on a day that is, in our times, established through Minhag, will be expounded upon later). In other words, we do not enact and celebrate an additional day because of 'doubt'; we clearly know in advance what day the fifteenth is, yet, we continue to celebrate the Yom Tov of Simchas Torah based on the profound power of Minhag.*

* According to the Rambam, "Every place that the messengers *would* reach, they would make the festival a one day Yom Tov — as is written in the Torah": *Kiddush haChodesh*, 3:11. In other words, a new city that was built in Israel would need to keep two days of Yom Tov, as no messengers had ever been sent there: *Kiddush haChodesh*, 5:12. See also *Shu'T Sheilas Ya'avetz*, Siman, 168. Yet, most Rishonim and the Geonim hold that today the distinction between celebrating a one-day and a two-day Yom Tov is the difference between Eretz Yisrael and the Diaspora; in Eretz Yisrael, there is one day, and in the Diaspora there are two. This is the opinion made popular by the Ritva: Ritva, *Rosh Hashanah*, 18a. Ritva, *Sukkah*, 43a. See also *Shu'T Eretz haTzvi*, Siman, 41. הקב"ה ציוה את משה עבדו והוא אמר לישראל, כי בארץ יהיה / להם יום אחד, ובחו"ל שני ימים, וכן היה מעולם "HaKadosh Baruch Hu commanded Moshe, who told it over to Klal Yisrael, that in the Land they will have a one-day Yom Tov, and in the Diaspora they will have two days, and that is the way it was established": Rav Saadia Gaon, quoted in *Shu'T Mishpetei Uziel*, 3, Orach Chayim, 47. *Otzar haGeonim* (4) Beitza, Teshuvos. In other words, this distinction already existed from the time of Moshe. Rashi writes that it is an injunction of Chazal — חכמים קבעום לחובה על בני גולה לעשותם שני ימים טובים לדורות: *Beitzah*, 4b. The *Yerushalmi* explains the Pasuk in *Yechezkel*, 20:25 — וגם-אני נתתי להם חקים לא טובים ומשפטים לא יחיו בהם / 'Moreover, I gave

A UNIQUE HOLIDAY WITH ITS OWN NAME

Even if the second day was originally only established because of a 'doubt' regarding the correct day, still, the second day of Shemini Atzeres is in a sense its own Yom Tov and it is called by its own name, *Simchas Torah*. This is unlike the second Yom Tov day of *Shevi'i shel Pesach* / the 'Seventh of Pesach', which is simply called *Acharon shel Pesach* / 'the Last Day of Pesach'.

Simchas Torah is the name of this day (*Zohar* 3, 256b), although it is also the second day of Yom Tov. This implies that although it is merely the second day of Yom Tov in the Diaspora, it is its own Yom Tov, as it were, and referred to by its own name (*Likutei Sichos*, 9, v'Zos haBerachah 1, Note 12).

In a state of profound spiritual ecstasy, the Mitteler Rebbe once proclaimed; "No one can truly bear (the true light of) Simchas Torah. In the future, when Moshiach arrives, we will all recognize and understand its virtues, and we will yearn for

---

them laws that were not good and rules by which they could not live' — "This refers to the second days of Yom Tov in the Diaspora. 'What caused me to keep two days in Syria? It was the fact I did not keep one day in the Land. I was thinking that I would be rewarded for both, but I am rewarded only for one...' Rebbe Yochanan then invoked for them the Pasuk (*Yechezkel*, 20:25), 'I gave them laws that were *not* good'": *Yerushalmi*, *Eiruvin*, 3:9. Rebbe Chayim haCohen, a Talmid of Rebbe Chayim Vital, writes that this negative view of the second days of Yom Tov refers to the time when they were celebrated because of doubts, but today we celebrate second days because of Minhag, and therefore, the above negative teaching from the *Yerushalmi* does not apply: *Tur Barekes*, Orach Chayim, Siman 669.

it." He then added, "We must have compassion for the people of Eretz Yisrael, who celebrate Simchas Torah on the same day as Shemini Atzeres, as they 'mix vegetables with meat'" (*Sefer haSichos*, 5696, p. 302).

In other words, those who live in the Diaspora have an 'advantage' in that they have a full and separate day to truly celebrate Simchas Torah as its own 'dish'.

SIMCHAH AND SASON

We call the joy of the Torah, Simchas Torah, the Simchah / joy of Torah, but what exactly does Simchah mean?

During the celebration on Simchas Torah, as the *Sifrei Torah* / Torah scrolls are being brought back into the *Aron Kodesh* / ark, we sing a song, that begins, שישו ושמחו בשמחת תורה, ותנו כבוד לתורה / "Have Sason and Simchah on Simchas Torah, and give honor to the Torah...." This suggests that on the day of Simchah, we also need to experience Sason. Sason is colloquially translated as joy, but what is the subtle and perhaps nuanced distinction between the joy of Simchah and the joy of Sason?

There is a fascinating, enigmatic teaching in the Gemara in Sukkah regarding Sason and Simchah, upon which the Gra comments that the entire secret of the two Moshiachs, Redeemers — Moshiach ben Dovid and Moshiach ben Yoseph — is encoded.

"There were these two heretics, one named Sason and one named Simchah. Sason said to Simchah: I am superior to you, as it is written: "They shall obtain joy (*Sason*) and happiness (*Simchah*), and sorrow and sighing shall flee" (*Yeshayahu*, 35:10). The Pasuk mentions Sason first. Simchah said to Sason, 'On the contrary, I am superior to you, as it is written: "For the Jews there was happiness (*Simchah*) and joy (Sason)'" (*Esther*, 8:17). Sason said to Simchah: 'One day they will dismiss you and render you a messenger, as it is written: "For you shall go out with happiness (Simchah)'" (*Yeshayahu*, 55:12). Simchah said to Sason: 'One day they will dismiss you and draw water with you, as it is written: "With joy (*Sason*) you shall draw water'"

הנהו תרי מיני חד שמיה ששון וחד שמיה שמחה א"ל ששון לשמחה אנא עדיפנא מינך דכתיב) ששון ושמחה ישיגו וגו' א"ל שמחה לששון אנא עדיפנא מינך דכתיב שמחה וששון ליהודים א"ל ששון לשמחה חד יומא שבקוך ושויוך פרוונקא דכתיב כי בשמחה תצאו א"ל שמחה לששון חד יומא שבקוך ומלו בך מיא דכתיב ושאבתם מים בששון :יומא *Sukkos*, 48b. It seems from the next episode of Gemara that these are literal people, and as the *Maharsha* writes, כן דרך המינים לפרש הכתובים על עצמם לפי סכלותם והבלם).

Let us decipher this riddle.

DISTINCTIONS BETWEEN SIMCHAH & SASON

In a *Ma'amar* / Chasidic discourse (*Likutei Torah*, U'Sh'avtem Mayim), the Alter Rebbe lays down a few foundations that may help us decode this tale. In contrasting Simchah with Sason, the Alter Rebbe writes that Simchah is the spiritual Avodah, inner work, of the Tribe of Levi. The Levi'im were the ones who served in the Beis haMikdash by playing instruments and singing, among other tasks. As such, Simchah is associated with *Shir* / song and music, and it is connected with wine, a liquid which draws out joy. It corresponds to the 'outwardly' revealed *Torah she-b'Kesav* / the Written Torah, and it is the experience of outwardly revealed revelry. Simchah is connected with the world of *Binah* / understanding and analysis. It is also connected to Moshiach Ben Dovid, who will be revealed to the whole world. In other words, Simchah is a revealed, outward joy.

Sason, on the other hand, is the Avodah of the Cohen, the priests who served quietly inside the Beis haMikdash. As such, Sason is associated with the inner world of silence. Sason is also connected with water (*U'Sh'avtem Mayim b'Sason* / "And with Sason you shall draw water"), water being a liquid that enters inside a body to sustain and nourish its life. Sason corresponds to *Torah she-b'Al Peh* / the Orally Transmitted part of Torah, which is addressed more 'privately' to Klal Yisrael in comparison to the universally revealed Written Torah. The Oral Torah is developed through the wisdom of our Sages who intuit and decode subtle hints within the Written Torah. Sason is connected with the world of *Chochmah* / subtle wisdom and intuition. It is connected to Moshiach Ben Yoseph. In other words, Sason is the experience of a more inward, subtle, concealed expression of joy.*

---

* Sason is also perhaps a sudden joy, whereas Simchah is connected to a more 'processed' joy: *Sheim miShemuel*, Yom haKippurim. The Gra speaks of Simchah as a more internal demonstration of joy, whereas Sason is a more outward expression of joy. See also *Malbim*, Yeshayahu, 35:1: ויש הבדל בין שמחה ששון גיל, השׂשׂון הוא הפעולות החיצונות שיעשׂה להראות השׂמחה... והשׂמחה והגיל הם

THE TWO DYNAMICS WITHIN SUKKOS

Simchah is generally connected with an outward movement and Sason with an inward movement, as expressed in
the Shabbos *Piyut* / liturgy: שמחים בצאתם וששים בבואם / "They
have Simchah when they go out and Sason when they return."
Simchah is related to 'going out', as in growth and movement,
whereas Sason is a calmer form of joy, more like contentment
(The Alter Rebbe explains that Simchah is a revealed, outward joy, whereas
Sason is a more subtle and inward joy, connected with contentment: שכל
שמחה היא התגלות הפנימיית / "All Simcha is the revelation of inner realities": *Torah Ohr*, Miketz, p. 37b. The Gra writes that *Simchah* is a joy that comes from
Hischadshus / experiencing something new, whereas *Sason* is the completion
of something, as in a project, that brings joy in the completion: Gra, Iyov,
3:22. Gra, *Megilas Esther*, 8:16. The Bnei Yissaschar seems to say the opposite, Sason is the anticipation of something good that will happen, Simchah
is the joy attained when it happens: *Bnei Yissaschar*, Tishrei, Ma'amar 10:22.
Agra d'Pirka, 47).

נפשיים, לבד שהשמחה היא השמחה התמידיית הרצופה. See also *Pri Megadim*, Pesicha
Koleles, 2, 60. Yet, the Alter Rebbe clearly explains Simchah and Sason as
explored; Simchah is outward joy and Sason is a more inward joy. See also
Hisva'aduyos 5745, 4, Chag haShavuos, p. 2,181. The Zohar teaches, א"ר אבא
מאיד כתיב כי בשמחה תצאו וגו'. אלא כד יפקון ישראל מן גלותא שכינתא נפקא עמהון ועמה
יפקון. הדא הוא דכתיב כי בשמחה תצאו. ששון דא קב"ה / "Rav Ada said, 'It is written,
And you will go out with Simchah: When Klal Yisrael are redeemed from
exile, the Shechinah ('Simchah', so-to-speak), goes out with them, and together they emerge from captivity. And *Sason* refers to HaKadosh Baruch
Hu, the Holy Transcendent One (Above and 'concealed'): *Zohar*, 3, 212b.
Hence, Simchah is a more revealed attribute, *Kaviyachol* / so-to-speak, of
Hashem, whereas Sason is a more concealed attribute of Hashem.

Simchah is the joy of becoming, while Sason is the joy of being.

Simchah is the joy that comes from achieving goals, while Sason is the simple joy of being alive, awake, and conscious. Simchah includes ambition, drive, and desire. It is a type of joy that arises when things are moving along, going in the right direction. Simchah is therefore connected to *Tz'michah* / 'sprouting' or flourishing vegetation. On Sukkos, we take the Four Minim, four types of vegetation, and we also cover the Sukkah with vegetation, as they express and elicit Simchah, as explored earlier. Sukkos is pervaded with this kind of joy.

Sason is the relaxed joy of stopping and just being present. The Mitzvah of sitting in the Sukkah involved pausing and being present in the Sukkah. The blessing we recite when we sit in the Sukkah is לישב בסוכה / Leishev baSukkah / "to sit in the Sukkah," which also means 'to dwell', or 'to be settled', in the Sukkah. Sitting in the Sukkah is lingering in the Sukkah, simply 'dwelling' or 'being' there. Theoretically, one can still recite this blessing even if we are not going to actually 'sit' in the Sukkah, as *Leishev* also implies to pause and linger (אין ישיבה אלא לשון עכבה: *Megilah*, 21a). Indeed, the idea of dwelling in the Sukkah is to be there fully gathered in, embraced, and held in Divine space. To feel truly settled is to feel that you have found your place. This is the 'presence' and contentment of Sason.

On a deep level, to be happy is actually to be conscious of being-ness itself. Joy is the natural state of life and in fact of all reality; whenever someone or something is 'being itself' there is joy (*Ma'amarei Admur haZaken*, Ketzarim, p. 553).

Simchah is a more excited state of joy arising from 'becoming', such as falling in love, making a new discovery, or having a new insight, while Sason is more an innate strength and delight of being in your *Makom* / place: עז וחדוה במקומו / "Strength and joy are in מקומו / *Mekomo* / His Place" (*Divrei haYamim*, 1, 16:27). When a person is in his or her Makom, their 'right place' in the world, they are not only "in" joy, they *are* joy.

From the perspective of Simchah, everything comes from Hashem Above through *Hashgacha Peratiyus* / Divine and specific providence. The more we are aware of Hashgacha, the more Simchah we experience (Hence, the two fundamental teachings of the Baal Shem Tov, Hashchacha Peratis and the service of Hashem through joy, are linked).

On Simchas Torah, we read the final Parshah in the Torah, finishing the yearly cycle of Torah readings. It is a *Siyyum* / completion, as it were; we have achieved a significant goal and we are full of contentment and gratitude. This is the Sason element of Simchas Torah.

Simchas Torah also celebrates the beginning of a new cycle of Torah study, a new journey and goal, a new effort that will sprout deeper levels of insight. Indeed, as soon as we have completed last year's study cycle, we launch the coming year's cycle. This is why we sing, שישו ושימחו בשמחת תורה / "*Sisu* ('Sason') *vSimchu* ('Simchah') on Simchas Torah...." In the song, 'Sason' precedes 'Simchah', for we first celebrate the Sason of completing the Torah, reading its final portion, and then we celebrate the Simchah of starting a new cycle, beginning the Torah again by reciting the first section of Bereishis.

TWO HERESIES

In the Talmudic tale above, there are two 'heretics'; one the heresy of Sason and the other the heresy of Simchah. What does this allegory mean on a deeper level?

Simchah is the world of 'revelation', exemplified by the Written Torah, which we received from Above at *Matan Torah* / the Giving of the Torah at Mount Sinai. The 'heretic' of Simchah is thus the person who believes only in the Revealed Torah. He does not believe in the Oral aspect of the Torah, because he denies that human beings can participate in the unfolding of the Revelation of the Torah using the tools and principles of interpretation that we received at Mount Sinai. He believes in the Creator, but he does not believe in Klal Yisrael, nor humanity in general. This ideology asserts that only pure objectivity is valid guidance; there is no place for subjective human interpretation and creativity.

In essence, this heresy recognizes only the absolute Divine *Yediah* / knowing and predestination — rejecting any possibility of human *Bechirah* / free choice. In this worldview, everything is determined, and so we are like puppets playing out a Divine scheme. Moshe, too, is nothing more than an open channel for the Divine Wisdom that flows through his hands as the Written Torah.

Sason is connected with the Revelation of Torah she-b'Al Peh, which is revealed through the subtle wisdom and participation of the Sages, in the words of the Ramban, אלא יודעים האמת ברוח הקדש שבקרבם / "They know the truth through *Ruach haKodesh* / holy intuition, within them" (Ramban, *Baba Basra*, 12a).

The corresponding heresy believes only in an absoluteness of human subjectivity, human creativity, and Bechirah. It denies Divine Yediah and insists that the source of power is human intellect alone, insisting that the Creator is impartial or uninvolved in the world He created.

In this ideology, objective truth is denied, and reality and morality are defined subjectively, relative to one's own logic or emotions. One can 'choose' their own reality and do whatever they desire. In a world where nothing is absolute and everything is relative, everything goes, and in the end, nothing really matters.

In a world where everything is up to us, humans must manage the world on their own, and yet they are in a constant struggle with the forces of nature and history, and their own set of laws. If one wishes to survive, he must fight and grab what he needs, for he can only rely on himself.

THE TRUTH LIES WITHIN THE BALANCE
OF SIMCHAH & SASON

Paradoxically, הכל צפוי, והרשות נתונה / everything is foreseen *and* permission is granted" (*Avos*, 3:15), as Rebbe Akiva teaches (זה המאמר כולל דברים גדולים מאד וראוי היה זה המאמר שיהא לר' עקיבא): Rambam, *Pirush haMishnayos*). Both are simultaneously true; Yediah and Bechirah, Divine Providence and free choice, are not actually at odds. Certainly, in a dualistic apprehension of reality, it is difficult to live with this paradox. Our mind cannot make sense of the fact that we have free choice, and yet everything, including our past choices, was foreseen and meant to be. Yet, in truth, everything is foreseen *and* permission is compelled granted, and these two positions are united and harmonized.

In our personal Avodah, the reconciliation or the holding of this paradox plays itself out in the following way. While being overjoyed to know that everything occurs by Divine providence, we also take responsibility for our agency in life. Our happiness comes not only from submitting to Divine objectivity but also from engaging in personal development and growth. The more we subjectively feel like we are growing, succeeding, or advancing in any area of life, we will experience joy. We can have tremendous Simchah in our creativity, for example in our artistic projects or our innovative interpretations of Torah. And more generally, there is joy in being the 'creator' of your life, not being a victim or living at the 'effect' of life, but rather being the 'cause' of your experience. Indeed, a person would rather have one dollar earned than nine given. Still, our

Sason in achievement and engagement with the world can be partnered by Simchah, knowing that ultimately, Hashem rules the world, and gives us the achievements that we worked for, as well as the strength and skill to work for them.

SIMCHAS TORAH WITH A MEASURE OF SASON

The main Avodah of Simchas Torah is Simchah, celebrating the Torah that was gifted to us from On High. We are all connected with the Simchah of Torah, no matter our level of self-development, and no matter what depth of *Bechirah* / free choice we may have cultivated and what our previous choices have been.

We experience such great outward joy on this day that we all openly dance with the Torah, demonstrating our joy in the absolute perfection of the Torah and also in our personal relationship with it.

We sing exuberantly, like Levi'im carrying the Torah, and we celebrate with '*leChayims*' over wine or other intoxicating beverages. Many keep the thousand-year-old custom of going out into the streets and dancing with the Torah in the public domain.

Why do we begin the cycle of Torah reading on Simchas Torah and not on the Yom Tov of Shavuos when the Torah was given? It is because we are celebrating our full 'receiving' of the Torah. We only truly received and 'owned' the Torah in Tishrei, not when it was given many months prior, in Sivan.

Chazal tell us, ביום חתונתו זה מתן תורה / "'On the day of His wedding'; this (Pasuk from *Shir haShirim*) is referring to *Matan Torah* / the giving of the Torah." On Yom Kippur, we received the second set of *Luchos* / Tablets of the Torah from Moshe (*Ta'anis*, 26b. Rashi, *ad loc.*). This culmination of 'receiving' and absorbing what was 'given' only occurred on Yom Kippur, when we had owned our past mistakes with the *Eigel haZahav* / Golden Calf, and demonstrated that this time we truly desired to receive the Torah and live by it.

As explored earlier, the original Clouds of Glory ascended away from Klal Yisrael when some worshiped the Golden Calf, and the Clouds only returned following the atonement of Yom Kippur, with the giving of the second set of Luchos. These Clouds of Glory returned to us through our own *Teshuvah* / return and spiritual Avodah. They activated our *Koach haBechirah* / power to freely choose, and we firmly chose not to be defined and restricted by our past negative behaviors (Teshuvah is Bechirah, and thus the Rambam chose to convey the principles of Bechirah within his exposition of the laws of Teshuvah).

Through our desire to draw closer to Hashem and let go of idol worship, we merited Yom Kippur, the Second Luchos. Through our Teshuvah, the Clouds of Glory returned, and so, in a sense, through our Avodah the Clouds were 'created', leading to the Yom Tov of Sukkos, when the Clouds tangibly settle over us and upon us.

When we received the Second Luchos by means of our Be-chirah, we also received the *Torah she-b'al-Peh* / Oral aspect of the Torah more fully. By receiving the Torah she-b'al-Peh, we received the *Koach* / power to be a *Mechadeish* / innovator, exercising our creativity to form novel Torah interpretations in conjunction with the tools and principles given at Mount Sinai (בראשונות לא ניתן כח החידוש כלל אלא מה ששמע משה הלכות ידע מקורם בתורה שבכתב עפ״י חקים ומשפטים אבל לא ידע לחדש בעצמו אלא בדמוי מילתא למילתא ולא בחידוש הפלפול. משא״כ בשניות ניתן הכח לחדש הלכות בכל דור והיינו מה שתלמיד ותיק עתיד לחדש: *Ha'amek Davar*, Devarim, 4:14).

This is the 'Sason' dynamic of joy within Simchas Torah. Not only do we celebrate the written Torah, what was 'given' to us — but we celebrate Klal Yisrael's 'giving' of inspired in-terpretations rooted in the Written Torah. This is the joy of accepting and assimilating the Torah into our own lives and consciousness and being guided and enlivened by it *b'Penimi-yus* / inwardly.

Reb Baruch Ber, the great *Gaon* / genius and Tzadik and primary student of Rebbe Chayim Brisker, would dance on Simchas Torah grasping the published Torah innovations of his Rebbe, Reb Chayim. It would be wise to take this profound and moving example to heart. It resonates with the spirit of Simchas Torah to dance with a Sefer of the Chiddushim of one's *Rebbe* / chosen teacher, or for that matter, any Sefer that deeply speaks to us. The Torah teachings that are most precious to us are our personal 'Second Luchos', as it were. We should receive these personal revelations into the very core of our being, and rejoice exceedingly with them "for they are our life and the length of our days," literally.

Chapter 5
A MINHAG / CUSTOM AROUSES GREAT JOY ON HIGH

S IMCHAS TORAH IS NOT MENTIONED BY NAME IN THE
TORAH OR THE GEMARA, NOR IS ANY OTHER FORM OF
CELEBRATING THE COMPLETION OF A YEARLY CYCLE
of Torah study. The reason for this is quite simple. Reading and
studying the Torah every week is a tradition dating back to
the times of Moshe and the journey through the Desert (*Baba
Kama*, 82a); in fact, it was Moshe himself who instituted reading
from the Torah every week (*Yerushalmi, Megillah*, 4:1. *Maseches Sofrim*,
10:1. Ramban on *Vayikra*, 23:2). Yet, there was no one prevailing
custom of how much was read each week. Communities living

in *Eretz Yisrael* / the Land of Israel would read the Torah over the course of three years (לבני מערבא דמסקי לדאורייתא בתלת שנין: *Megillah*, 29b. Rashi, *ad loc.*). Those living in *Bavel* / Babylon had a custom to read the Torah over the course of a single year. Today, and for over a thousand years, the prevailing custom worldwide is to complete the Torah in one year (Rambam, *Hilchos Tefilah*, 13:1: ויש מי שמשלים את התורה בשלש שנים ואינו מנהג פשוט).

In order to read the entire Torah in one year, the Torah was divided into fifty-four *Parshiyos* / portions, one *Parshah* / portion for each week. Other sources speak of fifty-three Parshiyos (Nitzavim and Vayelech are essentially one portion, and they are only divided in order to separate the Parshah of *Ki Savo* from Rosh Hashanah: *Tikkunei Zohar*, Tikkun 13. The Zohar 1, p. 100, teaches that there are *fifty* Parshiyos. Indeed, by subtracting the weeks that have special *Yom Tov* / holy day readings, every year contains about fifty weekly readings. Centuries ago in Eretz Yisrael, where the Torah was read in a three-year cycle, Chazal living in Eretz Yisrael referred to 175 Parshiyos of the Torah: *Maseches Sofrim*, 16:19).

In other words, even though today we have fifty-three or fifty-four weekly Parshiyos, and even though the Torah reading follows a yearly cycle with a yearly celebration, the actual portions that we call today a Parshah are not delineated in the Torah scroll itself. There are, however, clearly indicated groupings of the text into very long 'paragraphs' or 'chapters', also called Parshiyos.

There are two types of Parshiyos delineated in the Torah scroll: those that are *Setumah* / closed and those that are *Pesuchah* / open. A Parshah that is Setumah is divided from the subsequent portion by an empty space the size of nine letters. Here, a new Parshah begins on the same line that the Parshah Setumah ended on. Since this leaves very little space between one Parshah and the next, the preceding Parshah is considered a 'closed' Parshah.

A *Parshah Pesuchah* / open portion is followed by empty space extending to the end of the line, so that the next Parshah begins on the following line; thus it is 'open' at the end. The previous Parshah ends before the end of the column, leaving a space at the end of the line, and the new Parshah begins at the start of the next line, albeit without an indentation. There are a total of 669 such open Parshiyos in the Torah. Obviously, these should not be confused with the fifty-three to fifty-four Parshiyos that today we call the 'weekly Parshah'.

Whenever there was a completion of a Torah reading cycle, there was a celebration, just as when one finishes learning a particular section of Gemara one celebrates with a festive Seudah (אמר רבי אלעזר מכאן שעושין סעודה לגמרה של תורה): *Medrash Rabbah,* Shir haShirim, 1:9. *Shabbos,* 118b. The *Ohr Zarua,* 2:320, writes: ובתשיעי ספק שמיני אנו עושין שמחת תורה ומסיימין התורה ומתחילין בראשי וחתני תורה עושין סעודה לכבוד גמר תורה. ובמלכותנו בשושני"א עושים חתני תורה סעודה גמורה ומזמנין מבני הקהל ונותנים להם מאכלים טובים אווזות ותרנגולין ומצאתי עיקרו של מנהג אני המחבר יצחק בר' משה נב"ה בתחילת ש"ם מדרש שה. Similarly, the *Shibolei haLeket* writes, וביום שני קורין וזאת הברכה ומנהג לומר פזמונים ורהיטין כשהעולה הקורא האחרון לקרות בתורה כמו שעושין לחתנים ונקרא חתן

תורה והיום נקרא יום שמחת התורה...ומנהג חתן תורה לעשות סעודה ושמחה ולחלק לצבור
מגדים ומיני מתיקה שכך מצינו באגדה חזית ויבא שלמה ויעמד לפני ארון ברית ה' ויעל עולות ויעש
שלמים ויעש משתה לכל עבדיו אמר ר' אלעזר מיכן שעושין סעודה לגומרה של תורה. ליהודים
היה שמחה ואורה: Seder Chag haSukkos, 372. Note that *Medrash Shir haShirim*
and what the *Shibolei haLeket* calls באגדה חזית are one and the same Medrash).

THE MINHAG / CUSTOM OF CELEBRATING SIMCHAS TORAH

Based on the above, it seems that the foundation of dividing
the Torah into a yearly cycle of readings, and the subsequent
emergence of the celebration of Simchas Torah, developed in
Galus Bavel / the Babylonian Exile. Simchas Torah is founded
upon *Minhag* / custom, and a *Minhag Yisrael* / custom of the
community of Klal Yisrael is Torah. At some point following the completion of the Gemara some fifteen hundred years
ago, a custom spontaneously congealed to celebrate the end of
the cycle of readings and the beginning of the new cycle with
heightened Simchah and jubilation.

In the later period of the Geonim of Bavel, a question was
posed to Rav Hai Gaon (939-1038) about a developing custom
of adorning the Torah with ornaments fashioned from wom-
en's clothing, and also adorning the individual who read from
the Torah. The question was twofold: having been placed upon
the Torah, do such ornaments become sacred objects, and does
placing these ornaments upon males transgress the prohibition
on men wearing women's garments? This is one of the earliest known records of the celebration of Simchas Torah, and it
suggests that it was performed with tremendous jubilation (See

Teshuvos haRashba, Siman, 260. *Zohar* 3, 256b speaks about Simchas Torah. See also *Siddur Rasag*. Tosefos, *Beitzah*, 30b).

Centuries ago, especially in old Ashkenaz (Germany), there were various modes of celebrating Simchas Torah. One practice was to dance while holding candles. Certain older Ashkenaz communities, such as in the city of Worms, would dance around a bonfire on Simchas Torah. It seems that youngsters would light a bonfire of the wood from the Sukkah (*Sifrei Maharil*, Minhagim, Seder Tefilos Chag haSukkos, 14, Shinui Nuschaos).

In Barcelona (Sefard), the Rashba (1235-1310) was asked whether the custom of placing the crown of the Torah upon the heads of the children was disrespectful. He begins his response by writing that as a child, his own mother placed a Torah crown upon his head.[*]

---

[*] שלשה כתרים הם, כתר תורה וכתר כהנה וכתר מלכות / "There are three crowns, the crown of Torah, the crown of priesthood, and the crown of royalty": Mishnah, *Avos*, 4:13. On Rosh Hashanah, we connect with the crown of royalty, as we crown Hashem as King. On Yom Kippur, we connect with the crown of priesthood, as the service in the Beis haMikdash of Yom Kippur was performed by the Cohen Gadol, the High Priest. On Shemini Atzeres, we connect with the crown of Torah in the celebration of Simchas Torah: the Rebbe, *Sefer haMa'amarim*, 5714, Lehavin Inyan Shemini Atzeres, 7. Hence, on Simchas Torah, there is a focus upon the physical crown on the Torah scroll. Incidentally, the crown of royalty and even the crown of priesthood are connected to all the nations of the world, as *Malchus* / royalty is a concept that is found among all nations, and in fact, King Dovid drew his power for Malchus from Rus, his great grandmother, the convert. Even *Kehunah* / priesthood is connected with the nations of the world, as the Torah itself calls Yisro a *Cohen* / priest. But the crown of Torah is only found among Klal Yisrael. אם יאמר לך אדם: יש חכמה בגוים — תאמן...יש תורה בגוים אל תאמן / "If someone says there is wisdom among the nations, believe

Not only is Simchas Torah a universal Minhag, but the details of its celebration are also saturated with multiple Minhagim. The most prominent of these Minhagim is Hakafos, circling and dancing around the *Bimah* / the table where the Torah is normally read, carrying the *Sifrei Torah* / Torah scrolls. This is an old Minhag mentioned in the Zohar, but it gained tremendous prominence through the teachings and practice of the Holy Arizal. After dancing Hakafos in his own Shul, he would walk home, stopping in every Shul on the way to join their Hakafos as well. Since then, all the great Tzadikim have shared the Ari's great esteem for the holiness and power of the Hakafos.

MINHAG: THE ESSENCE OF SIMCHAS TORAH

As Simchas Torah is bound to the yearly Torah-reading cycle, an obvious question is why do we begin this cycle in the month of Tishrei, the beginning of the year? Why not begin the Torah-reading cycle on Shavuos, or perhaps the first Shabbos following Shavous? Shavuos is the day we were given the Torah, so it would be a logical time or season to begin the readings. However, our cycle of Shabbos Torah readings begins on the Shabbos after Simchas Torah — precisely because of the context of Rosh Hashanah and Tishrei.

---

him...If he says there is Torah among the nations, do not believe him": *Medrash Rabbah*, Eichah, 2:13. Shemini Atzeres / Simchas Torah is a paradigm of "us alone with the King." On Shemini Atzeres there is a subtler, inner joy, while on Simchas Torah, the joy spills outward and is revealed.

Why, then, does the Torah cycle not follow the yearly cycle of days? It would seem that we should start a new year of Torah readings on Rosh Hashanah, the start of the new year. The answer is that we could not begin on Rosh Hashanah itself, as on Rosh Hashanah there is a special Torah reading for that day, and it is unrelated to the cycle beginning with Bereishis. Yom Kippur and Sukkos also have special readings. Furthermore, all three of these Yamim Tovim often fall on Shabbos, and when a Yom Tov falls on Shabbos, the special Yom Tov reading replaces the weekly Parshah. For this reason, the cycle of Parshiyos could only begin after the end of Sukkos, on the first *regular* Shabbos of the year. But two questions still remain: why end and begin the Torah cycle on Simchas Torah? And why does the Torah cycle not begin in the context of Shavuos?

Perhaps the outer reason that the cycle ends and begins on Simchas Torah is that we cannot begin earlier in Tishrei, as just explained. But even if so, nothing is mere coincidence, and certainly issues regarding Torah — what, then, is the connection between the last day of all the Yamim Tovim of Tishrei and the beginning of the year's Torah readings? And again, why does the Torah cycle not begin in the Month of Sivan, in proximity to Shavuos?

It is interesting to note that one of the most joyous days in the entire calendar is founded on a Minhag and not on Torah or even Rabbinic wisdom. As explained, the second day of Yom Tov for Shemini Atzeres is a Rabbinic Yom Tov in the Diaspora, but the celebration of Simchas Torah that takes place on it is not Rabbinic; it is a Minhag. Indeed there are profound depths of meaning in Simchas Torah coming at the peak of all the Yamim Tovim of Tishrei, and also in the fact that the day itself is a Minhag.

As explored, the reason we begin the cycle of Torah reading and celebrate with the Torah in Tishrei, and not in the month of Sivan when the Torah was given, is that we are not celebrating the 'giving' of the Torah, rather the 'receiving' of the Torah. Klal Yisrael truly received, assimilated, and owned the Torah in Tishrei, not on Shavuos.

Whereas the first set of Luchos was given in Sivan, the second set of Luchos was given on the first Yom Kippur observed in the Desert. The First Luchos were gifted from Above, while the Second Luchos were earned by us, 'below', through our Teshuvah. The First Luchos essentially included the Five Books of Moshe and the Book of Yehoshua — teachings flowing from 'above' *to* the people below. The Second Luchos included all of Torah she-b'Al Peh and all the *Chidushim* / novel interpretations that will be revealed throughout history *by* the people 'below', so to speak.

In receiving the Second Luchos and the Torah she-b'Al Peh, our Simchah is immense. It is a joy of returning, and the Second Luchos were 'created' through our Teshuvah, our Bechirah. The joy of someone who was distant and has become close again is a joy that comes from within the person, earned and owned by their hard labor. Free gifts are appreciated, but not as much as what one buys with their own hard-earned money. Torah teachings that we reveal from within our own human experience can ignite even more Simchah than Torah that we receive from Above, from outside our human experience.

Simchas Torah was established in the Diaspora on the second day of Yom Tov, being a Yom Tov of the Rabbis, of Torah she-b'Al Peh. Additionally, today, when we have calendars and know exactly when each new month begins, the second day of Yom Tov is practiced because of Minhag, and this is an even deeper level of Torah she-b'Al Peh, arising from the 'collective prophetic' unconscious' within the soul of Klal Yisrael. All of these factors together magnify the Sason and Simchah of this day to maximum levels.

INTIMACY IS THE UNION OF THE MASCULINE / GIVER & FEMININE / RECEIVER

Not only is Simchas Torah a celebration that is created by 'us' and our customs, but it is also a celebration of 'us'. Torah she-b'Al Peh, and even more so, Minhag, are rooted in our human relationship with the Giver of Torah, the Source of our Life.

The period from Elul, the month of Virgo, until Sukkos, represents stages of deeper intimacy between humanity and HaKadosh Baruch Hu. The peak moment of this intimacy is Shemini Atzeres / Simchas Torah, when we are alone with

Hashem, without any specific Mitzvos or 'garments', as explored (אבל בשמיני אינו צריך כי הוא עצמו הדר / "On Shemini Atzeres we do not need the Esrog (or any particular Mitzvah or 'garment'), for the day itself is *Hadar* / splendor": Ramban, *Emor*, 23:40).

In genuine intimacy and harmony between the Above and the below, each party shows up fully for the other. Torah she-b'Al Peh represents our desire to show up in general, and Minhag represents our passionate desire to show up even in the minute details of our life.

REVELATION IS LOVE FROM ABOVE. MINHAG IS OUR LOVE TO ABOVE

Imagine a kind father tells his child, 'My dear boy, please clean your room,' and the child follows orders and tidies his room. This child demonstrates a strong but basic level of connection; a willingness to put aside his own will, at least temporarily, to do his father's will. This is an analogy of Torah she-b'Kesav, the revealed Torah from Above, our commitment to following the dictates of our Father in Heaven.

Sometimes, the parent does not explicitly instruct the child to clean their room, but makes a friendly hint, such as, 'Good morning, my sweet-boy-with-a-messy-room!' The child picks up on the hint and cleans the room. This child demonstrates love and devotion to his parent. This is analogous to Torah she-b'Al Peh, and specifically the Mitzvos enacted by the Sages. The Torah does not overtly command these practices, yet hints at them through allusions in the Torah (note *Ta'anis*, 9a).

Finally, a child with a very high level of love, devotion, and sensitivity does not need to be given a command or even a hint to clean his room. This child anticipates what will bring joy to his parents, and without any encouragement, he immediately cleans his room whenever it has gotten slightly messy. This is analogous to following Minhagim, acts of selfless devotion arising from our intuition of what our beloved Parent truly wants.

BINAH, CHOCHMAH, MAKIF

In another analogy, Torah she-b'Kesav is the written words describing Hashem's desire and will. Torah she-b'Al Peh are the hints and allusions that are found within the words, and Minhag is the overall *Makif* / thematic root of those words and hints.

In this way, Torah she-b'Kesav is rooted in the world of Binah; language and actual letters. Torah she-b'Al Peh is rooted in the world of Chochmah, Divine intuition, beyond words and letters. And Minhag is rooted in the Makifim of Chochmah, the *Kelalim* / principles surrounding those intuitions (Alter Rebbe, *Likutei Torah*, D'rushim l'Sukkos, pp. 79d-80d).

Say, for example, your spouse asks you to take out the garbage. This 'instruction' is analogous to Torah she-b'Kesav, in which we are instructed to perform certain activities and refrain from certain activities, the positive and negative Mitzvos.

Torah she-b'Al Peh would mean to deeply and intuitively hear what your spouse is hinting at behind these words — such as you need to help out in the house more in general, although your spouse did not explicitly tell you this. If you understand this implied message, you might take out the garbage, but then also rinse the odor out of the basket with soapy water, let it dry, and insert a new trash bag in it. This would be analogous to Torah she-b'Al Peh. But then if you can hear even more deeply, you may sense the 'Makifim' of your spouse's words, a meaning that may not even be conscious on their part. For example, there might be an unspoken need: 'Please be more attentive to me; notice how hard I am working, and acknowledge me.' When you respond by taking out the garbage, rinsing the basket, inserting a clean bag, and then sitting down with them and giving them attention and kind words of acknowledgment, that is 'Minhag'.

A Minhag is an act of love for Hashem.* Our burning desire

---

* Although all the Four Minim (represent) the Holy One: "Esrog is the Holy One…Hadasim is the Holy One…Lulav is the Holy One…Aravah is the Holy One (*Medrash Rabbah*, Emor, 30:9: כפת ...פרי עץ הדר, זה הקדוש ברוך הוא תמרים, זה הקדוש ברוך הוא ...וענף עץ עבת, זה הקדוש ברוך הוא... וערבי נחל, זה הקדוש הוא ברוך). Yet, the Alter Rebbe writes in *Likutei Torah* (D'rushim l'Sukkos, pp. 88b-88c), that the Esrog represents the innermost love that HaKadosh Baruch Hu has for us, and the Lulav draws us to mirror that love for the Essence of Hashem (כי הנה ארז"ל פרי עץ הדר זה הקב"ה כו', וגם אמרו פרי עץ הדר הדר באילנו וכו' כי האדם עץ השדה. פי' האדם זה הקב"ה ...והוא ענין עץ החיים... והדר באילנו. הוא בחינת פנימיות האילן שהוא ענין פנימיות האהבה שיש להוי' עלינו...שהאהבה הוא עד"מ בבחי' פנימית נקודת הלב ישראל בתוונא דלבא יתבי ונפלאה אהבתו להם ...והאתרוג מחברים אותו עם הלולב שהוא גבוה במינו דהיינו השרש המושרש למעלה העושה פרי למטה בישראל בחי' לו לב להיות לב א' לו ית' לבד ולדבקה בו דהיינו לבחינת עצמותו ומהותו ית' בדביקה וחשיקה מעומקא דלבא). The Mishnah says (*Sukkah*, 4:4), מיד התינוקות שומטין את לולביהן ואוכלין אתרוגיהן / "Immediately (on Hoshana Rabbah, after fulfilling the Mitzvah

and love for HaKadosh Baruch Hu is what gives birth to the multitude of Minhagim we have, collectively and each community in their own distinct and particular manner.

MINHAG IS OUR COLLECTIVE 'LOVE POETRY'

Performing a custom is like telling Hashem, 'I want to go beyond the surface of this relationship. I want to be tangibly connected to You — I want to feel Your Presence in everything I do, beyond what I was commanded.' Performing a custom is presenting our individual or collective 'love poem' to HaKadosh Baruch Hu. It is our acted-out love poem or love song formed out of our yearning, as well as the yearning and creative inspiration carved into our spiritual genes by diverse communities of Klal Yisrael across geographical locations and times throughout space and time. As we present this behavioral 'poetry' to the Creative One, we are connecting to the flow of strength and love that supported those historical communities in their experiences of exile, and we too are strengthened.

For example, on Rosh Hashanah, as we walk to a body of

of Lulav and Esrog) the adults take the Lulavim (from the children) and eat their Esrogim" (הגדולים. ואוכלים...תינוקות של מידן התינוקות לולבי שומטים הגדולים אוכלים אין הגדולים אבל...שמחה משום נהגו שכך גזל משום בדבר ואין תינוקות. של אתרוגיהן לכולו הוקצה היום למקצת למצוה שהוקצה דכיון היום, אותו כל אתרוגיהן: *Bartenura,* ad loc.). Eating the Esrog is a Minhag of joy, and grabbing the children's Esrogim evokes the fact that "Joy breaks all boundaries." Eating an Esrog also demonstrates internalizing Hashem's love, and a child represents the natural love of a parent, much like Hashem's deepest love for us. When we eat this Estrog מיד / immediately, after the last time we can fulfil the Mitzvah of the Four Minim, we show that our love is burning bright we are ready to dance passionately with Hashem and His Torah, as Shemini Atzeres / Simchas Torah is about to commence.

water and cast our wrongdoings away during the Tashlich ritual, we are forging a profound connection with the holy Jewish
community of 14th-century Germany where this custom first
arose. This beautiful custom, born from a deep desire to tangibly connect with Hashem, carries the legacy of that community into our present-day lives. Whether we stand by the water
today and act out the sacred 'poetry' of our ancestors, we are
unifying across time and place, by these enduring traditions, to
our collective story. And when, in the early morning of Erev
Yom Kippur, we pass a live chicken over our head and look on
as it is slaughtered in the ancient custom of Kapparos, we are
connecting to the communities of *Bavel* / Babylon, and to the
souls of the Rishonim and the Mekubalim, who wrote in support of this ancient practice. Similarly, when we participate in
Hakafos, we join in song and dance with the faithful of earlier
eras, from the times of the Geonim to the days of the Arizal
and the vibrant streets of Tzfas. We are joining them today by
expressing their 'love poem' and dancing on Simchas Torah.

The collective desire of K'lal Yisrael to reach out and serve
Hashem in a time, a place, or activity where we are not commanded to, nor even hinted to, is of utmost importance and
shows on a living, alive, vibrant relationship with HaKadosh
Baruch Hu. This, indeed, is why Minhagim are part of our living tradition and extremely vital. Minhagim are the essence of
serving our Divine Beloved.

MINHAGIM ARE ROOTED IN KESER

Torah Law is an expression of the Torah she-b'Kesav, clear-

ly delineating what should and should not be done. Beyond
the letter of the law are the various Mitzvos established by
the Sages. Minhag comes from a root that is beyond all law
and rules, where our essence of self is one with the Essence of
Hashem (Minhag is sourced in our connection with *Atzmus* / Essence,
beyond Binah (written Torah) and Chochmah (oral dimension of Torah).
Likutei Sichos, 29, Hoshana Rabbah, Chap. 9).

Torah she-b'Kesav is generally connected with the *Sefirah*
/ spiritual and Divine 'attribute' of Tiferes, yet, its deeper root
is the Sefirah of *Binah* / understanding, analysis, and compre-
hension, that is, revealed intellect. As explained earlier, this attribute is the seat of Simchah. Torah she-b'Al Peh is rooted in
Chochmah, the concealed, more subtle level of intellect. This
attribute is the seat of Sason.

Minhag is rooted in *Keser* / the 'crown' above the intellect,
which is Divine *Ratzon* / will and desire, and *Ta'anug* / pleasure (*Siddur Im Dach*, Sha'ar haSukkos. The Written Torah is *Mochin* / Intellect of *Ima* / Mother / Binah. The Oral Torah is Mochin of *Aba* / Father
/ Chochmah; the *Hakafos Makifim d'Abba* / the higher *Makif Ohr of* Chochmah: Igros Kodesh printed in *Likutei Sichos* 29, Hosafos, Shemini Atzeres,
pp. 505-506).

Our relationship with HaKadosh Baruch Hu can be grounded in rationality; the better we follow basic instructions, the
better the relationship. When an employee has Binah, when
he understands and fulfills the employer's clear instructions,
the employer is happy, he has Simchah. This is even more so

when the employee 'goes beyond the letter of the law' and acts according to his Chochmah, his ability to grasp the employer's deeper will from his gestures and tone of voice while giving instructions. He brings Sason, a restful, satisfied happiness, to the employer, because he has fulfilled the employer's will without having to be told.

Yet, in both of these levels, their relationship is founded on an impersonal 'work contract', as it were. It is conceivable that a talented 'slave' or even an 'artificial intelligence' robot could do a good job following subtle instructions. There is still no real passion and 'desire' between the people. There is no *Geshmak* / 'relishing' of the relationship itself. It is more of a functional or 'utilitarian' dynamic; as soon as the performance of the employee falls slightly, he might be seen in a critical light and told, 'Could you please go back to how you were performing yesterday?'

On the deepest level, an employee understands his employer so well and resonates with his will so intimately, that his own will is one with the will of the employer, and his Ta'anug is one with his employer's Ta'anug. From this unification with the employer's 'Keser', the employee can initiate actions in the employer's name (This is a Mashal for the highest level within Keser, the idea of יחידה ליחדך / 'The essence of the soul is one with You, O Essence of Divinity.' See *Siddur al-Pi Nusach haAri*, Hoshanos, Yom Gimel. A Minhag creates a *Kesher Atzmi* / an Essential connection with HaKadosh Baruch Hu, as Malchus, when aligned, reflects the highest, deepest light of Keser).

Minhagim are rooted in a place that is beyond fixed systems of law, transcending even Binah and Chochmah. In this vibrant place of Keser, of aliveness and Geshmak, we are bound up with HaKadosh Baruch Hu, like inseparable lovers. Our whole life and all of our actions are spontaneously in harmony with the Living Presence of HaKadosh Baruch Hu, and we live in this Presence always and forever.

TORAH OF YOUR MOTHER

The Torah of 'law', and even the level beyond the letter of the 'law', are called *Toras Avicha* / Torah of your father. This is the Torah of order, structure, systems, and obligations. Minhagim are called *Toras Imecha* / Torah of your mother.*

---

* The Alter Rebbe explains in the name of the Zohar that the verse אל תטוש תורת אמך / "Do not forsake the Torah of your Mother" (*Mishlei*, 1:8) refers to Torah she-b'Al Peh: *Tanya*, Igeres haKodesh, 29. See also *Me'or Einayim*, Emor 3. This is in general, yet, more specifically, within Torah she-b'Al-Peh itself, תורת אמך / the Torah of *your* mother, refers to Minhagim: *Pesachim*, 50b. הני ביעי חשילתא שריין ואת לא תיכול משום ואל תטוש תורת אמך :Chulin*, 93b. דאפי׳ לאליהו זכור לטוב אין שומעין לשנות מנהג העם) :*Shu'T Maharik*, Siman 54). It also seems that according to the Rambam, there is a *Torah obligation* to follow a Minhag of our Sages. In other words, we are 'commanded' to follow Minhagim — הרי. אלו מצות עשה לשמוע להן והעובר על כל אחת מהן עובר בלא תעשה. הוא אומר על פי התורה אשר יורוך אלו הגזירות והתקנות והמנהגות שיורו בהם לרבים כדי לחזק הדת ולתקן העולם: *Hilchos Mamrim*, 1:2. This ruling contradicts the opinion of the Rambam elsewhere, where he rules that we do not recite a blessing on a Minhag, as a Minhag has no source other than being a Minhag, thus cannot say, *Asher Kiddishanu* / "...Who commanded us": *Hilchos Berachos*, 3:7. *Hilchos Chanukah*, 11:16. Perhaps the word *Minhag* in *Hilchos Mamrim* does not mean simply a Minhag, rather a ruling of the Sages. Note *Tur*, Choshen Mishpat, 368: מנ״ל דמנהגא מילתא שנאמר לא תשיג גבול רעך אשר גבלו ראשונים. *Sefer Chasidim*, 114. Although, see *Shabbos*, 85a.

This is the Torah of warmth, passion, and desire of 'non-obligatory' or freely chosen participation and engagement.

A Minhag expresses the unique, idiosyncratic ways that we relate to HaKadosh Baruch Hu, much like how each family has their own ways of doing things, their distinct sense of humor, or the way they celebrate their birthdays, etc. Minhagim are about how we, in our own personal manner, are drawn to relate to Truth, and therefore it is more intimate, warm, and pleasurable, like how one might relate to their caring mother.

The 'Torah of our mother', the Minhagim that we assumed throughout the ages and the places where Jews resided, are the deepest nourishment of the soul of Klal Yisrael (Indeed, Keneses Yisrael, the collective soul of Klal Yisrael is called 'mother'. *Sanhedrin*, 101a. *Zohar* 1, 77a. *Margaliyus HaYam*, Sanhedrin, ibid.). It is within the 'idiosyncratic' practices of the Minhagim that many of us feel most embraced and seen. In fact, long after some have sadly left the path of their ancestors, the ways of Torah and Mitzvos, many have nonetheless held onto some of their Minhagim, such as singing holy Nigunim and eating certain traditional foods. Indeed, through remaining in touch with the beautiful tapestry of their Minhagim, many have returned to observance. The mother's warm embrace draws wanderers back into her fold.

This is another reason that Minhagim are essential for the thriving of Klal Yisrael, and for our commitment to the path of Torah.

A person should never think, 'This detail of observance is not essential, it is just a Minhag....' The whole *Tzurah* / form of a Yiddishe home is the Minhagim. The way the house feels and looks, and how the foods taste, are part of the Geshmak of Yiddishkeit itself. They draw the heart to engage deeply with the world of Kedushah. Indeed, a person's very identity as a Jew is determined by their mother.

The Gemara (*Sotah*, 11b) narrates that the women (the mothers) of Klal Yisrael, while in Mitzrayim, had passionate *Bitachon* / trust that Hashem would redeem His People to the extent that they initiated a Minhag, so-to-speak: they took it upon themselves to prepare tambourines for the day when they would sing and dance at the Sea in gratitude for their redemption. The Ari haKadosh commented (*Sha'ar haGilgulim*, Hakdamah, 20) that in the same way, through the righteous women of our generation (and perhaps, by extension, those who keep Minhagim, the *Toras Imecha*), we will be redeemed, once again.

The Minhag of dancing Hakafos on Simchas Torah is a glorious revelation of Keser, the indelible connection and Ta'anug between Klal Yisrael and HaKadosh Baruch Hu. This Ta'anug is none other than Hashem's pleasure in creating the world, and it is the very *Tachlis* / purpose of Creation: that He should dwell here, in a world redeemed and transformed by freely-chosen human acts of love. May we hasten that redemption and Divine Indwelling as we rejoice with the holy Minhagim of Klal Yisrael on this 'crown' of all days.

Chapter 6

DANCING FOR HASHEM &
DRAWING DOWN BLESSING

THE REBBE RAYATZ ONCE SAID THAT SHEMINI ATZERES / SIMCHAS TORAH AND ROSH HASHANAH BASICALLY PARALLEL EACH OTHER, EXCEPT FOR ONE essential distinction. On Rosh Hashanah, we receive blessings through anxious supplication, bitterness, and serious inner reflection, while on Shemini Atzeres and Simchas Torah, we receive blessings through joy and jubilation (*Likutei Sichos* 2, Hosafos Shemini Atzeres, Simchas Torah, p. 646. See also *Hayom Yom*, 22 Tishrei. Following the days of Judgment, Rosh Hashanah, Yom Kippur, Hoshana Rabbah, on Shemini Atzeres / Simchas Torah we carry the Torah from a place of love, rather than from a place of fear of judgment: Rebbe Shlomo Kluger, *Kehilas Ya'akov*, Simchas Torah, Derush 4).

On Simchas Torah, not only do we receive blessings through joy, we also receive all the blessings bequeathed to us on Rosh Hashanah for the entire year, but the vessel to receive these blessings is not somber introspection and evaluation, rather elation, singing, and dancing.

Rosh Hashanah is a judgment for our entire year. It is divided into two parts: on 'day one' of Rosh Hashanah there is a judgment on *Neshamos* / souls, the inner aspect of reality, and on day two there is a judgment on the *Olam* / world, the outer reality and the body (*Ya'aros D'vash*, 2, Derush 1 and Derush 10, *Bnei Yissaschar*, Tishrei, 2:2. *Avodas Yisrael*, Derush Rosh Hashanah sheChal b'Shabbos. "On 'day one', there is an elevation of our internal dimension, the level of souls, and on 'day two', the external dimension is also elevated": *Sha'ar haKavanos*, Inyan Rosh Hashanah, Derush 2).

Yet, the blessings that we had received on Rosh Hashanah and Yom Kippur are revealed on Sukkos, and they are finally *materialized* on Shemini Atzeres / Simchas Torah, through our Avodah / spiritual, mental, and emotional work of joy. This is the meaning of the verse, תקעו בחודש שופר בכסה ליום חגנו / "Blow the horn on the new moon for our feast day" (*Tehilim*, 81:4). The "new moon" (blessing) is concealed (בכסה) on the first day of the month (בחודש) when we "blow the horn" (תקעו שופר), until the יום חגנו / day of our festivity, which is the Yom Tov of Sukkos (*Likutei Torah*, Rosh Hashanah, 54d. *Siddur Im Dach*, 235b).

On Rosh Hashanah, the moon is still (for the most part) concealed from our vantage point on earth. Since it is hidden specifically to 'us', we engage in a 'concealed' or inner type of Avodah, spiritual-mental-emotional work, introspection, self-evaluation, and prayer — all of these are by nature inner activities. Yom Kippur is similar in that it strongly emphasizes *Avodah Penimis* / internal work. Both Rosh Hashanah and Yom Kippur are also celebrated mostly in the Shul, the inner sanctum. Sukkos begins with the full moon, as it glows brightly for all to see, despite being night. This represents the revelation of the 'content' that was hidden with the concealed moon. The blessings and *Shefa* / flow of abundance that we received in those solemn days now becomes revealed. Sukkos is a Yom Tov we spend 'outside' our homes. We celebrate under the stars with outwardly revealed joy on Sukkos, revealing what we had achieved inwardly throughout Rosh Hashanah, Yom Kippur, and the days in between. The positive judgment, blessings, and forgiveness that we received on Rosh Hashanah and Yom Kippur are finally expressed externally in the physical structure of the Sukkah, which is a 'public display of affection', a visible Divine embrace. We go out of our homes, visible to neighbors and passersby to enter this Divine embrace, and spend most of the festival there, in an atmosphere of revealed joy.

Although there is a general Mitzvah to be b'Simchah on all Yamim Tovim, Simchah is given outstanding emphasis in the Torah's Pesukim regarding Sukkos. The Torah only tells us once to be joyful on Pesach, while it tells us three times to be b'Simchah on Sukkos (*Yalkut Shimoni*, Emor 247:654). In fact, Sukkos is defined as זמן שמחתנו / the Season of our Simchah.

As mentioned earlier, there are various types and grades of joy (*Avos d'Rebbe Nasan*, 43:9), and Simchah is one that is outwardly revealed and expressed: שמחים בצאתם / "They (the celestial spheres) are joyful when they go out." Simchah is a posture of "going out." In this way, on Sukkos, we outwardly reveal the Shefa that we inwardly absorbed on Rosh Hashanah and Yom Kippur, and we do this specifically through an Avodah of expressed joy and openly displayed dancing.

'PAYING OUR BILL' THROUGH DANCING

On Shemini Atzeres / Simchas Torah, the culmination of the holy days and feasts, we 'pay the bill', as it were, for all the spiritual and material blessings given to us on Rosh Hashanah. Hopefully we 'earned' all those great blessings through our hours of supplications and heartfelt Tefilos, firm resolutions, and commitments on Rosh Hashanah. If we were for some reason unable to engage in these vigorous forms of 'Avodah', or if we sense that we are for another reason bereft of spiritual currency and unable to 'pay' for the blessings that we received through Rosh Hashanah, then our dancing itself can 'generate the funds' and 'pay the bill'.

In the language of Chazal, the word *Hakafah* (as in the *Hakafos* / encircling the Bimah on Simchas Torah), means 'credit', as in חנוני המקיפו / storekeeper who gives credit (*Avodah Zarah*, 63b), and through the dancing on Simchas Torah, we are paying back the credit extended to us on Rosh Hashanah.

A story illustrates how dancing on Simchas Torah can serve as a 'payment' for the blessings offered to us when we were being judged for the coming year on Rosh Hashanah.

A man checks into a five-star hotel, books the penthouse, walks into the restaurant, and orders the most expensive entree and lavish delicacies, drinks, and dessert. He deeply relishes them. When it comes time to pay the bill, he says, "I'm so sorry, I don't have a credit card or checkbook, and I just now realized my bank account is in the negative and I don't have a dime on me." Fuming, the hotel owner reaches to call the police to arrest the man and throw him in jail. The man interrupts him: "Wait, please don't! What good would that do for you? My sitting in jail will not get you back your money!"

"Look, here's what I suggest," the man continues. "I will offer dance performances in the lobby free of charge (note *Baba Kamah*, 86a: דהוה מרקיד בי כובי). New customers will be attracted to stay here, and eventually, the owner will retrieve his losses...."

Similarly, we 'check in' to Hashem's Presence on Rosh Hashanah and 'order' the most luxurious blessings and the best of years. If we do not then give Hashem sincere service and heartfelt Avodah on Rosh Hashanah, Hashem waits patiently for our Avodah on Yom Kippur. Once Yom Kippur is over and we have again squandered the day, Hashem anticipates our Avodah on Sukkos. Finally, on the last day of the Festivals, Hashem says, 'Listen, I want to give you a good year but you have not offered a proper vessel to receive those blessings.

It is best for you that I withhold your blessings.' And we respond, 'True I messed up, true I have nothing to offer, but I could dance for You. And if I dance with fervor and passion, my dancing will inspire me, and inspire all those around me as well to reconnect and realign.

'Maybe I do not have the proper vessels to hold all the blessings I asked for on Rosh Hashanah and Yom Kippur, but, Hashem, I can dance for You! This will show others that the Torah is an excellent 'product' and attract them to it — they will see that the Torah is deeply desirable, and it brings so much joy. And maybe You will consider this itself a proper vessel, a 'payment', for the blessings that You showered on me.'

When people in the 'lobby' or the street, or even just in the Shul, see you dancing with elation, they are drawn in and want to know why you are dancing so ecstatically. You are drawing people closer to HaKadosh Baruch Hu simply by being happy and dancing. They 'want what you're having' and the 'Owner' is satisfied by the additional 'business' you brought in.

Some people have the concentration to pray, and some have the intellectual capacity to learn complicated Torah teachings, but most people have the ability to say a *l'Chayim* and jump up and down, or hold hands with others, and follow the circle turning around the holy Torah.

DANCING UP & DRAWING DOWN

Dancing is a means to draw great blessings down into proper vessels, and it is also a means to connect to the Source of Blessing, Above. When we jump upward in the dance, we connect to the Source Above, and when we land down, we draw blessings to the earth. Over and over, we jump up higher than our standing height, and then land on the ground with a thump, indenting the floorboards even if very slightly. We are viscerally rising above our normal consciousness, and also descending more deeply than normal into the earthly plane.

Through the Avodah of dwelling in the Sukkah, and that of waving the Lulav and Esrog, we have elevated and refined our personal space and the six directions extending all around us. Surrounded by elevated and refined space, the gravitational pull upon us toward physicality is diminished. As a result, we find ourselves 'lifting off the ground' on Simchas Torah, leaping and floating in the air with joy.

Dancing, as explored, is not only connected to the Hakafos of Simchas Torah but to every day of the *Chag* / Yom Tov of Sukkos.

חייב אדם לטהר את עצמו ברגל / "A person needs to purify himself on the *Regel* / holy day" (*Rosh Hashanah,* 16b). *Regel* / רגל literally means 'leg' or 'foot', as on Yom Tov one had to walk by foot up to the *Har haBayis* / Temple Mount and climb stairs to the Beis haMikdash on top. This, says Rebbe Elimelech of Lizensk, means that on Yom Tov a person needs to purify and elevate himself with his legs and feet, through dancing.

While this is true on Sukkos, how much more so on Simchas Torah. We become refined and elevated by dancing and aspiring for higher and higher levels of consciousness and action.

Whatever goes up must come down, and the higher it goes up the more impact it has when it falls. When we dance leaping up we also come pounding down upon the floor with our feet.* In this way, our joyous movements serve as a conduit, leaping upwards and then bringing the blessings all the way down to the physical earth.

---

* As explored earlier from the Zohar, the final sealing for *Geshem* / physicality is on Shemini Atzeres (Simchas Torah). Similar to dancing, clapping can draw down blessings from Above, just as one's higher hand claps upon one's lower hand. Certain Mekubalim mention that clapping with the right hand above the left is an act of sweetening Din, Gevurah, the left side (and the five fingers are five levels of Gevurah) by means of the right hand, which is Chesed (and the five levels of Chesed): *Ben Ish Chai*, V'Zos haBrachah, 18. In general, clapping and dancing create a *Hamtakas haDin* / sweetening of Din: *Likutei Moharan* 1, 10. Without getting into the details, while the Mishnah in *Beitzah* (36b) clearly states that we are not allowed to dance and clap on Yom Tov, Tosefos (30a), writes that today may be different. Certainly, with regards to Simchas Torah, in honor of the Torah, all agree that we may (and do) dance. Here are the words of the *Beis Yoseph*, Orach Chayim, 339: ולא מטפחין ולא מספקין ולא מרקדין משנה בפרק משילין ומפרש טעמא בגמ' שמא יתקן כלי שיר וכתבו התוספות בר"פ המביא כדי יין ומיהו לדידן שרי דדוקא בימיהם שהיו בקיאים לעשות כלי שיר שייך למיגזר אבל לדידן אין אנו בקיאין לעשות כלי שיר ולא שייך למיגזר עכ"ל. ואע"ג דבפ"ק דביצה אמרינן שאע"פ שנתבטל טעם הגזירה לא נתבטלה הגזירה התוס' מדמו ליה למשקין מגולים דשרו האידנא לפי שאין נחשים מצויים כמ"ש הם ז"ל בפ"ב דע"ז: וכתב מהר"י קולון ז"ל בשורש ט' בשם רבינו האי שביום שמחת תורה מותר לרקד בשעה שאומרים קילוסים דתורה דנהגו בו היתר משום כבוד התורה כיון דלית ביה אלא משום שבות. Based on this Maharik, the Minchas Elazar rules that any dancing that is in honor of the Torah, on any Yom Tov or Shabbos, is allowed: *Shu'T Minchas Elazar*, 1:29.

As mentioned earlier, in the Davening of Shemini Atzeres (which is also Simchas Torah in Eretz Yisrael), we begin to request rainfall for the winter: משיב הרוח ומוריד הגשם / "He returns the wind and draws down the *Geshem* / rain." When the holy Baal Shem Tov would say these words, he would gesture with his hands. While saying, "He returns the wind (the *Ruach* / spirit, the spirituality)," he would wave his hand upwards. And when saying, "and draws down the *Geshem* / literally, the physicality," he would move his hand downwards. He was expressing, 'Now, on Shemini Atzeres, Simchas Torah, after our intense inner and deeper spiritual Avodah on the days of Rosh Hashanah and Yom Kippur, Hashem, please receive our prayers, our *Ruach* / spirituality, On High, and please send the blessings that this Avodah produced down into the 'Geshem', the *Gashmiyus* / physicality of the material world.' Now is the time to draw down all the blessings that we received within a hidden, spiritual realm on Rosh Hashanah and Yom Kippur, and to extend them all the way down to the physical ground.

Shemini / the eighth day of עצרת / *Atzeres* means the day when all the light and blessings that were given to us from Rosh Hashanah through Sukkos are נעצרים ונקלטים / collected, retained and absorbed. The word *Atzeres* is related to *Otzar* / treasury, and on Shemini Atzeres, all the treasures from the previous Holy Days are deposited and held within a great royal treasure chest for us. Shemini Atzeres is thus the essence of the entire season of Yamim Tovim (*Ohr haTorah*, Sukkos, 1, 762. *Ohr haTorah*, Balak, 926. *Sefer haMa'amarim*, Ranat, p. 43. *Sefer haMa'amarim*

Melukat, Vol. 1, "BaYom haShemini"). All the potential revelations that poured down in the first twenty-one days of this month are finally absorbed within us on Shemini Atzeres, and now we can draw them all the way down to, and 'into' the ground, like *Geshem /* rainwater.

DANCING IS A SIGN OF LIFE

Dancing is a physical representation and embodiment of prayer, 'prayer in motion', drawing all light and blessings into the physical dimension. On a deeper level, dancing is aliveness itself. The more we are awake and alive, and the more we can 'move' dynamically in our world, the more we can draw Divine aliveness and *Shefa /* flow and blessings from Above to below. And yet, sometimes the dancing itself *generates* the aliveness and therefore the flow and blessings.

Once, on Simchas Torah, the Baal Shem Tov saw one of his students, Reb Shlomo Zalman, standing off to the side while all the other students were dancing with vigor and ecstasy. The holy Baal Shem Tov challenged him: "Why are you not dancing?" "Rebbe," responded Shlomo Zalman, "how can I dance and be happy when I have been married for so many years and have not been blessed with children?" The Baal Shem Tov told him, טאנץ מיט חיות, וועסטו האבן חיות / dance with *Chayus /* aliveness, and you will *have* Chayus (and hence you will become able to sire children)."

In order to procreate and create life, one needs aliveness. A lifeless act of intimacy cannot produce offspring. This is both literally and figuratively true; all creativity is a manifestation of aliveness. The more vital your spirit, the more you can produce and innovate. The Baal Shem Tov was telling his student, 'You are avoiding dancing because you have no Chayus, and you have not had children for the same reason. The solution is to simply get up and dance; dancing will generate Chayus in your system. Movement is both a sign of Chayus, and it is what stimulates Chayus. Dancing will bring more Chayus into your body, mind, and emotions, until you have built up the potency to create *new* life, and the vessel to receive the blessing of children.

The more we choose to cultivate and embody aliveness, the more vitality we will feel. And as a result, we will have more aliveness, creativity, and life-affirming qualities to contribute to our family and community, and more positivity and goodness to reveal this world.

WHEN ALL ELSE FAILS, STAND UP & DANCE

To live is to be alive, alert, and awake, to live with wonderment, passion, and openness. Sadly, many people are existentially asleep, walking through life half alive, half awake, resentfully dragging themselves through the drudgeries of life. So many people have blinded themselves to what authentic living means, to live with purpose, meaning, focus, and celebration of life.

With the Shofar on Rosh Hashanah, we blast powerful sounds to wake us up, to shake us out of our mental, emotional, and spiritual slumbers. At the beginning of each year, we rouse ourselves to life and to authentic living.

What do we need to do when we want to wake up a person who is so deeply asleep that even an alarm or loud blast of the Shofar cannot rouse him? We need to give them a shake. When a person faints on the floor and we shout his name in his ear and he still does not wake up, we take hold of him and shake a bit. This is the Na'anuim of the Lulav. If the sound of the Shofar did not wake us up to life, maybe a little shaking will.

If even shaking does not do the trick, we try to stand him up. This is Simchas Torah; we pick him up and pull him into the dance circle. The dancing itself awakens aliveness in him and he has a personal *Techiyas haMeisim /* resurrection of his spirit, so-to-speak.

There is a self-reinforcing loop in which the more we dance with Chayus, the more alive we become, and the more we become a conduit and instrument for the Divine Life Force to flow through us to others. May we dance with great vigor on Simchas Torah and celebrate the beginning of the new cycle of Torah readings with joy, הם חיינו ואורך ימינו, "for they are our aliveness and the length of our days."

Chapter 7
HAKAFOS: DANCING IN A CIRCLE BEYOND LINEAR REALITY

O N THE SEVEN DAYS OF SUKKOS, WE PLACE A TORAH SCROLL NEAR OR ON THE *BIMAH* / TORAH-READING TABLE, AND THEN CIRCLE THE BIMAH HOLDING our Lulav and Esrog. On Simchas Torah, we circle the Bimah carrying the Torah scrolls themselves.

In the *Hakafos* / circuits of Simchas Torah, we circle the square Bimah seven times carrying the Torah scrolls, and then continue to dance around the Bimah.

In both of these customs, there is an interplay between 'circles' and a 'square', and what these shapes mean. In a circle, there is no beginning or end, and thus there are no definable standalone points along the circumference. A square features several beginnings and ends — for example, each side of the square ends where another side begins. In this way, squares have many definable points along their perimeter.

Squares represent limitation, measurability, and definability, while circles represent a world of infinity, immeasurability, and undefinability. In our lives, the square represents boundaries, limitations, and the natural order, while the circle represents breaking boundaries and limitations, and going beyond the natural order.*

PROSE VS. POETRY, LAW VS. LORE

A square also represents 'prose', the linear, objective story of our life, while a circle represents 'poetry', the non-linear subjective experience of our life.

Objective 'law and order' is square or 'linear', while music and poetry are 'circular'. The Written Torah is called the Law and is in this sense linear, and yet the Torah is also called a *Shirah* / song: ועתה כתבו לכם את־השירה הזאת ולמדתה בני ישראל שימה בפיהם / "And now, write down this Shirah and teach it to the children of Israel and place it within their mouths" (31:19). This

---

* "There is no square in Creation," asserts Rabban Shimon ben Gamliel: *Yerushalmi*, end of Ma'asros, *Nedarim*, 3:2. *Shavuos* 3:8. A creation created by the Infinite One is, in its depth, also infinite. Whether this is also the opinion of the Sages, and whether 'square' literally means a 'perfect square', and whether it only refers to the realm of human experience, and so forth, are points that are greatly debated: the Rebbe, *Igros Kodesh*, Vol. 2, p. 360.

Pasuk delivers the Mitzvah, the positive command, to write the entire Torah (Rambam, *Hilchos Tefillin, Mezuzah, v'Sefer Torah*, 7:1. *Sanhedrin*, 21b). This Mitzvah is not just to write the particular poem or song expressed in that Torah reading (Rashi), but actually to write the entire Torah (כתבו לכם תורה שיש בה שירה זו, לפי שאין כותבין ע"כ כונת פרשיות: את התורה פרשיות: Rambam, *ibid.*, see *Tzafnas Paneach*, ad loc. התורה דצריך לכתוב התורה כולה ונ"מ אם בלתה התורה ונשתיירה השירה אם יצא: *Sha'agas Aryeh*, Siman 34).

In this way, the whole Torah is called a Shirah, although the main body of Torah is not poetry but rather law and instruction. In fact, the Torah is called 'Torah' from the word meaning *Hora'ah* / 'teaching', and this teaching is accomplished through direction, guidance, and law. Law is absolute, rigid, objective, impersonal, and 'linear', whereas song, music, and poetry are free-flowing, subjective, fluid, personal, and 'circular'. (The word Shir, in fact, means 'circle' כשיר מהו: *Baba Metziya*, 25a. The word *Shir* in Hebrew and Aramaic means 'a piece of round jewelry' like a bracelet: *Yeshayahu*, 3:19. *Targum*, Bereishis, 24:22. Mishnah, *Shabbos*, 51b. וסוס בשיר וכל בעלי השיר יוצאין בשיר ונמשכין בשיר). As such, the Torah is both law and a song.

TOP DOWN VS. BOTTOM UP

'Law' follows a strict linear descent from Above to below; it is imposed, and one must abide by it for one has no choice in the matter. In this descent, the line moves only in one direction; it is a 'top-down' relationship. While the whole Torah has this quality, it refers more specifically to the revealed Written Torah, the body of law that we humbly accept from On High. The oral aspect of Torah, which is revealed through human participation and involvement, subjectivity, is more akin to a circle. It is our addition, flowing from our devotion and inspiration, and becoming part of the *Mesorah* / 'Torah tradition' from past to present.

The Torah says, שימה בפיהם...כתבו לכם את־השירה / "Write for yourselves this Shirah… and place in their mouths." 'Writing down' is obviously Torah she-b'Kesav, the Written Torah, which is dictated and transcribed. But what does it mean to place the Written Torah "in their mouths"? This refers to the oral aspect of the Torah. "In their mouths" means transmitted through the mouths of the people, *Torah she-b'Al Peh* / literally, 'the teaching that is upon one's mouth'. Hence, the Baal haTurim writes that the words שימה בפיהם / "Place in their mouths" is the same numerical value as the words, זה תלמוד / "This is the Talmud." Talmud is the primary text of Torah she-b'Al Peh.

Within the Torah, the 'circular' dimension is not the top-down revelation at Mount Sinai, but rather the oral aspects of the Torah, which have become more and more revealed over time by the Sages below. Although, once there is a 'new' revelation of Torah from the Sages below, it retroactively loops back into Above-to-below movement, and is identified as part of the revelation from Above at Mount Sinai.

A CIRCULAR LINKAGE

Chazal tell us: "Even what a proficient pupil is destined to *Mechadesh* / innovate (*Megilah*, 19b), was already told to Moshe at Sinai" (*Yerushalmi*, *Pe'ah*, 2:4). This means every *Chidush* / au-

thentic innovation in Torah created by human beings throughout history 'below' was actually given by Hashem to Moshe on
Mount Sinai. This begs the question: if a teaching is an innovation, how can it be 'given by Hashem'? And if the insight was
originally given on Mount Sinai, how is it an innovation?

"Three links are linked with each other, Hashem, the Torah
and Klal Yisrael" ("Hashem, Torah, and Israel are one," is quoted frequently in *Chasidus* in the name of the *Zohar*, and it also appears in many
sources, such as the *Nefesh haChayim* and the *Ramchal*. However, it is not actually stated clearly anywhere in *Zohar* — see for example, *Zohar* 3, 73a). If
three ideas or objects are linked to each other, one on top of the
next, two links would suffice; why are three links? The answer
is that three links create a 'circle'. When Hashem is linked with
the Torah and the Torah is revealed to us, it is a 'linear' image,
with two links. But once we have received and internalized the
Torah, a third link can be revealed — our own understanding and oral expression of the Torah becomes Hashem's own
Torah revelation, linking us back to HaKadosh Baruch Hu.
These three links complete a never-ending 'circle'... 1) Hashem
is linked with the Torah, 2) the Torah is linked with the People
of Israel, and 3) the People of Israel is linked with HaKadosh
Baruch Hu.

Three millennia after the revelation at Mount Sinai, Klal
Yisrael continues to innovate Torah teachings in direct link-
age with the Infinite Creator, and the Creator continues to
'retroactively' reveal these innovations as His own words spoken to Moshe at Mount Sinai. This speaks of a perspective of

timelessness or eternity; true innovations spoken thousands of years 'after' the giving of the Torah, are rooted in the Timeless Eternal One, the Giver of Torah. Insofar as Torah and Klal Yisrael are linked with the Timeless Eternal One, both have an inherent aspect of timeless eternality within themselves, and they exist 'prior' to Creation or 'beyond' the unfolding of historical time. When that which is beyond time is manifest within time, an innovation can be paradoxically both 'new' in linear time, and eternal. This is the nature of the revelation of the Torah she-b'Al Peh, the 'Circle World'.

CUSTOMS ARISING FROM THE UNCONSCIOUS COLLECTIVE PROPHETIC SOUL

While this 'Circle World' dynamic within Torah is generally connected with the Oral Torah interpretations and innovations throughout the ages, the best example of 'Circle World Torah' is the collective 'poetry' of Klal Yisrael enacted within their Minhagim. Our inspirational adornments and detailed customs of how we most enthusiastically celebrate our Yiddishkeit and identity as servants of the Eternal One, also link back, retroactively, to the revelation of Divine Presence at Mount Sinai. Minhagim complete the eternal circle of revelation.

Minhagim well up from within our collective, deepest, holy subconsciousness. Klal Yisrael has an "unconscious collective prophetic soul" (אם אין נביאים הן בני נביאים הן / "If they are not prophets, they are the children of prophets": *Pesachim*, 66a), and when an authentic Minhag arises, it too becomes Torah from Sinai (note Rambam,

Hilchos Mamrim, 1:2). Hence, the statement, מנהג ישראל תורה הוא /
"A custom of Yisrael is Torah."* This statement does not specify
'a Minhag of the Sages or learned people', rather, it means the
customs of the collective Keneses Yisrael, the *People* of Yisrael.
The 'collective prophetic soul' of the People reveals prophetic
depth in everything that the People, as a collective, chooses to
do in service of Hashem.

CIRCLES AND MINHAG

From deep within human prophetic imagination, the Circle
Reality arises in the form of popular customs. There are two
fully Rabbinic holidays in the calendar: Purim and Chanukah.
The celebration of Simchas Torah on the first or second day
of Shemini Atzeres is not a Rabbinic Yom Tov (although it was
mentioned in the Zohar and recorded and documented in the writings of the
Geonim over a thousand years ago), but it, too, is a Yom Tov of sort
that has arisen from within the collective unconscious of the
Jewish People.

---

* *Tosefos, Menachos,* 20b, writes, ומנהג אבותינו תורה היא / "The custom of our
ancestors (Tosefos is specifically referring to the French Ashkenaz sages) is
Torah." See Ritva on *Pesachim,* 105a. Rosh on *Pesachim,* 10:13. Tur, *Orach
Chayim,* 591. (The Ramban writes (*Pesachim,* 7b) regarding the customs of
the morning blessings, ומנהג ישראל תורה היא / "and the custom of (Klal) Yisrael is Torah"). For hundreds of years now, a popular version of this statement
is מנהג ישראל תורה היא / "The custom of Yisrael is Torah." This does not say
'the custom of our ancestors', i.e. in the context of Tosefos, this particularly
refers to the customs of Ashkenaz — rather, 'the custom of Klal Yisrael',
all of Klal Yisrael.

Interestingly, the customs that arise on these auspicious days are connected with 'rounding' squares — making circles around a square, or converting squares into circles.

On all these three days, Chanukah, Purim, and Simchas Torah, there is a custom that is related to each of these days respectively, where we round off, encircle, create a circle, or take an object that is square and spin it to fashion a circle.

Squares are similar, energetically to lines, as squares represent rigidity, absoluteness, boundaries, hence, the world of law and order. The 'prose' of life, the pedestrian and routine. The things you 'have' to do in life. Whereas the circular represents the 'poetry' of life, the music, the non-linear, the passionate. The things you 'want' to do in life. You may love and want to cook a nice meal but you then have to clean up. Torah she-b'Al Peh, and more pointedly Minhag, is what we relish and love doing for our Beloved, not what we 'have' to do. On the other hand, Minhagim support and inspire us to relate to all areas of Torah, including obligations, with passion, vitality, and deep joy.

DREIDEL, GRAGGER, HAKOFOS

On Chanukah, there is an informal Minhag of uncertain origin: the custom of playing with a Dreidel. Though certainly not a Rabbinic Mitzvah, this is nonetheless a holy, and meaningful custom. The Dreidel is a 'spinning top' with a body of four sides. When you spin this 'square', its shape blurs into a circle — you make a circle out of a square.

A similar custom on Purim is to make noise with a *Gragger* when Haman's name is mentioned during the reading of the *Megilah* / Scroll of Esther. While the Dreidel is spun from a handle above, the Gragger is held and spun from a handle below. The body of the Gragger is shaped like a line or rectangle, and this rectangle is twirled around rapidly in a circle to make noise.

Simchas Torah has a very pronounced theme of circling around squares. The Bimah in the Shul is traditionally shaped as a square, like the *Mizbe'ach* / Altar in the Beis haMikdash. This is also where the Written Torah, from the world of lines or squares, is read. By dancing in circles around the Bimah we *encompass* a square with circles. Our 'poetry', so-to-speak, is revealed as the *Makif* / encompassing light around the linear 'prose' of the Written Law.

LINES / SQUARE & CIRCLES WITHIN THE TORAH

Dancing with a rolled-up, closed Torah scroll is also a way of making lines and squares into circles. The *Ksav* / script of the Torah is laid out in pre-indented, precise, horizontal lines on the parchment, called *Sirtut*, etched upon rectangular parchments. Sirtutim are etched into the parchments in order to ensure that all the letters stay aligned; it is of utmost importance for the letters of the Torah to be 'in line'.

When Torah is open and being read, one sees lines on a rectangle. On Simchas Torah, when we are dancing with the Torah scroll rolled up, these rectangles and lines are wrapped in tight, circular spirals. We dance in a circle around a square Bimah, carrying a closed Torah scroll, whose lines are now circles.

Simchas Torah is saturated with Minhagim, besides the day itself being a Minhag. Several older customs are no longer practiced, such as dressing up the Torah, placing the Torah crowns on the heads of children, taking a previously lit, long burning candle and lighting a bonfire with it, and as strange and spiritually insensitive at it may seem, having music played by non-Jews during the procession from the Shul to the home of the man honored with *Chasan Torah* / the final reading before starting again with *Bereishis*. Some older customs such as doing a backwards *Hagbah* / lifting the Torah with the letters facing outwards, are still practiced by many. The custom of calling many people up for a single *Aliyah* / being called up to the Torah is a custom that is prevalent today as well. A Chasidic custom is to flip the Chazan over, making him do a somersault in the air after he has taken three 'linear' steps back after the Musaf Amidah.

Some of these Minhagim 'push' a little beyond what we consider normal, although of course remaining within the framework of Halachah. A 'framework' is like a square, and doing a Minhag that seems a bit out of the ordinary, yet within Halachic requirements, is like a circle inside a square, infinity within the finite.

Minhagim represent our passionate 'love poetry' for HaKadosh Baruch Hu, while Halachah represents the more prosaic but healthy, respectful boundaries and even healthy fear. In a marriage relationship, both partners benefit from tapping into the playful, poetic freedom of love and an ability to loosen up and laugh with each other, yet they should never lose respect for the other, or violate healthy boundaries. This, too, is a joining of a 'circle' and a 'square', without breaking or destroying the square.

CORNERS AND EDGES CAN BE NEGATIVE OR POSITIVE, DEPENDING ON THE CONTEXT

Torah Law keeps us aligned and attuned with our own inner order, conscience, and awe of the Creator. Yet, when Torah is practiced as strict law alone, without spiritual desire, passion, and Deveikus, sadly, it can stifle a person's spirit and keep them inhibited, 'squared', and boxed in. The Baal Shem Tov said that sometimes *Chumros* / extra stringencies can deepen a person's *Katnus* / smallness, immaturity, and constricted, exiled consciousness. The trajectory of our practice should move us toward *Gadlus* / expansiveness, openness, and maturity. For this, we need to combine Minhagim and organic, 'circular' expressions of love for the Creator, even while staying in contact with the 'square' structures of precise practice and balanced Chumros.

In the Infinite Creator's world "there is nothing square" ("There is no square in Creation," *Yerushalmi*, end of Ma'asros, *Nedarim*, 3:2.

Shevuos, 3:8). Certainly, this is true of Hashem's Torah, which is One with HaKadosh Baruch Hu. Yet, sometimes, life and the path of Torah can seem like a confining box with sharp corners and harsh lines. And so, when we passionately celebrate the Torah, we roll the scroll into a circle and enter a state of expansive, holy, loving joy, placing the square Bimah into its proper context, as it were: in the center of a free-flowing, sometimes even humorous, circle dance.

This is another, embodied way to break out of the Kelipah of overly rigid and confining 'boxes' that make us smaller and hold us back from living our dreams. When we need to enter into a more 'circular', poetic relationship with the Infinite One, we take all that is 'square' and make circles around or within them, or wrap them in circles. We include both.

Sometimes we may require the opposite. There are times when we need to stabilize the expansiveness and flow of the poetry and passion in our life with the lines and angles of 'law'. For example, at the time of our wedding, when the poetry of life takes prominence and we feel more circle energy, we enter into a Chupah, which is a square. On Sukkos, too, we enter the Chupah of the Sukkah. Sukkos is the Time of our Joy, celebrating our 'wedding' with the One Above. We enter the 'square' of boundaries within marriage, so that healthy boundaries and structures will hold and guide the passion and poetry of our love.

Once we enter the Chupah, we take a step deeper, and as the 'Kallah' of Hashem, we make circles walking seven times around our Groom. This means that not only have we stabilized and guided our passion and poetry with healthy boundaries, but even within the square-ness of boundaries there is an aspect of boundlessness, passion, and desire. In the context of Sukkos, after we fulfill the law of sitting in the 'square' of the Sukkah for seven days, we step out of the Sukkah and begin dancing in circles on Shemini Atzeres and very intensively throughout Simchas Torah. Although, even within the borders of Sukkos, we march in circles around the Bimah, and especially on the day of Hoshana Rabbah.

Simchas Torah's theme of endless circles is illustrated by the Arizal, who, once he completed Hakafos in his own Shul, would enter and dance along with other Shuls who were still performing Hakafos until all the Hakafos were complete in all of the Shuls.

We do not find any parallel to this idea in other Mitzvos or Minhagim. For example, on Purim, once the Arizal heard the recitation of the Megilah in his Shul, if he passed another Shul in the middle of the reading, or about to start the reading, he would not enter that Shul to hear it again. This idea of joining the celebrations of other Shuls is unique to the custom of Hakafos. Hakafos are the fullest expression of the infinite 'Circle World', pervaded with the quality of no beginnings and endings. Hakafos are a manifestation of the energy of infinity, so the Arizal would dance throughout the night of Simchas Torah, as if it was never-ending and infinite.

Simchas Torah is intrinsically connected to the ultimate circle, representing the highest level of Makif, which encompasses and unifies everything. During Simchas Torah, everyone dances — not just the pious and the sages, as was done during Simchas Beis haShoeiva. We all dance together in an all-inclusive circle-reality where no one is closer to the center than another.

We dance holding a closed, rolled-up Torah, symbolizing our collective relationship with the Torah on the level of Makif. This is also why, on Simchas Torah, we may call up many people to the Torah together, in a group, unlike throughout the year when only one person is called up at a time. Moreover, on Simchas Torah, we seamlessly transition from the end of the Torah back to the beginning, connecting the end with the beginning, forming a continuous, unbroken circle.

The Light of Ohr Makif, which is infinite and transcends all higher and lower paradigms, is revealed on Simchas Torah (Alter Rebbe, Siddur). Remarkably, this Ohr Makif is generated by our performance of Mitzvos. Specific Mitzvos generate Makifim that are more connected to the world of Penimi, enveloping the specific person who performed the Mitzvah with an Ohr Makif connected to that particular Mizvah (Nefesh haChayim, Sha'ar 1, 12), whereas the entire body of Mitzvos as a whole produces a higher, more transcendent, infinite Makif.

Simchah, the joy we experience doing the Mitzvos is what generates these Makifim that are transcendental and infinite (*Bnei Yissaschar*, Ma'amrei Tishrei, 13), therefore, the ideal way to tap into this Ohr Makif is through Simchah, the joy of Simchas Torah.

Shemini Atzeres / Simchas Torah is the day of the Circle.* It is a time that reveals our timeless, eternal connection and unification with the Infinite One in an intimate embrace. It is a time when, with great joy, we celebrate our desire for HaKadosh Baruch Hu, and our participation, love, and commitment to the holy Torah and the Giver of Torah. Through this, may we generate an Ohr Makif that encircles and includes all of Creation, unifying all of humanity in the joyful revelation of the infinite Light of Torah.

---

* Shemini Atzeres, says the Chasam Sofer (*D'rashos*, Sukkos), is like the middle of a circle, and all of the other Yamim Tovim circle around it. On a different note, on the circumference of a circle, there is no defined midpoint: Reb Yitzchak Chaver, *Afikei Yam*, Moed Katan, 3a. In this way, a circle represents a quality beyond space, the idea of Infinity.

Chapter 8
CIRCLING THE TORAH VS.
CIRCLING WITH THE TORAH

AS EXPLORED, SUKKOS IS INTRINSICALLY CONNECTED
WITH THE 'WORLD OF CIRCLES'. THE WORD CHAG
MEANS 'A SEASONAL FESTIVAL' IN GENERAL, yet the
Torah uses it as a specific reference to Sukkos as well: שבעת
ימים תחג לה׳ / seven days it shall be a Chag to Hashem" (*Devarim*,
16:15). Chag also implies a festival on which people dance in a
Machol / circle dance (*Ha'amek Davar*, ad loc.). In fact, the Gemara
(*Chagigah*, 10b) too, suggests that to celebrate a Chag means to
dance in circles (*Chagigah*, 10b: "How do we know that וחגותם אותו חג
לה׳ / 'And you shall celebrate it as a festival to Hashem (*Vayikra*, 23:41)' is
referring (here) to an animal offering? Perhaps the Merciful One is simply

saying: חוגו חגא / 'Celebrate a festival,' (and) what would it mean to 'celebrate a festival? Perhaps to dance in circles." The word *Chag* is לשון מחולות: *Tosefos*, ad loc. The Ramban writes, שתחוגו שבעת הימים עם השנה ענין סבוב והקפה מלשון וחוג שמים: *Emor*, 23:40).

Throughout the seven days of Sukkos, we practice Hakafos, circling the Bimah during Hoshanos. On each of the first six days, we make one Hakafah, and then on Hoshana Rabbah, we make seven Hakafos. Before making these circles, we take the Torah from the ark and hold it or place it on the Bimah and then circle around the Bimah and the Torah, holding the Lulav and Esrog in our hands. On Simchas Torah, we again perform Hakafos, but instead of circling the Torah, we hold the Torah and circle the Bimah.

Throughout Sukkos, the highlights are the Mitzvah of Lulav and Esrog and that of dwelling in a Sukkah. These are the sacred items that bring joy and reveal our deeper connection with HaKadosh Baruch Hu during the seven days of Sukkos. On Simchas Torah, the main protagonist, as it were, is the Torah itself. The Torah is revealed on this day as the essential connection between us and Hashem, beyond all doing and even beyond Mitzvos. In this revelation, we realize that our essence is connected with the Essence of HaKadosh Baruch Hu.

Everything has an *Ikar* / main element and a *Tafel* / secondary element. When we circle around something, that thing is the Ikar of the practice. Whatever is being circled is considered more 'important' than the person or object that is circling it.

For example, when we circle the Bimah and the Torah next to it, we are giving deference and honor to the Torah. On Simchas Torah, we carry the Torah and circle just the Bimah itself. What does this represent?

The Torah is a manifestation of *Tiferes* / 'Divine Splendor', the Giver. The Bimah that holds the Torah (like the Mizbe'ach of the Beis haMikdash) is a manifestation of *Malchus* / the receiver or receptacle — the object that 'hosts' or holds the Torah.

Throughout the seven days of Sukkos, as we carry the Lulav and Esrog and circle the Torah, we are drawing the Light of the Torah into our practice of the Mitzvos. We are ensuring that the *Lichtigkeit* / illumination of Torah permeates all our activities in this world.

On Simchas Torah, we hold the Torah itself, and allow the Light of the Torah to draw out the wondrous qualities within Malchus itself. We are ultimately the Malchus to Hashem's Light and Hashem's Torah since we receive and uphold the Torah in the world. We are the 'Bimah' upon which the holy Torah is 'hosted', read, and revealed, so-to-speak.

When we hold and carry the Torah — holding nothing else in our hands — we are declaring, 'Please Hashem, I desire that the Light of Your Presence, embodied in Your Holy Torah, will now shine into my heart and soul, so that I will become an illuminated, transparent vessel of Malchus, and reveal Your

Light in the world. May the holy *Osyos* / letters of the Torah illuminate our souls and reveal the holy Osyos within the souls of Klal Yisrael.

Chapter 9
SIMCHAS TORAH: OUR JOY IN THE TORAH & THE TORAH'S JOY IN US

THE FINAL WORDS OF THE ENTIRE TORAH ARE, ולכל המורא הגדול אשר עשה משה לעיני כל־ישראל / "...AND ALL THE AWESOME POWER THAT MOSHE DISPLAYED BEFORE all Klal Yisrael" (*Devarim*, 34:12). What awesome power did Moshe display in front of all of Klal Yisrael? Rashi explains: "This refers to the shattering of the (First) Luchos before (Klal Yisrael's) eyes... And the opinion of the Holy One, blessed be He, regarding this action, agreed with his (Moshe's) opinion, as it is stated that Hashem said of the Luchos, אשר שברת / 'which you have broken' — (which implies) *Yishar Koach'cha* / 'May your strength be fitting (ישר כוחך, an expression of thanks and congratulation, popularly pronounced *Yasher Koach*) because you have broken them'" (Rashi, *ad loc. Yevamos*, 62a. *Shabbos*, 87a).

Surprisingly, this is how the Torah comes to a close — the 'crescendo' of all the Torah readings of the year is an account of Hashem thanking Moshe for breaking the Luchos, shattering the Torah. How could this be?

Chazal reveal the reason that Moshe broke the Luchos with a parable. "Once a king went overseas and left his wife with the maids. While she was with them, a negative rumor came out against her (that she was not loyal to the king). The king heard this and sought to kill her. Her maid heard (about the king's intentions), stood up and tore up her *Kesubah* / marriage contract, and reasoned: 'If the king says 'My wife did such-and-such,' we will respond, 'She is not yet your wife'" (*Tanchuma,* Ki Sisa, 30).

Moshe breaks the Luchos of the Torah, which is the Kesubah between Hashem and Klal Yisrael. And therefore, if Hashem rebukes Klal Yisrael for being disloyal and unfaithful by worshiping the Golden Calf, Moshe will argue, 'They were not married to You!' This is the great *Mesiras Nefesh* / self-sacrifice of Moshe, his burning love for his people, Klal Yisrael. The receiver and transmitter of Torah was ready to sacrifice everything, even the Torah itself, as it were, for our sake. This great deed is the pinnacle and completion of the entire Torah (*Likutei Sichos,* 34. p. 217. I was personally present when the Rebbe said this Sichah on Simchas Torah of 5747. The Rebbe wept profusely when he spoke, and there was a sense that he was speaking about himself, as well).

In this way, the peak and essence of Torah is Klal Yisrael. "There are two entities in this world that I love...the Torah and *Yisrael* / the Jewish people. However, I (Eliyahu *haNavi* / the Prophet) do not know which one of them came first. I told him, 'My son, the way of people is to say that the Torah came first...but I say that Yisrael came first.... When the Torah states, 'Speak to the Children of Israel...,' 'Command the Children of Israel...,' I know that Yisrael preceded all" (*Tana d'Vei Eliyahu Rabbah*, 14. See also *Medrash Rabbah*, Bereishis, 1:4. *Zohar* 2, 119b).

'Simchas Torah' does not only mean our Simchah in the Torah, but the Simchah that the Torah has *in us* (*Likutei Sichos*, 14, p. 168). Our Simchah in the Torah is stimulated when we have completed the cycle of Torah readings, and this inspires joyful celebration within us — and at the same time, we inspire Simchah within the Torah (See the Rebbe's Ma'amar *Lehavin Inyan Simchas Torah*, 5738. See also *Zohar* 3, 256b).

When we dance with the Torah and hold it high, we become the 'legs of the Torah', manifesting it in real-time, on the earth. Without Yisrael, there would be no Torah in the physical world. As much as the Torah carries our existence (הארון נושא את נושאיו: *Sotah*, 35a), we carry the existence of the Torah, and give life to its wisdom, ethics, light, and beauty.

"MY DAUGHTER, MY SISTER, MY MOTHER"

The Mishnah in Ta'anis says as follows: צאינה וראינה בנות ציון במלך שלמה בעטרה שעטרה לו אמו ביום חתנתו ... ביום חתנתו זה מתן תורה / "Go forth, daughters of Zion, and gaze upon King Shelomo, upon the crown with which his mother crowned him on the day of his wedding…" (*Shir haShirim*, 3:11). "On the day of his wedding" — this is the giving of the Torah (the Second Luchos on Yom Kippur)" (*Ta'anis*, 26b, Rashi).

"Go forth, daughters of Zion, and gaze upon King Shelomo, upon the crown with which his mother crowned him." Says the Medrash, Rebbe Yochanan said that Rebbe Shimon ben Yochai asked Rebbe Elazar the son of Rebbe Yossi, 'Have you heard from your father what is "the crown adorned by his mother?"' 'Yes… It is analogous to a king who had only one daughter, and he was very fond of her, and he would call her "my daughter." His love for her increased until he began to call her "my sister," and he kept cherishing her more and more, until he called her "my mother." The same is true with Hakadosh Baruch Hu's love for us, for Klal Yisrael. At first, He called us "My daughter," then he called us "My sister" and finally, He calls us "My mother" (*Medrash Rabbah*, Shir haShirim, ad loc. The Maggid says that there is a fourth level of love which is indescribable, a pure love beyond all metaphors — ויש עוד אהבה שאינו מושגת לאדם: *Magid Devarav l'Yaakov*, 37).

On the day of the giving of the Torah, referring to the giving of the Second Luchos on Yom Kippur and the full reception of them on Simchas Torah, HaKadosh Baruch Hu calls us "His Mother.'"* In this sense, the *Mekabel* / receiver of Torah becomes the *Mashpia* / giver, the mother or 'nurturer' of Torah.

When the Torah was given to us, it was given in such a way that if we make a *Kinyan* / reception of ownership of it, it 'belongs' to us (ולבסוף נקראת על שמו: *Avodah Zarah*, 19a). Certainly, then, we become the 'carriers' or nurturers of the Torah in this world. We become the feet and hands of the Torah as we hold the Torah with our hands and dance with our feet. In this way, *Simchas Torah* refers to the joy the Torah has in us, and in what we do for the Torah.

LIFTING THE TORAH & MAKING IT OUR CROWN

On Simchas Torah, we literally and metaphorically 'lift' the Torah up and carry it into the world. Lifting the holy Torah up to the level of our head, we 'crown' ourselves with it, receiving its light shining down from above us. In this way, Simchas Torah is *our* joy in the Torah, our rejoicing in what we receive from the Torah, just as much as the Torah is rejoicing in us.

When a parent wishes to enter their young child's world or play with them, they crouch down to the floor, descending to

---

* Alternatively, through our Teshuvah on Yom Kippur we are called "His mother," since the power of Teshuvah from love is such that it transforms malice and sin into merit: *Yuma*, 86b. A negative becomes a positive, a Mitzvah, as it were, certainly it becomes transformed into a *Hechsher Mitzvah* / a necessary preparation for a Mitzvah, which is like part of the Mitzvah itself. *D'rush b'Inyan Arvus Yisrael*, Pesicha, *Chidushei v'Shiurei Reb Baruch Ber*, p. 7-8. In this way, through our Teshuvah we 'added' a Mitzvah and became a Mashpiah, a bestower of nurture upon the Torah, 'giving' it additional Mitzvos, so to speak.

the child's level and bending towards them. Occasionally, the parent will scoop up the child, joyfully tossing them into the air or lifting them above their head, placing the child on their shoulders, and carrying them around. In doing so, the parent metaphorically 'crowns' themselves with their child; the child brings them immense joy, and they are illuminated by the light of their child riding high above them (עטרת זקנים בני בנים / "Grand-children are the Crown of their elders": Mishlei, 17:6. Also, many have a custom of placing their young children on their shoulders while dancing with the Torah, and the child himself often holds a 'make-believe Torah scroll').

When we read the Torah, we lay it on the table or Bimah and often need to bend down slightly to read it. But once we have completed reading the Torah portion of the week (Sefar-dim have a custom to do this before the reading), there is a moment of a 'miniature Simchas Torah', so-to-speak, and we perform *Hagbaha* / lifting up the Torah above the heads of the congre-gation so all might see its holy letters. On Simchas Torah, we carry the Torah usually near our chest, with its crown aligned with the top of our heads. But sometimes, amid our ecstatic dancing, we lift the Torah above our heads, and now the Torah itself becomes our crown.

In this loving relationship with Divine Revelation, may we both give to the Torah and receive from the Torah, multiplying our joy and the 'Joy of the Torah' in this unending circle.

Chapter 10

KAVANOS / INTENTIONS FOR HAKAFOS: ENCIRCLING WITHIN & EXCLUDING WITHOUT

A HAKAFAH, OR CIRCLE, SERVES A DUAL PURPOSE: IT ENCLOSES AND SECURES EVERYTHING WITHIN ITS BOUNDS, WHILE SIMULTANEOUSLY SHUTTING OFF and repelling all external forces. By dancing Hakafos, we symbolically block or even destroy negativity, while protecting and fostering positivity. Our Hakafos create both of these effects.

While every turn of our circle dance enacts both of these dynamics, sometimes our focus is on one and other times on the other. On all of our Hakafos, including the Hoshanos of Sukkos and the Hoshanos of Hoshana Rabbah, we circle around the *Bimah* / Torah-reading table. The Arizal teaches that the Bimah in the center of the circle embodies Malchus, the 'receiver', while the Torah stationed at the Bimah embodies

Tiferes (or the six Sefiros of Ze'ir Anpin, the 'giver'). Throughout Sukkos, we circle both the Bimah and the Torah, as we hold our Lulav and Esrog. On Simchas Torah, we no longer carry our Lulav and Esrog, rather we circle the Bimah while carrying the Torah.

A Lulav is shaped like a spear and an upright Lulav is a symbol of victory. Throughout Sukkos, culminating on Hoshana Rabbah, we circle the Bimah with the Lulav standing proudly, victoriously blocking and destroying all the negative forces from entering into our sacred space.

One of the sources for circling around the Mizbe'ach during Sukkos, and today around the Bimah, is from the story of the walls of Yericho. Yehoshua and his troops, circled Yericho for six days, every day a single circuit. On the seventh day, they circled seven times, and the walls of the city came tumbling down. In the same fashion, we circle the Bimah once on each of the first six days of Sukkos, and then on the seventh day, we circle seven times, and the 'walls', and all impediments and negative forces come tumbling down (Rabbeinu Bachya, *Kad haKemach*, Aravah. This is based on Yerushalmi — אותו היום מקיפין את המזבח שבע פעמים זיכר ליריחו / "On that day, Hoshana Rabbah, we circle the Mizbe'ach seven times, in remembrance of the walls of Yericho": Yerushalmi, *Sukkah*, 4:3).

On Simchas Torah, we no longer need to destroy walls or repel negativity, rather we focus completely on holding and creating positivity and positive space. On Simchas Torah, as we dance in circles carrying the holy Torah, we create and safe-

guard a sacred space filled with positive energy. Within this sacred circle, we are protected and able to be vulnerable, opening
ourselves to genuine growth and spiritual elevation.

The root of the word הקפות / *Hakafos* is הקף / *Hekef*. In numerical value, *Hekef* is 185. 185 is the full numerical value of
the name א"ל / E-1 (אלף למד = Aleph-Lamed 111+74 = 185). This
Divine Name of Hashem represents Chesed, the attribute
of boundless Divine kindness, as expressed in Tehilim: "The
Chesed of E-1 is present throughout the day" (52:3). In general,
through the Hakafos we draw down Chesed and become infused with Hashem's infinite kindness. More specifically, each
of the circles draws down and encloses us with another Divine
attribute, one of the seven Sefiros.

EACH CIRCLING DRAWS DOWN A
DISTINCT BLESSING

Rebbe Pinchas of Koritz, a student of the Baal Shem Tov,
illustrates how each circle corresponds to a certain Sefirah (see
Seder Hakafos l'Shemini Atzeres v'Simchas Torah. See also, *Eitz Chayim*, Sha'ar
HeKelalim, 1), and how each Hakafah draws that Divine quality
and blessing down by means of the angel connected to that
Sefirah, fulfilling specific human needs. For example, for people who have issues bearing children, he suggests dancing with
the Torah in the sixth Hakafah, corresponding to the Sefirah
of *Yesod* / 'connectivity', associated with the procreative organ.

If a person needs more power in their life or more protection, he should focus on the second Hakafah of *Gevurah*

/ strength or power, and if a person needs victory, such as in winning a litigation, he should focus on the fourth Hakafah of *Netzach* / victory and perseverance, and for wealth the seventh Hakafah, Malchus, and so on.

If you do not happen to have the opportunity to dance carrying the Torah scroll during the Hakafah that corresponds to your need, perhaps you can make a point to kiss it during that Hakafah while someone else carrying it passes by. In any case, you can quietly request your needs before Hashem during the dancing of the corresponding Hakafah — or simply celebrate as if your need is already fulfilled.

Here are the seven Hakafos and their corresponding energetic qualities:

First Hakafah: the angels are drawing down *Chesed* / Divine kindness and love.

Second Hakafah: the angels are drawing down *Gevurah* / Divine strength and *Shemirah* / protection.

Third Hakafah: the angels are transmitting *Tiferes* / Divine beauty, balance, and compassion.

Fourth Hakafah: the angels are bringing down *Netzach* / Divine victory and perseverance.

Fifth Hakafah: the angels are drawing down *Hod* / Divine splendor or humbleness, and *Chein* / grace.

Sixth Hakafah: the angels are transmitting *Yesod* / Divine intimacy or connectivity, and drawing down the power to get married or give birth or create greater domestic peace.

Seventh Hakafah: the angels are helping us establish *Malchus* / Divine receptivity, *Emunah* / faith, self-mastery, physical health, and *Osher* / wealth.

Each of these seven Sefiros are aligned with a vowel that we can meditate on when we recite the Name of Hashem in the liturgy of the corresponding Hakafah. In other words, when you pronounce the Name *Ado-noy* in the recitations before and after the dancing, you can visualize the letters Yud, Hei and Vav adorned by the featured vowel (for example Yud with a Segol is יֶ and Hei with a Segol is הֶ).

First Hakafah, the vowel Segol (ֶ), which is the *Eh* sound.

Second Hakafah, Sh'va (ְ) , which is the *Ih* sound.

Third Hakafah, Cholam (ֹ), which is the *Oh* sound.

Fourth Hakafah, Chirik (ִ), which is the *Ee* sound.

Fifth Hakafah, Kubutz (ֻ), which is an *Oo* sound.

Sixth Hakafah, Shuruk (ו), which is also an *Oo* sound.

Seventh of Hakafah, the non-voweled, silent Sefirah.

Human Need	Divine Remedy	Hakafah	Meditative Vowel
Lovingkindness from others or from oneself, a greater ability to give or say 'yes'.	Chesed	One / "Alef"	Segol / Eh
Strength, discipline, a greater ability to withhold or to say 'no'.	Gevurah	Two / "Beis"	Sh'va / Ih
To reveal one's spiritual beauty, to see beauty in the world, to have a sense of balance, to give or receive balanced compassion.	Tiferes	Three / "Gimel"	Cholam / Oh
Victory, perseverance, endurance	Netzach	Four / "Dalet"	Chirik / Ee
Grace in the eyes of others, humbleness	Hod	Five / "Hei"	Kubutz / Ooh
Marriage, children, creativity, focus	Yesod	Six / "Vav"	Shuruk / Ooh
Wealth, self-mastery, receptivity, faith, bodily health	Malchus	Seven / "Zayin"	No Vowel / Silence

In whatever way we may find connection, as we dance in the circles of Simchas Torah, let us connect with the circle of Infinity, the Ohr Ein Sof — and from there draw down all blessings all the way down into our body and mind, our family, relationships, communities, and into our purpose and Avodah in the world.

RETURNING TO THE WORLD OF LINES & SQUARES

After Simchas Torah is complete, along with its sustained, direct glimpse of the infinite Circle World, we gradually return to the linear world of 'squares', the conventional, linear, natural world of time and space. At the end of the following Shabbos, 'Shabbos Bereishis', we are finally fully empowered to go forward into the year, and declare, ויעקב הלך לדרכו / *V'Ya'akov Halach l'Darko* / "And Ya'akov went on his way" (*Bereishis*, 32:2. On Shabbos Bereishis, the Rebbes of Chabad had a Minhag to recite this Pasuk).

This transition is not always easy; we need to know how to successfully draw the spiritual sustenance from Tishrei into our personal life in the coming year. The principle is *L'Hazir Gedolim al haKetanim* / to allow our expanded states to illuminate us in our more 'mundane' or contracted states. One way to do this is to take mental pictures of the highest states you experienced during Tishrei or Simchas Torah. When you encounter a 'lower state', you can recall these images, feel the light of that inspiration or focus, and let this illuminate your experience in the present. For instance, if you were able to pray the Neilah service in an intense or expansive state of consciousness, you can recall where you were standing, how it felt, and what words or experiences are associated with that state. Then you can tell yourself, 'If I can Daven Neilah with expanded consciousness, it means I can Daven with expanded consciousness now, too.' This is not just living in the past. If you sufficiently saturated your consciousness with light in Tishrei, this light remains present and available to you throughout every day of the un-folding year.

Darko means 'our own particular way'. Most of the expe-riences we had during the Yamim Tovim may have been ex-perienced in community; with hardly any time to ourselves as individuals. Perhaps we were swept into the euphoria, the celebration, and the emotions of the community and we filled ourselves up together this way, but now we need to translate these experiences into our own life and integrate them into our individual *Derech* / path. This is the sacred work of integration: to translate the grandeur of the festival into the quiet steps of everyday life. To let the revelations of the Holy Days illumi-nate our personal way forward, not just in moments of ecstasy, but in the stillness of ordinary time.

In Cheshvan, we start Davening for rain, because in Ancient Israel, by that time everyone had returned home from the *Regel*, the Pilgrimage to the Beis haMikdash for the Yamim Tovim. In the month of Cheshvan, as the echoes of the festivals fade and we return to the quiet rhythm of our personal lives, we be-gin to pray for rain. The communal heights of Tishrei dissolve into the solitude of daily life, and it is precisely then, when the crowds have dispersed and the festivals subsided, that we begin to ask: Let the heavens open and nourish our ground.

This is not merely a request for physical rain, but a deep-er, more tender yearning, for spiritual waters to descend softly and steadily, saturating the furrows of our ordinary days. It is a plea that the awe, the cleansing winds, the profound love, and soaring joy of Tishrei now soak into the very soil of our being. Even if we no longer feel alight with inspiration or trembling in the wake of revelation, we pray that the impressions remain, like seeds nestled just beneath the surface, hidden but alive. May ask that the radiance of the festivals etch themselves into our inner landscape, ready to blossom again in unexpected moments, and to nourish the mundane with quiet holiness.

In this world of contrast, where peaks are followed by valleys and light gives way to shadow, spiritual heights may not endure in their intensity. Yet we hope that their trace, their impact, their fragrance, lingers on. That the elevated states we touched continue to shape us, subtly yet profoundly, guiding the rhythm of our days as we go on 'our path' through the unfolding year.

Now we 'hit the road', hopefully, carrying the inspiration from the Yamim Tovim into the world. Now all judgments have been exquisitely sweetened and all 'our ways' are Hashem's ways. We hope that we are now empowered to walk through the world not as wanderers, but as bearers of light, carrying the afterglow of Infinity into every place, every task, every interaction. Now, with Hashem's help, we will create, by means of all our daily activities, a revealed 'dwelling place' for HaKadosh Baruch Hu, a home for the Divine, right here in this physical world. This will be the ultimate integration of the Infinity and oneness of the Circle World with the limitation and multiplicity of the World of Squares — may it be soon, *Amein.*

Other Books by Rav Pinson

Rav Pinson on the Torah

Awakenings:
Drawing Life from the Weekly Torah Reading

The deeper teachings of the Torah reveal to us that the weekly Torah reading is connected to the unique energetic properties of that week. Every Torah portion, and thus every week, radiates with a particular quality, a distinct energy that, when understood and received, can bring tremendous guidance and assistance to every facet of our lives.

Delving into the weekly Torah reading and uncovering its overarching theme allows us to apply the power available on that week in our practical life.

We can learn how to harness the Ko'ach, power, of each unique Torah reading to expand consciousness, overcome challenges, gain control of our lives, and come to learn how to serve Hashem, self and others more mindfully, productively and effectively.

Weaving together the various facets of Torah interpretation, from the most esoteric (Kabbalah) and mystical (Chassidus) to the straightforward literal meaning (Peshat), this book is a multi-dimensional tapestry of practical, allegorical, philosophical, and mystical ideas and implications.

Rav Pinson on the Life Cycle

A BOND FOR ETERNITY
Understanding the Bris Milah

What is the Bris Milah – the covenant of circumcision? What does it represent, symbolize and signify? This book provides an in depth and sensitive review of this fundamental Mitzvah. In this little masterpiece of wisdom – profound yet accessible —the deeper meaning of this essential rite of passage and its eternal link to the Jewish people, is revealed and explored.

UPSHERNISH: THE FIRST HAIRCUT
Exploring the Laws, Customs & Meanings of a Boy's First Haircut

What is the meaning of Upsherin, the traditional celebration of a boy's first haircut at the age of three? Why is a boy's hair allowed to grow freely for his first three years? What is the deeper import of hair in all its lengths and varieties? What is the meaning of hair coverings? Includes a guide to conducting an Upsherin ceremony.

THE JEWISH WEDDING:
A Guide to the Rituals and Traditions of the Wedding Ceremony

The Jewish Wedding: A Guide to the Rituals and Traditions of the Wedding Ceremony.

This guide is based on the teachings of Torah, Talmud, Medrash, Zohar,

Halacha, Poskim, Kabbalah and Chassidus. By quoting these teachings, we actively draw down the 'presence' of these holy souls who revealed these teachings, thus extending blessings to the bride and groom and all in attendance at the Chupa.

THE MYSTERY OF KADDISH
Understanding the Mourner's Kaddish

The Mystery of Kaddish is an in-depth exploration into the Mourner's Prayer. Throughout Jewish history, there have been many rites and rituals associated with loss and mourning, yet none have prevailed quite like the Mourner's Kaddish Prayer, which has become the definitive ritual of mourning. The book explores the source of this prayer and deconstructs the meaning to better understand the grieving process and how the Kaddish prayer supports and uplifts the bereaved through their own personal journey to healing.

THE BOOK OF LIFE AFTER LIFE

What is a soul? What happens to us after we physically die?

What is consciousness, and can it survive without a physical brain?

Can we remember our past lives?

Do near-death experiences prove immortality?

What is Gan Eden? Resurrection?

Exploring the possibility of surviving death, the near-death experience and a glimpse into what awaits us after this life.

(This book is an updated and expanded version of the book; Jewish Wisdom of the Afterlife)

Rav Pinson on Kabbalah

REINCARNATION AND JUDAISM
The Journey of the Soul

A fascinating analysis of the concept of Gilgul / Reincarnation. Dipping into the fountain of ancient wisdom and modern understanding, this book addresses and answers such basic questions as: What is reincarnation? Why does it occur? And how does it affect us personally?

INNER RHYTHMS
The Kabbalah of Music

Exploring the inner dimension of sound and music, and particularly, how music permeates all aspects of life. The topics range from Deveikus/ Unity and Yichudim/Unifications, to the more personal issues, such as Simcha/Happiness and Marirus/ sadness.

THIRTY–TWO GATES OF WISDOM
Into the Heart of Kabbalah & Chassidus

What is Kabbalah? And what are the differences between the theoretical, meditative, magical and personal Kabbalistic teachings? What are the four paths of interpreting the teachings of the ARIzal? What did Chassidus teach? These are some of the fundamental issues expanded upon in this text. And then, more specifically, why are there so many names of G-d and what do they represent? What are the key concepts of these deeper teachings?

The book explores the grand narrative of the great chain of reality, how there was and is a movement from the Infinite Oneness of Hashem to a world of (apparent) duality and multiplicity.

––––––––––

PASSPORT TO KABBALAH
A Journey of Inner Transformation

Life is a journey full of ups and downs, inside-outs, and unexpected detours. There are times when we think we know exactly where we want to be headed, and other times when we are so lost we don't even know where we are. This slim book provides readers with a passport of sorts to help them through any obstacles along their path of self-refinement, reflection, and self-transformation.

––––––––––

THE SEVEN PRINCIPLES:
Towards a Life of Meaning and Purpose
A book on the Seven Mitzvos of Noach

These seven principles will open you up to a new and empowering way of thinking and being in this world.

486 | EMBRACED IN DIVINE SPACE

It will inspire you to engage in life proactively with openness, care, clarity of consciousness and attachment to the Source of life and fulfillment. Overflowing with thought provoking insights, Divine guidance and practical exercises, The Seven Principles is a manual to leading a life of purpose and joy.

THE GARDEN OF PARADOX:
The Essence of Non - Dual Kabbalah

This book is a Primer on the Essential Philosophy of Kabbalah presented as a series of 3 conversations, revealing the mysteries of Creator, Creation and Consciousness. With three representational students, embodying respectively, the philosopher, the activist and the mystic, the book, tackles the larger questions of life. Who is G-d? Who am I? Why do I exist? What is my purpose in this life? Written in clear and concise prose, the text, gently guides the reader towards making sense of life's paradoxes and living meaningfully.

THE POWER OF CHOICE:
A Practical Guide to Conscious Living

It is the essential premise of this book that we hold the key to unlock many of the gates that seem closed to us and keep us from living our fullest life. That key we all hold is the power to choose. The Power of Choice is the primary tool that we have at our disposal to impact the world and effect change within our own lives. We often give up this power to outside forces such as the market, media, politicians or peer pressure; or to internal forces that often function beyond our conscious control such as ego, anger, lust, greed or jealousy. Making conscious, compassionate and creative decisions is the cornerstone of living a mature and meaningful life.

MYSTIC TALES FROM THE EMEK HAMELECH

Mystic Tales of the Emek HaMelech, is a wondrous and inspiring collection of stories culled from the Emek HaMelech. Emek HaMelech, from which these stories have been taken, (as well as its author) is a bit of a mystery. But like all good mysteries, it is one worth investigating. In this spirit the present volume is being offered to the general public in the merit and memory of its saintly author, as well as in the hopes of introducing a vital voice of deeper Torah teaching and tradition to a contemporary English speaking audience

----

Rav Pinson on Meditation

MEDITATION AND JUDAISM
Exploring the Jewish Meditative Paths

A comprehensive work encompassing the entire spectrum of Jewish thought, from the sages of the Talmud and the early Kabbalists to the modern philosophers and Chassidic masters. This book is both a scholarly, in-depth study of meditative practices, and a practical, easy to follow guide for any person interested in meditating the Jewish way.

TOWARD THE INFINITE

A book focusing exclusively on the Chassidic approach to meditation known as Hisbonenus. Encompassing the entire meditative experience, it takes the reader on a comprehensive and engaging journey through this unique practice. The book explores the various states of consciousness that a person encounters in the course of the meditation, beginning at a level of extreme self-awareness and concluding with a state of total non-awareness.

BREATHING & QUIETING THE MIND

Achieving a sense of self-mastery and inner freedom demands that we gain a measure of hegemony over our thoughts. We learn to choose out thoughts so that we are not at the mercy of whatever belches up to the mind. Through quieting the mind and conscious breathing we can slow the onrush of anxious, scattered thinking and come to a deeper awareness of the interconnectedness of all of life.

Source texts are included in translation, with how-to-guides for the various practices.

SOUND AND VIBRATION:
Tuning into the Echoes of Creation

Through our perception of sound and vibration we internalize the world around us. What we hear, and how we process that hearing, has a profound impact on how we experience life. What we hear can empower us or harm us. A defining human capacity is to harness the power sound -- through speech, dialogue, and song, and through listening to others. Hearing is primary dimension of our existence. In fact, as a fetus our ears were the first fully operating sensory organs to develop.

This book will guide you in methods of utilizing the power of sound and vibration to heal and maintain mental, emotional and spiritual health, to fine-tune your Midos and even to guide you into deeper levels of Deveikus / conscious unity with Hashem. The vibratory patterns of the Aleph-Beis are particularly useful portals into our deeper conscious selves. Through chanting and deep listening, we can use the letters and sounds to shift our very mindset, to induce us into a state of presence and spiritual elevation.

VISUALIZATION AND IMAGERY:
Harnessing the Power of our Mind's Eye

We assume that what we see with our eyes is absolute. Yet, beyond our ability to choose what we see, we have the ability to choose how we see. This directly translates into how we experience life. In a world saturated with visual imagery, our senses are continuously assaulted with Kelipa/empty/fantasy imagery that we would not necessarily choose. These images can negatively affect our relationship with ourselves, with the world around us, and with the Divine. This volume seeks to show us how we can alter that which we observe through harnessing the power of our mind's eye, the inner sanctum of our imagination. We thus create a new way to see and experience the world. This book teaches us how to utilize visualization and imagery as a way to develop our spiritual sensitivity and higher intuition, and ultimately achieve Deveikus/Unity with Hashem.

CONTEMPLATING AND TRANSCENDING MIND

Hisbonenus: The Meditative Path of Chabad

What is Hisbonenus / meditative contemplation? And how is it actually practiced? The illustrious first Rebbe of Chabad, the Alter Rebbe, aimed for the deepest teachings of the Torah and Chassidus to be internalized and deeply contemplated.Hisbonenus, the process of focused contemplation, begins by training your mind to dwell, for example, on the unity of Hashem, for extended periods. This practice engages the entire spectrum of your intellect-your Chochmah (wisdom or spark of intuition), Binah (analysis and understanding), and Da'as (knowledge and integration). As you progress, your thoughts will naturally stir your heart and emotions. When your mind contemplates lofty concepts such as the unity of the Creator with all of Creation, emotions of profound love for Hashem and a deep sense of wonder will arise. These emotions become more refined and subtle as you delve deeper, eventually leading to Ayin (transparency of self) and Deveikus ('conscious' unity with the Divine).

When the mind reaches its full potential for concentration and contemplation, it may 'implode' from exhaustion, so to speak, leading to a state of Ayin. This phenomenon shows that we don't have to circumvent or invalidate the intellect to transcend it. Rather, we can use the mind itself as a bridge to the Beyond.

Achieving 'intellectual exhaustion' allows us to transition into a state of Ayin- consciousness and mystical union more easily than trying to leap over the mind or stop thinking entirely. This advanced stage of Hisbonenus involves moving from Binah (understanding) back to Chochmah (supra-rational wisdom), and beyond.

Rav Pinson on The Holidays

THE HAGGADAH:
Pathways to Pesach and the Haggadah

"In every generation a person must regard oneself as having gone out of Mitzrayim / Egypt." This means that when recalling the Exodus, which occurred thousands of years ago, we also need to envision ourselves as being taken out of Mitzrayim and freed from enslavement.

Introducing the Haggadah and the themes of Pesach, this book delves into the greater context of the Festival and the Seder, allowing us to tap into the profound inspiration and Koach / power that Pesach and Seder Night offers.

EIGHT LIGHTS
8 Meditations for Chanukah

What is the meaning and message of Chanukah? What is the spiritual significance of the Lights of the Menorah? What are the Lights telling us? What is the deeper dimension of the Dreidel? Rav Pinson, with his trademark deep learning and spiritual sensitivity guides us through eight meditations relating to the Lights of the Menorah, the eight days of Chanukah, and a fascinating exploration of the symbolism and structure of the Dreidel. Includes a detailed how-to guide for lighting the Chanukah Menorah.

THE PURIM READER
The Holiday of Purim Explored

With a Persian name, a masquerade dress code and a woman as the heroine, Purim is certainly unusual amongst the Jewish holidays. Most people are very familiar with the costumes, Megilah and revelry, but are mystified by their significance. This book offers a glimpse into the hidden world of Purim, uncovering these mysteries and offering a deeper understanding of this unique holiday.

The High Holiday Series:

A CALL TO MAJESTY:
The Mysteries of Shofar & Rosh Hashanah

The Shofar is the preeminent symbol of Rosh Hashanah, waking us up to a time of deep introspection and celebration. But why do we blow the Shofar on this most special of days? While the Torah decrees that the Shofar must be blown, it does not provide a reason. On the deepest level, the Shofar is of course beyond reason altogether, and yet, from within its shape, sound and story, a constellation of "reasons" emerge. Rebirth. Responsibility. Radical Amazement. On a primal vibrational level, the Shofar calls each of us to a place of deeper consciousness and community as we crown the King of All Creation.

A CALL TO MAJESTY delves deeply into the world of Rosh Hashanah and its primary Mitzvah, the sound of the Shofar. Weaving together a multi-dimensional tapestry of practical, allegorical, philosophical, and mystical ideas and implications, the teachings collected herein empower us all to answer the higher calling of the Shofar.

A LIGHTNESS OF BEING:
Your Guide to Yom Kippur

Yom Kippur is unabashedly transformative; the power of the day beckons us to work toward fundamental transformation and Teshuvah / return to who we really are. Often, the word Teshuvah is unfortunately translated as 'repentance'. It is more accurately rendered as 'return', meaning both a return 'from' our states of spiritual alienation and exile, as well as a 'turning to' experiencing our deepest selves. Yom Kippur empowers us to return to our essence, reclaim who we truly are, and live from that place.

A LIGHTNESS OF BEING delves into the powerful and transformative day of Yom Kippur. Weaving together a multi-dimensional tapestry of practical, allegorical, philosophical and mystical ideas and implications, the teachings gathered herein empower us all to enter Yom Kippur and truly feel enlightened, elevated, lighter and transformed.

THE FOUR SPECIES
The Symbolism of the Lulav & Esrog

The Four Species have inspired countless commentaries and traditions and intrigued scholars and mystics alike. In this little masterpiece of wisdom both profound and practical - the deep symbolic roots and nature of the Four Species are explored. The Na'anuim, or ritual of the Lulav movement, is meticulously detailed and Kavanos,, are offered for use with the practice. Includes an illustrated guide to the Lulav Movements.

Rav Pinson on Prayer

INNER WORLDS OF JEWISH PRAYER
A Guide to Develop and Deepen the Prayer Experience

While much attention has been paid to the poetry, history, theology and contextual meaning of the prayers, the intention of this work is to provide a guide to finding meaning and effecting transformation through the prayer experience itself.

Explore: *What happens when we pray? *How do we enter the mind-state of prayer? *Learning to incorporate the body into the prayers. *Discover techniques to enhance and deepen prayer and make it a transformative experience.

This empowering and inspiring text, demonstrates how through proper mindset, preparation and dedication, the experience of prayer can be deeply transformative and ultimately, life-altering.

ILLUMINATED SOUND:
The Baal Shem Tov on Prayer

In the year 1698 a great light was revealed to the world with the descent of the holy soul of the Baal Shem Tov. In time, the Baal Shem Tov became one of the most important and influential teachers of Torah in all of history, and the founder of Chassidus.

Amongst the vast repository of profound and revolutionary teachings of the holy Baal Shem Tov, the teachings on the path of Tefilah / Prayer are the most elaborate. The teachings of the Baal Shem Tov on Tefilah include some of his most innovative expressions, or Chidushim. Tefilah is the essential and central tenet from which all other teachings flow.

In this masterful and practical text, Rav Pinson revives the awe-inspiring and transformational teachings of the Baal Shem Tov, and illuminates his unique path to Tefilah.

Rav Pinson on Jewish Practice

RECLAIMING THE SELF
The Way of Teshuvah

Teshuvah is one of the great gifts of life. It speaks of a hope for a better today and empowers us to choose a brighter tomorrow. But what exactly is Teshuvah? How does it work? How can we undo our past and how do we deal with guilt? And what is healthy regret without eroding our self-esteem? In this fascinating and empowering book, the path for genuine transformation and a way to include all of our past in the powerful moment of the now, is explored and demonstrated.

WRAPPED IN MAJESTY
Tefillin - Exploring the Mystery

Tefillin, the black boxes and leather straps that are worn during prayer, are curiously powerful and mysterious. Within the inky black boxes lie untold secrets. In this profound, passionate and thought-provoking text, the multi-dimensional perspectives of Tefillin are explored and revealed. Magically weaving together all levels of Torah including the Peshat (literal observation), to Remez (allegorical), to Derush, (homiletic), to Sod (hidden) into one beautiful tapestry. Inspirational and instructive, Wrapped in Majesty: Tefillin, will make putting on the Tefillin more meaningful and inspiring.

SECRETS OF THE MIKVAH:
Waters of Transformation

A Mikvah is a pool of water used for the purpose of ritual immersion; a place where one moves from a state of Tumah; impurity, blockage and death— to a place of Teharah; purity, fluidity and life.

In SECRETS OF THE MIKVAH, Rav Pinson delves into the transformative powers of the Mikvah with his trademark all-encompassing perspective that ranges from the literal, Pshat observation and Halachic implications of the texts, to the allegorical, the philosophical, and finally, to the deep secrets of the Mikvah as revealed by Kabbalah and Chassidus.

This insightful and inspirational text demonstrates how immersion in a Mikvah can be a transformative and life-altering practice, and includes various Kavanos—deep intentions—for all people, through various stages of life, that empower and enrich the immersion experience.

THE MYSTERY OF SHABBOS
Shabbat Rediscovered

Delving into the transformative power of Shabbos. With an all-encompassing perspective that ranges from the literal, Pshat observation and Halachic implications of the texts, to the allegorical, the philosophical, and finally, to the deeper secrets as revealed by Kabbalah and Chassidus, creating an elegant tapestry of thought and experience. THE MYSTERY OF SHABBOS is a profound meditation on the meaning of Shabbos and demonstrates the physical, emotional, mental and spiritual possibilities available and given to us with the gift of Shabbos. Studying and contemplating this inspired text on the depths of Shabbos will unveil a redemptive light in your experience of the Seventh Day -- and by extension, every day of your life.

Rav Pinson on Time

THE SPIRAL OF TIME:
A 12 Part Series on the Months of the Year
VOL 1: THE SPIRAL OF TIME:
Unraveling the Yearly Cycle

Many centuries ago, the Sages of Israel were the foremost authority in the fields of both astronomical calculation and astrological wisdom, including the deeper interpretations of the cycles and seasons. Over time, this wisdom became hidden within the esoteric teachings of the Torah, and as a result was known only to students and scholars of the deepest depths of the tradition. More recently, the great teachers, from R.Yitzchak Luria (the Arizal) to the Baal Shem Tov, taught that as the world approaches the Era of Redemption, it is a Mitzvah / spiritual obligation to broadly reveal this wisdom.

"The Spiral of Time" is volume 1 in a series of 12 books, and serves as an introductory book to the basic concepts and nature of the Hebrew calendar and explores the special day of Rosh Chodesh.

_____

VOL 2: THE MONTH OF NISAN:
Miraculous Awakenings from Above

The month of NISAN is the first month of the lunar cycle of the year, a month that brings in the spring and a month of redemption. Spring represents a time of plenty, abundance, sunshine, hope, and possibility. Redemption, on whatever level, feels palpable and accessible. In spring, the world is redeemed from the cold winter, the flower is redeemed from the tree, the grass from the earth, and we too feel that redemption is possible. A whole complex of ideas, including newness, redemption, going out of Egypt, and being freed from slavery, is intricately bound with the idea of Aviv / spring and the powerful month of Nisan.

_____

VOL 3: THE MONTH OF IYYAR:
EVOLVING THE SELF
& The Holiday of LAG B'OMER

The month of IYYAR is the second month of the spring, a month that connects the Redemption from Egypt in Nissan with the Revelation of Torah in Sivan. The Chai/ Eighteenth day of the Month is the day we celebrate the Rashbi (Rabbi Shimon Bar Yochai) and the revealing of the hidden aspects of the Torah. This is the 'Holiday' of Lag b'Omer. The book explores the unique quality of this special month, a month that has a Mitzvah of counting the Omer every day. In addition, the book explores the roots and significance of the mystical 'holiday' of Lag b'Omer. Including the customs & Practices of Lag b'Omer, such as, bonfires, bows & arrows, parades, Upsherin, and more.

———————

VOL 4: THE MONTH OF SIVAN:
The Art of Receiving:
Shavuos and Matan Torah

Sivan is the third month of the lunar cycle. One is a singularity. Two is division. Three is harmony, a unity that synthesizes individuality and multiplicity, Heaven and Earth, Spirituality and Physicality. During this month we celebrate Shavuos and the giving of the Torah, the ultimate expression of the unity of the Above and Below and we aspire to connect with the Keser/Crown of Torah that Transcends and yet includes all Worlds. Learning how to truly receive Higher wisdom in our Lower faculties is the mental, emotional, and spiritual exercise of the month.

———————

VOL 5: THE MONTHS OF TAMUZ AND AV:
Embracing Brokenness -
17th of Tamuz, Tisha B'Av, & Tu B'Av

Each month and season of the year, radiates with distinct Divine qualities and unique opportunities for growth and Tikkun.

The summer month of Tamuz and Av contain the longest and hottest days of the year. The raised temperature is indicative of a corresponding spiritual heat, a time of harsher judgement and potential destruction, such as the destructions of the first and second Beis HaMikdash, which began on the 17th of Tamuz and culminated on the 9th and 10th of Av.

A few days later, on Tu b'Av, the darkness is transformed and reveals the greatest light and possibility for new life. During these summer months of Tamuz and Av we embrace our brokenness so that we can heal and transform darkness into light.

VOL 6: THE MONTH OF ELUL:
Days of Introspection and Transformation

Each month of the year radiates with a distinct quality and provides unique opportunities for growth and personal transformation. Elul, as the final month of the spring/summer season is connected to endings. Elul gives us the strength to be able to finish strong, to end well. Elul also serves as a month of preparation for the New Year/Rosh Hashanah.

We inhale our past year, ending with wisdom and then we also gain the wisdom to begin anew and exhale a positive year into being. The mental, emotional, and spiritual objective of this month is introspection and the reclaiming of our inner purity and wholeness.

VOL 7: THE MONTH OF TISHREI:
A Time of Rebirth & Upward Movement

Each month of the year radiates with distinct Divine qualities and unique opportunities for growth and spiritual illumination. As Tishrei begins the new yearly cycle, it is an appropriate month to introspect, reflect and resolve to move forward and preserve moving forward into the more inward months of the winter. This month creates the space to unburden ourselves from our negativities, and enter a more sacred, grounded sacred space. In Tishrei we are given the gift of forgiveness and then the ability to truly regain our space and inner joy.

VOL 8: THE MONTH OF CHESHVAN:
Navigating Transitions, Elevating the Fall

Directly on the heels of the inspiring and holiday-filled month of Tishrei, Cheshvan is a month that is quiet and devoid of holidays. In the month of Cheshvan we use the stored up energies of the previous months to self-generate our inspiration and creativity and provide ourselves with the strength to rise up after a fall. In Cheshvan we are entering into a stormier, wetter and colder season. It is a month of transition. The mental, emotional and spiritual objective of this month is to weather the transitions, learn to self-generate and stand tall. And if we do fall, we use the quality of this month to get back up and do so with more conviction, strength, wisdom and clarity.

VOL 9: THE MONTH OF KISLEV:
Rekindling Hope, Dreams and Trust

Kislev is the final month of the fall. Throughout this month, daylight progressively shortens, and the temperatures drop. Towards the end of the month, at the darkest hour, the winter solstice arrives and we begin the celebration of Chanukah. We commemorate the miracle of a small jug of oil that burned for eight nights, and as we celebrate, daylight expands. In the month of Kislev-despite the darkness, or perhaps because of it-we have the ability to tap into the Ohr HaGanuz, the hidden light of hope that rekindles our dreams and aspirations.

VOL 10: THE MONTH OF TEVES:
Refining Relationships, Elevating the Body

The quality of Teves is generally harsh—much like its counterpart Tamuz in the summer, thus the tendency for many is to hunker down, retract, curl up and wait for the month to pass by, only to reemerge when the harshness has dissipated. Think for a moment about the 'easier' months of the year, which, like gentle waves in the ocean, carry us where we want to go. We can ride these energies easily and they can propel us forward effortlessly, we just need to go with the overall flow, so to speak. The harsher months, on the other hand, can be compared to the more powerful waves that emanate from the belly of the ocean, which come forcefully crashing down and can easily drown a person before they even realize what has happened. However, those who want to utilize the momentum of the powerful energy that is available during such times can, with caution and creativity, harness these intense waves and ride them higher and farther than other, more gentle circumstances may allow. However, harnessing the power of Tohu, the raw energy of the body, does in fact need to be approached with great care and attention.

VOL 11: THE MONTH OF SHEVAT:
ELEVATING EATING
& The Holiday of Tu b'Shevat

Each month of the year radiates with a distinct Divine energy and thus unique opportunities for growth, *Tikkun* and illumination. According to the deeper teachings of the Torah, all of these distinct qualities, opportunities and natural phenomena correspond to a certain data set. That is, the nature of each month is elucidated by a specific letter of the Aleph Beis, a tribe, verse, human sense, and so forth. The month of Shevat is particularly connected to food and our relationship to bodily intake. During this month we celebrate Tu b'Shevat, the New Year of the Tree, and aspire to create a proper and physically/emotionally/spiritually healthy relationship with food.

––––––––––

VOL 12: THE MONTH OF ADAR:
Transformation Through Laughter & Holy Doubt

Each month of the year radiates with distinct Divine qualities and unique opportunities for growth and spiritual illumination. As Adar concludes the monthly cycle of the year, as well as the solar phenomena of the winter, it is an appropriate month to think about our essential identity, before moving out to meet the world come spring. This month we strive to create a healthy relationship with holy humor, unbounded joy, and a general sense of lightness of being. Through the work of Adar we transform negative, crippling doubt and uncertainties into radical wonderment and openness.

New Release!

––––––––––

PROCESS AND PRESENCE
Life in Balance

In the world of process, the self and the world are broken, and we ambitiously strive to improve and to better.
In presence reality, all is now, everything is perfect, and there is

nowhere to progress and certainly no reason to fight or strive.

This book offers the gift of a balanced life, wherein the path of process and the pathless path of presence are lived in unison.

www.ingramcontent.com/pod-product-compliance
Lightning Source LLC
Chambersburg PA
CBHW040410110426
42812CB00012B/2512